Lawman

Harry N. Morse, circa 1870. Courtesy Jack Reynolds.

Lawman

THE LIFE AND TIMES OF HARRY MORSE, 1835–1912

By John Boessenecker

UNIVERSITY OF OKLAHOMA PRESS : NORMAN

Also by John Boessenecker

Badge and Buckshot: Lawlessness in Old California (Norman, 1988)
(with Mark Dugan) *The Grey Fox: The True Story of Bill Miner, Last of the
Old-Time Bandits* (Norman, 1992)

Published with the assistance of the National Endowment for the Human-
ities, a federal agency which supports the study of such fields as history,
philosophy, literature, and language.

Library of Congress Cataloging-in-Publication Data

Boessenecker, John, 1953–
      Lawman : the life and times of Harry Morse, 1835–1912 / by John
Boessenecker.
            p.   cm.
      Includes bibliographical references (p.) and index.
      ISBN 0-8061-3011-3 (alk. paper)
      1. Morse, Harry N., 1835–1912.   2. Sheriffs—California—Alameda
County—Biography.   3. Frontier and pioneer life —California—Alameda
County.   4. Alameda County (Calif.)—Biography.   5. Crime—Califor-
nia—Alameda County—History—19th century.   I. Title.
F868.A3B64   1998
363.28'2'092—dc21
[B]   97-35009
                                                                   CIP

The paper in this book meets the guidelines for permanence and durability
of the Committee on Production Guidelines for Book Longevity of the
Council on Library Resources, Inc. ∞

1   2   3   4   5   6   7   8   9   10

ADB-9020

For my parents,
Edward and Joan Boessenecker

A man had better have the devil after him than Harry Morse.

—Anonymous bandido,
quoted in the *Oakland Daily News*,
January 5, 1874

Contents

Illustrations

FIGURES

MAPS

Preface

FOR nearly half a century, Harry N. Morse was one of the most celebrated lawmen of the Old West. From 1878 until his death in 1912 he was the most famous private detective on the Pacific Coast. Before that, as sheriff of Alameda County, California, from 1864 to 1878, he became a legendary figure as he killed or captured some of the worst outlaws west of the Sierra Nevada. Harry Morse was a gunfighter, manhunter, and sleuth whose career is without parallel in the history of the American frontier.

The story of Harry Morse, his life and times, had never before been told. His days ended at a time when interest in the frontier was on the wane and the era of great Hollywood westerns had not yet arrived. Beginning in the 1920s and for the next four decades, there was a flood of books and motion pictures about real and fictional outlaws and lawmen of the Old West. Although many western writers and filmmakers lived in southern California, they seldom used California topics or personalities as subjects for their works. Most were unaware that California once had a Wild West past and instead produced books and films set in states with more of a "western" flavor: Texas, Montana, Wyoming, Arizona, New Mexico. The California frontier has been settled long before, and most of the pioneers who helped tame California, including Harry Morse, were long dead. Thus by the 1920s the stories of California's great lawmen were all but forgotten, buried in dusty newspaper archives and crumbling court records.

Those novelists, screenwriters, and popular historians of the period 1920–60 rehashed over and again timeworn stories about such legendary gunmen as James B. "Wild Bill" Hickok, Wyatt Earp, and Bat Masterson. They thus created a myth of the wandering lawman/gunfighter who drifted from cow town to border town, taming the badmen and then moving on. In reality, neither Hickok nor Earp nor Masterson was a professional lawman. They wore badges in termittently and made a living primarily by gambling. They rarely settled for long in one place and associated with the saloon and sporting element. They were just as ready to use their guns in a personal quarrel as in enforcing the law.

Harry Morse was cut from another cloth. He was a solid, public-spirited citizen, a sober family man of moral as well as physical courage. His career as a lawman spanned five decades. Instead of drifting from place to place, he remained in his community and took an active hand in civic leadership. He never once pulled the trigger in a personal quarrel, but only as a last resort when making a lawful arrest. His companions were not gamblers and gunfighters but judges, lawyers, journalists, and prominent businessmen. During his lifetime Harry Morse was far better known on the West Coast than Wild Bill Hickok, Wyatt Earp, or Bat Masterson. For half a century his name was prominent in the newspapers, and even Ned Buntline, who discovered William F. "Buffalo Bill" Cody, made Harry Morse a dime novel hero.

Alameda County—Sheriff Morse's bailiwick—is today a study in contradictions. Nestled in the Oakland-Berkeley hills are the expensive mansions of Montclair and Piedmont, but only a mile away, in the Oakland "flats," are the crime- and poverty-ridden streets of one of the worst slums in the western United States. There, drugs, prostitution, and street crime of every type are a daily fact of life, as is one of the highest murder rates in the nation, triggered by rival drug gangs battling for supremacy. To the south are the sprawling, middle-class housing tracts of San Leandro, Hayward, and Fremont. Just over the towering hills to the east light industry and office parks have sprouted up like weeds in once-rural Pleasanton and Livermore; and cattle, grain, grapes, and nuclear energy are nurtured side by side in the fertile valleys of Amador and Livermore. Congested freeways snake to and fro throughout the county, Oakland's port is one of the busiest in the country, and the land teems with the burden of its million inhabitants.

The strange anomaly that is modern Alameda County is perhaps not so strange when one compares it with the tableau that Harry Morse first encountered when he arrived in California in 1849. The ugly urban sprawl of the East Bay flats was then a wild, fertile plain, covered with thick growths of mustard and wild oak, interrupted only by scattered cattle and Indian trails and occupied by a few wealthy dons and a handful of ornery squatters, while the rest of the county was left to cattle, sheep, and Indians. For it would not be until the mid-1850s that towns like Oakland and San Leandro would blossom. It is difficult to imagine that this once pastoral setting became the scene of one of the great dramas of the Old West: Sheriff Harry Morse's epic struggle to exterminate the murderers, *bandidos*, cattle rustlers, horse thieves, and highway robbers who blocked development and retarded growth in California during the rapid immigration and expansion of the frontier era.

The modern crime problems faced by Alameda County's computerized, motorized police and sheriff's departments, employing several thousand personnel, are utterly dwarfed by the challenge that faced young Harry Morse when he first became sheriff in 1864. As a lone horseman on the windswept hills, armed with nothing but raw courage and a Colt revolver, his only armor a silver star pinned to his breast, he squared off against a small army of desperadoes and beat them at their own game. He shot to death the notorious bandidos Narato Ponce and Juan Soto, outgunned and wounded the vicious Narciso Bojorques, captured Joaquin Murrieta's nephew, Procopio Bustamante, a preeminent bandit chieftain, and pursued the Tiburcio Vasquez gang for two months in one of the frontier's longest and most tenacious manhunts. Later, as a private detective, Morse captured Black Bart, America's greatest stagecoach robber, and played a leading role in many of the most sensational criminal cases of the day: his investigations of the Dupont Street Frauds, implicating San Francisco's mayor in political corruption; the Harkins Opium Ring, resulting in the prosecution of a corrupt federal magistrate; the case of Theodore Durrant, San Francisco's most infamous murderer; the Selby Smelter Robbery, one of the biggest thefts of that era; and the mysterious death of the philanthropist Jane Stanford in 1905.

For the most part, Harry Morse enjoyed good press during his lifetime. But in retrospect a close look at Morse's life raises questions about his character that must be examined. Did he treat fairly the Hispanic community, or was he a racist who trampled the rights of frontier California's largest minority group? Was he overzealous, and did he use unreliable evidence against some men he arrested? Did he deliberately frame the outlaw Bartolo Sepulveda for murder? Was he a parsimonious reward-monger? A publicity hound who helped manufacture his own legend? These questions can be answered only by examining both his life and the times in which he lived.

Harry Morse's story is told here, whenever possible, in his own words. Fortunately for the historian, Morse loved to tell tales of his adventures, and he was frequently interviewed by newspaper reporters. During the early 1880s, in an effort to publicize his fledgling detective agency, Morse wrote a series of long articles about some of his most famous manhunts. These accounts, rich in the color of the horseback era and written only a decade after the events they portray, are the most complete and detailed contemporary narratives of a frontier lawman known to this writer. Because of their rarity, their historical importance, and the sense of drama, immediacy of action, and insight into Morse's personality that they provide, these memoirs have been woven into the narrative. They appear here with some editing and annotation. Minor errors in grammar and spelling have been corrected, and several accounts have been reduced in length to eliminate redundant or extraneous material. Morse's words and their meaning have not been changed or altered.

This book is a look—actually, a glance—at a long-forgotten era and a vanished way of life, a time when the old Spanish-Mexican social order was in rapid decline and Anglo power and influence were on the rise. It was a time when that clash between the disenfranchised Hispanic and the land-hungry Anglo reached its inevitable nadir, catching men such as Harry Morse viselike in the middle. And it was a time when social upheaval resulted in extraordinary crime and murder rates.

This is also a look at the dark underbelly of life in the two Californias of that time. One was a frontier world of cantinas, gambling halls, brothels, and fandango houses where *aguardiente* and blood flowed freely and where men lived and died by pistol and poniard, a lawman's world of rugged wilderness peopled by elusive mounted bandits, of thousand-mile manhunts, bone-wearying horseback rides, and heart-stopping gun battles. The other was an urban world of burgeoning young towns and cities, burdened by grafters, bribe takers, tinhorn politicians, corrupt officials, smugglers, counterfeiters, forgers, and confidence men, a world of smoke-filled back rooms reeking with the stench of moral and municipal corruption.

This, then, is a glimpse at the life and times of Harry Morse.

Acknowledgments

IN 1972 I published a magazine article on Harry N. Morse and conceived the idea of writing a full-length biography. But it was not until 1985 that I began researching the story in earnest. While piecing together Morse's life I became indebted to many people for their generous help and encouragement.

First and foremost, I must acknowledge the help of my great friend William B. Secrest, *the* authority on the outlaws and lawmen of frontier California. Bill has aided me in so many ways I doubt he even remembers them all. He provided everything from advice to research help to copies of rare photographs. Bill's broad knowledge of California history coupled with a deep insight into frontier lawlessness and a knack for uncovering long-forgotten source material have proved invaluable to me. This book could not have been written without his generous assistance.

I also owe thanks to four pals from the San Francisco Corral of Westerners for their aid and advice over the years: Bob Chandler, Dick Dillon, Kevin Mullen, and Al Shumate, gentlemen, scholars, and authors all. Each provided data and encouragement so many times I lost count.

I owe a special word of gratitude to Jeané Isoard, great-granddaughter of Harry N. Morse; her father, Widber de la Montanya, ran the Morse Detective Agency in San Francisco for many years.

Of particular help have been Bill Sturm and Larry Odoms, of the Oakland Public Library History Room, who allowed me unfettered access to all the materials in their collections, and the late J. E. (Jack) Reynolds, who generously shared with me his research on Harry Morse and Tiburcio Vasquez.

Conrad Yamamoto, of the San Mateo County Library, has helped me for years in obtaining countless items on interlibrary loan.

I extend many thanks to Joseph P. Samora of the California State Archives, Ann Doss of the Amador-Livermore Valley Historical Society, Barbara Bunshah of the Livermore Heritage Guild, Julia O'Keefe of Santa Clara University, Maggie Schaus of the Stockton Public Library, David R. Bricknell, retired commander of the Alameda County Sheriff's Department, Sybille Zemitas of the California State Library, Dr. Ron Limbaugh of the University of the Pacific, Roberta Hagood of the Marion County Historical Society in Hannibal, Missouri, and the staffs of the Bancroft Library at the University of California, Berkeley, the Huntington Library in San Marino, the California Historical Society Library in San Francisco, the Society of California Pioneers Library in San Francisco, the Oakland Museum, the Haggin Museum in Stockton, and the Ralph Milliken Museum in Los Banos.

I also owe special thanks to Chris Brewer, Harold G. Davidson, Harold L. Edwards, Peter Frusetta, John D. Gilchriese, Mark P. Hall-Patton, Phil Hudner, Bruce Levene, Greg Martin, Tom Martin, Roger McGrath, Gary Ogle, Robert Olsen, Marc Reed, Colin Rickards, Joseph G. Rosa, William B. Secrest, Jr., Bart Sepulveda, Boyd Stephens, M.D., Monroe Stinson, Richard K. Tibbals, and Troy Tuggle.

Last, I owe more than I can express to my wife, Marta S. Diaz, a trial lawyer, who helped with everything from Spanish-language translations to guidance regarding criminal jurisprudence while running a household, raising two boys, and managing a law practice at the same time. Her patience and understanding allowed this project to come to fruition.

Lawman

Prologue

A bitter January wind howled up Corral Hollow and sent shivers through the three horsemen as they made their way carefully down the arroyo bed, their mustangs stepping skittishly on the wet rocks and the muddy adobe clay. The lead rider blew into his cupped hands and hunched himself over against the wind as the sun slowly dropped behind the looming shadow of the Coast Range. They said little as they spurred their horses gingerly down the trail, once part of El Camino Viejo and long used by Indians, mustang runners, and cattle drivers as an entrance into the San Joaquin Valley.

The leader was a clean-shaven, boyish, twenty-three-year-old Californio with fair skin, a distinctive Roman nose, and dark curly hair protruding from his flat-brimmed sombrero. A brace of Colt Army .44s were shoved into a red sash around his waist, and from his bootleg protruded the ivory handle of a razor-sharp poniard. Behind him rode a youth about the same age, a strikingly handsome Sonoreno, lean and lanky, with the grace of a man born to the saddle. He too was heavily armed, with a long-barreled six-shooter in the waistband of his trousers and a knife shoved into the top of the goatskin leggings that covered his lower legs. They were followed by a heavyset vaquero with coal black hair and features of a mahogany hue. Swaying gracefully in their saddles, the trio used their spurs sparingly on their mustangs as they cantered down the rocky arroyo.

It was dark when they approached the spot where Corral Hollow opens up onto the great broad plain of the San Joaquin Valley. About three hundred feet from the trail stood the small wood cabin owned by the cattleman Aaron Golding, a stable and corral adjoining it. The three horsemen dismounted, removed their spurs, and tied their animals to a creekside scrub oak. The sun's last rays dimmed like a snuffed candle behind the western mountains, and the darkness swallowed up the three as they walked silently toward the cabin.

Moments later a woman's terrified shriek shattered the night air.

3

It was followed by the crash and din of a violent struggle, punctuated by excited shouts in Spanish and the hysterical crying of a young child. Finally the muffled thud of gunshots echoed inside the clapboard cabin, accompanied by the sickening slash of knife blades plunging into flesh.

Then all was quiet. Three shadowy figures emerged at a trot, their high-heeled boots slipping precariously in the adobe mud. Behind them a wall of flame leaped up from the cabin, silhouetting them against the night sky as they swung lithely onto their mustangs and retraced their tracks up Corral Hollow toward the Livermore Valley. Their saddlebags heavy with coin, they rode hard to distance themselves from the scene. By the time they reached the Alisal at midnight they were in a jubilant mood. Tethering their horses near a crumbling adobe, they vanished into a cantina and were lost to the tinkling of glasses, the clink of coin at the monte tables, the laughter of señoritas, and the music of the fandango.

As the first rays of dawn stretched across the great valley the charred remains of Golding's cabin appeared like a blackened gash on the landscape. Inside, burned beyond recognition, were the cindered bodies of Aaron Golding, his Mexican wife, Cossuth, his adopted son, Santero, and his vaquero, Pedro.

And the wind seemed to moan for vengeance as it whipped across the tules and through the lonely scrub oak of Corral Hollow.

CHAPTER 1

A Teenage Argonaut

HARRY Morse came from a long line of Puritan pioneers. His ancestors settled in New England in 1735 and were among the founders of Dedham, Massachusetts. A penchant for soldiering ran in their blood: Morse's great-grandfather served in the French and Indian wars, his grandfather fought in the Revolutionary War, and his father, Abraham Washington Morse, saw service as an eleven-year-old drummer boy in the War of 1812. Abraham Morse, a merchant tailor, married Charlotte E. Speight, a native of Leeds, England, and they made their home in New York City, where their son Henry Nicholson Morse was born on February 2, 1835. He had an older half-brother, George P. Goff, from his mother's previous marriage, and a sister, Charlotte Morse.

Harry, as his parents called him, spent his boyhood in New York City, attending Public School No. 7, in Christy Street, until he was ten years old. But the boy had a yen for travel and adventure, and he longed to go to sea. In 1845, with his parents' blessing, he shipped before the mast, not as a cabin boy, but as a common sailor. For four years he sailed between New York and Liverpool. Early in 1849, while on a visit home, he and his father took a walk on Wall Street, then abuzz with the topic of the day—the discovery of gold in California. Abraham Morse remarked, "Harry, how would you like to go to California?"

A voyage to the gold fields—"to see the elephant" in the vernacular of the times—would be the adventure of a lifetime. The boy was so excited by the idea that he immediately went down to the wharf and signed up as a seaman on the East India packet *Panama*. The *Panama* had been purchased by a company of gold hunters, each paying their share. The written prospectus, issued by the leaders of the company, declared optimistically that the ship would "sail to the mines direct, anchor in the river, and be a home for the passengers while they gathered up the gold," and then return them to New

Left to right: Harry Morse's father, Abraham W. Morse, his sister Charlotte, and his mother, Charlotte Speight Morse. This image was taken in New York City in 1849. From original daguerreotype in author's collection.

York. Many, like young Morse, were experienced sailors but could not afford to purchase a share in the company, and they were more than happy to go "by the run," to work for their passage to California. The *Panama* left New York on February 4, 1849, with Captain Russell S. Bodfish at the helm. On board were two hundred males and four females—an indication to the Argonauts of the paucity of women they would find in California.[1]

The voyage to the West Coast lasted six months. The journey around Cape Horn alone took six weeks because of strong head winds. This was the most difficult and terrifying part of the journey, and one of the passengers left a vivid description in his diary entry of April 17:

> Never before have we witnessed anything like what presents itself to view this morning. The wind has howled to such an extent that we have lived through a day of suspense and fear. The sea seems determined to overwhelm us, and appears to be one bed of froth. The towering masses of water, when we get in the trough of the sea, appear on both sides of us, like a dreary mountainous country when covered with snow. At one moment our jib-boom points to the regions above, the next moment toward the devil's home as if undetermined whether to send us to hell or heaven. . . . Oh! To see those huge white-capped mountain waves as they would curl, threatening us with instant destruction, when our noble ship, true to her helm, would bound and glide over them, and mounting high on another, quiver for an instant, then plunging down the receding wave, bury her head in a sea of foam, deluging her decks, she would again advance up another wave.[2]

Captain Bodfish was a seasoned mariner, and he made slow but safe headway. They lay at port in Talcuahana, Chile, a full month to rest, repair the ship, and take on fresh water and supplies. The *Panama* finally approached San Francisco on August 8, 1849, having lost not a soul to sickness or drowning. As the ship entered the Golden Gate, Harry Morse caught his first glimpse of his new home. But what he saw was not the village of San Francisco, which was hidden from view by the rocks and hills of the southern promontory of the Golden Gate. Instead, peering through the Gate, he saw what the Spanish had named the Contra Costa, the opposite shore, directly across the bay. Harry Morse never forgot that first glimpse of his future home.

There was something strangely attractive to the ship's crew in the long, low sweep of coast on the shore opposite San Francisco. The vivid green of the live oaks looked in the dim distance like an oasis in the midst of a great, brown countryside. The low shoreline was backed up by high hills upon some of whose ridges grew immense redwood trees. The crew's curiosity about the Contra Costa grew, and finally a few of us determined on an exploring expedition. Obtaining one of the ship's small boats, we set sail on the fair morning of August 15, 1849, and landed at about the foot of Oakland's present Broadway. That is how I came to see the oak groves and the site of the city in all of its untouched, original beauty.

We walked up from the waterfront into the edge of these mighty trees and gazed about us with a feeling of surprise and pleasure at the beautiful vistas spread before us. There was nothing to break the solitude of the place except the occasional lowing of semi-wild cattle or the bleating of calves belonging to the herd. Over the broad acres as far as the eye could reach there was no sign of man or his habitation. The undergrowth was full of quail, while now and then a deer would start up and bound away, giving a startled, almost reproachful look at the intruders. The country was lovely, the climate delightful. Here in the Contra Costa nature had been most prodigal. Here on this ideal site for a great city, Oakland was to be born as a town in 1852 and incorporated as a city two years later.[3]

The *Panama*'s crew deserted shortly after she made port, and the ship, like scores of others, was left abandoned at anchor in the bay. Goods of all kinds were scarce, and prices and wages were very high. Young Morse spent his first month in San Francisco, cooking for sailors at the munificent rate of $5 a day. Although he had never done any cooking before, he managed to earn enough to save a small grubstake and soon departed for the mother lode. He spent the winter working the placer mines at Carson Creek in Mariposa County, then drifted from Angels Camp to Mormon Gulch, Sonora, Jamestown, and Woods Creek. It was hard work for a fourteen-year-old boy who stood but five feet tall, but young Harry was of sturdy build and never shied from heavy labor. However, he quickly realized that the wild stories of easy riches he had so eagerly devoured in New York had been great exaggerations. Like most Argonauts he did not strike it rich, but he did save enough money to return to San Francisco and buy several small boats. For a year the energetic youth lightered coal to departing ships and ferried passengers ashore from arriving steamers to the foot of Mission Street. The work was hard, but Morse always remembered that time with fondness.

Harry Morse at age four-
teen. Copied from a da-
guerreotype taken in New
York before he left for California in 1849. Courtesy of
the Oakland Museum of
California.

I was the owner of a sloop in those days called the Flat Iron. *John Ross
[owner of the sloop* Bobtail] *and myself made up a race one day to sail
from the foot of Broadway out to the bar at the mouth of Oakland Creek
and return. We started out all right amidst great excitement among the
boys. I kept near enough to the* Bobtail *in beating out to the mouth of the
creek to give me hopes of winning the race, but when we turned and got
to running before the wind, Ross's boat soon left the* Flat Iron *behind and
to save the good name of our boat and a bad beating we deliberately per-
mitted our boat to capsize, compelling the* Bobtail *to put back to our rescue. We had lots of fun over it at supper the same evening.*[4]

Although Morse earned a good income with his vessels, his restless streak led him through a series of varied occupations. In mid-
1851 he sold his boats and went to work for Dallum Brothers' bakery
driving a delivery wagon. In 1852 he left San Francisco for the tiny
village of Redwood City, situated twenty-five miles to the south on
the Redwood Creek slough. It was a principal shipping point of lumber that was sent up the bay on schooners for the rapid building in

San Francisco. Here he constructed the town's first hotel, the Eureka House, at the corner of Main and Bridge streets. It was a substantial wooden building, two stories high, measuring fifty by thirty feet, and it would stand at least another forty-three years. Morse drew the plans, and although he had never done any carpentering before, he performed all the labor himself, a remarkable achievement for a seventeen-year-old youth.

He took on a partner, a young friend named Daniel W. Balch, and they ran the hotel for a year. There were a score of lumber mills in the heavily wooded hills, and from eighty to one hundred teamsters arrived at the embarcadero daily with lumber for the San Francisco-bound schooners. The two young innkeepers did a land-office business. Not satisfied with building the first principal structure in town, Morse also constructed the first bridge across Redwood Creek. In those years the social and political life of every American village revolved around its volunteer fire department, and Harry Morse and his partner were among the first to join the fledgling settlement's fire brigade.[5]

I was only seventeen then. Everything was bright and I thought the world was mine. One thing in particular I have not forgotten was the town's first fire department. The machinery consisted of one long pole with a hook and chain attached, one long ladder, and about a dozen buckets. William Holbrook was foreman and I was assistant foreman. Those of the members whom I can recall were Dan Balch, Charley Perkins, George Thatcher, John Voorhies, Charley Ayers, and William Holder.

The first call we had after the company was organized was for a fire that broke out in Holbrook's office. Billy used to tally lumber at the landing and had a 6x8 redwood shanty near the creek. One day he went out to lunch, leaving a hot fire in his stove, and the result was that the office caught fire and the department was called out. Off we went in a mad rush, some of us with the ladder and some with the long pole with hook and chain attachment.

The first move was to thrust the long pole into the office. Then away we started, pulling the office after us, and Billy following, screaming cuss words and trying to get us to let up on the destruction of his home. There was not much of the office left when the fire department got through with it.[6]

Although they were too young to vote, both Morse and Balch were active in local politics. But things went sour for them in June

1853, when financial difficulties arose. The two boys had unwisely signed as security on loans for some insolvent business associates, and when the loans came due, the creditors came after them. Balch's brother bailed them out, but Morse had to turn over to him all he owned, including the hotel. Everything he had worked for during the past four years had suddenly vanished. Disgusted and disenchanted, young Morse left Redwood City for the rapidly growing port town of Oakland, where he hoped to start anew. He went to work for an uncle there who had opened a butcher shop. By then he had grown another ten and a half inches, all gristle and muscle.

Like most forty-niners, young Morse certainly spent some time in saloons and gambling halls. These were important social centers for young unmarried men in antebellum America. Volunteer fire companies, militia units, and political organizations also provided gathering places where men shared company, cemented friendships, drank together, fought together, and garnered each other's respect. In California during the 1850s the scarcity of women made such places even more attractive than they were in the East. In that bachelor subculture a cult of masculinity arose in which physical prowess and personal honor were exalted. Honor and respect had to be earned; a man had honor only if other men said so. If a man's personal reputation was challenged, if he was accused of being a coward or a liar or a cheat, only an act of valor or retribution could restore his honor and his position among his peers. Thus minor disputes were often resolved in rough and tumble fights; formal duels, fought over matters of personal honor, occurred frequently in 1850s California.

Although Harry Morse carried a revolver for self-protection during the gold rush, he had little use for guns, preferring brawn instead. The years of hard labor had made him tough and strong. California's male-dominated culture firmly embedded in his personality the rough ethics of honor and of refusal to back down from an enemy. He picked up the fine points of that most popular of sports among young men, the "manly art" of bare knuckle boxing. Morse's strength and agility made him a natural pugilist. His honesty, courage, and willingness to fight when necessary won him a host of friends.[7]

The humdrum labor of a butcher seems to have held little attraction for Harry Morse. Now eighteen and imbued with that restlessness of spirit that had seized an entire westering generation, he craved adventure and excitement. Both were sorely missing from his lackluster life as an innkeeper and butcher. In his spare time he ea-

gerly listened to stories of the many brigands who infested Alameda
County: Joaquin Murrieta, who reportedly once lived in an adobe in
Alameda Canyon, now Niles Canyon, thirty miles south of Oakland;
Murrieta's brother-in-law Claudio Feliz, who raided John W. Kot-
tinger's rancho in the Livermore Valley in 1852 and later was slain
with several of his *compadres* in a bloody gunfight with a posse near
Monterey; Jack Powers, who with his vaqueros made many trips
from San Francisco through Oakland and the Livermore Valley, to
and from the mines; Tom Gear, noted as the chief of a band of cattle
thieves at Mission San Jose until two Mexican gang members were
lynched in 1855; and Ramon Anzavierra, who was tracked down and
slain in 1853 after killing Dr. John Marshall in one of frontier Oakland's most celebrated murder cases.

Listening to Oakland's storefront yarn-spinners tell of such blood-
curdling events must have injected at least a particle of color into the
youth's otherwise drab existence. And it was not long before Harry
Morse had his own electrifying encounter with a notorious bandido,
one that he not only recalled in minute detail more than thirty years
later but, more significant, seems to have marked him indelibly.

*On a bright morning in the spring of 1854, just as the little ferry
steamboat* Clinton, *which then plied across the bay of San Francisco, was
about leaving its wharf at Oakland, on its first trip for that day, a Mexican, mounted on a spirited mustang, galloped down the slight declivity
which leads to the embarcadero and rode over the gang-plank onto the
steamer's deck. He was a dashing-looking fellow, and sat on his horse with
that easy grace that a life spent in the saddle gives to all native Californians or Mexicans. It was evident that he was anxious to conceal his identity, for his broad-brimmed sombrero was drawn well down over his eyes,
and his face was closely muffled in a large woolen comforter, and as he
dismounted he studiously kept his back toward the throng of passengers.
No sooner had he reached the deck than the gang-plank was drawn in, the
lines cast loose and the little steamer commenced slowly to drift away from
the dock.*

*At that moment some one of the passengers who thronged the forward
deck cried out, "Look out, boys! Here's Felipe! Here's Felipe!"*

*The liveliest commotion followed this exclamation. The passengers
rushed in a body toward the spot indicated by the individual who had discovered the presence of the obnoxious horseman, and for a moment there
was a fine promise of work for the coroner.*

"Shoot him!" "Knock him down and tie him!" "Pitch him overboard!"
were the cries that came from the crowd as it surged in a mass toward the
object of this popular demonstration. But the Mexican was not idly waiting for his enemies to put their threats into execution. At the first indication that his identity was discovered, he sprang into his saddle, drew his
six-shooter and flourishing it in a threatening manner over the heads of
passengers who crowded near him, clapped his spurs into the sides of the
little mustang and made a rush for the open space between the boat and
the wharf. It was a bold attempt, but the horse cleared it in a bound,
dashed with his daring rider up the road and was out of sight before the
astonished multitude had recovered from their alarm.

The hero of this escapade was Felipe Carabajal, a notorious Mexican
desperado, whose name was a terror to the rancheros of that section of the
state. He had committed numerous murders and robberies, and yet so cun-
ningly had he succeeded in covering up his tracks that it had been found
impossible to procure sufficient evidence to convict him of any of the
crimes he had perpetrated.

My introduction to Felipe was shortly subsequent to his adventure on
the ferryboat, and when I was yet in the heyday of youth. It was a bright
moonlit night in September. I was returning home from a visit to the village of Alameda, about three miles distant. The sky was clear and the
stars shone like myriads of gems in the deep blue canopy that rounded in
the wonderful fullness of its mystic depths above. It was one of those clear,
crisp nights peculiar to the California climate just before the rainy season
sets in. Not a living thing was in sight as I drove along under the great
massive oaks that grew in and about the little slumbering town. The road
leading between Alameda and Oakland ran through a dense growth of
wild mustard, which at that time grew profusely all over the valley, and at-
tained on this rich land a height of eight or ten feet.

Where the road enters what is now East Oakland, stood a notorious
rendezvous and fandango house known all over the country as the
"Chileno Gate." This institution had in connection with it a bull pen,
where throngs of Mexicans assembled on Sundays to witness the exciting
spectacles of bull-fighting, horse racing, cock-fighting and other equally
interesting and sanguinary exhibitions. The Chileno Gate was an earthly
pandemonium nightly. Pretty women were in attendance to attract patrons, and the discordant scrapings of an asthmatic violin excited the
Terpsichorean proclivities of the gathered rabble who alternately danced
and drank of the vilest of liquors until the full break of the coming day.

As my little buckskin horse quietly jogged along the Alameda road I lit *a cigar and under the gentle influence of the balmy air and peaceful starlight my thoughts wandered back to the old folks at home in the East. While thus meditating, the sound of galloping horses broke upon my ears. I could hear the clatter of the animals' feet approaching behind, but owing to the dense shadows thrown out from the great oaks, I could not distinguish the comers. I was unarmed, and preferred my own company to that of any bushwhacking greaser who might be out on a raid after plunder, and I was prompted by a due regard for my personal safety to chirrup to the little buckskin nag to accelerate his pace. The horse responded at once, and in a few seconds I was in the open country. Looking back, I observed two horsemen coming rapidly toward me and a moment later one of them hailed me in Spanish.*

"Espere vosotros un instante!" he shouted. [Wait a moment!]

I paid no attention to his command, but touched my horse on the flanks with the whip and started him on the dead run through the wild mustard. It was well I commenced in earnest when I did to get out of the way of my pursuers, for one of them was already swinging his lasso, and both were urging their horses to their utmost speed to overtake me. I was now thoroughly alarmed, for I saw that my only chance to escape was in the speed and endurance of my horse. When I got fairly into the mustard I noticed that the road was so narrow and the vegetation so high it would be almost impossible for my pursuers to swing their lassos with any effect. My little horse fairly flew over the ground, and was fast taking me to a place of safety. I could hear my Mexican friends as they galloped along after me. The gallant little buckskin, seeming to partake of the excitement of the chase, responded to every touch of the whip, and in a few moments I was through the mustard and in sight of Chileno Gate, where a fandango was going on in full blast.

I rode up to the door, fully confident that among the many persons within I should find someone who would assist me if the knights of the road returned to assail me there. Almost the first person I met was a man named James D. Arlington, whom I knew in Oakland, who, although I knew he associated generally with a rough class, still I thought he could be depended upon for an emergency of this kind, where it was Mexican against American. I told him about the chase up the road, and as the men did not put in an appearance, Arlington advised me to wait awhile. I was desirous of finding out who my pursuers were, so that I would be able to recognize them whenever we might meet again, in town or elsewhere.

I remained at Chileno Gate about an hour and in company with Arlington rode into Oakland. From the description I gave of the man who swung the reata, my companion expressed the opinion that he was Felipe. I arrived home without further adventure, and fully made up my mind that I would in the future keep better hours, and if business or pleasure again took me out late at night, I would go prepared to make a respectable defense.[8]

Felipe Carabajal appeared in Santa Barbara County, where he stole a band of horses. A posse tried to capture him on his return to Oakland, but he escaped after a sharp gunfight. In 1855 Carabajal robbed and murdered the owner of a trading post in Santa Clara County. His career came to an abrupt end on February 14, 1856. After stealing a horse near Oakland, he was pursued by a posse of citizens and cornered under a bridge across Indian Creek near what is now the head of Lake Merritt. Carabajal wounded one citizen, but when he tried to flee he was shot in the head and killed.

Such excitement seems only to have underscored young Morse's boredom and restlessness. When his uncle died, Harry Morse carried on the butcher business by himself. Later he took on a partner, who one day departed with the firm's funds to buy cattle and was never seen again. His hopes once more shattered, Morse was cheered when Dan Balch arrived from Redwood City. The youths journeyed north to Trinity County where Morse tried his hand again at butchering. In 1855 he returned to Oakland and got work driving a butcher wagon. Things brightened considerably for the young Argonaut that year, as he met and wooed sixteen-year-old Virginia Elizabeth Heslep, a striking, petite brunette and the daughter of Judge Augustus M. Heslep, a noted San Francisco lawyer and occasional journalist. Descended from a prominent family—her grandfather was the Revolutionary War hero General Brice Viers—Virginia was born in Brook County, Virginia, on August 5, 1838. When Virginia was still a child the family settled in Illinois, but in 1849 Augustus Heslep and his two brothers came overland to California. He left his wife, Editha, and children behind.[9]

Heslep was extremely ornery and an outspoken critic of men and events. Although a physician by profession, he thrived on conflict and found that lawyering was more to his liking. He soon became an attorney, and although he failed to obtain an appointment to the district court, he was ever after known as Judge Heslep. In 1853 he brought his wife and children across the plains to California, and the family settled in San Francisco. Heslep wrote often for the San Francisco and Sacramento newspapers. His sharp tongue and pen made him many enemies. The judge's cantankerous personality also caused friction between himself and his wife. In 1854 Editha moved with her children to San Jose so they could attend school there. The judge paid for Virginia's education at the College of Notre Dame in San Jose, a school that educated many of the belles of California's early days.

Despite his many faults, Heslep was a charitable man. He took into his San Francisco home a destitute British seaman, Edward Griffiths, and his wife and daughter. The judge was unable to find work for Griffiths in San Francisco, so he sent him with a letter of introduction to his brother, Joseph Heslep, who was the treasurer of Tuolumne County in Sonora. He too befriended Griffiths and offered to help him. On January 18, 1855, Griffiths repaid the Hesleps' kindness by murdering the treasurer with an ax and robbing his safe of $6,000 in county funds. The next day, when the stolen gold was discovered in Griffith's hotel room, an enraged mob lynched him. The grieving judge wrote an open letter to a San Francisco newspaper, the *Alta California,* warning the public about "extending their sympathies and charities" to strangers.[10]

Judge Heslep was not pleased when he learned of Virginia's romance with Harry Morse. He was in no frame of mind to welcome a stranger seeking his daughter's hand. The judge also believed that the rough-cut young butcher was not worthy of his educated and well-bred daughter. Virginia, however, was eager to escape from her parents and their unhappy marriage. When Harry asked for permission to wed Virginia, her father refused. Headstrong and impulsive, young Morse was hardly fazed by the judge's decision. He climbed through a window of the Heslep house at night and exited with tiny Virginia in his arms. On September 14, 1855, before the judge could interfere, they were married in Oakland.[11]

Augustus and Editha Heslep divorced, and soon after he remarried in San Francisco. His ex-wife and children, Virginia included, severed their ties with him. That same year, 1856, Heslep joined the San Francisco Committee of Vigilance, which was organized after the murder of the newspaper editor James King of William. Heslep helped prosecute Judge Edward "Ned" McGowan, a notorious scoundrel, on a charge of accessory to that killing. Although McGowan was acquitted, he never forgave Heslep or the other vigilantes. He published a newspaper, with the principal objective of

Virginia Morse and
daughter Emma in a
photograph printed
on leather, 1858.
Author's collection.

publicly humiliating as many vigilantes as possible. In 1858
McGowan claimed in print that Heslep had "debauched his own
daughter," a charge that he had falsely made against at least one
other vigilante. Heslep sued for libel, but in a courtroom brawl
McGowan thrashed him with a cane. Heslep's next fracas almost
cost him his life. When handling a land title lawsuit in 1863 against
Captain Charles M. Weber, the pioneer founder of the city of Stockton, the two quarreled. Weber drew a derringer and shot the unarmed lawyer in the back, a wound that would plague him for the
rest of his life.[12]

   Harry Morse and his teenage bride made their home in Oakland
and began a stable fifty-two-year marriage. Ten months later the
newlyweds welcomed their first child, George Balch Morse, who was
not only his father's greatest pride but also would be the cause of his

greatest anguish. Harry Morse continued to labor as a butcher, but the crime and violence of the California frontier continued an inexorable pull on him.

On the north side of Broadway between First and Second Streets was a wholesale and retail butcher shop owned and carried on by a French Basque named Bartolo Baratie. He was a jolly good soul and quite prominent in Oakland at the time he resided here in 1856. The way I came to know Baratie so well was because Felix Chapelet and myself used to slave for him in those days. I use the word slave advisedly, for slave we two certainly did. We were up and at work at 4 o'clock each morning and worked until 8 and 10 and sometimes as late as 12 o'clock at night.

Two such faithful workers Baratie never had before, and I believed he recognized the fact, from the amount of work he piled upon us at times. However, we were young and tough and so survived it, and Baratie grew rich, so rich that in about a year's time, he, together with his wife and one or two servants moved from Oakland into San Luis Obispo County to the Rancho San Juan Capistrano, which he had purchased, intending to go into the business of raising cattle.[13]

More than forty years later Harry Morse would recall in vivid detail the horrible fate of his former employer. On May 12, 1858, a month after the Baratie party and his partner, M. Jose Borel, had settled on the rancho, they were attacked by the Jack Powers–Pio Linares bandit gang. Baratie and Borel were murdered in cold blood, the rancho was looted, and Baratie's wife, Andrea, was kidnapped and raped. This savagery electrified the citizens of San Luis Obispo, who had long tolerated lesser outrages. They formed a vigilance committee and quickly broke up the gang, lynching seven, killing Pio Linares in a bloody gunfight, and driving Jack Powers into Mexico where he was later slain.[14]

Although Morse had ceased working for Baratie the previous year, the shocking news of the Basque's murder seems to have deeply impressed on him the human toll of violent crime. But the young butcher had no way of knowing that the killing of Baratie was merely symptomatic of California's unsettled society of the 1850s, a cauldron of social and racial unrest that resulted in a homicide rate sixteen times greater than the current national rate.[15]

In 1858 Harry and his young wife welcomed another child, Emma Charlotte. But even marriage and family seem not to have quelled

Morse's restless spirit. He continued to drift from one venture to another. Leaving his butcher business, he became an expressman for Bamber & Co.'s Express. He soon began his own express company, delivering newspapers and packages throughout the western part of Alameda County and also across the bay to San Francisco. In 1858, while making a return trip from San Francisco, Morse chanced to be the lead player in a dramatic incident that provided a glimpse of that strength of character and purpose which wold soon thrust him into the public eye. An eyewitness related the episode twenty years later:

On a pleasant, balmy day in the year 1858, I happened to be a passenger on the old ferry boat *Contra Costa* which then made her regular three trips per day between the big city of San Francisco and the little town of Oakland. It was the middle, or noon, trip. We had left the wharf on the 'Frisco side and the boat was about midway between the city and the Oakland bar, opposite Goat Island. I stood on the upper deck watching the ponderous walking-beam of the low-pressure engine and listening to the regular drumming of the paddle wheels as they revolved and the buckets struck one after another into the deep, green water. All nature seemed to be doing its best to make the day beautiful and enjoyable. The hills and mountains of the Oakland side were covered with rich green verdure and flowers of all the different hues of the rainbow.

On the lower deck of the steamer were little groups of men gazing out toward the shore. Close up in the bow of the boat stood a small team of horses, hitched to an express wagon which was loaded with bundles and packages of various kinds. On the seat of the wagon sat a young man apparently about twenty-two or twenty-three years of age, busily engaged in noting down in a little memorandum book his various business engagements of the day. His clothing was that of a laboring man, consisting of a blue flannel overshirt, pants of coarse material, the legs of which were encased in the uppers of a stout pair of "stogy" boots, and on his head he wore a rather broad-brimmed black hat which fitted well down over his face, and from under which protruded a profusion of silken dark brown hair. The face was entirely devoid of any beard and was as smooth as that of a girl. A long, thin nose denoted shrewdness in its possessor, and a pair of dark-blue eyes, slightly inclined to grey, looked fearlessly into your own when they were turned toward you. The square, finely cut jaw indicated great firmness of character. In fact, the face was one which most people would take a second look at when meeting its owner for the first time. He was well known to all on board the boat as a quiet, determined young fellow who was always ready to fight for his friends and as equally ready to forgive an enemy. And he had many friends, for he had been through many a tough set-to in protecting the helpless weak against the tyrannical strong.

On the starboard side of the boat, leaning with his back against the rail that was placed across the forward gangway, was a lad of about twelve years of age. He was a light-hearted, merry little fellow, eyes beaming with the mischievous sport of boyhood, and was a great favorite with the Oakland people, to whom he was well known; and he was fairly idolized by his mother and father. Full of youthful exuberance, the youngster could not remain quiet, but kept pushing with his back against the rail. Suddenly a cry of horror went up from the throng of passengers. The rail had lifted from its place and the little fellow, who had stood there a moment before, full of life and buoyant enjoyment, fell with a piercing shriek backward into the deep waters of the bay.

All was confusion on the instant. A simultaneous rush was made to the side of the steamer, the passengers fearing that the boy would be struck by the paddle wheel and torn into pieces. But so terrible a fate was not to befall him. Luckily, he fell just far enough from the vessel's side to escape such a horrible death.

The bell was instantly rung to "stop her," then "back her." While this was being done, the quick stern voice of Captain Ned Lewis was heard ordering the forward boat to be cleared away. The order was promptly executed and the boat was swung overboard over the rail of the steamer, ready to be lowered at a signal from the captain. By this time the headway of the steamer had carried her a long way past the struggling boy. As soon as the vessel had come to a standstill, the boat was lowered into the water, the tackles unhitched, and the steamer commenced backing in the direction of the lad, who was now far astern. In the hurry the men had forgotten to put the plug into the drain hole in the bottom of the boat, and she began to fill rapidly with water. A hasty search was made for the plug

Harry Morse in a
photograph printed on
leather, circa 1858.
Courtesy Jack Reynolds.

but it could not be found, and one of the thole pins was used
as a substitute. This left them nothing but the plain gunwale
to work the oar upon. For all the benefit the steamer's boat was
likely to be in the emergency, the boy might have drowned.
The steamer by this time had backed to within about fifty
yards of the drowning boy, who was doing his best to keep his
head above water.

"In the name of God, why don't that boat get there?" exclaimed the excited passengers. "The boy will sink before they
reach him!"

"Clear the way there," said a low, quiet voice. "Clear the
way, and I will save the youngster."

All looked toward the speaker. It was the expressman. He
was stripped of his hat, shirt, and boots. A resolute look shown
out of his now wide-awake eyes. All made way for him. Rushing forward through the throng, he seized a small gang-plank
that was lying on the upper deck, dragged it to the side of the
steamer, and with a quick, dextrous movement, threw it over

the side into the water and plunged over head first after it. Quick as a flash he rose to the surface, grasped one end of the gang-plank and struck out toward the boy, pushing the float ahead of him.

"Keep up, Jimmy! Keep up a second more and I will be there!" exclaimed the swimmer, encouragingly.

When within a few feet of the little fellow the expressman observed the boy was about exhausted and almost ready to sink, and with a renewed effort, he increased his pace and came up to him just in time to save him. A wild hurrah of delight went up from the passengers on the steamer as they saw the little fellow clinging to the gang-plank, supported by the strong arm of the gallant expressman. The small boat soon came up and took them aboard the steamer, where both received the congratulations of the passengers. The boat was hoisted on deck and the *Contra Costa* continued on her way to the Oakland side.

That little boy is now [1878] a six-footer and lives in Los Angeles County. His name is James Howard and he is the son of Volney E. Howard, a prominent lawyer of that part of the state. The expressman's name was Harry N. Morse.[16]

CHAPTER 2

Bandidos Californios

HARRY Morse operated his express business for four years and took in a partner, Jeremiah Tyrrel. He sold out to Tyrrel in 1862 and ran a grocery store for a year. To alleviate his boredom, he took an active role in county politics and joined the newly formed Republican party. He was strongly pro-Union, and with the outbreak of the Civil War he helped to organize the Oakland Guard, the first military unit in Alameda County. The company was mustered in on August 31, 1861, with James Brown, a Mexican War veteran and later city marshal of Oakland, as captain. Harry Morse held the rank of first corporal, but he was soon promoted to first lieutenant. Later, in 1864, he was elected captain, a position he held for four years.[1]

California's citizens were sharply divided over the rebellion, and although the state remained loyal throughout the war, there were large numbers of Confederate sympathizers, known as Copperheads. Many of them were commonly believed to have banded together into such secret societies as the Knights of the Golden Circle. The Oakland Guard, like other local militia units, expected to be called into active duty if the bloodshed spread to the coast. This danger never materialized, and Morse and the others were reduced to drilling, parading, and otherwise making a show of force to demoralize the rebel sympathizers in their midst.

Harry Morse's activity in the Oakland Guard was a great benefit to him politically. He became widely known in Oakland and San Leandro as a staunch pro-Union man, and in 1863 he was appointed deputy provost marshal of Alameda County, with the principal duty of enrolling men for a California draft that never materialized. That same year, at age twenty-eight, he was unanimously nominated as the Republican candidate for sheriff. The *Alameda County Gazette*, which endorsed him and would be his staunchest supporter, reported that while his Democratic opponent, James Beazell, campaigned actively, Morse "did not canvass the county and made but little effort in any

way to secure votes for himself." In the election on September 2 he
garnered 1,309 votes to Beazell's 820. He sold his grocery business
and took office on March 7, 1864, becoming one of the youngest
sheriffs in the state's history.[2]

This was to prove the most important turning point in Morse's
life. But although he was extremely proud to be chosen sheriff, his
political opponents did not think it much of an honor. One of his enemies, John Scott, editor of the *Oakland Daily Transcript*, later recalled,

> At the time Harry was first nominated the office was not
> considered to be worth much. Fees were small and business
> light. The office had been carelessly conducted, and as a con-
> sequence there was the "deuce to pay" generally. Laxity of ad-
> ministration produced its legitimate results. The sparsely settled
> valleys of Livermore and Amador were overrun by bands of
> horse-thieves and desperadoes, and the incursions of these law-
> less men even penetrated the thickly settled regions on this side
> of the hills. The settlers were at the mercy of the villains, and
> could only sit quietly in their homes and see their horses, cat-
> tle, and sheep taken in droves, thankful that their humble
> homes and lives were spared. Of course, with the existing state
> of affairs, aspirants for the office of sheriff were not numerous
> and clamorous.[3]

Morse appointed twenty-five-year-old Peter R. Borein undersheriff. Borein was Morse's good friend and a fellow member of the
Masonic fraternity. (Borein's son Edward, born nine years later in
San Leandro, would achieve fame as one of the great artists of the
American West.) The undersheriff's principal duties involved bookkeeping, running the jail, and managing the civil duties of the sheriff's office.[4]

Sheriff Morse's new bailiwick was some eight hundred square
miles, fairly small for a California county. Its population was a little
more than ten thousand. The principal towns were Oakland and
San Leandro, the latter the county seat until 1873, when the courts
and county offices were moved to Oakland. South of San Leandro
were the tiny villages of Hayward, Alvarado, and Mission San Jose,
which, confusingly, is located fifteen miles north of San Jose in
present-day Fremont. To the east was a rugged range of tall hills, an

Morse's friend Peter R.
Borein, undersheriff of
Alameda County from
1864 to 1874. Courtesy
Harold G. Davidson.

arm of the Coast Range running north and south and effectively dividing the county in half, both geographically and culturally. The west side of these hills (today's East Bay flats) was well settled by the 1860s, with rapidly growing towns and prosperous farms, dairies, mills and saltworks along San Francisco Bay. The settlers here were mainly Anglos, and they constituted the large majority of the county's population.

Across the hills to the east lay the expansive Livermore and Amador valleys. Although a horseman on a good mount could ride the twenty-five miles from San Leandro to Livermore in several hours, Murray Township, as the eastern portion of Alameda County was officially known, was another world entirely. Here, prior to the early 1870s, Anglos were a small minority; the residents were mainly native-born Californians, known as *Californios*.[5] The land had been settled a generation before by Mexican rancheros—the Amadors, the Bernals, the Sunols, the transplanted Englishman Robert Livermore, and others. In the lush valleys and along the verdant mountain ridges they grazed their vast herds of cattle and sheep, isolated from the rest of the world until the arrival of the railroad in 1869, which brought rapid Anglo settlement and disheartening change for the rancheros. In 1860 the township's population was just over 500; by 1870 the number jumped to 2,400.

Small settlements appeared on the major ranchos in the 1850s and 1860s: Sunol; Dublin (first called Amador or Dougherty's Station); Pleasanton, known as the Alisal; and Laddville, later incorporated into the city of Livermore. A mile north of Livermore was a cluster of adobes known as "Mexico" or "Little Mexico." These settlements sprang up gradually along the main trails into the Livermore and Amador valleys: the Stockton Pass Road near Mission San Jose (now Interstate 680) and the Hayward Pass Road to the north (now Interstate 580). Two even older routes ran through the Livermore Valley. One, El Camino Viejo, the Old Highway, began in southern California and passed along the old Mexican settlements of the San Joaquin Valley's west side before it entered the Livermore Valley through Corral Hollow. Another, La Vereda del Monte, the Mountain Trail, ran north through the remotest parts of the Coast Range, crossed the Livermore Valley, and ended at Point of Timber near present-day Brentwood in eastern Contra Costa County. During the 1850s and early 1860s these ancient trails were used mainly by *mesteneros*—mustang runners—who hunted the huge herds of wild horses in the San Joaquin Valley and drove them to markets in the northern and southern parts of the state. When the wild mustang herds were depleted, many of the mesteneros used the trails for a less legitimate calling: the herding of stolen livestock to markets north and south.

Between Los Angeles in the south and the Livermore Valley in the north were many small, isolated Hispanic settlements, some dating back to the 1820s. There, peons eked out a living tilling the soil; vaqueros and *borregueros,* or sheepherders, raised a few cattle or sheep. During the 1850s and 1860s these settlements became the stomping grounds for bandidos, horse thieves, and cattle rustlers. Among the most notorious was Poso Chane, located on El Camino Viejo, six miles east of present-day Coalinga on the west side of Fresno County. Its name, which literally means "watering hole of the Chane Indians," aptly described what was once a lush oasis in the arid west side of the San Joaquin Valley; today the well is dry and nothing remains. Just as notorious was Rancho de los Californios, known to Anglos as the California Ranch, a settlement of adobe huts in a dense willow thicket situated on the San Joaquin River near what is now Kerman

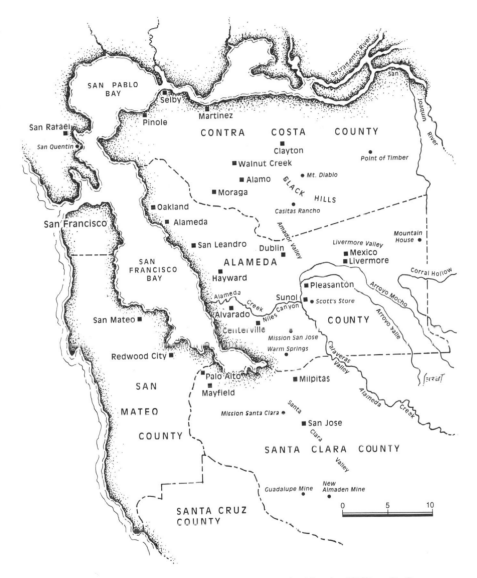

The San Francisco Bay Area as Sheriff Morse knew it. Map by William B. Secrest.

in Fresno County. Robbers and stock thieves, both Hispanic and
Anglo, made their headquarters in a stockade built of logs that had
floated down the river from the Sierra Nevada forests. There were
many other such settlements: at San Emigdio and Panama in Kern
County, at Pueblo de las Juntas and Firebaugh's Ferry in Fresno
County, at the New Almaden and Guadalupe quicksilver mines in
Santa Clara County and the New Idria mine in San Benito County.
All were popular hideouts for bandidos and other fugitives.

North of the Livermore Valley were the Black Hills, and beyond
them the towering expanse of Mount Diablo. To the south of the Livermore Valley was the heart of the Coast Range, studded with rugged,
4,000-foot peaks, yawning chasms, and impassable saddlebacks. Several deep canyons—the Arroyo Mocho, Arroyo Valle, and Calaveras
Canyon—sliced deep into the mountains. Their creeks drained this
part of the Coast Range. They ran north into the Livermore Valley,
spilling onto the plain and ensuring ample water for crops and grazing. These mountains and arroyos were ideal hiding places for fugitives and stolen stock. Here and there were *jacales*, or huts, some
made entirely of brush and others of adobe, where honest vaqueros
and borregueros as well as horse thieves and cattle rustlers lived.

*In March, 1864, I was sworn in and took possession of my office. At
the time the northern and eastern portion [of Alameda County] was infested by a gang of Mexican and white horse thieves, highwaymen, and
cutthroats of the most reckless character. These scoundrels, in the most
reckless manner, perpetrated the most outrageous crimes, with no one
seemingly interested enough to hunt them out or make them afraid. The
mountains around Livermore Valley were well suited for the rendezvous
of these outlaws, the canyons and ravines being all densely wooded, and
each and every jacal containing one or more of these desperadoes or their
sympathizers.*

*These mountains and canyons were in early days [the 1850s] the hid-
ing places for such men as Joaquin Murrieta, Jack Powers, Tom Bell, Pancho Altamirano, Pancho Ruiz, Joaquin Olivera, Pancho Blanco, Obispo
Arcia, and a host of others of the same bad stripe. These men created a
holy terror among the people of the valley and it was considered almost
certain death for an officer of the law to venture among them for the purpose of ferreting out a criminal who happened to be in any way connected
with this gang. Sunol Valley, and what is known as the Black Hills, north
of Livermore, were particularly infested by these thieves.*

Harry Morse's California. Map by William B. Secrest.

The only houses of any note, at this particular time, in or about Liv-
ermore Valley, were the old rancho houses of the Livermores and Bernals
and Martin & Dougherty's. Tom Hart's hotel, a small wayside inn, situ-
ated about half way between Dougherty's Station [Dublin] and the old
Livermore Rancho, on the road leading from Hayward to Stockton, was
the only place of any note where a man could be well and safely cared for
overnight. Tom was a good fellow and did not allow any of this gang to
frequent his place. A cantina, or fandango house [Yreneo Ramirez's
Old Stockton House], situated about two miles northeast from Liver-
more, and built near a thick clump of willows, was a noted place for these
outlaws to hold their hilarious frolics. It was here they met, night after
night, to plan their robberies and murders and enjoy themselves after fill-
ing up with "sheepherders delight," dealt out to them by the Don [Ramirez]
who presided at this den of criminals.

It was not safe for a man who was known to have any money about
him to pass through that region even in broad daylight, as these cutthroats
would waylay and murder him. They would run off whole bands of
sheep, cattle, and horses from the rancheros living in the vicinity, and the
law-abiding citizens were afraid to organize to capture them.[6]

Most of the outlaws worked as herders or laborers. They did not
belong to organized bandit gangs but instead would gather together
and make a raid when the opportunity arose and then return to their
honest occupations. Of all the bandidos who infested Alameda
County in the early sixties, the two most dangerous were Narciso
Bojorques and his compadre, Tomás Procopio Bustamante. Harry
Morse would become their nemesis.

Narciso Bojorques was a reckless, devil-may-care sort of a fellow, and
was known about the Alisal—now Pleasanton—as a man who feared
nothing. In personal appearance, he was a magnificent-looking Mexican,
about nineteen years of age, five feet ten inches high, very light complex-
ion, large Roman nose, hair black as night, eyes large and full and in color
a red brown, skin fair and smooth, the red showing through it, giving to
his face a fresh and healthy look, stout built, with muscles laid up like wire
rope, easy and graceful in his movements, the strength of a lion, and
withal, one of the best horsemen in the country. Bojorques—better known
among his fellows as Narciso—held supreme sway in and about Liver-
more Valley.

Procopio and Narciso were about the same age but entirely different in build and temperament. Procopio was six feet tall, slim, a handsome face, brown-gray eyes, brown hair, and, in general appearance, looked more like an American than a Mexican. A close observer, however, would soon detect the devilish look in the eyes of the Mexican desperado as he swaggered about among his fellows. In temperament, Narciso was hot-headed, impulsive, easily excited, and at times very violent and brutal. Procopio, on the contrary, was cool, cunning, and deceitful. Between the two they were a terrible team for almost any man to tackle. I might add that Procopio was a nephew of the much dreaded and notorious Joaquin Murrieta, Procopio's mother being Joaquin's sister.[7]

Although Morse's information about Procopio's ancestry has been dismissed by most modern writers, research by the late Frank F. Latta has fully confirmed it. Procopio (then a popular Hispanic name, after the Byzantine historian, Procopius) was born Tomás Procopio Bustamante in Sonora, Mexico, in 1842, the son of Vicenta Murrieta, Joaquin's older sister, and Tomás Bustamante, a stage driver on the route between Ures and Hermosillo. In 1852 a band of Yaqui Indians attacked his stage and killed the elder Bustamante. By this time Joaquin Murrieta had joined the gold rush to California. He was not yet a bandit but rather a mestenero, catching wild horses in the broad San Joaquin Valley and driving them to Mexico for sale. After one such visit home he brought his grieving sister and ten-year-old Procopio back to California with him. Joaquin reputedly owned a small rancho in what is now Niles Canyon in southern Alameda County. Here he brought his sister, and according to Murrieta family legend (which conflicts with all reliable accounts) it was in this adobe that Procopio and his mother buried Joaquin after he was allegedly wounded by lawmen in 1853. Joaquin Murrieta remains America's most noted Hispanic outlaw.[8]

According to Latta, Procopio and his mother lived for some years in the Niles Canyon adobe. By the time Procopio reached adulthood he was fast following in his notorious uncle's footsteps. The story of Procopio's career, which has been greatly eclipsed by that of Tiburcio Vasquez, demonstrates that he was perhaps even a worse desperado than Vasquez and one of the most dangerous Hispanic bandit chieftains. Procopio often used an alias, Tomás Redondo. However, to lawmen he became known as "Red Dick" or "Red-Handed Dick" because of the number of men he had slain.

By the early 1860s Procopio's mother had remarried, and since he

This adobe in Alameda Canyon (now Niles Canyon) was reputedly the home of Procopio. True or not, it depicts a typical *jacal* of that era. Author's collection.

was not on good terms with his stepfather, the youth moved to Los Angeles County. There, on November 17, 1862, John Rains, owner of the Rancho Cucamonga, was lassoed from his wagon, dragged across the cactus, and shot to death. This was one of southern California's most sensational frontier era murder cases. Procopio and two compadres, Manuel Cerrada and a youth known only by his nickname, Tal Juanito, were suspected. Procopio and Tal Juanito promptly fled north. When Cerrada was captured several months later he laid the blame on Procopio, Tal Juanito, and three other young vaqueros. He claimed that Don Ramon Carrillo, a prominent ranchero and enemy of Rains, had paid them $500 to do the deed. Cerrada was eventually lynched; Carrillo was examined in court but released for lack of evidence.[9]

Meanwhile Procopio and Tal Juanito had made a hard ride up El Camino Viejo to distance themselves from the hemp-hungry Los Angeles vigilantes. Tal Juanito dallied at Firebaugh's Ferry, where he was shot to death on April 4, 1863, while attempting to steal a horse from an Indian. Procopio had continued north and returned to his old haunts in the Alisal, meeting up with Narciso Bojorques. They lost no time joining with Chano Ortega, a desperado of the worst stripe. On January 29, 1863, the trio rode into Corral Hollow. At the spot where the canyon opens up onto the broad plain of the San Joaquin Valley they attacked the small ranch of Aaron Golding, butchering the cattleman, his wife, his adopted son, and his vaquero and burning the cabin to the ground. The quadruple murder horrified California's citizens; the *Stockton Daily Independent* rightfully termed the atrocity "one of the most horrible and barbarous outrages ever recorded in California's annals of crime." To many it seemed to epitomize the deep antagonism and racial conflict between Hispanic and Anglos.[10]

Borjorques and Ortega were arrested but soon released; all the witnesses to the brutal multiple murder were dead. Harry Morse later learned that the three killers had been observed riding toward Golding's cabin the day of the murder and that they had returned to the Alisal late that night flush with coin, spending it freely in the cantinas. It developed that Ortega had once quarreled with Aaron Golding over money, and the raid may have been an effort to settle this score. In any event, Ortega soon fled to Mexico, but Procopio and Bojorques lingered in the Alisal.

Things were quiet for a while about Livermore Valley after this awful murder. One day Narciso and a Mexican named Quarte disappeared from their usual haunts.[11] It was whispered among the Mexicans that they had gone into the northern counties to make a "raise." In a few days they as suddenly returned, each of them mounted upon a splendid horse, with trappings new and complete. Each was rigged out with a new and stylish suit of clothes. Each was also armed with new ivory-handled, eight-inch Colt six-shooters [the .44-caliber 1860 Army model]. They were welcomed by their companions in the usual hilarious way, and passed a merry night. On the day following their arrival at the Alisal, Narciso and Quarte went to the Arroyo Valle for the purpose of dividing some horses and other property, which they no doubt had stolen on their northern trip. Narciso returned to the Alisal the same evening, alone. When asked about Quarte, he replied that he and Quarte had parted at the Arroyo Valle, Quarte going to the Twenty-five Ranch [in Fresno County] to look out after some horses that he had left there some months before.

Narciso stayed around Alisal several months carousing with the women and spending his money freely, and he seemed to have an inexhaustible supply of it. About this time some cattlemen, while hunting lost stock in the Arroyo Valle, discovered hid away under some brush in a little ravine, the dead body of a Mexican, who had evidently been murdered. He had been shot through the head from behind; his pockets were turned inside out; his clothing was nearly new, and close by the corpse lay an ivory-handled eight-inch Colt pistol. The body was identified as that of Quarte. Of course Narciso killed him, but there was no legal evidence of that fact, so nothing was done about it.

About a month after the finding of Quarte's body [in August 1863], a Mr. Pope, living in the Arroyo Valle, lost a band of his best cattle. Narciso, Procopio, and a young Californian whose residence was at the old Mission San Jose had been seen together a few days before the cattle were missing in the vicinity of Pope's ranch, evidently reconnoitring Pope's premises and herds. At any rate, the cattle were stolen, and these Mexicans were suspected of being the thieves. Diligent search and inquiry developed the fact that a band of cattle corresponding in number and description to those stolen from Pope had passed through the hills by the old Stockton and San Jose road [now Interstate 680] and down into the Alameda Valley, taking the direction of Alvarado [now part of Union City].

It was necessary to be very careful about making inquiries, as the thieves had their friends and spies on the lookout all the time, and the movements of strangers were carefully noted and immediately given notice of to the thieves. Avoiding all Spanish houses and diligently searching all the country in the vicinity of Alvarado, Mr. Pope learned that a tall, good-looking Mexican named Procopio and a stout-built, fair-complexioned Mexican with a Roman nose and whose name was unknown to his informant, had on the night before, with the assistance of a Spanish boy who lived at the Mission San Jose, driven a small band of cattle into a corral at Alvarado and had offered the same for sale to a butcher.

The informant also stated that the butcher, being suspicious that all was not right, had delayed purchasing the cattle, hoping an owner might put in an appearance and claim them, but no owner having come, the butcher had finally agreed to take and pay for the cattle the following day at noon. Mr. Pope immediately interviewed the butcher, who confirmed all that had been told to Pope before, and added that Procopio's real name was Tomaso Redondo [actually, this was an alias] and that his companion's name was Narciso Bojorques, both of whom he said were bad and dangerous men, and at the same time he warned Mr. Pope that if he attempted to arrest these Mexicans he should be on his guard all the time, or they would make fight and get away. Pope promised to be cautious, and going to the county seat of San Leandro, he swore out a warrant for Procopio, et al.

The warrant being procured, it was placed in the hands of Constable

Orlo B. Wood for service. Wood was a good officer and a brave man, and after being duly posted as to the character of the men to be arrested, Pope and Wood proceeded to Alvarado at once, so as to be on hand when the thieves came to the butcher after the money. It had been arranged between Procopio and the butcher that the former should be at the latter's place at precisely two o'clock in the afternoon to be paid for the cattle. Pope again cautioned Wood what kind of men he had to deal with, and it was agreed that Wood should hide in the butcher shop and await the arrival of Procopio and his companions, and that at the very moment the butcher should commence payment of the money, but before it had changed hands, Wood should step from his hiding place, cover Procopio with his pistols, make him hold up his hands, and with the assistance of the butcher's clerk, handcuff him.

All being arranged to the satisfaction of Wood, it only remained for the plan to be carried into effect. Promptly at two o'clock the tall, stately form of Procopio appeared in sight alone. He sauntered quietly up to the butcher shop, looked up and down the street, drew a cigarette from his pocket, lit it, and after taking a few puffs, stepped quickly into the shop. The butcher asked Procopio into the back room to receive the money for the cattle. Procopio laughingly assented. The moment he entered the back room Wood covered him with his pistol and ordered him to hold up his hands. Procopio, finding that he was caught in a trap and at the mercy of the officer, complied at once with the request, not a muscle of his face betraying the least emotion. Thus they stood looking at each other, the officer thinking over in his own mind how best to secure his prisoner and the desperado, no doubt, revolving in his quiet way a plan for escape.

Suddenly a self-satisfied and diabolical gleam shot across the eyes of Procopio. His plan was made. He immediately changed to a quiet look of resignation, and said to the officer, "I surrender. I am unarmed."

As he uttered these words, Wood lowered his pistol and returned it to its scabbard. As soon as the constable had done this, Procopio, as quick as lightning, drew his own weapon, and covering the officer with it, commenced to move backward toward the door. Wood sprang forward to stay the desperado's departure, and as he did so, Procopio fired. The unexpected assault, the blinding flash of the pistol into his face, and the crashing of the ball through Wood's arm stunned and confused him for an instant.

As soon as Procopio fired he sprang into the street and started off at full speed, and he ran like a deer. He attempted to gain the main county road leading toward Centerville [now part of Fremont], and where Narciso was in waiting for him with their horses ready saddled. The firing of *the shot and the yells of the frightened people at the butcher shop soon brought to the street a crowd of excited people. Seeing a man running at full speed toward them flourishing a pistol, they gave way before him, but not until they turned him from his original course and obliged him to take the left-hand road toward Mount Eden* [now part of Hayward].

At the north end of the main street a deep creek or arm of the bay [Alameda Creek], *makes up into the town, and which is spanned by a draw-bridge. Procopio made as fast as possible for this bridge, hoping to cross it and get into the thick willows that grew on either bank of the creek and where he would be completely safe. Before he could reach the bridge he was headed off by some people who had heard the shot and were coming into the town to see what was the cause of the shooting.*

Nothing daunted, he quickly sprang down the bank of the creek, and although he was shot at several times he never faltered, but managed with considerable difficulty to reach the opposite shore and make for the willows. [According to most accounts, Procopio swam the creek with his six-gun clenched in his teeth]. *Again he met with opposition, and turning to the left, he sped away toward the salt marsh with a hundred people after him. By this time the whole town had become aroused, and taking what firearms they could lay their hands upon, they all started out in pursuit of the fleeing desperado.*

Meanwhile Procopio sped on at a terrific gait, but his pursuers being many, soon surrounded him. Many shots were fired at him, but without effect. Procopio returned the fire until his ammunition became exhausted, when he threw up his hands and walked toward his pursuers and gave himself up. He was immediately secured and escorted back to the place where Wood was having his wound dressed. Narciso and the Spanish boy were awaiting the return of Procopio with the money, in fancied security. Procopio would tell nothing, but the people, knowing from what Pope told them that there were two others concerned in the robbery, suspected that they could not be far off and started out in search of them. They were soon found, and being surprised, surrendered without resistance.

The whole party was taken to San Leandro and locked up. Upon the trial of the case, Procopio assumed the whole blame and declared that the others knew nothing about his stealing the cattle and that he only hired them to help drive them, and that they were entirely innocent. Upon this statement and the inability of the prosecution to show otherwise, Narciso and the boy were turned loose. Procopio was convicted of grand larceny and resisting an officer in the discharge of his official duties, and in the fall [September 4, 1863] *was sent to the state prison for a term of nine years.*[12]

Harry Morse, from a
carte de visite taken in
San Francisco about 1863.
Author's collection.

Harry Morse had been elected sheriff just two days before Procopio entered San Quentin. During the six-month interim between
the election and his taking office in March, Alameda County continued to be the scene of raids by bandit gangs. On November 23,
1863, a band of Mexican desperadoes thundered into Alvarado, six-
shooters flaming. They thoroughly shot up the village, then fled
with a posse of enraged citizens in hot pursuit. Just as they had
caught Procopio, the Alvarado men managed to rope in one of this
band. He was brought back to town and placed under guard at the
Brooklyn Hotel. That night, however, a band of vigilantes seized the
bandido and lynched him from the bridge over Alameda Creek. On
January 15, 1864, a party of Yankee brigands armed with pistols and
Bowie knives attacked the Mountain House, a popular hotel and tav-
ern owned by Simon Zimmerman and located on the old Stockton
road, near the San Joaquin County line. After looting the house and
roughing up its occupants they escaped, but two were later captured and lodged in San Quentin.[13]

These raids, occurring only weeks before Morse was sworn into office, should have given him reason to reconsider his new profession. They also illustrated that Procopio and Narciso Bojorques were probably just the worst outlaws in the Livermore and Amador valleys, not the only ones. Many more dangerous ruffians lived in the mountains or in the deep arroyos that ran north into the Livermore Valley. Others drifted in from elsewhere: recently released convicts from San Quentin, southern California desperadoes on their way to San Francisco, and Monterey and San Jose bandidos looking for greener pastures. Among the latter, the two most notorious were Tiburcio Vasquez and Juan Soto.

Today Tiburcio Vasquez has the distinction of being, next to Joaquin Murrieta, California's most famous Hispanic bandit. He was descended from an old Californio family. His grandfather and namesake came to the California frontier as a young soldier in 1776 and was one of the first settlers at San Jose in the heart of the lush Santa Clara Valley. He sired thirteen children, among them Hermenegildo Vasquez, father of the future bandit chief. Hermenegildo served as a soldier and later settled in Monterey County, where Tiburcio was born about 1835. Tiburcio's parents were respectable people, but the youth had a wild streak, coupled with a hatred of Anglos. As Vasquez once explained,

> My career grew out of the circumstances by which I was sur-
> rounded. As I grew to manhood I was in the habit of attend-
> ing balls and parties given by the native Californians, into
> which the Americans, then beginning to become numerous,
> would force themselves and shove the native born men aside,
> monopolizing the dance and the women. This was about 1852.
> I had numerous fights in defense of what I believed to be my
> rights and those of my countrymen. . . . I believed we were un-
> justly and wrongly deprived of the social rights that belonged
> to us. . . . I went to my mother and told her I intended to com-
> mence a different life. I asked for and obtained her blessing,
> and at once commenced the career of a robber.[14]

When still in his teens Tiburcio fell under the influence of Anastasio Garcia, one of the most vicious outlaws of the 1850s. At a Monterey fandango in 1854, Garcia, young Vasquez, and Jose Higuera took part in the murder of Constable William Hardmount. A mob promptly strung up Higuera, but Garcia and Vasquez succeeded in escaping. Garcia was eventually captured and lynched in Monterey in February 1857, after reportedly confessing to fourteen murders. Six months later Tiburcio was arrested for horse theft near Los Angeles and sent to San Quentin. For the next thirteen years he was in and out of the old stone cellblock in Marin County, several times managing to break out in mass escapes. On two occasions Tiburcio and other prisoners attempted to escape by commandeering schooners docked at the prison wharf.

Tiburcio was a romantic and reveled in his role as a horseback bandit. He wore expensive clothes and fine boots and always sported a large gold watch and chain. He rode the best horse that could be bought or stolen. Women were attracted to him, for Vasquez loved music and dancing and wrote evocative poems to his female admirers. He seduced many young women but quickly abandoned them Although his name would not become a household word until 1873, his exploits eventually made Tiburcio Vasquez a folk hero among his people.

Like Vasquez, Juan Soto was a member of an old and very large Californio family. His grandfather, Ignacio Soto, also came to California in 1776, and ten years later he too settled at San Jose. Ignacio Soto fathered thirteen children, including Jose Francisco Soto, who was born in 1825 and baptized at Mission Santa Clara. Jose Francisco Soto eventually married Maria Carmen Flores and settled at what is now Milpitas, south of Mission San Jose. Their son, Juan Bautista Soto, was born in February 1846 and baptized a few days later, on February 22, at Mission Santa Clara. Either one or both of his parents had Indian blood, for Juan Soto had strong mestizo features. Juan's father worked as a vaquero. Juan's uncle, Sebastian Flores (his mother's older brother), was a noted bandit and a member of the Francisco Garcia band of highway robbers in Santa Clara County during the mid-1850s. By 1860 young Juan Soto was working as a laborer and vaquero for Daniel C. Murphy, a wealthy stock farmer who owned a large ranch near Gilroy in the southern part of Santa Clara County.[15]

The Sotos' neighbors were the Sepulveda family, and Juan grew to adulthood with Bartolo Sepulveda, six years his senior, and Bartolo's younger brothers, Miguel and Nicolas. The Sepulvedas were a wild bunch, all expert vaqueros and rope makers, and each of the sons would end up in serious trouble with the law. But it was Juan Soto who by the mid-1860s was one of the most daring bandidos of the Santa Clara Valley. He had grown into a terror of a figure—six feet tall, two hundred pounds, and a ferocious, pockmarked countenance. Although badly cross-eyed, he was nonetheless a dead shot and a peerless horseman. His temper was legendary, and even his own followers were said to be in dread of him. He was filled with hatred for the Anglo. R. B. Hall, undersheriff of Santa Clara County, knew Soto well and later wrote that the badman and his compadres "herded cattle as vaqueros part of the time and gambled and robbed travelers for the rest.[16]

In the spring of 1865 Soto and three other bandidos were levying tribute on the road from San Jose to the New Almaden Mine. On May 4 they held up Julius Wetzel, stealing his horse and money. Undersheriff Hall investigated the crime and suspected Soto's involvement. He found the bandit on Daniel Murphy's ranch, rounding up cattle for branding. Hall arrested Soto without trouble and jailed him in San Jose. The court records show that although the outlaw was indicted for robbery, the case was never brought to trial and he escaped punishment.[17]

Tiburcio Vasquez and Juan Soto were both symptom and symbol of an epidemic of crime that engulfed California's Hispanic community between the 1850s and 1870s. A large and disproportionate number of California's outlaws were Hispanic. In 1855, for example, almost one in four convicts in San Quentin were Spanish-speaking, despite the fact that Hispanics at that time represented less than 13 percent of the state's population. One historian who studied the San Quentin prison records for the period between 1851 and 1880 found that the prison averaged 13 percent Hispanic convicts during those years whereas the state's Spanish-speaking population between 1860 and 1880 was by then only about 4 percent.[18]

Numerous theories have been propounded to explain why so many Hispanics turned to crime in frontier California. The most bigoted pioneers simply assumed that Hispanics were, at best, too lazy to earn an honest living or, at worst, inherently evil. Perhaps the most accepted explanation during that era was summarized by a commentator in 1888 who combined insight with a touch of racism:

There was, perhaps, a peculiar reason for the existence of this class of outlaws. The native Californians had seen their peaceful, pastoral homes overrun by a horde of greedy for-

eigners, who were bringing innovation and change. Little by
little their lands were passing into the possession of strangers,
their institutions were disappearing, and their ancient supremacy becoming a thing of the past. Accustomed to lives of
idleness and ease, the grim specter of work presented itself as
the only alternative to starvation, if they hoped to hold their
own with the bustling stranger, who, beside injury actually in-
flicted, added insult thereto by terming them "greasers" and
treating them with contempt. To these considerations were
added the bitter feelings engendered by the war with Mexico.
It was the old story of animosity, taken advantage of by the less
responsible and more desperate members of the community to
excuse and justify their warfare on society.[19]

To this may be added the view of the writer-historian Joseph Henry
Jackson:

During what has been called the Pastoral Age of California,
the great *ranchos* supported among the thousands of hangers-
on; it was Mexican habit to cluster in family groups, and every
large ranch had attached to it hundreds of ostensible "workers"—men who had little to do but whose keep, with cattle
multiplying uncounted on the hills and corn and beans pro-
ducing several crops a year in the mild climate, amounted to
very little. By the time the gold rush began, however, the era
of the great ranches was over. The enormous land-grants were
beginning to break up; the free and easy days were gone. And
these thousands of vaguely employed Mexicans found themselves with nowhere to go, displaced persons without quite understanding what had happened to them.[20]

That old Los Angeles Ranger, Horace Bell, aptly observed that in
Mexico "the line of demarkation between rebel and robber, pillager
and patriot, was dimly defined." And so it was for many California
Hispanics, who provided help and harbor to the bandidos. One of
the simplest and most logical explanations for such banditry has
been offered by the historian Leonard Pitt, whose watershed work,
The Decline of the Californios, remains a basic source on the Hispanic
experience in frontier California: "For many Spanish-American
youths, California represented a place that had robbed them of their

birthright, but had meanwhile provided innumerable opportunities to steal back parts of it."[21]

The California bandidos and stock thieves of the 1860s and 1870s were merely carrying on a tradition of banditry that existed as far back as the 1820s, during the Mexican era, and gained momentum during the gold rush of 1849. The early 1850s were wide open, flush years when fortunes were made at the swing of a pick, the shake of a washpan, or the flip of a card. Many reckless wanderers and adventurers flocked to California from all over the world, motivated by lust for money and adventure. Many who did not strike it rich—not just Hispanics—turned to crime. Society was in flux, and the proliferation of brash young males without the settling influences of women, family, and established community resulted in extremely high crime rates and an extraordinary level of violence. Near the bottom of the social heap were the poorest of the Hispanics. Driven from the mines, mistreated by callous Anglos, and denied a means to earn their living, it is hardly surprising that many Californios and other Hispanics turned to robbery and theft. As the outlaws of the 1850s were slain or imprisoned, others quickly replaced them. By the 1860s increasing settlement and socialization in California contributed to somewhat reduced crime rates, but there were still badmen aplenty.

In more recent years a new theory has been proposed to explain, and even excuse, Hispanic brigandage: the "social bandit" concept. This theory holds that such early California bandidos as Joaquin Murrieta and Tiburcio Vasquez were avengers or revolutionaries and therefore "social bandits," who struck out in self-defense against the conquering Anglos. Proponents of this concept contend that "they were forced into a life that was outside of the newly imposed Anglo-American law; theirs was a banditry in the form of retribution and for purpose of survival." When one considers that most of California's bandidos preyed on Hispanics as well as Anglos, the social bandit concept seems to be somewhat unsound. But when its proponents excuse such banditry and view these outlaws as noble avengers and as "sources of pride to their people," their concept goes seriously awry. As we will see, some of the bandidos were indeed lionized and protected by their people, but that hardly makes them eligible for historical justification, nor can it excuse their many horrible murders and other crimes.[22]

One of the most basic reasons that California bandidos received succor and a degree of respect from Hispanics was that the state's Spanish-speaking community of that era was a close-knit one. Californio families were very large and interconnected by blood and marriage. They tended to remain loyal to *los hijos del pais* (native sons) who had trouble with the law, and excused their wrongdoing, especially if it involved theft of livestock from the gringo, who had stolen land and cattle from the Californio in the first place. Tiburcio Vasquez, for example, had scores of relatives from Sonoma County in the north to Los Angeles County in the south. Coupled with a large contingent of loyal amigos—all of whom were happy to harbor him—it is no wonder he was often able to evade capture. Even bandidos who were not native Californians, such as Mexicans and Chilenos, were often supported by sympathetic Californio families.

Heroes to some, hellions to others, Procopio, Narciso Bojorques, Juan Soto, and Tiburcio Vasquez were among the most cunning and infamous bandidos of that era, appearing and vanishing as suddenly as the violent, unpredictable Santa Ana winds. Elusive as they were, each would meet his match in Alameda's cocky young sheriff.

CHAPTER 3

El Muchacho: The Boy Sheriff

HARRY Morse's first experiences in law enforcement had nothing to do with Hispanic outlaws. During the Civil War years Morse was active in battling secessionist sentiment in the county, first as a member of the Oakland Guard and later as deputy provost marshal and sheriff. When he ran for sheriff he promised to "rid the county of traitors." His efforts were often a source of controversy and afterward were described by a reporter for the *Alameda County Gazette:*

> At the outbreak of the rebellion there were in Oakland plenty of rough, brutal fellows, Southerners, who would revile the Unionists, frequently offer personal violence, and who tried to make themselves a terror to the community. About that time Harry Morse was a young man in the express business, an ardent Unionist and afraid of nobody. More than one of those bullying secessionists felt the force of his powerful arm. A man, who in his presence howled that Lincoln was the son of a dog, would find himself prone upon the sands.[1]

During the war the state legislature passed emergency laws that made it illegal to display the rebel flag or to publicly cheer for the subversion of the United States. Said Charles G. Reed, an old friend of Morse's, "No man in California was a more ardent supporter of the Union sentiment or revered the flag of our country more than Morse. Wherever he went, if he heard anything said against the flag, it meant fight." Harry Morse had grown into a lean, muscular young man, standing an inch short of six feet. Though his weight stood at only 155 pounds, he was tough to beat in a scrap.[2]

Morse's actions were widely supported by pro-Union men, but his political enemies—local Democrats—accused him of being a political bully, or "shoulder-striker." Some years later the editor of the *Oakland Daily Transcript* charged,

The war was in progress, belligerent blood was boiling. Morse was a young, athletic, and notoriously pugnacious man, who had made himself somewhat conspicuous by the vigor of his arguments for the Union cause, and withal was considered the most decent of the fellows who were "on the shoulder," and some of his friends desiring to reward his fidelity to the Union party, brought him forward as a candidate for sheriff.[3]

In response to this assault on his character, the Republican editor of the *Oakland Daily News* attempted, somewhat futilely, to refute the charges:

But he did knock down a man occasionally, and every respectable Union man applauded him. During the first year of the rebellion there were others besides Mr. Morse who would not be bullied and browbeaten by the secessionists, who were then a terror to the community. We believe we can prove that he has never struck a man except for reviling the flag of his country, and cheering for the Southern Army.[4]

The charge that Harry Morse was a bully during the war years was one that would surface repeatedly while he held office. In Morse's defense, his friend Reed said simply, "He was not quarrelsome, but if any man tried to impose on him, he simply got knocked out and that ended the matter."[5]

Morse no doubt played a prominent role in several colorful incidents involving the Oakland Guard. During the war a small cannon stood at Twelfth and Fallon streets in Oakland and was fired to celebrate Union victories. One day it disappeared, and suspicion centered on Jack Cohane, a leader of the county's Copperheads. Members of the Guard arrested Cohane, marched him to the foot of Broadway, and threw him unceremoniously into the Oakland Estuary. Cohane, to save himself from drowning, revealed the hiding place of the gun, which was found sunk in the water off a nearby wharf.[6]

On another occasion, in 1863, Morse and a squad of Oakland Guardsmen reportedly raided a building at Eleventh and Madison streets and captured three members of the Knights of the Golden Circle, who were packed off to the military prison on Alcatraz island. According to one account, Morse seized "plans that had been

Officers of the Oakland Guard at the general state encampment in Alameda, 1863. *Left to right:* James Brown, Harry Morse, Jeremiah Tyrrel, and Henry Hillebrand. Author's collection.

mapped for the taking of the State government, which the plotters intended turning over to the South." During civil disturbances in San Francisco which followed the assassination of President Abraham Lincoln in 1865, the Oakland Guard joined other militia units in patrolling the city's streets to prevent further outbreaks of violence.[7]

Despite his reputation for riding herd on Copperheads, Harry Morse was a good-natured and popular sheriff. But he was undeniably contentious when it came to wartime loyalty. His buggy was a common sight on the muddy streets of San Leandro and Oakland, his horse at a canter, his booted feet resting easily on the dash, a broad-brimmed hat perched jauntily on the back of his head, cigar in one hand and whip in the other, bellowing lustily a refrain he knew was guaranteed to boil the blood of any secessionist within earshot:

Hurrah! Hurrah! We bring the jubilee!
Hurrah! Hurrah! The flag that makes you free!
So we sang the chorus from Atlanta to the sea,
While we were marching through Georgia.

Morse claimed many times in later years that he spent his first two-year term as sheriff carefully mapping out his campaign against the outlaw bands that infested the Amador and Livermore valleys and surrounding mountains. The earliest such account appeared in the *San Francisco Chronicle* in 1872. In a long, laudatory article about the sheriff's career, the *Chronicle*'s writer introduced Morse's version:

He exhibited his eminent fitness for the responsible position from the very onset of his official career, and the "beardless boy," as he was at first contemptuously denominated by the outlaws who were overrunning the eastern portion of the county, soon rendered himself notorious, alike for the exhibition of shrewdness, energy, and high qualities of courage, coolness, and readiness of resources in face of peril.[8]

Harry Morse's claims were later recorded by Morse himself in 1885 and by various other writers, including George Beers (1875), D. S. Richardson (1888), Charles Howard Shinn (1890), and Joseph Henry Jackson (1949), and they form a major component of the Morse legend as modern writers continue to repeat them. But Morse's attempts to place himself in the best light possible have greatly distorted the facts behind his first futile and bumbling efforts as Alameda's new chief lawman.[9]

The truth is that Morse's first two years as sheriff were marked by a lamentable lack of law enforcement and outlaw-catching activity. In writing of the period immediately after Morse took office, William Halley, the county's first historian, said, "During the month of May [1864] the county jail was without a prisoner, notwithstanding the many lawless characters that frequently found their way over here from San Francisco." Even more notably, a search of the issues of the *Alameda County Gazette* for the years 1864 and 1865 failed to reveal any accounts of arrests by Harry Morse, save two Chinese thieves he picked up for stealing clothes. His sheriff's fee book for this period shows but a handful of arrests for petty offenses. As Morse himself once frankly admitted, "I was as green in the business as a man could be, having had no experience whatever in that line before."[10]

The profession of policing was still a relatively new one in 1864. There were no organized, professional police departments in the United States before 1845. Law enforcement in America tended to follow the example set in England. American policing had been done by watchmen at night and constables by day; some were volunteers, others were paid. Policing was not a profession, and citizens were expected to help enforce the law. As villages turned into cities the old system became increasingly unable to cope with the rising crime rates, social unrest, and rioting that occurred in the urban centers of the East in the 1830s and 1840s. In 1829 the London Metropolitan Police was created, and it formed the model for New York City and Philadelphia to establish full-time, night and day police forces manned by regular officers. Other communities soon followed suit: San Francisco in 1849, New Orleans and Cincinnati in 1852, Boston in 1854, Chicago in 1855, and Baltimore in 1857. Harry Morse, like other pioneer law enforcers, was bound to learn his new profession by trial and error.[11]

Just as is true today, a rookie policeman needs several years of experience to achieve sufficient acumen to become an effective law enforcer, and it is quite clear that Alameda's new sheriff was completely unprepared for the dangerous challenge that confronted him. Not only was he inexperienced as a lawman, he was overwhelmed by the considerable civil duties required by his office. Morse seems to have devoted most of his time during his first term of office to serving legal papers, making attachments, subpoenaing witnesses, and managing the county jail, which frequently held prisoners arrested by the Oakland police. He commented some years later, "A sheriff cannot afford to neglect the civil business of his office, however urgent the demands may be upon his attention otherwise. He is liable upon his bonds for any neglect to promptly execute civil processes placed in his hands."[12]

The new sheriff's civil duties were not always routine. During the 1850s and 1860s Alameda County was the scene of protracted litigation over land titles originating in the old Mexican land grants. Squatters settled on disputed land, and violence often resulted. One of the most obnoxious squatters in the county was A. W. Powers, a medical doctor from Vermont. He engaged in numerous quarrels and squatted on various parcels of land. He was suspected of arson and of stealing his neighbors' cattle. Finally he squatted on a section

of land near San Leandro that was claimed by the prominent Estudillo and Castro families. Powers threatened to kill anyone who
tried to eject him. When the capitalist F. D. Atherton took over the
disputed claim, he brought an ejectment action against Dr. Powers
and other squatters who had settled on various portions of the old
rancho. The writs were handed to Sheriff Morse for service. This was
exactly the type of challenge that Morse loved, and in December
1864 he successfully ejected Powers and twenty-three other men
from Atherton's lands. Powers never carried out his violent threats
and soon settled in what was to become San Benito County. More
than twenty years later, Harry Morse would have good reason to remember Dr. A. W. Powers.[13]

Morse desperately wanted to bring the Corral Hollow murderers to
justice, but he lacked the ability to thoroughly investigate the crime
and track down the killers. The young sheriff's primary law enforcement activity in 1864–65 appears to have been his efforts to keep local
Copperheads in line. Morse's world was the streets, storefronts, and
political meetings of San Leandro and Oakland. He knew little about
the rugged mountains, remote ranchos, and dusty adobe settlements
in the eastern portion of the county and absolutely nothing about investigation of crime and apprehension of criminals. He little understood the language, customs, and habits of the vaqueros, from whose
ranks so many of the robbers and rustlers came. Too, he lacked skill
with both horses and firearms. As sheriff, provost marshal, and militia captain, Morse had used his brawn and his fists to subdue disorderly Copperheads. But such physical prowess was of little advantage
against a heavily armed bandido mounted on a swift California mustang. The bandidos looked on the beardless young lawman with dis-
dain and mockingly nicknamed him El Muchacho, "The Boy."

Harry Morse *would* begin an epic campaign against the outlaw
gangs—but not for more than two years. In the meantime his performance as the county's new sheriff was woefully inadequate. The
Livermore and Amador valleys and the surrounding mountains continued to be overrun by horse thieves, cattle rustlers, fugitives, and
criminals of every stripe, both Anglo and Hispanic. The cantinas and
fandango houses there were a favorite stopping place for convicts recently released from San Quentin.

In 1860 the population of Alameda County was 8,926; by 1870
it had increased almost threefold. More settlers poured into Murray
and Washington townships, and the frequency of stock theft increased as the thieves found increasing numbers of easy victims.

Oakland in 1869 had many modern three-story brick buildings. This view shows Broadway, Oakland's main street, looking north toward the coastal hills from Twelfth Street. Courtesy of the California History Room, California State Library, Sacramento.

Many of the settlers were afraid to oppose the rustlers; some who did found their stock poisoned or their houses and barns burned.[14]

The settlers, evidently unimpressed with the new sheriff's ability to deal with the outlaws, decided to take matters into their own hands. The *Gazette* reported on April 8, 1865:

> Pursuant to a public call a large number of the citizens of Washington Township assembled at Milton's Hall [in Centerville, now part of Fremont] last Saturday and formed a Vigilance Committee, for the purposes of protecting the people of that community against horse and cattle thieves, stock poisoners, and incendiaries. . . . We think this action of the people will have a salutary effect upon a set of vile scoundrels who have been prowling about that neighborhood, thieving and worst of all poisoning the stock in the pastures.

Yet the vigilance committee and the $500 reward they offered for stock poisoners seem to have had little effect on crime, as the outlawry continued unabated. Probably the most brazen theft took place on the night of October 20, 1865, when Narciso Bojorques and another noted badman, Joaquin Olivera, descended on the rancho of William Knox, near Hayward, and drove off five hundred head of sheep from his corral while his borreguero slept. The two desperadoes silently moved the huge herd all night up into the mountains behind Mission San Jose. Following old trails, the pair drove them south to the New Almaden Mine in Santa Clara County where they sold the animals to an unsuspecting rancher. Within a week Knox managed to track down and recover his missing herd at New Almaden, but the thieves escaped.[15]

That same month saw a bold raid led by Juan Soto against Charles Garthwaite's ranch and trading post one mile west of Pleasanton. Soto, Manuel Rojas, a young ex-convict named Alfonso M. Burnham (alias Fred Welch), and another bandit attacked the house, but Garthwaite's wife, Mary, who was alone, put up a stiff fight and shot and wounded Burnham. The bandidos overpowered the plucky woman, bound her hand and foot, and escaped with money, jewelry, and her six-shooter. Burnham departed for San Francisco, where he quickly recovered from his wound. He celebrated by embarking on a spree with his share of the spoils but was picked up by the police for carrying a concealed weapon. While Burnham languished in jail a fellow prisoner "peached" on him and Sheriff Morse was notified. He brought Mrs. Garthwaite to the San Francisco city prison and she unhesitatingly identified him as one of the robbers. Burnham confessed and was sentenced to eighteen months in San Quentin. Although he refused to identify his compadres, he gave a lame account of how they had forced him, under pain of death, to assist in the holdup. For the time being Juan Soto was a free man, unsuspected of this latest outrage.[16]

All this was a great embarrassment to Harry Morse. The inexperienced young sheriff was helpless against these brigands, who seemed to emerge wraithlike from the midnight blackness, plundering at will and escaping as if by magic. However, Morse's greatest embarrassment during his impotent first term involved not these elusive bandits but a group of disgruntled jailbirds in his lockup. On the Fourth of July, 1865, he had negligently left the jail unguarded, going to San Francisco to celebrate the holiday and allowing his undersheriff, Peter Borein, to spend the day in San Lorenzo. Morse returned to San Leandro at midnight but went directly home without bothering to check the jail or to lock the prisoners in their individual cells, as was the custom.

The jail held six inmates, the most notorious being Agustín Avila, known as "El Capitán," a dangerous ruffian and horse thief. Four of the prisoners—El Capitán, Jose Ramon Peralta (the black sheep son of a prominent Californio family), William Ward, and John Hanley— had been busy in his absence. With a smuggled saw they managed to cut off two bars from a window and then urged the two remaining prisoners, both Chinese, to join them in escaping. The Chinese refused, and one tried to raise an alarm, for which he received a sound beating. The four prisoners fled the jail at 1:00 A.M., and the battered Chinese crawled out of the window and made his way to Morse's house to try to warn the sheriff. But Morse "supposed him to be some drunken brawler and paid no attention to him," not bothering to investigate and not even recognizing the man as one of his own prisoners. The Chinese prisoner went through town trying vainly to arouse the sleeping citizens and finally returned to the jail and crawled back inside. When the sheriff arrived at the courthouse in the morning, he was stunned to find that all that remained of his erstwhile charges was a waggish note they had left behind, telling him that they "didn't relish their Fourth of July dinner, and so they thought they would leave."[17]

Such discouraging episodes only made Harry Morse work harder to master his new duties. He later said, "I was young and strong, and ambitious to be proficient in my new office, and I was determined that I would be." Despite his lack of effectiveness, he was reelected on September 6, 1865, by garnering 1,399 votes and outpolling his opponent, Ed Neihaus, by a margin of almost two to one. This was more a victory for the Republican party than it was a victory for Harry Morse. It is probable that any Republican candidate, no matter who he was, would have won in that political atmosphere of 1865, due to the strong anti-Democrat public sentiment that prevailed in California in the wake of the Civil War. Too, Republicans outnumbered Democrats in the county by a substantial margin from 1861 to 1876, ensuring Morse's ability to retain his office.[18]

It was during this second term that Harry Morse truly began his epic campaign against the sheep thieves, cattle rustlers, and highway robbers of Alameda's backcountry. Gradually he acquired the skills he would need to fight them on their own terms. He learned, however slowly, to speak and understand Spanish, to read sign and follow a track, to memorize countless faces and nicknames, and to recall the descriptions of scores of wanted men. He struggled to become an ex-

Jose Ramon Peralta.
Peralta escaped from
Morse's jail in 1865.
Courtesy Christian de
Guigne IV.

pert horseman, capable of making long, hard rides without rest and of galloping the rocky, precarious mountain trails like a Californio. He practiced until he was a dead shot with both his Winchester rifle and his Colt Army .44, able to hit a moving target with the Winchester at a range of 150 yards and to draw quickly, cock, and fire the heavy single-action revolver with deadly accuracy at close quarters. He slowly managed to develop a network of criminal informants who kept him posted on the comings and goings of the badmen. Harry Morse was fast learning the ways of the mountain bandits.

One of the worst cattle thieves in the country was Eduardo Gallego, a hard-riding vaquero who, according to the *Gazette*, "[was] an old and hardened sinner, and had made his boast that no white man could ever take him." In May 1866 Morse learned that Gallego was wanted on a warrant issued in San Joaquin County which charged him with stealing a large herd of cattle. He had a clue to Gallego's whereabouts and immediately secured the help of two close friends: Oakland police officer Richard B. Richardson and Contra Costa County undersheriff George Swain.

Both men would figure prominently in Harry Morse's early exploits. Dick Richardson was a strapping, handsome man, twenty-nine years old, who had joined the Oakland force two years earlier. Amiable and popular, he lived in Oakland with his wife and two children and had a reputation for fearlessness. George Swain, thirty-one years old, was the ablest lawman of Contra Costa County's pioneer era. Dashing and steel-nerved, as a very young man he had been *mayordomo*, or foreman, of Dr. John Marsh's huge ranch in eastern Contra Costa County. There Swain was charged with riding herd not only on thousands of cattle but also on the rancho's reckless vaqueros and the many rustlers who preyed on Marsh's stock. Swain was a superb vaquero, and it was said that he could outride and outrope even the saddle-born Californios. Dr. Marsh was murdered by two of his vaqueros in 1856, and young Swain was later appointed a deputy sheriff. Harry Morse called Swain "a brave and thoroughly reliable officer, one of the kind of men who never got tired or discouraged if the hunt was a long one. He was impetuous in his way, but under proper control a very useful man and could always be depended upon to do his full duty when in a tight place."[19]

On May 24 Morse, Richardson, and Swain set off after Gallego in a light wagon. The wily vaquero fled into the San Joaquin Valley, and the lawmen trailed him south more than 100 miles. They fell behind when a wheel spoke snapped. Switching to saddle horses, they trailed Gallego to Fresno City and then to Zapato Chino Creek in the Coast Range, where they lost the track. They returned north, having been on the trail for twelve days. On their hard ride into the Coast Range they had covered 180 miles in less than three days.[20]

Morse was weary but not yet ready to give up. On the night of July 14 he received a telegram from Captain John H. Adams, sheriff of Santa Clara County, that the fugitive could be found at a jacal in a canyon at the foot of Mount Diablo. Gallego was reportedly accompanied by two notorious compadres of Juan Soto, Pancho Caravantes and Pancho Ruiz, who had escaped from the Contra Costa County jail a year before. Caravantes had reputedly been a member of Joaquin Murrieta's band.[21]

Morse telegraphed to George Swain, and the undersheriff and his brother, David, met him the following day at Dublin after making a hard ride south from Martinez. The three lawmen raided the out-

Oakland police officer Dick
Richardson. A close friend
of Harry Morse, he was
shot and killed while
making an arrest in 1867.
Author's collection.

law hideout at first light and were surprised to find a crowd of more
than thirty armed vaqueros saddling their horses, which were hob-
bled in front of the jacal, "hitched like a cavalry troop," according to
the *Oakand Daily News,* and their riders "ready to mount their animals and start out on a plundering expedition." But Morse's little
posse had the element of surprise, and he knew they had to act
quickly. He spotted Gallego in the crowd, struggling to cut the hob-
bles from his horse's feet with a long knife. Drawing a bead on the
badman, the sheriff barked, "Hold up your hands!"

Gallego, not dreaming that a lawman would have the nerve to
venture into the canyon, was caught completely off guard. George
Swain galloped up to him, put his six-gun to his head, and relieved
him of his knife and a Colt Navy revolver. The officers quickly
slapped a pair of handcuffs on the outlaw's wrists, shackled him to
his horse, and whisked him away before his *compañeros* had time to
react. Pancho Caravantes and Pancho Ruiz were not present. Both

were soon captured, however (Caravantes by Undersheriff Swain in October), and sentenced to terms in San Quentin.[22]

A month later Harry Morse was again in the saddle after cattle thieves. On August 23 three rough hombres, Jesus Ruiz, Roderigo Chapo, and Pedro Martinez, stole twenty-five head of cattle from a butcher near San Jose and drove them north. The butcher immediately notified Sheriff Morse, who rode into the Amador Valley and sent Constable Orlo B. Wood to search the Moraga Valley in Contra Costa County. Wood cut their trail, rounded up a posse, and trapped two of the rustlers at a jacal on San Pablo Creek. The constable had learned a valuable lesson from Procopio three years earlier, and when one of the outlaws drew a pistol, Wood promptly shot him in the back. The two badmen were jailed in Martinez, and their compadre was nabbed a few days later by Dick Richardson of the Oakland police.[23]

These successful manhunts greatly encouraged the young sheriff. He must have sensed that at last the boredom and lack of purpose that had plagued him for so long were gone forever. He had tasted the adventure of a fruitful manhunt, the public acclaim that followed it, and the resulting sense of pride and accomplishment, and he thirsted for more of the same. Harry Morse had now truly found his calling, one he would later call "a labor of love."[24]

These arrests, however, hardly put an end to banditry in the Amador and Livermore valleys. The *Alameda County Gazette* reported in the fall of 1866,

> There are, daily, a set of villainous looking Mexicans, booted and spurred, armed with large navy revolvers and long knives, traveling back and forth through the valleys of [Murray] township, with no visible occupation, insolent and indolent and the terror of peace loving and law abiding citizens. Of late their insolence has extended even so far as to walk into the small stores and trading posts scattered throughout Sunol and Amador valley, taking from the shelves and hooks such articles as pleased their fancy, and walking off without payment.[25]

It was as if the mountain bandits were daring the new sheriff to a test of his mettle. It was a grievous mistake, for El Muchacho was ready to strike a bloody blow against the very worst of them.

CHAPTER 4

First Fire

NARCISO Bojorques had continued to make himself the terror of the Amador and Livermore valleys. He thumbed his nose at local lawmen. As Harry Morse later recalled, "He had been heard to make some fearful threats about what he would do to any officer who attempted to arrest him, and swore that if his arrest was attempted, he would never be taken alive."[1]

It was not long before the young sheriff saw a chance to avenge the Corral Hollow murders. One day Narciso had angry words with John Gunnell, a butcher at Alisal, and threatened to kill him. A few days later, on the evening of August 25, 1866, Gunnell started on horseback from Pleasanton to Mission San Jose. Three miles down the trail he was accosted by a mounted bandido wearing false whiskers, a slouch hat, and a sarape.

Pistol in hand, the road agent demanded money. Gunnell denied having any and put spurs to his horse. At that, the bandido fired, sending a ball through his arm. He pulled the butcher off his horse, relieved him of $120, and galloped away. Gunnell, whose wound did not prove serious, returned home and reported the crime.[2]

I was called upon to ferret out and bring to justice the robber, if such a thing was possible. Gunnell was quite certain that the robber was Narciso, but would not swear to it for the reason that it was dark at the time and he was not certain as to his identity, and therefore was not willing to take the chances of swearing out a warrant for him. I made the most diligent search and inquiry in the vicinity of the attempted murder but could not find a single particle of evidence outside of what Gunnell said to substantiate the fact of Narciso's being the man. I did not care to arrest him on mere suspicion, as I knew I could not hold him, and it would make matters worse, and I would be laughed at for my trouble. Besides, I wanted to be certain of my man being the right one, and then I would be taking no chances in case he should resist arrest.

Narciso Bojorques.
A woodcut from a lost
photograph, circa 1865.
Author's collection.

One day while sitting in my office my undersheriff brought me a letter from the post office. Upon opening it I saw to my great joy that it was a warrant from one of the southern counties, charging Narciso Bojorques with the crime of grand larceny, and commanding me to forthwith arrest the said Narciso. The warrant came into my hands at 10 A.M. [on September 19, 1866]. Arranging my business so that I could be absent for a few days, I went to my stable, and putting the saddle on a big, strong California mustang that I owned, I was ready to move out at eleven. Changing my everyday clothing for an old grey shirt, pair of cavalry pants, an old coat, and a broad-brimmed slouch hat, and arming myself with a large-sized Colt's revolver, I started out for Narciso's rendezvous.

A three hours' ride brought me to the old Mission San Jose, just twenty miles from my starting point, my objective point being the Cajon, a large creek emptying into Sunol Valley [today known as Alameda Creek], and where Narciso was generally to be found. Putting my horse in a stable to rest and feed, I sauntered about the old Mission, making inquiries as to when Narciso had been there. I soon learned that Narciso had been in the Mission that morning, and at noon had been seen riding through the old Stockton Pass road toward Sunol Valley, his usual hiding place. Leaving the old Mission at 5 P.M., I took the old Pass road and went quietly on, turning over in my own mind my plan of attack in case I should come on to Narciso in the canyon. I will confess that I felt nervous now that I was getting so close to the place of action, as this was the first really bad man that I had yet tackled, and I was somewhat inclined to doubt my own courage in relation to the matter. However, I kept on, and rode through the Pass—which, by the way, had been the scene of many an awful murder and robbery.

About sundown I emerged from the hills and entered the beautiful little valley of Sunol. To the right the Cajon made its way out of the mountains, running through the center of the valley, and turning to the left, cut its way through the inner Coast Range to the Bay of San Francisco. To the east, and directly in front of me, could be seen the continuation of the road as it rose over the hill in the direction of Livermore Valley and Vallecitos. Crossing the Cajon and riding on a mile or more, I came to where the road to the Alisal turned to the left. At this point, and to the right, was situated a small trading post kept by an Italian named George Foscalina. [This spot is still shown on maps as Scott's Corners and is located at the intersection of Highway 680 and Vallecitos Road.]

There were about thirty people at and around the store, mostly Mexicans. It then struck me for the first time that I had done a very foolish thing in venturing on such an errand alone. However, it was too late to repent now. While engaged in taking the saddle from off my horse, John Foscalina, a son of the storekeeper, came into the stable to assist me in taking care of my horse. While chatting with the young man, he remarked, "I wish you had arrived a few minutes sooner. You would have met a very bad man—a fellow by the name of Bojorques. He is always making trouble," he continued, and expressed a wish that he could be got rid of.

I pretended that I did not know who Bojorques was.

"Why," said Foscalina, "he's an awful bad and desperate man, and it is suspected that he is the chap who attempted to kill John Gunnell. I wish he was away from here. We are afraid of him. I'll bet anything that the cuss is bent on some mischief now, as he seems to be preparing for a journey of some kind. As he rode by here a few moments since on a little bay horse he had a new saddle and in addition he had an extra saddle, also new, on behind him."

"What kind of a horse did he have?" I asked. "Was it a good one?"

"Yes, it was a strong built native horse and one I never saw him ride before," replied Foscalina.

"Which way did he go, John?" I asked.

"He rode over the hill toward the Vallecitos, sir."

"Do you think he will return this way?"

"Oh, yes, he lives in the canyon, about three miles from here, and must return this way to get to his camp."

"Now, John," I said, "I want you to do me a favor, will you?"

"Certainly I will, if I can," replied the young man. "What is it?"

"Well, when Narciso comes back I want you to entice him from his horse into the store. I've heard a great deal about this fellow but, as yet, I have never got a good look at him. It is so dark that I cannot see him outside, so I want you to get him in where it is light, so that I can see him well."

My real object was to get him into the store, away from his horse, as he was a splendid horseman, while I, at that time, was a very indifferent one, and I well knew that I would be at a great disadvantage if I attempted to gather him in while he was on his horse.

"All right," said Foscalina. "I will ask him into the store to take a drink when he comes."

Had the young man known my real intentions to Narciso, I don't think he would have been so willing to assist me, as all of these people had a mortal dread of this one man. However, it was arranged that I should stay behind the corner of the house, out of sight, until Narciso rode up and got into the store, when I was to come out and go in after him. Everything being fixed to my satisfaction, I took my position behind the house and began to prepare my mind for the encounter.

To say that there was not a nervous fear about me would not be telling the truth. I was a little alarmed about the final result of the thing and really wished it was over and I was well out of it, but such an idea as backing out never for a second entered my mind. I was fully determined to bring the bandit to justice, if possible, yet I could not help but wish that I had brought some good, trusty man with me to assist me. I felt myself fully able to cope with the desperado as long as no firearms or other weapons were brought into use, for I was young and strong. But I did doubt my ability to cope with him otherwise, as I had never been used in all my life to weapons of any kind, while on the contrary, Narciso was considered to be quite an expert in the use of them.

I sat on an old box near the west corner of the store, anxiously watching for the coming of Narciso. It was quite dark, and I had been waiting and watching for perhaps half an hour, when suddenly I heard the jingling of spurs and the sound of a voice singing in Spanish. Looking up toward the top of the hill in the direction of Vallecitos, I could just discern the form of a man galloping toward the store, the musical jingle of his spurs keeping time to the galloping feet of his horse as he came swiftly onward toward me.

Harry Morse owned several revolvers. This one is a Colt 1849 Pocket Model, serial no. 96432, manufactured in 1854. The backstrap is inscribed "H.N. Morse" and the buttstrap, "New York—Cala. To See the Elephant." The holster is a civilian half flap model. Author's collection.

"Is that the man, John?" I asked.

"Yes," he replied.

I then drew back out of sight. At the same time my heart certainly commenced to beat faster. Narciso drew up in front of the store and John invited him to dismount and take a drink.

"No, señor," said Narciso. "I don't wish to drink. Have you any candy in the store?" Dulces [sweets] he called them.

"Yes," said John.

"Well, bring me out a quarter's worth."

"I've no time," said John. "Go in and get them."

"Pendejo!" [Imbecile!] exclaimed Narciso, and turned to ride away.

Fearing that he would escape me, I came quickly forward from my hiding place, intending to seize the horse's bridle rein and give it a sudden jerk backward, thus setting the horse down on his haunches, and then to reach out, take Narciso by the throat, and pull him off his horse to the ground. Once there I would feel that I had him secure. But I never got him there.

I had taken perhaps six steps toward the desperado and had got almost within reach of his horse's head, when Narciso seemed to suddenly discover who I was and, divining my intention, suddenly drew his horse back out of my reach and at the same time, with the rapidity of lightning, he drew his revolver, and cocking it, thrust it into my face, at the same time exclaiming, "No poder, señor!" [It can't be done, sir!].

God, what a shock it gave me! Caught in my own trap and completely at the mercy of the desperado, looking in to the end of his eight-inch six-shooter, held by the hand of a man who would not stop a moment at taking my life to make his escape! "He who hesitates is lost." How the thought did flash through my brain. I did not even have my pistol out, but like a foolish schoolboy, I had it safely in the scabbard at my side. I expected each instant to see the flash and feel the bullet crash through my flesh. My plan was made instantly. I was bound that if I did get shot I would take it in front and not behind, and at the same time I was aware that if I let this fellow get away with me, that my usefulness as an officer was gone and I would have to take the chances of a fight with every scrub thief that I had to arrest hereafter, as well as being the laughing stock for all the greasers in the country. If I could have gotten out of the scrape safely by letting the fellow escape, and no one to know of it, I am not certain but what I would have adopted that mode out of my difficulty, but my pride kept me fast to the spot.

Lord! How quick my mind worked! It occurred to me, if I could only get my pistol out, cock and shoot it, no matter in what direction, the effect upon the desperado might be demoralizing, and if he hesitated a moment longer to shoot I could get the best of him. He did hesitate, and that saved my life. Seizing my pistol with my right hand, I drew it from the scabbard, and raising it quickly into a vertical position, with my thumb upon the hammer, I brought the pistol down to the line of fire, the weight of the pistol coming down cocking it, and shot.

The effect was electrical. Narciso exclaimed, "No tiras!" [Don't shoot!] and striking spurs into his horse, he, like an excited fool, dodged around behind the store, whereas if he had taken the straight road in front of him he could have ridden away from me. I began to get mad now, to think that the fellow would not stand up and take what he had intended for me, but run away at the first declaration of war, in the shape of a harmless shot fired at random. I knew, from the position of the house and grounds, that there was no escape now for Narciso, unless he shot me or jumped his horse over a four-board fence, and made his way into the hills in rear of the store.

As Narciso started to run I took three or four steps toward the direction he had taken, and seeing his dim outline in the darkness, I drew my
revolver down upon him and fired. Just as I did so Narciso went down
over the side of his horse, in regular Comanche fashion, to escape the
shot. The shot seemed to have no effect and I thought that I had missed
him. I expected each second to get his return fire but it did not come. I
got him into a corner and attempted to fire again, as he was busy sock-
ing the spurs into the sides of his little horse in his earnest endeavor to
jump the fence. To my horror I found that an exploded cap had caught
in the cylinder of my pistol and it would no longer revolve. I was bound
that he should not escape me; so, seizing my weapon firmly in my right
hand, I raised it aloft and made a rush toward him, intending to strike
the desperado over the head with it and knock him from his horse. I was
within two steps of the bandit—almost within reach of him—when he
sunk the spurs deep into the animal's sides, who, with a desperate spring,
cleared the fence and began to run swiftly toward the hill, I after him on
foot.

I thought he had gotten clean away, but no—he had jumped his horse
into a large corral used for keeping cattle in at night when passing that
way. I followed quickly after the fleeing criminal, calling upon him to stop.
The fence on the upper side of the corral was rather too much for the little horse, for after making one or two ineffectual attempts to jump it, and
seeing that I was getting very close to him, the desperate man suddenly
abandoned his horse and took to the hills afoot, with me in quick pursuit.
I followed him for quite a distance by the jingle of his spurs. Finally I lost
the sound of the spurs, and fearing that he might have stopped behind some
bush to await my coming and then shoot me as I went by him, I thought
it the better part of valor to slow down. This I did, and searched very carefully through hills and ravines for about an hour, but without success. The
cuss had got away from me, and I returned to the store.

As I stated before, there were some thirty or more Mexicans and white
people at the store when I first rode up to it. When the shooting commenced such a scattering as took place in a second not a person was visible. Upon my return to the store all was excitement. One old Spaniard
asked me if I had found Narciso. I told him that unfortunately I had not.

"Your shot struck him," said the old fellow.

"I don't think so," I replied.

"I am certain of it," answered the old chap, "for the reason that when
you fired the second shot I was standing quite near to him, and I heard the
ball strike him and I also heard him groan."

Scott's Corners in 1880, looking south. The large building at far right is the store built by Thomas Scott in mid-1871. Directly across the Old Stockton Road, and partly obscured by trees, is the old store built by George Foscalina, which was the scene of Sheriff Morse's shooting of Narciso Bojorques in 1866 as well as of the murder of Otto Ludovisi by the Juan Soto band in 1871. The four-board fence and corral described by Morse can be seen at the lower right. The building in the center with the windmill and water tower is Thomas Scott's home. Courtesy of the Oakland Public Library.

I then recollected that he did not return my fire as he most certainly ought to have done, and it occurred to me that perhaps I did hit him just when he was leaning over on the side of his horse to escape my shot. If I did hit him then, he might have dropped his pistol, and which would account for his not returning my fire. Stooping down, I drew my hand along on the ground, and when I came to where Narciso was when I fired I found his pistol lying on the ground, full cocked. The handle of the pistol seemed quite wet. Taking it to the light, I found that it was covered with fresh blood.

I was certain that I had wounded the desperado, but how bad the wound was of course I was unable to determine. I immediately concluded to continue the search for Narciso as best I could in the darkness and not give him a chance to escape if I could possibly help it. Borrowing an old-fashioned United States musket from Foscalina, and taking young John Foscalina with me, I instituted a brisk search of the surrounding hill, canyon, and brush for about two hours. Our search was necessarily slow. It was dark and we did not know what moment the wounded bandit would spring from behind some bush, and one of us would receive a fatal shot. However, our search was fruitless. We could not hear or see the least sign of him.

Returning to the store, I secured the horse that Narciso had left behind him. It was now about twelve o'clock and the moon was just making its appearance over the mountain tops east of Sunol. I determined to leave the animal, just as he was, in the big corral, as a bait for the wounded bandit, hoping that he might venture back into the night to regain his horse. Foscalina and I hid ourselves in a straw stack and within easy shot of the corral and waited and watched until broad daylight but no one came for the horse. As soon as we got some coffee I started off again to see if I could get any trace of the wounded robber.

Starting from where Narciso left his horse on the upper side of the corral, I very readily tracked him by drops of blood that had dripped from his wound. I followed the blood tracks for about a mile along the foot of the hills when they suddenly turned to the left, up a deep ravine. Following on about 200 yards, I came upon an old dead trunk of a large tree. Here I found a large pool of clotted blood. The wounded man had evidently rested here and attempted to bind up his wound, as I also found pieces of a linen duster that he had torn into strips and which was saturated with blood. Notwithstanding I kept up the search most diligently, I could discover no other trace of the fugitive. Satisfied that I could do nothing more alone, I concluded that I would return to San Leandro, organize a posse, and make a thorough and complete search of the mountain country, where the robber must of necessity be hid.

My trophies, upon inventory, consisted of one eight-inch Colt revolver, a new saddle, a new serape of fancy colors, one new reata, and a stout mustang horse—one of the kind all nerve, yet as gentle as a lamb, so gentle that any child could handle it. Many a curious glance was taken at me

by the Mexicans as I passed their jacales with my trophies, as all of them
by this time had heard of the fight and seemed surprised that "El Muchacho" had got away with Narciso.

Arriving at San Leandro, I proceeded at once to organize a posse of good
men to assist me in my search. Calling to my assistance S. J. Marston,
Otho Morgan, Steve Johnson, B. F. Granger, E. S. Allen, N. Crowell, Joe
Rooker, and several others whose names I do not at this moment recall, we
started out on our hunt for the wounded desperado. Each man of us was
mounted on a good horse; each of us had a roll of blankets and grub
enough to last us three or four days. Our first day's search was through the
steep and rugged mountains east of Sunol Valley, and which was known
to contain at that time some of the very worst characters in the state. They
were hid and scattered about in the various deep ravines situated in these
mountains. We searched all day, taking in a circuit of about fifteen miles,
visited all the shanties, and rolled great rocks down into the canyons
wherever it looked like a place where a person might be hid, but our search
was unavailing. Not a single clew could we get to our man.

Retracing our steps, we camped for the night at the ranch of Charley
Garthwaite, who very generously provided the whole party with food for
ourselves and horses. We were in the saddle again at daylight. Making our
way to the Alisal, we searched all the huts in that vicinity. Finding nothing, we struck out for the Casitas, near the Black Hills in Contra Costa
County. The Casitas was a collection of small houses and was the hiding
place of many a bad man. We searched this country thoroughly but without success. Making our way east, we crossed the Livermore Valley, which
at this time was almost uninhabited, toward the Arroyo Valle, and camped
for the night at the ranch of Green Patterson [about 2 miles southeast
of present-day Livermore].

After supper I called the men around and explained to them the topography of the country that we were to explore in the morning. I had concluded to divide the party in the morning and make a complete search of
the Arroyo Seco and also the Arroyo Valle. The first party was to cross
the mountains in a southerly direction, leaving Pine Mountain, or as the
Mexicans called it, Monte Pino, to the left and meet posse number two
high up on the Arroyo Valle and near the old Mendenhall Rancho [lo-
cated 12 miles south of Livermore].

The Arroyo del Valle is a steep canyon whose rough and mountainous
sides are covered with dense underbrush and large oak trees. A beautiful
stream of clear, sparkling water makes its way through the rocky bottom
and sinks near the Livermore Valley. Scattered here and there in the

canyon were little Mexican huts, whose inhabitants had no visible means
of support and of necessity must have lived by preying upon the herds of
the cattle and sheep men who herded in these mountains. These huts were
the rendezvous of all the horse thieves in the state. Bands of horses and
cattle, stolen from the northern part of the state, would be run into these
almost unpenetrable canyons and secreted and rested, and when sufficiently recuperated they would be driven south to a market, and the same
performance would be gone through with for animals stolen from the
southern parts of the state.

In the arroyo I certainly expected to hear something of my valento-
nado [boaster], or if we got no trace of Narciso, I was quite certain to
come into contact with some of the gang. Our camp was in close proximity
to a den owned by a Mexican named Juan Camargo, reputed to be a notorious tapadera [literally, a cover; a slang term for one who fences
stolen goods] for all the horse thieves in the country. No matter at what
time you visited Juan's house you would be certain to see three or four
ugly-looking cutthroats hanging about. Juan, himself, was no beauty,
having as villainous a looking face as was ever put upon a man's shoulders.
He was of stout build, about forty years of age, bowlegged, dark complexion, hair long and coarse, heavy black moustache, pointed at the end;
his nose was of the Roman order, eyes large, black, with a decided squint,
and when the least excited they sparkled and burned like coals of fire.
Take him altogether, he was one of the most cruel and most desperate-
looking men I ever saw. A man of his peculiar personal appearance could
not help but attract all the thieves and cutthroats in the country to his
domicile.

In the morning I divided the party, sending half up the Arroyo Seco.
With me went Rooker, Morgan, Crowell, Johnson, and Allen. The trail
leading from our camp to Camargo's house passed through an open country, so that we had to approach it with great caution so as not to be seen
until we got close to the house. Making our way up through a little ravine
leading in the direction of Camargo's house, we got within about 300
yards of it without alarming either the dogs or the people. Another moment
and we would be upon an elevated piece of ground and in full view of Camargo's house. Halting my men, I told them to prepare their arms for immediate use, as there was no telling who we would meet at the house, and
that when we came in view of it to dash forward at full speed, and if anyone attempted to leave the house, to stop them at all hazards.

Being all ready, I gave the order to go forward. In about thirty steps we
were in full view of the house. I gazed sharply toward the den and saw

three men rolled up in their blankets and lying on a dried hide under a
large tree that grew close by the jacal. They did not seem to notice us at
first and we rode silently toward them. Suddenly the sharp yelp of a cur
dog sounded in the still crisp morning air. Immediately a head was raised
up from under the blankets. The head rested upon the man's elbow for a
second. He sat up, rubbed his eyes, and took a good long look at us. Still
we rode silently on toward them. Suddenly the sleeper jumped to his feet,
pulled on his boots, buckled on his six-shooter, and without waiting to put
on his hat or coat, started on the dead run for a horse that was picketed
in the rear of the house. He had but a hundred feet to run to the horse,
while we were yet about 200 feet away from him. When I saw him buckle
on his pistol and start to run I gave the order to dash forward. We did so
at the top of our speed. The man got to the horse and was making a desperate effort to untie the animal from the picket pin. He did get him untied and then attempted to spring upon the horse's back. He made two or
three efforts and failed each time, the horse shying away from him, and the
last time he fell, sprawling upon the ground.

By this time we were upon him: Morgan, Rooker, Crowell, and Allen
taking the rear of the house and I taking the front. Rooker drew down
upon the Mexican with his double-barrelled shotgun. The Mexican placed
his hand upon his pistol, as if to draw, but seeing Morgan, Allen, and
Crowell all had him under cover of their guns, he changed his mind, stood
up a moment as if to surrender, but suddenly darted around the corner of
the cabin and ran toward the front door, evidently thinking that part of the
house was not guarded. I had just dismounted from my horse and stood,
pistol in hand, keeping the Mexicans who were inside the house from coming out and at the same time keeping the two Mexicans, who were still
rolled in their blankets under the tree, still. The fleeing Mexican ran toward me, pistol in hand. As soon as I saw him I recognized him as a notorious horse thief named Agustín Avila, alias "El Capitán," and an escapee
from our jail at San Leandro. He was so close to me by the time that he
saw me that my pistol, which I thrust into his face, almost touched his
forehead.

I called him by name and told him to hold up his hands and surrender.
He did so at once. Still keeping him under cover of my pistol, I ordered him
to drop his weapon to the ground. He did so. I then ordered him to walk
away from it and he obeyed. Picking up his pistol and putting it into my
own belt, I took a pair of handcuffs from out of my pocket and put them
on him. He made no resistance, but Lord, how he did curse and swear in
Spanish. He was tearfully angry and excited and his eyes snapped like fire.

El Capitán said that he recognized me as soon as he raised his head from his blankets and, knowing that he was an escapee from jail and that an indictment for grand larceny was hanging over him, was the reason for his desperate effort to escape. It was the greatest wonder in the world that Rooker did not kill him when he dodged around the corner of the house and it was a fortunate thing for all of us that I was dismounted and at the front door. Had El Capitán managed to get inside the house he was just desperate and mean enough to have made fight on us. He, being on the inside, would have had the advantage on us ten to one, and that too without danger to himself. He could have picked every one of us off in detail, with hardly a single chance of being killed himself, and he was just the kind of an excitable Mexican to do it, too.

As soon as I had El Capitán properly secured, I had his horse brought up and the saddle put on him and ordered the prisoner to mount and prepare for a long ride, as I intended to take him with us on our scout in the mountains. Securing one of his wrists to the pommel of the saddle with the handcuffs, I tied his legs together under the horse's belly. I took my mescarte [hair rope] and tied it around the neck of the prisoner's horse, drove it through the leather curb of his bridle bit, and taking a turn around the pommel of my saddletree, we rode triumphantly off, leaving Juan Camargo and the rest of the gang looking after us in a dazed sort of way.

We kept the trail almost due south for a mile or more and then turned in an easterly direction, entering the Arroyo Valle canyon near the house of old man Mariano Higuera. Here we made diligent search and inquiry but no one had seen anything of Narciso. Leaving Mariano's house, we proceeded up the canyon about ten miles, searching all the way as we went, but not a sign of Narciso could be found. Still, I was sure that he was hid away in these mountains somewhere and I knew that it would be almost impossible to unearth him.

At noon both parties met again. There being plenty of good feed here we went into camp for an hour to rest our horses and get lunch. We then started over the mountains in a westerly direction, toward Indian Gulch. The mountain trails here were frightfully steep and our horses were very much exhausted by the time we reached the summit. We made a thorough search of Indian Gulch and arrived at Foscalina's store in Sunol Valley about dark, tired and worn out. At nine o'clock I started with El Capitán for the county jail at San Leandro, arriving there at two o'clock in the morning, having ridden eighty miles that day. El Capitán pleaded guilty to grand larceny and was sentenced to the state prison for three years. He

served out his full term and was discharged, but not cured. I heard of him
many times in Southern California, working at his old business—horse
stealing.
    I kept up my search for Narciso for several months but I never suc-
ceeded in capturing him. I learned from a Mexican friend of his that the
ball from my pistol had struck Narciso in the arm near the elbow, ripping
the flesh up to the wrist and coming out through the center of his hand.
After the wound healed the arm and fingers were permanently crippled.[3]

    Narciso Bojorques soon met his end. In February 1867 he and an
ex-convict, One-Eyed Jack Williams, quarreled over a card game in
a cantina near Copperopolis, Calaveras County. Each was armed
with a Colt revolver, and they agreed to settle the dispute in a frontier duel. Each was to exit the cantina, one by the front door and the
other by the back, and when they met outside they would open fire.
The agreement was carried out to the letter. The two met at the rear
of the cantina and pulled triggers. Narciso's pistol ball creased One-
Eyed Jack's scalp but did no further damage. Jack's aim was better.
His first shot slammed into Narciso's right arm and lodged in his
heart, killing the bandido instantly.
    Narciso's mother lived in Stockton, and there his body was taken
and turned over to her for burial. Sheriff Morse visited Stockton to
view the body and to confirm that the Corral Hollow killer was
dead. He felt compassion for the outlaw's mother and later said, "She
was a tough citizen herself but a good mother to him, and stuck to
her degraded son to the last."[4]
    His shooting of Narciso Bojorques proved a turning point in
Harry Morse's career. For the first time he recognized that a quick
mind coupled with boldness and skill with firearms were enough to
overcome even the most dangerous and desperate of outlaws. Those
qualities would serve him well in the years to come.

CHAPTER 5

El Diablo

HARRY Morse's victory over the worst of his bandit adversaries was short-lived. Just nine days after the Bojorques shooting, on September 28, 1866, at exactly the same spot where Narciso had held up John Gunnell, a pair of heavily armed bandidos held up S. P. Doane, a wealthy Livermore Valley farmer. Doane was en route by buggy to Sunol from Mission San Jose, where he had picked up his $250 payroll, when two well-dressed, well mounted brigands rode up next to him, pointed a six-gun at his head, and ordered him in Spanish to halt. Luck was with Doane, however, for at that instant a teamster hove into sight. The two horsemen gave a cry of alarm, wheeled their horses, and putting spurs into their flanks, vanished in a cloud of hoof dust.[1]

Morse was unable to capture this pair. He must have taken this brazen daylight holdup as a direct challenge from the bandit gangs, as it was too much of a coincidence that these highwaymen had selected for their holdup the exact spot Gunnell was robbed. In any event, it showed the young sheriff that he had a great deal of work ahead of him if he expected to rid his bailiwick of its untamed outlaw bands.

After thoroughly scanning the situation, I commenced to "gather them in" as fast as occasion should require me to do so. But first I must get thoroughly acquainted with the country infested by these fellows, and I resolved to become thoroughly posted as to the roads and trails leading in and out of their mountain hiding places. Accordingly, every few days I would mount my horse and visit every canyon road and trail, riding leisurely along through the country as though I had no particular business except to see the horses and cattle grazing on the hills. In a short time the whole country became as familiar to me as my own hand. I managed to see and know all the gang by sight, and at the same time I was becoming posted on the past and personal character of every one of them, which I

71

*found of great value to me in my future operations. This I learned, even
to the most minute particular.*

*Having familiarized myself with their names, history, faces, and other
necessary facts in regard to the bandits, as well as to the topography of
their chosen hiding places, I began to make hostile demonstrations. I fully
recognized the great responsibility that rested upon me, and resolved to be
equal to the task.*

*Meanwhile, the desperadoes regarded my movements disdainfully,
laughing at the seeming interest of the sheriff, or El Muchacho as they
called me, took in the mountains and canyons. They never suspected
that they had anything to fear from me. At least, they never showed it if
they did. Whenever I got ready to take in one of the gang, I always made
certain that his retreat was cut off before I ventured to tackle him. One
after another, and without a moment's warning, they began to get
"nipped" and brought into camp. They were astonished, and began to
open their eyes. El Muchacho was getting away with the business, and
they could not help themselves or account for it.*

*The arrests grew systematic, and the bandits began to get alarmed, and
made threats of getting even with me. My bump of combativeness being
largely developed, and there being something in my nature that gave me
intense delight in following up and bringing these fellows to justice, I de-
fied them. Whenever word of a threat against me by any of these exas-
perated cutthroats reached my ears, I took especial pains to go after that
particular one. If I could fasten no local crime upon him, I would corre-
spond with the officers in the counties where this particular man had for-
merly resided, and would generally be rewarded with success by receiving
a warrant for the man in question. So exciting did this business become
that I spent every spare moment in hunting these criminals. I took no little pride in mystifying and outwitting these conocidos [suspects]. They
also had their spies out watching my movements but somehow I always
managed to outwit them.*

*Whenever I made up my mind to raid one of their camps, I would
make it a point to be seen sauntering carelessly along through the streets
of San Leandro, about dusk in the evening. As soon as it grew quite dark,
I would quietly slip away, saddle my horse, and at daylight the next morning I would dash into one of their camps, thirty miles away, and another
one of the band would be "nipped," and brought to justice. They could
never tell when El Muchacho was coming, or how soon. Meanwhile, my
friends, while they appreciated my devotion to duty, began to fear that I
was getting too reckless for my own safety, and were in constant appre-*

Harry Morse, from a carte de visite taken in Oakland about 1867. Author's collection.

hension of my being killed by some of this formidable gang. They little suspected the amount of caution I used in these adventures, for full well I
knew that in the exercise of this faculty lay the secret of my success and
safety.[2]

Morse's next exploit plainly showed the bandidos the stuff he was
made of. And it gave him an opportunity to repay George Foscalina
for the help his son had given him the day he shot Narciso Bojorques.

In July, 1866, a well-to-do cattle raiser, the owner of a large rancho
near Mount Diablo in Contra Costa County, had stolen from his place
ten head of fine steers. The thieves, whom I subsequently traced, drove the
stock through the mountains of the Black Hill country on the southern
slope of El Monte Diablo toward Livermore Valley, striking that valley at
or about the old Hiram Bailey or Casitas [Little Houses] Rancho, thence

across the Livermore Valley to the Arroyo Valle, where they camped for
the night. On the following day they struck across the mountains and entered the Vallecitos, near the old Stockton road. Traveling along this road
for a mile or more, they came to the cluster of houses where George Foscalina kept his little store.

Here the thieves sold to the storekeeper one of the stolen animals and
urged him to purchase all of them, telling him that they had bought the
stock from a farmer on the San Joaquin at a very low price, and offered
the whole lot to him for a small cash sum. The Italian declined to purchase, saying he desired only one head, as that would be sufficient for his
immediate wants. Prudence ought to have dictated to him that he was taking very serious risks in buying cattle from strangers in a country where
cattle stealing was a common occurrence, and to which severe penalties
were attached, not only to the thieves, if arrested, but also to the receivers
of stolen property, if found in his possession immediately after the theft,
and he not able to clearly and honorably account for its presence.

Foolishly, however, Foscalina accepted the statement of the strangers
in good faith, and purchased one of the steers. The thieves thereupon left
with the remainder of the herd. Turning north on the old Alisal road, they
crossed Alameda Creek near the farm of Charles Hadsell and made their
way up Cathcart Canyon [known later as Sunol Glen and today as
Sinbad Creek Canyon]. Proceeding up the canyon for about three miles,
they came to a hut built in a steep ravine and owned by one Juan Robles,
alias Seda Chaleco [Satin Vest], who was a very clever and well known
horse thief of those times. Here the cattle were left by the Mexicans to be
hidden in the canyons until the excitement of the theft and the search for
the thieves had ceased.

A few days after the loss of his cattle, the ranchero, in searching for
them, discovered the hide, with his brand on it, of one of his best steers
hanging upon the corral fence of the Italian storekeeper. There was only
one inference to be drawn from this discovery and the owner was not slow
in drawing it. It was then a lonely place, well adapted by its isolation to
be a haunt for cattle thieves, and it naturally occurred to the victimized
stock raiser that he had come upon the rendezvous or home of one of them,
at least.

Riding to the store, he dismounted, entered the house, and demanded
the return to him of the stolen cattle and the delivery of the thieves to the
officers of the law. Foscalina was as much startled at the accusation implied in this demand as the other was confident of his criminality. The
storekeeper disclaimed all knowledge of the whereabouts of the remainder

of the herd, nor could he tell who or where the men were who had sold him the animal whose hide was hanging on the fence of his corral. He declared that he had acquired the steer honestly by purchase from two Mexicans who had passed his house with ten head of cattle a few days previously. He described the Mexicans to the owner, told him in what direction they had gone after leaving his place, and said he would endeavor to ascertain what their names were that they might be brought to justice, and ended by saying he would pay the owner for the steer he had purchased from the thieves. This, however, did not satisfy the owner of the cattle, who insisted upon Foscalina paying him for the whole herd, intimating very strongly that the storekeeper was an accessory to the larceny. The latter, however, was firm in his refusal to pay for more than the one animal. The owner was naturally much incensed over the loss of his cattle and rode away in a very angry frame of mind. He continued his search through the mountains for several days, but without success, and finally, worn out and discouraged, he returned to his rancho at Mount Diablo.

The first information I had of the loss of the cattle was through a letter from the rancher giving a full description of them and also a detailed account of his search and what he had found at Foscalina's corral. He stated his suspicions that the storekeeper knew more about the affair than he was willing to tell and he ended his communication with the declaration that he believed Foscalina was accessory to and connected with the gang of cattle thieves who then infested the Black Hills near the line of Alameda and Contra Costa Counties. This last declaration surprised me much. I did not credit it. I knew Foscalina well, and had in my experience with him found him to be fair and upright in his affairs. If some well known disreputable character showed up in his vicinity he was prompt in his notification of the fact to me. No man in the country was better situated to furnish important information to the officers of the law than he and he always did so cheerfully. On the other hand, no man had better opportunity to shield the outlaws had he been so inclined.

No trains of cars were then bowling along every few hours through Livermore Valley. It was a rough ride on a half broken mustang or not get there at all. Saddling up my bronco, I at once started for the scene. I was fully satisfied that when I saw Foscalina he would tell me all he knew.

Passing along the county road from San Leandro, I turned to the left through Castro Valley and struck the old stage road about three miles east of Haywards. Continuing on to the Palomares Canyon, I took to the ridge and was soon on the top of the mountain overlooking a vast expanse of country, including the whole of Livermore Valley and the Vallecitos. Gal-

loping along the ridge for a few miles, I came to the Cathcart Canyon, which led directly to Sunol Valley and Foscalina's store.

Cathcart Canyon is a deep gorge in the inner Coast Range and west of the great wall-like mountains which loom up in their silent majesty west of and almost overlooking what is now known as Pleasanton, but at that time known all over the country as the Alisal. Riding through this deep canyon, the scenery is very beautiful. In places the mountains almost come together, overtopping one hundreds of feet. In the bed of the ravine a stream of clear sparkling water rushes merrily along over a gravelly bottom, making its way to the greater Alameda Canyon [now called Niles Canyon], and thence to the waters of the bay of San Francisco.

Along the sides of this deep mountain gorge for several miles there grows a dense forest of oak and other timber. Numerous ravines make their way into the gorge from the surrounding mountains, the sides of which are covered with a heavy growth of underbrush. Now and then there reaches out from the head of these ravines small plateaus, upon which a luxurious growth of wild oats and other grasses is always to be found. It was upon these mountain plateaus that the cattle and horse thieves hid and rested the stolen animals. This important fact, of course, was well known to me.

I arrived at Foscalina's store about four o'clock in the afternoon and was much surprised to learn that he had been arrested by an officer from Contra Costa County that morning upon a warrant sworn out by the owner of the cattle, charging him with the crime of grand larceny. Upon my advice the unfortunate storekeeper waived preliminary examination, gave bail, and awaited the action of the grand jury. I impressed upon his mind the seriousness of the charge that had been brought against him and explained to him that the possession of property recently stolen was a strong point for the prosecution. With other circumstances which might go to show that he knew the animals were stolen at the time he bought the steer, he would likely be convicted of receiving stolen property.

I also informed him that the owner was determined to fight the case against him to the bitter end. If he was innocent I would assist in clearing him of the charge, but he must tell me the whole truth about the matter. Foscalina then related to me the same circumstances that he had first told the ranchero, adding, however, that since then he had ascertained the names of the thieves, who were two Mexicans named Juan Robles and Jesus Cruz. After a description of the men I informed him that I knew the parties well and promised to soon have them in custody.

Part of my success in this case was due to chance and part to patience and hard work. My first step was to take up and try to follow the trail of the stolen cattle from the time the thieves left Foscalina's place. This was a difficult thing to do, as some six weeks had elapsed. However, I went diligently to work, resolved to solve the problem now uppermost in my mind. I called to my assistance George Swain, undersheriff of Contra Costa County. I felt that the officers of Contra Costa County were also entitled to representation and credit in the pursuit and capture of the men who had stolen property from their county.

We met at Dougherty's Station [now Dublin] as per agreement. Together we rode down the west side of the Alisal about ten miles to the place where the stolen cattle had crossed Alameda Creek and made their way into the mountains. Leaving our horses at the foot of a steep canyon, we climbed the mountain side to the hut of Juan Robles. This hut was situated about 200 yards up the mountain side and in a dense thicket. Juan was not in the hut but we found there a Portuguese woodchopper whom we closely questioned. We learned from him that about a mile further up the canyon, high up on the side of the mountain, on one of the plateaus, some Mexicans had, about six weeks before, driven nine head of cattle. Leaving them there, they had ridden hurriedly away. He had not seen them since.

When pressed for their names, the woodchopper said that he had met them once before at a fandango at Alisal, and that one was named Juan. This was all he knew, and it corresponded exactly with what Foscalina had told me. Everything looked encouraging. Returning to our horses, we rode up the canyon and soon came to the place indicated by the Portuguese, but no cattle greeted our expectant gaze. Crossing the plateau, however, we came to a deep ravine in which we saw several head of cattle grazing and which, upon closer inspection, proved to be part of the stolen herd. We did not stop to see more and as it was not at all likely that the thieves themselves were there, we made our way back to Alisal, which was the general rendezvous for all the hard characters in the country.

As we came into sight of the little village of Alisal we noticed quite a crowd of men gathered there, apparently considerably excited. We were within about 200 yards of the crowd when we saw two men clinch each other and fall on their knees. As they fell a horseman dashed toward them at full speed, and striking the uppermost with his horse's breast, knocked him at least ten feet, where he fell headlong to the ground. Another man rushed up to the man who had been knocked down by the horse, and taking something from his hand, ran away with it.

By this time Swain and I were in the middle of the crowd inquiring the cause of the turmoil. We were informed that a half-breed Indian had attempted to kill Presentación Bernal, and that thereupon Abelino Bernal, Presentación's brother, seeing the danger his brother was in, had made the sudden dash on horseback at the would-be murderer, placing him hors de combat.[3]

The Bernals, knowing this particular Indian's character for treachery, and fearing future injury from him, refused to prosecute. Finding that justice was about to be balked, I took the Indian by the nape of the neck, and leading him out to the rear of the office of the justice of the peace, I applied my boot vigorously to his rear fifteen or twenty times, shouting at the top of my voice, "Vamos!"

"Si, señor," he said, and off he started. It was fun, indeed, to see him leg it over the hill, into a canyon and out of sight.

As I turned toward the road again I heard loud and angry voices in front of the justice's door. Passing quickly through the room, I found a large crowd of men collected about two mounted Mexicans who were striking at each other furiously, one with a reata, the other with a heavy stick. Both men were somewhat under the influence of liquor, and each was doing his utmost to unhorse the other.

One of the men was a stranger to me, but the other was a well known ex-convict and stage robber named "El Macho" Feliciano. El Macho [The Man] had been shot through the hip in one of his nefarious expeditions and could not walk very well. Consequently, he had to do his fighting on horseback. He was a quarrelsome and dangerous fellow when in liquor, but whether sober or drunk he was a capital horseman.

Nearly all the crowd were Mexicans or native Californians. A few were Indians or Americans. All seemed to be enjoying the fight, and none ventured to interfere, as Feliciano was known to them as a bad man to deal with. Both men were skillful riders and handled their horses dexterously. As long as they did nothing more than dash at each other with their horses, I did not interfere. After a few moments of rough jostling, Feliciano received a terrible whack across the shoulders from the stick wielded by his antagonist. Up to this time the fight had been rather a tame affair. But when Feliciano received the blow his great black eyes fairly gleamed with fire, and before anyone could prevent it he had thrown the loop of his lasso over the neck of the other man, and taking a turn over the pommel of his saddle, he put spurs to his horse and attempted to drag him to the ground.

When the poor devil found himself in the loop of the reata he dashed toward Feliciano and endeavored to keep as close to him as possible.

They run around in a circle, the one trying to drag the other from his horse and the other frantically endeavoring to release his neck from the dangerous loop. At one time Feliciano got a steady pull on the reata and it seemed to me that the other Mexican's neck would be broken. The man finally succeeded in relieving himself from the rope and dashed up to Feliciano's side. Leaning over on his horse, he made a clutch for Feliciano's leg, intending to throw him from the saddle, but Feliciano, wheeling quickly away, prevented him from doing so.

I was now convinced that the contest would be likely to result in a shooting or cutting scrape, and stepping forward, I commanded them to desist. Their blood being at fever heat, they paid no attention to me. I grasped the bridle of Feliciano's horse, and as I did so he turned toward me and attempted to run the animal over me. I stepped quickly aside, and going to a buggy which stood near, I took from its socket a good gut and bone whip, and approaching Feliciano, I struck him a quick, sharp blow across the face with it. He turned and glared at me, and as he did so I gave him another just as hard as I could lay it on. He wheeled and attempted to jump his horse upon me. At that moment someone in the crowd cried out, "Cuidado! Esta el jerife!" [Look out! It's the sheriff!]

Again Feliciano tried to run over me. I grasped the bridle with a firm hand and swung my whip with terrible force full in the desperado's face. I repeated the blow again and again until his skin was covered with large, white ridges. Still he fought and endeavored to ride his horse over me. He struggled desperately until I had given him about fifty lashes when he cried, "Bastante, señor!" [Enough, sir!]

He promised that if I would quit the punishment he would go quietly away. I released my hold upon the bridle and Feliciano rode out of the town amid the jeers of the crowd. Ordinarily this whipping was not the proper thing to do, but I was on the track of the cattle thieves and under the circumstances it was the best possible course to pursue.

An hour's search and inquiry led us to believe that Robles and Cruz were in hiding in the canyons of the Black Hills near Mount Diablo. Mounting our horses, we struck across Livermore Valley toward the Casitas, and from there into the Black Hill country. Riding along the ridges we espied a thin column of blue smoke coming out of the chaparral near the foot of the mountain. Creeping carefully down the canyon, we were soon in the vicinity of a camp. Peeping through the bushes, we saw two Mexicans sitting upon the ground, chatting and smoking cigaritos. We at once recognized them as Juan Robles and Jesus Cruz. In an instant Swain had the two men covered with his Winchester, while I handcuffed them together.

The Mexicans admitted stealing the cattle and exonerated Foscalina of having any knowledge of the theft. They also told us where the stolen cattle were to be found—the whereabouts of which we had already learned. Swain and I recovered the stolen animals and a few days afterward Robles and Cruz were punished and the reputation of the unfortunate George Foscalina was cleared of all suspicion of being a receiver of stolen property.[4]

The cowhiding Harry Morse administered to El Macho did nothing to improve the desperado's temperament. Six months later, on June 6, 1867, at a fandango at Joe Livermore's Rancho Agua Puerca, he made the mistake of bullying George Foscalina's twenty-one-year-old son, Simon. Young Foscalina tried to escape on horseback from the knife-wielding badman, but El Macho repeatedly spurred his mustang after the youth, slashing wildly with the poniard. Unable to outride El Macho, Simon Foscalina finally drew his six-gun and shot the outlaw dead.[5]

Harry Morse's adventures now were becoming grist for the newspapers. More important, he was quickly making himself a terror to evildoers. No longer would he be an object of derision and laughter; no longer was he El Muchacho. Now the cutthroats, cattle thieves, and mountain bandits had a new nickname for the young sheriff: El Diablo—The Devil.

CHAPTER 6

A Bullet for a Bandido

THE courts in Alameda County during the 1860s and 1870s functioned effectively to punish evildoers. By the same token, competent local attorneys were available to defend those accused of crimes. In that era many lawyers charged low fees for their services, so that even the poorest horse thief was often able to obtain effective legal counsel. Judges also appointed lawyers to represent indigent defendants without charge. Nonetheless, some injustices did occur. And although some revisionist historians have claimed that Hispanics routinely received unfair treatment in the courts of that era, there is scant evidence to support this view. Most of the unfair punishment of Hispanics was perpetrated by vigilance committees and lynch mobs rather than by the judicial system. Substantial anecdotal evidence suggests that Hispanics received due process in California courts and that judges gave equal prison sentences to Anglos and Hispanics.[1]

One such incident involved Chrisanto Altamirano, one of the best horse thieves in the Alisal. Morse saw a chance to send him "across the bay" when a Livermore Valley rancher, John Brophy, swore out a warrant charging him with stealing one of his horses. The sheriff picked up Altamirano on December 8, 1866, and confiscated his mount. However, at the preliminary hearing Morse was in for a surprise. As the *Gazette* reported, "The horse turned out not to be Brophy's at all, and the prisoner and his horse were released. For Brophy's carelessness in swearing out the warrant the Court made a 'little order' that he pay for the costs, which after many groans and some profanity and a little compromise he did."[2]

Sheriff Morse himself surely entertained few modern notions of racial egalitarianism. He was very much a product of his times and shared the prevailing religious, cultural, and racial prejudices of that era. However, his duties brought him into daily contact with the Hispanic community and he made many Spanish-speaking friends. He would work just as hard to bring justice to a Hispanic victim as to an Anglo. The pioneer Higuera family of the Livermore Valley was the recipient of Morse's aid on several occasions.

On June 25, 1864, at a bullfight near Robert Livermore's rancho, Emilio Higuera, the twenty-five-year-old son of the family patriarch, Mariano Higuera, was shot and killed by Jose Chorín. According to the *Gazette*, "A warrant was issued and placed in the hands of a constable for his arrest. In the chase, said officer became enamored at a roadside deadfall of a beautiful, but uncertain game of seven-up, and the culprit escaped."[3]

Morse, who had just begun his impotent first term as sheriff, was no more diligent than the errant constable. Three years later, however, he was not the same lawman. He renewed the manhunt and managed to trace the killer to a rancho in Sonoma County, ten miles from Petaluma. On May 29, 1867, Morse rode out to the rancho with Petaluma's crack city marshal, Jim Knowles, and the constable of Olema, Felipe Jose Garcia. Jose Chorín spotted the mounted lawmen and leaped into the saddle, but Garcia lunged after him, gun drawn, and a moment later the three officers had the killer in handcuffs. Although the *Oakland Daily News* termed the killing of Higuera "deliberate and entirely unprovoked," at Chorín's trial in July he was acquitted on grounds of self-defense, much to Morse's disgust. Such verdicts of self-defense were common in that era. Most men carried knives or guns for self-protection, and juries often acquitted killers on the legal theory that a man had no duty to retreat from an antagonist and instead could stand his ground and kill his attacker.[4]

Another member of this family, Lazaro Higuera, was shot and badly wounded by a dangerous cutthroat, Jose Delores Ruiz, during a card game at Laddville. Ruiz escaped. Morse, believing he had fled to southern California, notified officers there to look out for him. Three years later Los Angeles County Sheriff Jim Burns captured the badman and returned him to Alameda. Ruiz was indicted for assault with intent to murder Higuera, but he too claimed self-defense. He was convicted of the lesser crime of assault with a deadly weapon and was sentenced to fourteen months in San Quentin. On another occasion, eight horses were stolen from the Higuera rancho, a serious financial blow to the family. Morse began an immediate search for the culprits. His hunt was so aggressive that several nights later the rattled thieves returned the horses to the Higuera pasture.[5]

The year 1867 would prove one of the busiest and most memorable in Morse's career. He kicked off the new year by bagging cat-

The Alameda County courthouse in San Leandro, circa 1867. The building was destroyed in the earthquake of 1868. Author's collection.

tle thief William "Bub" Hagan, an ex-convict who had broken out of the Oakland city jail. Hagan took refuge at his father's house, where, as the *Gazette* reported, "he was escaping from a rear window when Sheriff Morse's revolver brought him to terms."[6]

Morse lodged Hagan in his lockup with a notorious cattle rustler, Jose Valenzuela, alias Jose California. On the night of March 7 the sheriff locked the prisoners in their cells, but he was unable to find the key to Hagan's cell. Morse had made the mistake of allowing the jailbreaker to sweep up his office, and now he suspected that Hagan had stolen the key. He carefully searched Hagan and the prisoners' cells. Inside one cell he found that the leg of an iron bedstead had been broken off, making a dangerous truncheon. Morse bolted the cell doors shut and left Undersheriff Borein in charge. When he returned to the courthouse in the morning, Morse was greatly chagrined to find that the two prisoners had tunneled out of the jail and shaken the dust of San Leandro from their boots. Once again Borein had left the jail unguarded. The *Gazette* reported that he had gone to Oakland to attend a Masonic ball, but Borein denied this, declaring that he had gone there "upon official business." Either way, his bad judgment was responsible for the escape and the embarrassment it caused Sheriff Morse.[7]

In July Morse was busy politicking for the Republican primary election, but he still had time to nab a pair of stock thieves. In the Arroyo Mocho he ran down Pancho Castillo, who was wanted for cattle theft in Napa County. Castillo misjudged the lawman's honesty, as reported in the *Gazette:*

> On the way to the jail, he made special inquiry as to the sheriff's compensation, and being informed that it would amount to about $25, he coolly offered to make it a hundred, with the privilege of slipping into the chapparal while the sheriff looked the other way. This proposition was courteously declined, and the unfortunate speculator has returned to Napa in disgrace.[8]

The following day, July 20, Morse's endurance and horsemanship was put to a severe test when a ranchero, Victor Castro, reported that his vaquero, Jose Escobar, had stolen one of his horses near Hayward and fled toward Dublin. Morse picked up the trail at Hayward and tracked Escobar twenty-five miles north to Alamo, nabbed his man and the stolen horse, then returned to San Leandro and lodged Escobar in jail at 2:00 A.M. Morse had covered forty-five miles through steep terrain in nine hours, a tough feat for a horse and rider.[9]

A few weeks later the sheriff teamed up with his friend Dick Richardson to make his most important capture yet. Joaquin Olivera had remained at large since he and Narciso Bojorques had stolen William Knox's herd of five hundred sheep near Hayward two years previous. Olivera (alias Alexandria Morales, alias Antone Savage) was one of the worst outlaws in the Bay Area. A gray-bearded, fifty-seven-year-old Portuguese, "Old Joaquin" was an agile horseman and experienced cattle thief and highway robber who rode with bandidos half his age. "He is regarded by his own gang as one of the most desperate ruffians and thieves in this region, and it is said that it has long been his boast that no officer could arrest him alive," reported the *Oakland Daily News.*[10]

When Olivera stole seven head of work oxen from the Livermore Valley rancho of Samuel Martin, Sheriff Morse traced him to a hideout at the New Almaden Mine, ten miles south of San Jose. The New Almaden was one of the richest quicksilver mines in the world. It employed some five hundred Cornish and Mexican miners who lived in two separate camps of rude wooden cabins, Cornish Camp halfway up Mine Hill and Mexican Camp at the top of the hill. Mexican Camp had been a favorite rendezvous for bandits since the 1850s, and its cantinas and gambling houses were the scene of frequent brawls, gunfights, and cutting scrapes. Outlaws like Old Joaquin could find ready succor from the gamblers, prostitutes, and other hangers-on in Mexican Camp.

Morse and Officer Richardson met Santa Clara County Under-sheriff R. B. Hall in San Jose on August 8, 1867, and proceeded with him to the New Almaden Mine. Hall was an astute lawman, best known for his role in helping to break up Captain Rufus Ingram's band of Confederate guerrillas and stage robbers three years earlier. Hall had captured several of the gang, including the notorious Jim Grant, whom the lawman shot and wounded when Grant drew a shotgun on him.[11]

By this time Morse's raids against the bandidos had made him well known to them. Now, to avoid being recognized by Old Joaquin and his compadres, the young sheriff wore an old slouch hat and false whiskers, a guise he would adopt many times in the future. The three lawmen surrounded the small cabin where Morse suspected Olivera could be found. Stepping to the door, Morse threw its six occupants off guard by quietly mentioning the name of a fictitious person and inquiring about his whereabouts. This simple ruse was all he needed to get a quick peep through the doorway. Inside he spotted Old Joaquin, lying in bed, covered with a blanket, and feigning sickness. Morse motioned to Richardson, and in an instant he was at the sheriff's side, covering the outlaw with a double barreled shotgun. With a quick jerk, Morse snatched the blanket from the bed, revealing a Colt Navy six-gun at full cock in Old Joaquin's shooting hand. But the badman took a long look down the barrel of Richardson's shotgun and wisely surrendered.

Two months later Joaquin Olivera and a compadre, Francisco Ochoa, were brought to trial for stealing the oxen. The jury found Ochoa not guilty, but Old Joaquin was convicted of grand larceny and sentenced to two years in San Quentin. On his release he returned to the road, and in 1875 the sixty-five-year-old outlaw joined up with such noted bandidos as Isador Padilla and Ramon Ruiz. They robbed numerous stagecoaches in the mother lode country until Old Joaquin was captured by Calaveras County Sheriff Ben K.

Joaquin Olivera, captured
by Sheriff Morse at the new
Almaden Mine, 1867.
Author's collection.

Thorn and returned to San Quentin for another long respite from
brigandage.[12]

The weeks following his capture of Old Joaquin brought Harry
Morse more good luck. Bub Hagan, missing for five months since his
escape from the county jail, was picked up by an alert lawman at Fort
Yuma, Arizona Territory. Morse made a quick trip by steamer to Los
Angeles to return him to San Leandro, where Hagan was promptly
tried and sent to San Quentin for jail breaking. Then, on September 4, Morse again won reelection by a wide margin, polling 1,533
votes to the 1,050 garnered by his Democratic opponent, John
Gieschen.[13]

But the best news arrived two weeks later, when the sheriff received a wire from the Marysville police that they had arrested
Manuel Rojas, the long-missing compañero of Juan Soto. Rojas had
been a fugitive since the robbery of the Garthwaite ranch three
years before. On one occasion he had been captured at the mining
camp of Sonora in the Sierra foothills, but he managed to escape.
Still later Rojas was jailed in Petaluma, but before Morse could pick

him up, several of his amigos tunneled inside the calaboose and freed him. Hunted down by a constable from Bodega, Rojas managed again to escape after a brief shootout. While in the Marysville jail the elusive bandido almost managed to again slip from Morse's grasp. Rojas gave "leg bail" by knocking down a guard and bolting down the street. Police officer Henry L. McCoy, one of the best lawmen of the California frontier, chanced to be on duty, and with his six-shooter barking, he overhauled the fleeing desperado and dragged him back to the station house. The next day Morse brought Rojas to San Leandro to stand trial for the Garthwaite robbery. The badman pled guilty to a reduced charge of burglary, and in an example of lenient treatment of a Hispanic outlaw, he was sentenced to a scant thirteen months in San Quentin.[14]

A few weeks later Harry Morse's string of good luck was interrupted by a tragedy that brought home to him the great risks inherent in his new calling. John Thomas, a sixty-year-old black man who was squatting in a house at the corner of Ninth and Castro streets in Oakland, quarreled with its rightful owner and drove him off with a shotgun. On October 22 a warrant was sworn out for Thomas's arrest and placed in the hands of Officer Dick Richardson to be served. Richardson rode out to the house and knocked on the door. Thomas's wife opened it and seeing the policeman, slammed it shut. When Richardson shoved the door open, John Thomas took aim with a double-barreled pistol and dropped one hammer. The barrel was loaded to the muzzle with balls, and the heavy charge struck the officer in the side of the throat, almost decapitating him.

Thomas was arrested immediately and a lynch mob quickly gathered, howling for vengeance against the popular officer's killer. He was first lodged in the Oakland jail, but as lynch threats spread like wildfire, the murderer was rushed to the county jail and turned over to a stunned Harry Morse. Grief-stricken by the loss of his close friend, Morse nonetheless provided a secure guard for the jail, effectively discouraging any would-be lynchers. Thomas, enfeebled and in poor health, remained safely in Morse's jail for five months while awaiting trial and finally died in his cell of natural causes a few days before his trial was to begin.[15]

Morse attended Dick Richardson's funeral the day following the murder, but he had little time for mourning. An electrifying series of events, ignited by a brutal killing three weeks earlier, were about to plunge him into two of the deadliest encounters of his life.

At two o'clock in the morning of October 3, 1867, four men clustered around a gaming table at Greavenor's Saloon, located near the railroad depot in Hayward. Among them were an inoffensive old man, William Lewis Joy, and Narato Ponce (pronounced "Ponsay"), a hot-tempered, thirty-five-year-old Chileno. Ponce was a noted ruffian and horse thief whom the *Alameda County Gazette* called "a more desperate character than the notorious Joaquin [Murrieta]." Although the *Gazette*'s comment was hyperbole, Ponce was nonetheless a desperado of the first water.

When a quarrel broke out over the game of poker, Ponce cashed in his chips and stomped out of the saloon. A few minutes later he burst back in, six-gun in hand, and opened fire at the card players. A pistol ball tore a hole through Joy's left side, passed through both lungs, and lodged in his right arm. Joy staggered into an adjoining room and crumpled to the floor.

At the first sound of gunfire one of the patrons blew out the lamp. When it was relit moments later, Ponce coolly stepped up to the bar and took a drink. Eyeing the other gamblers calmly, he asked them if they "wanted anything," then strode back out the door. The men in the saloon, too frightened to follow, examined Joy and found that he was dead. The murderer fled on foot toward the Hayward hills, leaving his horse behind in a nearby corral. Harry Morse was notified of the killing a few hours later and began a systematic search for Ponce. "The sheriff is on the warpath," declared the *Oakland Daily News,* "and if any man can secure the criminal, Harry is the man."

For several weeks Morse hunted Ponce in the bandit's favorite haunts in San Francisco, San Jose, and the New Almaden Mine. He kept a nightly watch at the various ranchos, adobes, and fandango houses that Ponce was known to frequent, but the killer was nowhere to be found. Finally Morse got one of the fugitive's compadres to "peach" on him and learned that Ponce was holed up in the Black Hills and was planning to ride down into the Alisal on Friday night, November 1. The sheriff instructed his informant to ride along with Ponce but to wear a white linen duster so that he would be recognized in the dark.

Morse asked John Conway of the Oakland police to join him in an attempt to capture the outlaw. Conway had been appointed a few days before to fill the position vacated by the death of Dick Richardson. A veteran police officer, he had served eight years on Captain William Douglass's watch in the San Francisco Police Department.

Conway agreed to assist Morse, but he discovered that he was required to first obtain permission from both the mayor and the city marshal of Oakland, as the manhunt would take them far outside the city. Approval was granted, and the two lawmen bundled into a buggy and headed into the hills, first through Hayward Pass and then down into Dublin. Here they obtained mounts and riding rigs and headed east on horseback along the telegraph road toward the Black Hills.

At a spot known as the Willows a side road connected with the main highway, closed off by a gate. Here Morse expected that Ponce would pass that night. On either side of the gate was a large haystack, and the lawmen tied the gate securely, then concealed themselves as best they could next to the haystacks and waited for darkness. (This spot is in the approximate area of the present intersection of Highway 580 and Tassajara Road.) They did not have long to wait. At 9:30 Morse heard the sound of hoofbeats approaching from the north, and soon he could plainly hear two riders conversing in Spanish. The sheriff was certain that Narato Ponce was close at hand. Although the night was extremely dark, Morse wanted to be sure that Ponce did not see the two lawmen until he was almost upon them. Dropping to the ground and clutching his shotgun close to his body, Morse rolled over and over until he was in the middle of the road, flat on his belly.

Ponce rode quickly up to the gate. Reaching down, he untied the latch, swung the gate open, and continued riding directly toward Morse, his compadre behind him. Morse allowed the outlaw to come on until his horse was but ten feet away. Then he suddenly leaped to his feet and yelled "Stop!"

Ponce reacted instantly. Jerking his six-gun, he opened fire on Morse, at the same time whirling his horse around to escape. Conway sprang from his hiding place behind the haystack, his six-shooter spitting lead at the bandit's shadowy form. Ponce banged away twice at Conway, and Morse, unable to see his target, aimed at the flashes from the outlaw's gun muzzle. The sheriff's shotgun roared, and thirteen buckshot slammed into Ponce's back. At the same time a ball from Conway's revolver struck the outlaw's little mare in the thigh, and animal and rider collapsed in a heap. Sprawled in the road, Ponce raised his pistol and continued to blaze away at the lawmen. Morse fired his second barrel at the muzzle flash, then drew his own six-gun and fired again.

Three balls from the lawmen's pistols struck the Chileno desperado. Conway by this time had emptied his revolver, which misfired on his sixth shot, and he ran back to the haystack after his Henry rifle. This gave Ponce the chance he needed, and although badly wounded, he struggled to his feet and ran along the fence, disappearing into the blackness. By now his compadre had long since thundered away, as fast as horseflesh could carry him.

Morse set fire to both haystacks. Huge flames leaped skyward, lighting up the valley a great distance in each direction. But he and Conway could not see a trace of Narato Ponce. They mounted their horses and hunted for him until 2:00 A.M., without success. At daylight, with the help of eight vaqueros, they searched the hills and discovered the Chileno's coat, soaked with blood and riddled with buckshot. A half mile farther on they found his boots, which for some reason he had abandoned.[16]

Morse and Conway returned to San Leandro, frustrated that their quarry had escaped but not yet ready to admit defeat. Morse kept up a lookout for any trace of the killer, and in the meantime Governor Frederick Low offered a $500 reward for his arrest. A month later Morse received a letter from Sheriff Henry Classen of Contra Costa County, advising him that he had information about Ponce and requesting that the Alameda lawman come immediately to Martinez. Morse arrived in Martinez that evening, and Sheriff Classen told him that he had been informed that Ponce was holed up at Cisco in Placer County, at that time the railhead on the Central Pacific overland route.

In the morning Sheriff Classen assigned Morse's friend, Undersheriff George Swain, to assist him. Morse and Swain rode to Antioch, planning to take a riverboat to Sacramento. But in Antioch they received new information that Narato Ponce was recovering from his wounds at an adobe in Rigg's Canyon in the Black Hills, near the southeastern foot of Mount Diablo. The two lawmen boarded the first boat for San Francisco and then crossed the bay by ferry to Oakland, where they were joined by John Conway. The trio continued to San Leandro, obtained saddle horses, and crossed the hills, arriving at Rigg's Canyon at eleven o'clock on the night of December 12. They surrounded the adobe hideout and at daylight moved in and searched it, but Ponce had vanished.

Morse and his companions scouted all day through the canyons and ridges of the Black Hills, but it was not until the next day that they finally hit paydirt. Morse stumbled on a suspicious vaquero whom Conway and Swain promptly identified as Antonio Martinez, alias Jesus Torres, an ex-convict and cattle thief. The lawmen also discovered an "old Spaniard," whom they suspected of having harbored Ponce and nursing him back to health. Exactly what methods Morse may have used to extract information from the old man are not known; the *Alameda County Gazette* reported vaguely that Morse "questioned and threatened" him. At any rate, the *viejo* (old man) told Morse that Ponce was "somewhere in Pinole."

Morse, Conway, and Swain returned to San Leandro, arriving on December 14, and lodged Martinez in jail. That night the trio boarded a Sacramento-bound riverboat and disembarked at Martinez. The next morning, December 15, they rode the eleven miles south to Pinole, at that time a tiny village on the shore of San Pablo Bay, with small adobes scattered up Pinole Valley. Two and a half miles up the canyon, on a small ridge on the south side of Pinole Creek (now known as Adobe Road), stood the impressive hacienda built in the 1830s by Ignacio Martinez, grantee of the Rancho El Pinole.

Morse and his men searched one house in the village, then rode up the canyon, searching all the jacales as they went. Finally they arrived at the adobe of Jose Rojas, located next to the creek near the upper end of the canyon. Morse spotted a man climbing the hillside across the creek from the house, a bundle in one hand and a shotgun in the other. Telling Conway and Swain to cover Rojas's adobe, Morse spurred his horse after the man on the hill. At the same time Conway and Swain crossed the creek and dismounted in front of the jacal. While Conway covered the front, Swain entered the adobe and carefully searched three rooms but found them empty. Entering a fourth windowless room through a very narrow doorway, Swain lit a candle and checked several beds. Suddenly he spotted the upper torso of a man inside a hole dug in the dirt floor under one of the beds.

Jerking his six-gun, Swain ordered, "Come out!"

At the same time his eyes caught the glimmer of a pistol and he quickly backed outside, yelling to Conway, "John, he is here!"

Swain burst out of the front door, immediately followed by Narato Ponce, six-shooter in hand. Swain whirled around and snapped a quick shot at the fleeing killer, but the bullet missed its mark and Ponce kept on at a dead run, his sarape thrown over one arm. Conway and Swain ran after Ponce, the undersheriff crying, "Stop and throw down your pistol and we won't shoot you!"

The notorious bandido Narato Ponce. Ponce was slain in a gun duel with Harry Morse in Pinole Valley, December 15, 1867. Courtesy Christian de Guigne IV.

But Ponce paid them no heed. Swain emptied his revolver at the murderer while Conway fired at him with a Spencer rifle. Swain borrowed Conway's pistol, and the two lawmen continued running after and firing at Ponce. Meanwhile Morse, at the sound of the first shot, wheeled his horse and raced back down the hill in an attempt to head off the outlaw. Reaching a fence, Morse leaped from his horse, grabbed his Henry rifle, and jumped over. The creek was flooded from winter rains and Morse was unable to cross. Directly opposite him Ponce was dashing along the muddy bank, about one hundred yards from the adobe.

"Stop and lay down your pistol!" Morse shouted, but still Ponce kept running. The sheriff drew a bead and fired, but the wily bandit had used his sarape to good effect. It flapped in the wind behind him, concealing his torso and making it difficult for Morse to aim a shot into his body. Three more times Morse fired; each time he missed. Conway's aim was better, and a ball from his Spencer smacked into the outlaw's right hand. Ponce threw his pistol into his left hand, then raced desperately up and down the creek bank several times in a last-ditch effort to escape. Seeing that he was cornered, the killer threw down his sarape, stepped to the edge of the creek, rested his six-gun across his wounded arm, and took dead aim at the sheriff.

Ponce was already in Morse's gunsight, and the young lawman knew that his life depended on his next shot. He squeezed the trigger and the Henry rifle roared. The .44-caliber ball rammed into Ponce's pistol belt, tore through his abdomen, and exited just left of the spine. As the desperado pitched face-first into the mud, Swain exclaimed to Conway, "He is keeled over! Morse's last shot has killed him!"

Morse managed to splash across the creek as Conway ran up and snatched the fugitive's pistol, still tightly clutched in his fist. In five minutes Narato Ponce was dead. Morse examined the body and found wounds from the thirteen buckshot and three pistol balls from their first encounter with the outlaw. Morse sent a message to Justice of the Peace A. F. Dyer, who summoned a coroner's jury of four Anglos and two Hispanics. They held an inquest into the killing. After taking detailed testimony from the officers and several local men who identified the corpse, they ruled that Morse had acted justifiably.

The young sheriff received high praise from the newspapers. The *Oakland Daily News* observed, "It appears to be just as feasible for a thief to escape Morse as for a camel to get through the eye of a needle."[17]

The killing of Narato Ponce did much to thrust Harry Morse's name into the public eye. Coupled with his many arrests during the previous year and his shooting of Narciso Bojorques, it gave him a statewide reputation as a deadly gunman and a relentless tracker of outlaws. Unlike the gunfighter heroes of fiction who slay scores of enemies, in the Old West just one killing was enough to elevate a man to the status of a dangerous foe; several victorious gunfights could launch a lawman into legend.

Especially among superstitious Indians and Mexicans, Harry Morse became known as an invincible, charmed figure, who could not be harmed by a bullet. The fear in which the outlaws held Morse can be measured by the fact that they obtained copies of a picture of the sheriff from a San Francisco photograph gallery. To identify the young lawman and to protect themselves from a surprise visit, the bandidos, stock thieves, and tapaderas kept this photograph handy in their remote jacales high in the Coast Range.

CHAPTER 7

Triumphs and Tragedies

DESPITE a hectic schedule that often kept him in the saddle and away from home, Harry Morse managed to father and raise a large family. Besides George and Emma, he and Virginia had welcomed another son, Henry, in 1860 and a daughter, Annie, in 1863. They added another boy, Lincoln, in 1869, but tragedy struck two months later, on July 22, when the infant died. Reeling from the loss, the Morses did not have time to recover before the unbelievable occurred: on October 11 nine-year-old Henry died of a heart condition. Their heartbreak was still not over. Ten months later, on August 26, 1870, they were overjoyed by the birth of yet another son, Charles, but their joy was quickly replaced by anguish, for in a scant five weeks this infant too was dead. Morse's parents, Abraham and Charlotte, came to California to console their son and daughter-in-law and remained for the rest of their lives.[1]

These tragedies, coupled with Morse's frequent absences from home and hearth, proved a great strain on his wife and family. Morse appears to have devoted less time than a father should to his son George, who became increasingly troublesome and rebellious. The boy seemed to crave attention, and he developed into a braggart and a liar. The busy sheriff tried to make time for his last son, but his efforts were too little and too late. He even allowed the boy to accompany him on a number of manhunts, an unwise decision considering the danger involved. George loved horseback riding, but when he was twelve he fell from his mount and injured his head. He suffered what today would be called a traumatic brain injury, which caused psychiatric problems. The youth became subject to erratic behavior and fits of violent anger.[2]

Harry Morse had an emotional stability that matched his physical strength and endurance. This quality helped him cope with the travails that he and Virginia faced. Easygoing and good-natured, he had a great sense of humor and a love of practical jokes. The reputation for pugnacity that he had earned during the Civil War years was a political liability, and he worked hard to overcome it. Other than the instances in which he used necessary force to uphold the law, he avoided physical and verbal conflict. "As long as I held an official position," he once explained, "I made it a point never to notice a criticism of my official acts, either by newspaper or individual."[3]

The Morses had spent the first ten years of their marriage in modest surroundings. Only after Harry had become sheriff did he achieve any pecuniary success. Now his salary, including fees, could reach $6,000 a year, then a munificent sum. But the early years of sacrifice, of little money and many mouths to feed, were hard on Virginia. Well bred, well educated, and raised by a prosperous father, she was little prepared for a union with a fiercely independent and proud young man who was determined to make his own way in the world. Yet their modest lifestyle, the financial hardships, and the many heartbreaking tragedies they faced served to strengthen her character. Though small and dainty, Virginia Morse became as strong-willed as her husband, with a sharp tongue and a sense of humor to match that of her husband.

Harry loved to boast of his mother's cooking, and on one occasion he complained to his wife, "Virginia, I wish you could make bread like my mother."

A twinkle in her eye, she snapped back, "Well, Harry, I wish you could make 'dough' like my father!"[4]

Virginia had a one-horse buggy, which she enjoyed driving alone through Oakland and San Leandro. She cared not a whit that her pastime thoroughly scandalized the proper matrons of the East Bay communities. On one occasion she had their Chinese stableman hitch up a spirited but somewhat skittish animal to the buggy before setting off with a lady friend for a visit to Fruitvale. It was a gorgeous spring afternoon when they drove along Adams Avenue (now East Fourteenth Street, in the southern part of Oakland). It was open country, interrupted only by scattered farms and houses. As Virginia and her friend approached Fruitvale Avenue the horse suddenly spooked and bolted into a dead run. Virginia could not control the animal, and the buggy careened wildly down the road. A Mexican vaquero spotted the runaway and galloped after them, but before he could reach them the buggy struck a rut and the two ladies were thrown from the lurching seat. Swinging his lariat, the vaquero managed to lasso the animal and bring the buggy to a halt. Although bruised and shaken, Virginia never lost her taste for buggy driving.[5]

On one of Morse's many absences from home, Virginia, alone at night in the front room of their San Leandro home, heard a suspicious noise in the rear of the house. Taking up one of her husband's six-shooters, she spotted a burglar attempting to crawl through a back window. Virginia immediately raised the large revolver, but her tiny hands were not strong enough to cock the weapon's heavy action. The ruffian took one look at the gun-wielding woman and cried, "Don't shoot!" He leaped to the ground and fled into the darkness.[6]

Virginia was a member of the Congregational church. Her husband, however, although raised in the Protestant faith, was not a churchgoing man, a fact that did not sit well with many in the community. He was far from an agnostic and held strong religious and moral beliefs. He had an idealistic faith in everything American, especially the system of justice. He was particularly opposed to vigilantism. On one occasion a group of rowdy Chinese set up a gambling house in Alvarado. Soon they were raking in the earnings of the area's numerous Chinese laborers, and many fights resulted. These disturbances aroused the ire of the community, and one night a mob drove out the gamblers and destroyed their house. Not satisfied with that, the vigilantes then drove every Chinese from town and vandalized their homes. Sheriff Morse investigated but was unable to identify the members of the mob. He offered a $250 reward from his own pocket for information leading to their arrest, but there were no takers.[7]

This reward offer was unusual for Morse, for he was extremely frugal and kept careful records of all his personal expenditures. He carefully invested his money, and with his brother-in-law, Philander Heslep, opened a flour mill in Hayward. It was destroyed in the great earthquake of October 21, 1868, causing the pair a serious financial loss.

One of Morse's outspoken critics was John Scott, the editor of the *Oakland Daily Transcript,* who strongly disliked the sheriff and ran occasional editorials railing against him. Scott accused Morse of parsimony and of favoring saloons over churches:

> The most depraved and profligate of men will occasionally contribute something to religious institutions as a sort of conscience money. Morse has never contributed to any church in

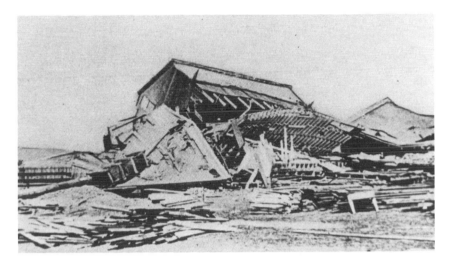

Harry Morse's flour mill in Hayward, destroyed in the great earthquake of
October 21, 1868. Author's collection.

this county. He may have spent some money around saloons
about election times; but usually he has found this unnecessary,
as in most all the saloons his "exploits" are so well known that
as soon as he enters there is someone who would consider it an
honor to "treat" so important a personage. Hence, the sheriff's travelling expenses are light—and around San Leandro,
where he is well known, no one accuses him of throwing away
his money.[8]

The editors of the *Alameda County Gazette* of San Leandro and
the *Oakland Daily News* were, however, good friends and strong supporters of the sheriff. They carefully chronicled his many exploits
and were generous in their praise. Early in his career Morse realized
the importance of good press, and he took pains to ensure that each
important arrest was carefully detailed in the local newspapers, thus
keeping his name in the public eye and helping to assure his reelection every two years.

Morse had left school at the age of ten, and in many ways he was a
self-educated man. He was a voracious reader of books, newspapers,
and magazines and kept a 250-volume library in his home. He was fas-

cinated by the law, and from his many attorney friends he learned how to read and interpret both statutory and case law. As sheriff and later as businessman, he was involved in a great deal of litigation and always retained the best lawyers to represent him. He enjoyed politicking and storefront yarn swapping and loved to tell his children stories of his adventures. This led to an interest in writing, nurtured by his journalist cronies. From his earliest years he had kept diaries in which he recorded his daily business. His habit of regular diary keeping developed into a writing avocation, and in later years he published several journals and was a frequent contributor to the San Francisco and Oakland newspapers. Yet his diaries, memoirs, and other writings reveal very little about his emotions or his personal life. Harry Morse was not a man of emotional complexity. He was a man of action, and he lacked the time and the inclination to indulge in deep introspection.

Many lawmen besides Sheriff Morse were active in running down bandidos. Morse's friend Jim Knowles, city marshal of Petaluma, arrested Tiburcio Vasquez for store burglary and sent him to San Quentin in January 1867. San Jose lawmen broke up Juan Soto's gang. In April 1867 Soto and another bandido, Pancho Galindo, stole a $100 horse from rancher Gordon Chase. Another of the band, Rafael Mirabel, robbed an express wagon, and gang member Abelardo Salazar stole a horse, saddle, and bridle from a San Jose livery stable. On June 1 Deputy Sheriff Robert McElroy spotted Soto at the New Almaden Mine, riding a horse reported to have been stolen at Mayfield. Soto opened fire on the deputy and escaped. He was later arrested and his old amigo Bartolo Sepulveda posted his $500 bail. Soto retained Frank E. Spencer, a very capable San Jose lawyer, to defend him. Spencer, who would represent a number of noted Hispanic outlaws, was unable to convince a jury of Soto's innocence. Soto was convicted of grand larceny and sentenced to one year in San Quentin. At the same time Rafael Mirabel and Abelardo Salazar were convicted of grand larceny, and on November 26 Sheriff John Adams took all three to San Quentin.[9]

On his release, Juan Soto was returned to San Jose to stand trial for assault with a deadly weapon on Deputy Sheriff McElroy. He was found guilty and sentenced to another two years. His compañero, Pancho Galindo, was convicted on charges arising out of the same case and received a six-month prison term. In December 1868 the two outlaws crossed the bay to San Quentin.[10]

In the meantime other members of Juan Soto's band continued

to plague Harry Morse and his fellow lawmen. Soto's Anglo compadre, Alfonso Burnham, remained a thorn in Morse's side. Of all the
badmen Morse encountered, Burnham probably had the most unusual background. He was born Alfonso Mason Burnham in Massachusetts in 1839, the son of Simon P. Burnham, a master mariner and
state senator. The elder Burnham brought his family to California in
1849. He bought a large rancho and prospered. In 1855, he was
elected county assessor in San Francisco and later served as a judge
of the district court. He died in 1859 after a long illness.[11]

Alfonso's youth was spent with local Californio boys, and he
learned to speak Spanish fluently and to ride like a vaquero. But after
his father's death he fell into bad company, later associating with the
likes of Juan Soto, Manuel Rojas, and Antonio Valacca, alias Red Antone, who had reportedly murdered twenty Chinese. About 1862,
with Rojas and Red Antone, Burnham was suspected of murdering
a party of Chinese miners near Oroville. The next year he landed in
San Quentin with a two-year term from San Francisco on a charge
of grand larceny. Released in 1865, he adopted the alias Fred Welch
and immediately fell in with Soto and Rojas, followed by the ill-fated
raid on the Garthwaite ranch in October. On his discharge from
prison in 1867 he returned to his old ways. But Burnham's story had
a remarkable twist that Harry Morse would never have believed had
he not seen it himself.

*Happening to be in San Jose in company with another officer in search
of some cattle that had been stolen (we had started out just at the break
of day), and turning the corner of a street, we ran against Alfonso Burnham, who was with as ugly a looking specimen of a Mexican as I ever saw.*

*"Hello," I said. "What are you doing here at this time of the morning?"
No one was yet astir in the town.*

*"I am going after my horse," he replied. "I am working on a ranch out
on the road a piece."*

*I suspected that they were up to some mischief, so we searched them
and on each we found an eight-inch Colt's revolver.*

*"Rather nice tools to work with," I remarked. "I guess I will take you
in and turn you over to Sheriff Adams."*

*We did so, and they were fined for carrying concealed weapons, and
having no money, were compelled to serve thirty days in the county jail.
He told me afterwards that our causing their detention prevented them
from carrying out a plan to run off a band of fine horses.*

One day I received a dispatch from one of the northern counties, stat-ing that a valuable American mare had been stolen from that county, and asking me to keep a lookout for her, as the thieves were coming my way. I soon found not only the animal described in the dispatch but several oth-ers, and found them too with Burnham, and in my own county. He was held and the horses were returned to their respective owners. This time he again pleaded guilty and was let off with one year's imprisonment in the state prison.[12]

He served out his term and was liberated. Afterward I met him occa-sionally, but he would only pull his hat down over his eyes and try to avoid me. Later I heard of him at San Jose, and that he was about to be mar-ried. On the very day of his wedding he was arrested on a charge of hav-ing stolen six horses from a farmer in the central portion of the state. He was detained in jail about four months and was finally discharged, there being no evidence to convict him. He really had nothing to do with the stealing of those horses, as I afterward recovered the animals, arrested the real culprit, and had him sent to the state prison.

He was released from the San Jose jail, everybody believing him to be the real thief. I lost sight of him for more than a year, when one day as I was coming from the upper country on the Central Pacific Railroad the train stopped at a station, and who should get aboard but Alfonso Burn-ham. He saw me and, as usual, tried to escape my notice. After the train had got well under way I left my seat and went and sat beside him and en-tered into conversation with him. I asked him what he was doing and all about himself. He told me he was married and had quit the old business forever. Of course, I thought that was barely probable, as very few of his class forsake their unlawful calling. But he assured me it was true, and that he had done nothing of the kind for several years.

In reply to my question of what he was doing, he said he was on his way to town [San Leandro] in search of work; that employment had been promised him and he expected to get it. He further stated that he, with his wife, had a room where they had been living at the station at which he had boarded the train and that all that he and his wife had had to eat for four days was some soda crackers, with only water to drink. The tears started in his eyes as he told me this. The train stopped and we both got off.

"Now," said I, "if what you tell me is true, and you really intend to be-come an honest man, I will help you to be so. If you don't find the work you expect, come to me and I will see what I can do for you."

He thanked me and left. In about an hour he came to me. I saw at a glance that he had been disappointed.

Alfonso M. Burnham, alias Fred Welch. Compadre of Juan Soto, he reformed and turned informer for Harry Morse. Author's collection.

"What success?" I asked.

"None," he replied. "I could not get the work."

Calling him into my private office, I had a long talk with him and at the end took a handful of silver from my pocket and handed it to him, saying, "Here, take this. It will keep you for a few days, and in the meantime I will try to get you work to do."

He took the money, and looking me full in the face for a second, turned suddenly away into a corner of the room and burst into the most sorrowful cry I ever heard. He sobbed as though his heart would break. As soon as he could master his emotions, he turned and came toward me, and taking my hand, said, "May God kill me if ever I do wrong again! I'll die of starvation in the streets first!"

"Stay here a little while," I said. "I will see if I can get you the work you want."

In half an hour I had obtained for him a job to drive a six-horse team. His face lighted up with the satisfaction he felt. He drove the team for about two months and then got a job driving a sand cart. He finally secured easier employment. Since that time I have entrusted him with the care of property, where had he been so disposed, he could have stolen hundreds of dollars, but he was true to his resolution. He has never returned to his old companions or their evil ways.[13]

Alfonso Burnham would figure again in the sheriff's campaign against the bandidos. But rarely did Morse's cases end so rewardingly. Many of the crimes he investigated could not be solved at all. Most frustrating to the sheriff was the difficulty in securing evidence in murder cases in which there were no eyewitnesses. In those days, before fingerprint and forensic analysis, an obviously guilty man would often go free because of a lack of evidence sufficient to convict him.

On March 4, 1868, Morse received word that the body of Henry Kreiger, a one-armed German vegetable peddler, had been found in a creek bed half a mile from Hayward. Kreiger's throat had been cut in two places, his head battered, the stump of his bad arm deeply gashed by a knife, and his pockets turned inside out. Morse examined the body and carefully questioned Kreiger's friends and neighbors. He learned that Kreiger was a peaceable, hardworking man, thirty-seven years old. After losing part of his left arm a year previously in a threshing machine accident, his friends bought him a team and wagon so he could work selling produce. He had last been seen nine days before when he told neighbors he was going to San Francisco and would return in a few days.

Morse learned that at the time Kreiger's body was discovered, Frederick Griebnow, a Hayward saloonkeeper, had attempted to persuade the men who thronged to the creek to view and retrieve the body that the German had killed himself. He had seemed particularly anxious that they believe Kreiger had committed suicide, although it was obvious to all that Kreiger had been murdered. Griebnow pointed out the gash on Kreiger's left arm and described how the German must have cut through the straps on his false arm to slash himself there. Recalled Charles Breeze, one of the men present, "I told him he had better go home and say nothing more about that."

The sheriff learned that Griebnow had told others that he had had nightmares about Kreiger having committed suicide. He told several persons that he had seen Kreiger going into the hills east of Hayward, not San Francisco, as the German peddler had told his neighbors. To others Griebnow reported that Kreiger had been drinking heavily before his disappearance, but Kreiger did not have a reputation as a drinking man. One of the dead man's friends, suspicious of Griebnow, asked him if he knew what had become of $130 Kreiger had been carrying, but Griebnow denied any knowledge of the money.

It was quite evident to Morse that Frederick Griebnow had murdered the German peddler and invented the suicide theory to cover his guilt. The sheriff placed Griebnow under arrest and found in his pockets $80, which his prisoner admitted belonged to Kreiger. Griebnow claimed that the German had given him the money "to keep for him."

Griebnow's preliminary hearing on a charge of murder was held before Judge Stephen G. Nye. Numerous witnesses testified to Griebnow's suspicious actions. Griebnow, of course, swore that he knew nothing about the peddler's death. But the testimony, other than casting a strong suspicion of guilt, provided neither direct nor circumstantial evidence linking Griebnow with the crime, and Judge Nye had no choice but to order his release. The district attorney requested that the grand jury indict him, but that body failed to return a true bill. Much to Morse's disgust, Griebnow was now a free man.[14]

Only a month later Morse became embroiled in another frustrating homicide investigation. This time it was a thirteen-year-old murder case involving one of the state's most prominent Californio families and one of the most infamous killings of the 1850s. For Californios, the slaying of Jose Sunol in 1855 epitomized their ill treatment by land-hungry Anglos and symbolized the cheapness of Hispanic life. Savage as it was, young Sunol's murder was but one bloody page in the sorriest chapter of Anglo California's persecution of her Hispanic people. Although Harry Morse was himself accused of ill treatment of Hispanics, his attempt to bring Jose Sunol's killer to justice was the only such effort made by any lawman during the long Anglo persecution of the Berreyesa-Sunol family.

The tragic story began many years earlier, during the Bear Flag Revolt. On June 28, 1846, an elderly ranchero, Jose de los Reyes Berreyesa, crossed San Francisco Bay in a small boat, en route to visit his son, the *alcalde* (mayor) at Sonoma. He was accompanied by his twin nephews, Ramon and Francisco de Haro. As they landed their boat on the beach near San Rafael, they were spotted by Kit Carson and two other men from John C. Frémont's command. Carson and his companions shot down the three Californios in cold blood, then rode off, leaving their bodies to rot on the beach. Carson's act was in retaliation for the torture, murder, and mutilation of two Americans a short time before.[15]

This was but the first of countless atrocities perpetrated on this Californio family. The murdered Jose de los Reyes Berreyesa had owned the San Vicente rancho in Santa Clara County, and his six sons continued to live on separate portions of the ranch with their families. In July 1854 the body of a murdered Yankee was found there, and a vigilance committee seized Encarnación Berreyesa, strung him up, and repeatedly raised and lowered him in an attempt to extract a confession. Realizing they had the wrong man, they returned to San Jose, leaving Berreyesa half-dead with a permanent rope scar on his neck.

A few days later, on July 21, 1854, another band of vigilantes returned to the rancho at night, dragged Encarnación's brother, Nemesio, from his house, and lynched him from a tree. The other brothers fled in terror with their families to southern California and Mexico. Encarnación took his wife and children to her parents' home in Ventura, but tragedy was soon to follow them. In February 1857, during the huge manhunt for Mexican bandits after the crime spree led by Juan Flores in Los Angeles County, a band of Los Angeles vigilantes headed by Ezekiel Rubottom visited Ventura and heard rumors of Encarnación and the attempted lynching near San Jose. They immediately assumed that he had escaped from a vigilance committee. They seized the hapless Californio and, seeing the rope scar on his neck, promptly hanged him.

More tragedies followed. Nicolas Berreyesa, brother of Jose de los Reyes, brooded over these callous murders. When squatters and defective land titles robbed him of his share of his beloved Rancho Milpitas, his mind snapped, and he died of insanity in 1863. Several of his sons were also driven insane by Anglo injustice. During the 1850s two other members of this extended Californio family, Juan Berreyesa and Jose Galindo, were murdered by Anglos. Yet another, Damaso Berreyesa, turned to banditry and was slain leading a mass break from San Quentin in 1861.[16]

Jose Sunol was a cousin of the Berreyesas. His father, Antonio Maria Sunol, was a prominent resident of San Jose and part owner of the enormous Rancho El Valle de San Jose, in southern Alameda County. Jose was the eldest Sunol son, and he settled in an adobe on his father's land, still standing in the town of Sunol and located near what is now the Water Temple of San Francisco's Hetch Hetchy water system. Sunol's adobe was for many years the home of Charles Hadsell, a prosperous rancher.

Like most Californio landowners, Jose Sunol had trouble with Yankee squatters on the ranch. The most troublesome of these was John Wilson, a dangerous frontiersman who had once lost a front tooth in a fight with a grizzly bear. Sunol and Wilson had several quarrels over land. On March 7, 1855, Wilson, armed with a rifle, shot the young Californio out of his saddle, killing him instantly. The killer outrode a pursuing posse and disappeared.[17]

Thirteen years passed, and the murder was all but forgotten when Sheriff Morse received information that a Californio who had known both Sunol and Wilson had spotted a man in San Luis Obispo, 250 miles to the south, whom he believed was the long-missing murderer. Morse immediately contacted San Luis Obispo County Sheriff Jose de la Guerra and requested information about the suspected murderer. The Alameda sheriff was advised that he was known as John Slack and that his physical description was identical to that of John Wilson, even down to the missing front tooth. A former resident of San Jose, Slack had settled in San Luis Obispo ten years before. He made his living as a wheat raiser and professional gambler and was known as a hard case who had many run-ins with Californios, then the dominant cultural group in San Luis Obispo. Alexander Murray, who ran a gambling house in the pueblo, had hired Slack to ride herd on the vaqueros who frequented his tables. Slack himself boasted of his many conflicts with Hispanics, and later claimed that they put a price on his head: "Any 'Mex' who could get me was to get $250."[18]

As Slack's appearance and temperament matched exactly that of the long-missing killer, Morse obtained an arrest warrant and boarded a southbound stage, arriving in San Luis Obispo on May 7, 1868. He had no trouble locating the murder suspect, for as he and Sheriff de la Guerra were standing in the street, Slack rode into the little pueblo on horseback. Morse stepped up to him and announced, "You are my prisoner."

Slack angrily demanded an explanation, but Sheriff de la Guerra urged him, "Don't make a fuss."

Slack eyed the warrant in Morse's hand, the six-gun and handcuffs at his belt, the no-nonsense glint in the lawman's eye, and wisely submitted to the arrest. While Slack was in jail, awaiting the northbound stage, his brother-in-law, Othar Kamp, threatened to kill Morse if he attempted to take Slack into the stage wearing irons. Morse ignored the threat but agreed to allow Slack's father-in-law to accompany them north so that he might testify on Slack's behalf.

The following morning, as Morse brought his shackled prisoner to the stage, Othar Kamp drew his gun on the Alameda lawman, but Kamp's friends overpowered him and wrestled the gun away. The stage rumbled north out of town and headed up the Cuesta grade. The road was slippery from recent rains, and the driver ordered all the passengers to get out and help push the coach uphill. Morse and the others clambered out, but Slack and his father-in-law refused. Slack glared with hatred at the sheriff.

"You are taking me to Oakland on a false charge, and you know it," he declared. "I'm going, but I ride!"

For John Slack it was a moment of triumph. While Morse, grunting and cursing, his boots slipping in the mud, helped push the lumbering coach through the mire, Slack and his father-in-law jubilantly leaned back inside the coach, alternately howling with glee and glowering at their supposed tormentor.

The sheriff lodged Slack in jail at San Leandro. Slack was so confident that he would be exonerated that he declined to hire a lawyer, and only did so at the urging of the district attorney. At his preliminary hearing on May 18 before Judge Nye, two witnesses, one of them the murdered man's brother, swore positively that John Slack was the killer. Numerous other prosecution witnesses thought that Slack and Wilson were the same man, but none were certain. Three witnesses testified on Slack's behalf, and all swore that he had been known since his arrival in California in 1854 only as John Slack. A San Francisco man named Cooksey testified that he had known Slack since his childhood in Missouri and that he had never used the name Wilson. Finally the hearing was postponed for a week to allow the prosecution to produce several missing witnesses.

When the hearing was resumed the new witnesses were divided in opinion: one was certain that Slack was Wilson, but another believed they were not the same man. The testimony completed, Judge Nye ruled that there was insufficient evidence that Slack was the fugitive, and he ordered him released. Declared the editor of the *Alameda County Gazette*, "This is the most remarkable case of mistaken identity that has ever come under our observation."[19]

John Slack returned to his farm in San Luis Obispo. He claimed that the real John Wilson later saw a newspaper account of his arrest and wrote to him from Arizona, advising "that he had shot Sunol in self-defense, but left, for he knew that among the greasers at Mission San Jose he stood no chance for fair play." Slack claimed that he forwarded the letter to Sheriff Morse. True or not, the slayer of Jose Sunol was never brought to justice.

In speaking of the court hearing some fifty years later, John Slack said, "Twenty-one 'greasers' were introduced as witnesses by Morse." Slack claimed that Morse refused to let him procure an alibi witness who lived in San Francisco and had mined with him in the Sierra at the time of the murder. But Slack's gravest charge against Morse was that when the sheriff brought a Californio witness into the jail to identify him, he overheard the two conversing in Spanish. Morse told the witness that he had to swear that Slack was Wilson, but the Californio protested, "But Wilson had lost a front tooth, and this man has all his teeth."

Slack claimed that he later told Morse that he spoke Spanish and had understood the entire conversation. According to Slack's version, "Morse slunk off. But $4,000 reward was offered for Wilson, and lie though he must have known it to be, he went on trying to turn [me] into Wilson."[20]

The accuracy of Slack's claim is subject to question. He obviously harbored a great deal of resentment against Morse, which made him far from an impartial witness. His claim that Morse was motivated by a $4,000 reward is not credible; there was no mention of such a reward in the 1854 or 1868 news accounts, and if such a reward had been issued at the time of the murder it is unlikely that the offer would still be outstanding thirteen years later. Contrary to Slack's story, he, like Wilson, had lost a front tooth, which he demonstrated to Judge Nye in open court. Last, that many witnesses believed Slack and Wilson were the same man is evidence supporting Morse's actions. Although Slack's allegations should perhaps be taken with a generous grain of salt, they nonetheless raise questions about the methods Harry Morse may have used in his effort to secure a conviction. This was not the last time the Alameda sheriff would be accused of manufacturing evidence.

Whether or not Morse acted overzealously, his effort to bring
Jose Sunol's killer to justice demonstrated both moral and political
courage. Given the prevalent racism of the era, many voters could not
be expected to understand a lawman's desire to convict an Anglo for
the long-forgotten death of a Hispanic. Morse deserves credit for ig-
noring the racial overtones of the case and risking his political security by his effort to avenge Jose Sunol's death.

By 1869 the Central Pacific Railroad had been built through the
Livermore Valley. William Mendenhall, pioneer rancher, conveyed
twenty acres of land to the railroad company on which to place a
train depot. This spot, located half a mile west of Laddville, he called
Livermore. A townsite was laid out, and lots sold quickly. The town
grew rapidly. By 1876, the year it was incorporated, it had a population of 830, with 234 buildings, including a flour mill, three grain
warehouses, four blacksmith shops, six hotels, and features that no
frontier town could exist without: one brewery and thirteen saloons.

But in 1869 Livermore was still so small that the trains did not
make regular stops, and the engineers, especially if they were running behind schedule, would not stop if there was only one passenger waiting. "Hence the delegation plan," reported the *Gazette*.
"The shrill whistle of an approaching train brings the whole town
to their feet. If it occurs at meal-time, they drop knife and fork and
rush for the doors. If there is only one passenger, fifteen or twenty
citizens accompany him or her to the station, which is merely a road
crossing, when all participate in signaling the train."[21]

Laddville and its Hispanic counterpart, Mexico, had always been
havens for hard hombres. But now, with the influx of railroad workers and others into the new town of Livermore, the incidence of
crime greatly increased, and the citizens became frustrated with
the ability of their local constables to deal with it. Sheriff Morse, as
a consequence, had his hands full maintaining order, which was
made doubly difficult by the fact that, even with the railroad now
in place, Livermore was still a two-hour trip from his office in San
Leandro.

Among Hispanics and the rougher class of Anglos, one of the
most popular sports was the bull and bear fight. In those years grizzly bears were still common in the Coast Range. These brutal affairs,
which took place in a bullring and usually resulted in victory by the
bear, were both widely attended and the scene of heavy wagering.
The *Gazette* reported:

Livermore in the early 1870s. Author's collection.

About once a month the inhabitants of this vicinity, irrespective of race, sex, or color, are treated to one of those chaste and classical entertainments, a bull and bear fight. A wise and discriminating legislature, whose conscientious scruples would not permit a wanton desecration of the Christian Sabbath, passed a law some years ago prohibiting these brutal exhibitions from being held on Sunday. Let the Society for the Prevention of Cruelty to Animals come to the rescue.[22]

In August 1869 Morse received a complaint that a bull and bear fight was illegally scheduled to take place on a Sunday. The *Gazette* reported with tongue in cheek, "The sheriff, who is continually interfering with the pleasures of the orderly and law-abiding citizens of Laddville, notified them that the Act to 'prevent barbarous and noisy amusements on the Sabbath' would be rigidly enforced, hence the day was changed to Saturday. A large attendance is confidently expected."[23]

The other principal mode of entertainment seemed to be fighting with knives and guns. During 1869 Laddville was the scene of numerous cutting and shooting scrapes. On one Sunday in March the little village saw three fistfights and one homicide, when a hostler, John Alty, shot and mortally wounded a Mexican whom he thought was attempting to break into his stable. "It was considered a poor day for fights," was the *Gazette* editor's facetious comment.[24]

Later that month the *Gazette* railed against the lawlessness in the Livermore Valley and the incompetence of the township's two constables:

> Murray Township is infested with horse thieves, robbers, and desperadoes guilty of every crime known to the law, and they seem to congregate about Laddville. Horses are stolen, men are robbed and beaten on the public highway, and the perpetrators of the crimes escape. The peaceable and respectable people have to rely upon their own vigilance for self-protection. The officers of the law in that vicinity must be culpably negligent to allow such a state of affairs to exist so long.[25]

The following week a correspondent from the Livermore Valley wrote the *Gazette*, "This valley has become the great lying-in hospital for the flood of rogues that graduate at San Quentin. What we want here is more display of nerve, and less brandishing of revolvers and handcuffs—in a word, we want an officer and not a braggart."[26]

Such a man was elected constable of Murray Township in September. His name was Ralph Faville, and not only did he retain this office for the next eight years, he soon was appointed deputy sheriff by Morse and became his right-hand man until Morse left office. Faville was one of the best lawmen of Alameda's frontier era, and he would take part in many of Morse's toughest manhunts.

As Sheriff Morse struggled to cope with the lawlessness of his bailiwick and the personal tragedies that had befallen his family, across the bay at San Quentin Juan Soto, Procopio, and Tiburcio Vasquez whiled away the dreary months. By day they labored in the shoe shop, the door factory, and the brickyard; at night they huddled in their bunks, with threadbare blankets their only protection from the foggy cold. From the balcony of the old stone cellblock they gazed longingly across the sparkling bay waters at the Contra Costa and its rolling foothills, with Mount Diablo rising behind them in the distance, an ever-present reminder of the freedom that would be theirs one day. From time to time they would receive a visitor from the opposite shore, always that young sheriff of Alameda. With a new prisoner in tow, he would rarely fail to call on one or another of them, sometimes at their cells, sometimes in the yard or the commissary. He would engage them in idle conversation, his sharp gray eyes seeming to soak in their every detail—their walk, their voices, their faces. And then he would be gone, and they would return to their dreary labor and their dreams of freedom, of fast horses and faster women, of good cigars and aguardiente, and of easy pickings in the pueblos and ranchos and along the roads and trails of that distant mountain fastness.

CHAPTER 8

Thousand-Mile Trackdown

"MURDER! Wife, I am shot!" These were the last words of Morgan Leighton, an old rancher who was gunned down by Joe Newell on September 20, 1868. His killer was, in Harry Morse's words, "a wild, reckless fellow," one of "an exceedingly rough class of white desperadoes" who lived in Cathcart Canyon, in the mountains north of Sunol. Newell, his brother-in-law, Al Wild, and another ruffian, Bill Powers, were passing Old Man Leighton's house with a wagonload of hay when Newell's bulldog attacked the rancher's little watchdog. When Leighton tried to separate the animals, Joe Newell draw a large Colt revolver and shot him in the left eye, a mortal wound. The killer fled. And Harry Morse embarked on his longest and toughest manhunt yet.

Morse immediately sent out wanted posters bearing a full description of the murderer and his horse, for in those days many people would pay more attention to a good saddle animal than to its rider. The sheriff was tipped that Newell may have gone to the Mount Diablo coal mines, where he had once worked. Morse and his friend Lewis C. Morehouse, constable of San Leandro, used a basic lawman's tactic. Instead of riding directly there, they made a wide circle on horseback, knowing that with luck they would eventually cut the fugitive's trail. They first rode through the Livermore Valley and down Corral Hollow, then north through the San Joaquin Valley and east through Livermore Pass. Searching all the way, they rode back to the San Joaquin River, then west to Point of Timber and the coal mines near Clayton. Newell was not there, but the lawmen learned that he had recently been offered a job by a friend named McMullen at a gold mine in Soledad Canyon in Los Angeles County.

To complete the circle, Morse and Morehouse rode to Oakland, checked with the police and ferrymen to make sure Newell had not crossed the bay, and then headed south to Santa Clara County. They searched the mountains west of San Jose, the New Almaden and

Guadalupe quicksilver mines, and the pueblo of San Jose, and then rode south to Gilroy. Here they at last picked up the trail. From Billy Berger, the city marshal, they learned that on September 26 a man matching Newell's description had passed through. Berger, thinking he might be riding a stolen horse, questioned him carefully, then let him go. The stranger asked Berger for directions to the mines in Los Angeles County. This was the information Morse needed. He and Morehouse had ridden two hundred miles in four days. They returned to San Leandro to rest and prepare for a long manhunt.[1]

As soon as I could arrange my business so as to permit of my absence, I was ready to start after the fugitive. From Walter J. Stratton of San Leandro I procured a team of little wiry mustangs, grey in color, ribbed up close and snug. They were gentle and true to pull and both were good feeders. With this team of plugs we made the round trip of 1,200 miles, and although the animals were thin in flesh when we returned with them, yet to show the endurance of these native horses it will only be necessary to state that the last day's drive made with them was sixty-five miles, from Gilroy, in Santa Clara County, to San Leandro, in Alameda County.

Duncan Cameron of Brooklyn [now part of Oakland] furnished us with a light, covered spring wagon. Our outfit consisted of crackers, bacon, coffee, tea, three pairs of good, thick Mission blankets, one double-barrelled shotgun, one Henry rifle, with the necessary ammunition; each of us wore a grey flannel shirt, broad-brimmed slouch hat, and rough stogy boots, into which the tops of our pants were stuck. In addition to all this, each of us had a change of underclothing. All this preparation, in my opinion, was absolutely necessary, for I was satisfied that we would have to go clear to the lower end of the state to find Newell and that he might possibly go over the line into lower [Baja] California, and if he did we had fully made up our minds to take the chances of following him there and bring him back with us.

We left San Leandro at 9 A.M. on the morning of the 14th of October, 1868, and drove direct to Haywards. Here we got a full and accurate description of Newell. We visited the tailor who put a patch in the knee of Joe's pants and he described them to us thoroughly. Next the shoemaker was interviewed and from him we got the description of the boots that he had made for Newell. They were of fine calf, double soles, very long heels, nearly three inches in length; the soles were put on with copper brads and in the center of each sole was made with these copper brads a large heart. All this description was necessary, for Newell was a newcomer in

MURDER!

On the evening of September 20th, 1868, one Joseph Newell
murdered Morgan Leighton in Alameda County.

Description of Murderer:

Newell is a man of Dark complexion; about twenty-
three years of age, nose inclined to Roman; about five feet six
or seven inches in height; slight lisp in conversation; shaved
clean; thick, dark moustache; full, black eyes; soft, white
hands. Dressed when last seen as follows: In light, mixed coat;
light colored, checked pants; white shirt; light hat, broad brim
and low crown; high heeled boots No. 6, with small heels. Rode
a Roan mare. 6 or 7 years old, about 13½ or 14 hands high, and
branded, [J. R.]
Arrest and detain said Newell until warrant can be sent.

HENRY N. MORSE,
Sheriff of Alameda County.
Dated, San Leandro, Sept. 21st, 1868.

The wanted poster Morse issued for Joe Newell. Author's collection.

my part of the country and was entirely unknown to either Morehouse or
myself. I also found that Joe invariably lisped when using a word having
the letter "s" in it.

With this information we started and drove on to San Jose, thirty miles
distant, where we rested the team. At 4 P.M. we started out again and
camped that night seven miles south of San Jose, on the old San Jose and
Gilroy road, having driven forty-three miles that day. We turned off the
road and pitched our camp under a very large black oak tree, on the opposite side of which were encamped a party of emigrants who were on
their way to Southern California. A very heavy north wind, such as we
usually have before the rains set in, was blowing, and had been all day,
which made things very uncomfortable for both man and beast. We had
picketed out our horses, had our supper, and were just preparing to roll up
in our blankets for the night, when we were startled by a sudden and
awful crash. We jumped to our feet just in time to see a large limb of a tree

*under which we were encamped fall with a tremendous crash into the very
center of the emigrant party. We expected, of course, to see the life crushed
out of some of them, but except for the smashing in of the top of one of
their wagons and a slight scratch on the knee of one of the party, there was
no damage done. We took the precaution, however, of removing our blankets to a place where no limbs of trees could fall on us.*

*We had breakfast and drove out the next morning, long before our em-
igrant friends had turned out of their blankets. The morning was very cold
and a thick frost lay upon the ground. At 11 A.M. we drove into Gilroy
and stopped an hour to rest and feed our team. I sought out the marshal
to see if he had made any new discoveries but he had made none of any
importance to us. At one o'clock we hitched up the team and started for
Pacheco Pass, the high Picachos to the south of the pass standing out in
the clear, blue sky in bold relief, everlasting guides to the weary traveler
making his way from the Santa Clara to the San Joaquin Valley.*

*A drive of twelve miles brought us to the Laguna, better known as Soap
Lake [now called San Felipe Lake]. Here we made close inquiry for Joe's
having passed there. They thought such a man as we described had passed
that way at the time we stated, but it being three weeks before, they
would not be certain about it. We drove on six miles further and entered
the mouth of the pass. Driving into the pass about two miles, we went into
camp for the night under a large oak tree, a nice clear spring of pure water
being close by. Morehouse unhitched the team and staked out the horses
while I pitched the tent and made the camp fire.*

*I visited a sheep camp that we had passed about 200 yards down the
canyon. From the sheepherder's description of a man who had stolen his
red blankets I was certain that it was Newell, and therefore we were on
the right track. But Joe had a long start on us—twenty days. Now, a
twenty-day start, over a much-traveled road, is a pretty cold trail. So
many people pass and repass that it is hard for the folks living on the road
to remember so far back. But we must follow on as best we could. At the
tollgate, in the pass, we thought certainly that they would remember Joe's
passing, but they did not and were certain that no such person had gone
that way. Yet that could be easily accounted for. Joe no doubt had avoided
the tollgate by going up on the side of the mountain and coming down into
the road again after he had passed the gate.*

*We drove on again, the road keeping near the bed of the deep canyon
creek. After a drive of about a mile the road turned a little to the left and
up onto the side of the steep mountain, this being the commencement of
the ascent to the summit of the pass. Just before taking the higher road we*

came upon a large flock of quail. The gun being loaded, I got out of the wagon and took a shot at them, bringing down six, just enough for the supper of two hungry men. Picking up the birds, I put them in the wagon and started on afoot up the mountain road, my gun across my shoulder. I had walked perhaps half a mile up the grade when I came upon a six-horse team just swinging one of the turns of the road. The driver, as soon as he saw me, stopped his team. He was a great, raw-boned, slab-sided individual, with a long, dirty red beard. His hair was of the same dirty color and came down to his shoulders. It looked as though his face had not been washed, nor his hair combed, for a year. On his head was an old slouched hat, the rim of which had apparently lost all the stiffness that had ever been in it, and it looped down over his face and neck as to almost entirely conceal them.

As I walked up to pass the wagon, this driver gave me a mean ugly look and said, "You look-a-har! Did you fire that 'ere gun off in the canyon down thar just now?"

"Yes, sir," I replied. "I suppose it was me. I shot some quail at the foot of the hill a few moments ago."

"Well now, you look-a-har. If yer fire that 'ere gun off agin and skar this 'ere team of mine, I'll make it mighty warm for you. You har me?"

I had to smile at the cheek of this butternut [backwoodsman], as I thought of the hornet's nest he had got into without knowing it and of the results that might follow in case he should attempt to carry his threat into execution.

"Keep cool, old fellow," I said. "I had no intention of frightening your team. I did not even know there was a team on the road. Besides, we are strangers in this part of the country and are not acquainted with the ways of the natives hereabouts. But judging from your style of addressing people, I should set you down for a tough."

"No sass, now, young feller, but move right along. Mighty quick, too, or I'll be after you! You har me?"

And as he said this he placed his hand upon the handle of a large six-shooter that he had strapped to his side.

Seeing that the fellow meant mischief and not caring to take any chances with him, I quietly swung my shotgun from my shoulder into the hollow of my arm, in such a manner as to present the muzzle toward him and so that he could look into the end of the barrels. At the same time cocking the piece and placing my finger upon the trigger, I said, "Now, Mr. Butternut, if you don't remove your hand from that pistol you will never get over the hill with your team, because this gun will certainly go off, and it might scare your horses and make them go over the grade, wagon and all."

And at the same time I raised the gun, ready for action.

Whether it was the ominous click of the cocking of the gun or something in my actions he did not like the looks of, I don't know. But the ruffian turned white at the mouth, looked undecided, and slowly took his hand away from the pistol, and taking up his whip, he swung it at the leaders in a very spiteful way and yelled out, "Get up there you, Dick! What's the matter you, Bally!"

The horses slowly straightened their traces and the great heavy wagon, with its load of lumber and butternut driver, commenced to move slowly up the hill. He did not notice us any more and we drove on by him, laughing to ourselves at the way the blustering fellow backed down. The little team of ours trotted briskly up the grade toward the summit and we soon lost sight of the combative teamster.

As we came over the top of the mountain and looked over the great broad valley of the San Joaquin, a most beautiful panorama was presented to our view. As far as the eye could reach there lay spread out before us a great level plain. Far away to the east we could see the towering, massive range of the wild, romantic Sierra Nevada Mountains. Their great peaks and deep gorges, covered and filled with the everlasting snow, were brought vividly to our view through the transparent atmosphere, the bright, shining sun pouring its silvery rays upon them from its meridian height. Along the center of the great valley thus spread before us wound and crept the deep, muddy waters of the San Joaquin River, its banks fringed with aliso [alder] and oak trees, whose dark green foliage in the great distance was marked and well defined and indicated to a certainty the course of the river. At intervals of ten or fifteen miles a similar streak of green foliage could be seen running at right angles with the main river and told of smaller streams making their way from the great snow-clad mountains beyond down into the creeping muddy waters of the main stream.

It was a grand sight, and we sat in silent admiration of it for about twenty minutes and until the crack of the whip of the butternut teamster coming behind us brought us down out of dreamland and was notice to us that if we wished to avoid further trouble we had better drive on. Touching our little grays with the whip, we drove on down the steep grade toward the San Luis Rancho. The road wound and twisted toward all points of the compass. We let the horses go and soon found ourselves at the base of the mountain and in a small, basin-like valley that was almost completely surrounded by mountains of the Coast Range.[2]

A drive of seven miles brought us to the old rancho. Passing it, we drove to the stage station, about a mile further on, where we fed our team and made some coffee for ourselves. After lunch I had a talk with the hostler at the station and from him learned that about three weeks before a man riding a small roan mare had stopped at the station and asked for a feed of barley for his animal. The hostler at first refused him but the man told such a pitiful story about being out of funds and having such a long ride to make before reaching his friends that he finally relented and allowed him to feed his mare and also to sleep in the stable. The description of this man, as given by the hostler, was that of Newell.

"Did you notice the direction taken by this man when he left your station that morning?" I asked.

"Yes, he told me he was going to Visalia, and when he left here he took the road leading in that direction."

At 4 P.M. we left the station, taking the Visalia stage road going south. A drive of eight miles brought us to the sheep ranch of the Woods brothers, and here we went into camp for the night. We were now in the great San Joaquin Valley, not a tree or shrub of any kind within ten miles of us. Water here was hard to find, except at the sheep camps or at the river, ten miles away. Feed was dry and not very plentiful but with what barley we gave the horses they seemed to get along pretty well.

Morehouse took care of the team while I fixed up the tent. Then we both gathered up the cattle chips to make our campfire with. The fire made, we proceeded to get supper. The quail that I had killed in the morning were nicely cleaned and ready for the frying pan. The water in the coffee pot was boiling merrily and every now and then spurted out into the fire. Four or five slices of nice sweet bacon were cut and sizzling in the frying pan. The quail were laid in alongside the bacon, then a great big onion was cut into slices and put in the pan. Over the frying pan we then placed a tin plate and let it all slowly cook for about twenty minutes when we took it off, done. Such a delicious supper! Why, it would actually have made a bald-headed man's hair curl.

After supper we cleared away the wreck and sat at the little fire there was left, smoking our pipes and talking about the fugitive and our plans in the future in regard to him. Then we walked out to where the horses were picketed to see if they were all right for the night and found that they had eaten their fill and were lying down, resting themselves. This is good, for a horse that never lies down to rest cannot stand long and continuous driving. Getting back to camp we found that during our absence we had had a visitor in the shape of a shepherd dog, and who on leaving carried off a large piece of bacon with him.

We had breakfast next morning and were on the road by daylight. A

Morse's deputy Lewis C.
Morehouse, who played
a prominent role in
the manhunts for Joe
Newell and Jesus Tejada.
Author's collection.

drive of ten miles brought us to a dry creek, on the banks of which we saw
a fine flock of quail. Taking out the gun, I got two flying shots at them,
bringing down four as the birds rose in a bunch from the ground and two
more with the second shot as they were flying away. With these we had
enough for another good quail supper tonight. Could there be any better
living than that?

At noon we drove up to the ferry house at Firebaugh's, unhitched the
horses and led them to the river to drink, and then gave them a good feed
of barley. No one at the ferry house remembered having seen Joe pass. I
then went to the stage station close by and asked. A teamster who was
hauling grain for the stage company informed us that he had seen Newell
(describing him) and stated that there was another man with him. He saw
them on the main stage road and about five miles north of the ferry.
They inquired their way to Los Angeles. At two o'clock we started for the
Fresno Slough ferry and heard of Newell again as having passed about two
miles south of Firebaugh's. He was going south toward Fresno Slough.

We crossed the slough ferry at dark and went into camp. We could not
find wood enough to make a fire and tried to purchase some but the
owner would not sell us any and was very gruff and cross. We tried the

whiskey argument on him and succeeded, getting all the wood we wanted. 'Tis a shame to tempt a man with spirits. Its effects are demoralizing, we know, but we were not on a cruise, trying to reform the world. It can't be done by us. Wood we had to have was wood we got, while the wood man got our whiskey in exchange. The wood helped us to a good quail supper and our whiskey helped the wood man into a good humor.

We got away from the slough at daylight—destination Elkhorn Station, thirty-five miles distant. About two miles from the ferry we came to a water-hole full of ducks and shot two nice fat ones. After watering our team we started on over the worst alkali I ever saw. In the road the earth was as white as snow and ground up as fine as flour. Every time the horses planted their feet in this powdered earth it would squish out from under their hooves and fly in all directions, covering the horses, harness, wagon, and ourselves until we all looked as though we had been run through a flouring mill.

At eleven o'clock we arrived at the old Hawthorn Station. It is a perfect garden spot—with the garden left out. The place is situated in the center of an alkali plain. The wind was blowing at the rate of at least thirty miles an hour, while the thermometer stood 112 in the shade. The water in the well would make a pig squeal to drink it, so strongly was it impregnated with alkali.[3]

At one o'clock we started again for the next station, Elkhorn, distant fifteen miles. This fearful alkali and hot, drying winds caused us and our team to suffer very much, but at three o'clock we got into a better road. Green feed—a sort of wire grass—made its appearance and was very pleasant to look upon. At 5 P.M. we drove up to Elkhorn Station. We fixed our camp on the bright greensward and prepared out supper. We were very hungry and ate with great relish.

At daylight we were on the road, intending to make Visalia that night. But mistaking the road, we got lost and had to retrace our steps almost back to Elkhorn. We saw quite a band of antelope but did not get near enough to shoot at them. A very large coyote came close to the wagon as we were getting lunch. After making a satisfactory reconnaissance, he lay down upon his belly and looked at us. I took a shot at him with my Henry rifle and just creased him across the back, making his hair fly. The old chap jumped about four feet straight into the air. When he landed he started off on a dead run and was soon out of sight.

A few hours rest and we started again. The appearance of the country here had changed. From dry alkali plains we had come into a heavily wooded and well-watered country. Passing along through the Twenty-five

Rancho, we came to Cross Creek and camped for the night. Our mistaking the road this morning compelled us to camp here and not at Visalia as
we intended when we broke camp in the morning.[4]

In the morning we started bright and early and at 11 A.M. drove into
Visalia. Here we made vigorous search and inquiry for Newell but found
no trace of him whatever. At sun-up the next morning we were on our
way south and crossed Tule River, thirty miles from Visalia, at two o'clock
and reached Fountain Springs, twelve miles farther on, just before dark,
and went into camp. Here I found a track of Joe. Mrs. Hilton, the lady
of the house, informed me that she remembered seeing him perfectly well.
The high-heeled boots drew her particular attention to him and she also
noticed that he was riding a small roan mare. This was the first certain
information that we had of Newell for 150 miles.[5]

We were off at daylight again. About two miles from our camp the
roads forked, one going across the valley via Kern River Island [now
Bakersfield] and Fort Tejon to Los Angeles, and the other across Greenhorn Mountain to Havilah. If Newell had taken the Kern River Island
road he would have to keep on to Los Angeles and was probably there at
the present time. But if he went across the mountains he might be in the
vicinity of Havilah; so if we took the lower road, and he at Havilah, we
would miss him. Thinking the matter over, we came to the conclusion to
go over Greenhorn Mountain and thereby not lose a chance, although it
would be at least sixty miles further.

Turning to the left, we crossed White River and White River Mountain
through Linn Valley and Glennville to the foot of Greenhorn Mountain,
which is a part of the Sierra Nevada range. We soon reached the snow-
clad summit and took the down grade for Kernville, alias Whiskey Flat—
rightly named, too, for most every man we met in town (it being Sunday)
was full of the material of which the town was named after. We made diligent search and inquiry for Newell but failed to get the least clue of him.[6]

Driving down the river about a mile, we met an old friend of mine
named Joseph Venable, who, in early days, lived in Oakland. Upon his invitation, we took supper with him and his wife. The latter we found to be
a very bright and intelligent lady. The remembrance of her ladylike greet-
ing of welcome to us and the splendid supper of her own cooking that she
sat before us is still fresh in my own mind, although so many years have
passed, and I often, in thinking over the events of this trip, call to mind the
very pleasant evening spent in the company of Mr. Venable and his good
wife.

The next day we drove into Havilah, the county seat of Kern County,

and which we found to be a thriving village. We found the people pleas-
ant and willing to give all the information necessary as to roads and trails.
Leaving Havilah, we passed on through Walker's Basin and camped on
the mountainside, about a mile from the basin. At sunrise we were on the
road again, making for the head of the San Joaquin Valley. The country
that we were passing through was a spur of the Sierra Nevada and was
very steep and rugged. A large grizzly bear had crossed the road just be-
fore we passed along. His footprints measured twelve inches in length.
About noon we reached the summit and commenced the down grade to-
ward the valley. On the left of the road we observed a little mound of earth
and a cross stuck up at the head of it. Upon inquiry at the tollgate a few
miles further on we were informed that a man, unknown to any person,
was found murdered on the road and that the people buried him at the spot
and put the cross at his head. Poor fellow, shot down on the road; no per-
son knew who he was or where he came from. His body lies mouldering
where strangers buried it—high up on the side of the Sierra Nevada.

We camped at [Fort] Tejon. It is a beautiful place, situated as it is in
a deep canyon, surrounded by high mountain peaks. The little plat where
the government buildings stand is covered with green grass, made so by the
clear, sparkling water rushing out from the immense springs that lay ad-
jacent to the old fort. Great, magnificent oaks grow up and cast a plea-
surable shade over the old military quarters and parade grounds. What a
waste of Uncle Samuel's money has taken place here. It must have cost
at least $1,000,000 to fix up Tejon.[7]

We left Tejon the next morning at six o'clock for the Mojave Desert.
After leaving the fort, the road opened out into a fine-looking country.
Large oaks lined the road on either side of us, the little valleys being well
watered with springs and lakes, while the wild oats grew waist high and
furnished splendid feed for horses and cattle, of which the country was
full. A drive of twenty miles brought us to the Liebre Rancho, owned by
Captain Edward F. Beale. Here we found an old gentleman named
Handcock who informed us that Newell had passed his place about ten
days previous and that he had inquired for the Soledad mines. He de-
scribed Newell and his roan mare so accurately that there could be no mis-
take about its being him.

We ate lunch with the ranchero, fed our team, and at one o'clock we
started for Mud Springs, on the west side of the desert and distant twenty
miles. We passed through a dense growth of Spanish bayonet cactus,
which in the distance resembled a growth of dwarf pines. At six in the
evening we went into camp at Mud Springs. The north wind swept across

the desert like a perfect hurricane and made it somewhat difficult for us to light our campfire, but we finally succeeded, and after cooking our supper we turned into our blankets, tired and anxious, and slept soundly and as only tired men can sleep, til daylight in the morning.

At sunrise we were on the road again, and after a drive of twenty miles over heavily sandy road, reached Llano Verde, a station on the desert, about noon. Here we found, turned out to die, the little roan mare that had carried the fugitive for many a weary mile. The little animal was footsore, stiff, and worn down to skin and bone. She came up to us and we gave her a feed of barley, as she seemed to be sadly in need of it. She looked at us with her great melancholy eyes, which said, "Thank you," as plainly as though she had spoken it. The station-keeper informed us that Newell had left the mare at the station some eight or ten days previous and had started over the mountains afoot for the Soledad mines, where, as he said, he had friends.

Morehouse and I held a consultation and talked over the situation. We were getting warm on Newell's trail. If he had gone to his friend McMullen, and was still there, we were at the time not more than fifteen miles distant from him. From Llano Verde to Soledad by the regular road it was about twenty-four miles, but by the trail that led over the mountains it was but fourteen miles. It was finally agreed upon that Morehouse should take the wagon and drive around by the road, while I was to go over the mountain trail to the mines and see what I could discover.

It may be guessed that after our long tramp through so much rough country we did not present the most tidy appearance imaginable. We could discount the ordinary tramp in our personal makeup. So, taking a pair of blankets from the wagon and buckling on a six-shooter, I bade Morehouse good-by, slung the blankets over my shoulder, and started off over the mountain trail alone for the Soledad mines in "search of work." It was getting well along in the afternoon when I reached the summit of the mountain. Here I rested for about ten minutes and at the same time examined the country. Directly in front of me and at the bottom of the mountain was spread out a beautiful little valley, the trail running through the center of it and leading directly to the little village of Soledad. Some of the jacales I could just see from my elevated position. Away to the right and high up on the mountainside I could see the dumps at the mouth of the tunnel where the miners were working.

I started on toward the miners' camp. I walked along the mountainside, and before reaching the tunnel, I took the precaution to cross over the mountain and come down to the mine from the upper side. I did this for two reasons. One was that I could get closer to where the miners were working without being seen so soon; and secondly, if Newell was there, and seeing me, should attempt to run, it would be a downhill race and not an uphill one. I was tired and was getting foot-sore, having on thin-soled boots, and I knew, or was afraid, that if it came to a foot race, Newell, knowing the country and being fresh, would most likely get away from me, while if he was forced to go downhill I imagined that I could outrun him.

Well, upon my arrival at the mines I found our man had been there but had left for Los Angeles two weeks before. A brisk walk of an hour and a half brought me to Soledad where I found Morehouse camped in the willows and busy getting supper. The next day we drove down the Soledad Canyon forty miles and camped at San Fernando Valley, and the day following drove on to Joe Rice's and finding good feed, concluded to stay there the balance of the day and rest our tired horses. About dark a teamster came in from Los Angeles and went into camp near us. After supper Morehouse and I walked over and had a talk with him. He said he was hauling bullion from the Cerro Gordo mines [in Inyo County] and was on the road most of the time. I then described Newell to him and asked him if he had met such a man on the road.

"Why, of course I did," he replied. "The man you describe rode into Los Angeles with me on my last trip down about ten days ago. I noticed particularly his high-heeled boots. He had a soldier's blue overcoat and had two pair of blankets—a gray pair and a pair of red ones rolled up inside the gray ones.

"Those are the blankets he stole at Pacheco Pass," I remarked to Morehouse. "Did he tell you what part of the country he came from?"

"Well, I asked him, and he told me that he came from the coal mines in Contra Costa County."

"Do you think he is still in Los Angeles?"

"That I cannot tell you," replied the teamster, and added, "He told me he was going to chop wood on the Ballona Rancho, and he may be there now. I have not seen him since he rode into Los Angeles with me. I noticed that he was dreadful uneasy all the time and got off my wagon outside of town, saying he would walk the rest of the way in, as he might find a job of work by so doing."

I then told the teamster why Newell was so uneasy.

"Killed a man named Leighton!" said the teamster "Why, that's my name. It seems funny, don't it," he continued, "that he should kill a man named Leighton and should also have man of the same name unconsciously assist in helping him away from the scene of the murder."

"Yes," I replied. "It is rather a singular coincidence. Did he tell you what his name was?"

"No, I never asked it and he did not tell me. I have told you all I know about it, and I hope you will catch the fellow."

The following day we drove into Los Angeles. Here we obtained a fresh team and started for the Ballona rancho [now Culver City], but found that Newell had not been there at all.

The next four or five days were spent about Los Angeles and vicinity in a useless effort to get on Newell's trail. He was not in Los Angeles; of that we were fully satisfied. He must have pushed on father south and, alas, we must follow. Even if he had gone across the line into Mexico we intended to follow and bring him back. Hearing at Los Angeles that they were employing a large number of men building the Los Angeles and Wilmington Railroad near Wilmington, about twenty miles off, Morehouse and I concluded that before we started further south we would go through the railroad camps.[8]

We left Los Angeles early in the morning, behind a spanking team of mustangs, and were soon well on toward Wilmington. Stopping at a wayside inn to water our horses, we learned that a chap answering Newell's description, wearing very high-heeled boots, had passed there about two weeks before and told the innkeeper that he was going to try and get work on the railroad. We drove to Wilmington and learned that the railroad camps were out five miles. Driving out to the first camp, I very fortunately found an old friend of mine named McDonald in charge of the men as boss. I stated my business to him. He could not remember any such man as I described but he said that men were coming and going all the time and added that the man might be in one of the camps and he not be aware of it. We searched them all but found no one.

Then McDonald spoke up and said, "There is a young fellow who came here about three weeks ago and has been working on the road, but he sprained his wrist three or four days ago and is now up at the camp assisting the cook. You can go and see him if you like, but he can't be the man. He is too nice a fellow to do such a deed as you tell about."

We rode on to the camp. McDonald dismounted and tied his horse while I jumped out of the buggy, leaving Morehouse to hold the horses. While approaching the camp I kept my eyes vigilantly at work to notice that no person left the place without me seeing him. Our buggy had stopped just in front of the kitchen and dining room, if such you could call it, being a large frame, the top of which was covered with canvas, while the sides were left open. Running length-wise along this canvas-covered frame were three long tables, on either side of which were long wooden benches for the men to sit upon. At the extreme far end was a brush-covered shanty in which the cooking was done.

"Where is the man you spoke about, Mac?" I said.

"That's him, back near the cooking department—he with the knife, assisting in cutting up the meat."

I looked in the direction pointed out by McDonald and saw, as he described, a rather nice, pleasant-looking young man. As soon as he saw us looking in his direction he immediately turned his back on us.

I whispered to Mac, "Can't we make some excuse, without exciting suspicion, to get into the cooking department? I'll ask you for a drink of water, Mac, and then you say, 'Yes, plenty of it. Come this way,' and then you lead me back there."

This was done and Mac and I went to the cooking place, passing close to the young man in question. After getting my drink of water I turned around, expecting to get a good, square look at the man. But when I turned around I discovered that he had found something at the front of the place to look at, for his back was toward me still. I made up my mind at once to interview him.

Turning to McDonald, I said, "Mac, what name is this young man working under here?"

"I don't know, but wait a moment and I will find out from the storekeeper."

In a few moments he returned and informed me that he was on the books as George Hartley.

Walking toward the young fellow, I said, "George, I want to talk with you a few moments. Lay down your knife and step this way, so that we can sit down to it."

He obeyed at once and followed me out to where the benches were on each side of the dining tables.

"Sit down, George," I said, pointing him the place to sit. He did so and I took my seat just opposite him. We sat facing each other and not more than two feet apart. Leaning over toward him, I looked him squarely in the eye and thus gazed at him without speaking a single word. This I kept up for at least three minutes. I saw his eye quail and give way before mine. I noticed that large drops of perspiration commenced to come out on each side of his nose. Finally taking my eyes from his for a moment, I cast them down toward his feet. Quickly I noticed that he wore a pair of checkered pants, on one of the knees of which was a large patch. On his feet he had what had once been a pair of fine boots, but now the tops had been cut off, they had been slit down the instep, and the heels had been knocked off. Reaching quickly down, I

Joe Newell in a photograph
taken shortly after he
was captured by Morse.
Courtesy of the San Jose
Historical Museum.

*seized one of his feet and held it up so that I could see the sole of the boot.
Great God! How it did startle me, and at the same time how exultant I felt.
For in the center of the sole was a figure of a heart, made in there with cop-
per nails. I knew in a second that I had the murderer of Morgan Leighton.*

Dropping the foot, I said to him, "George, what is your true name?"

"George Hartley," he replied.

"How old are you, George?"

"Twenty-eight."

"Where were you born?"

*"San Francisco, sir," he replied, and in saying it he lisped in using the
letter "s".*

"Are you certain that you are not mistaken in this, George?"

*"Of course I am. And," he added, "why do you look at me so strangely,
and why do you ask so many questions?"*

*"I will tell you why. It is because you have been lying to me. Your name
is not George Hartley. It is Joseph Newell. You are not twenty-eight years of*

age. You are but twenty-four. You were not born in San Francisco. You are an Australian by birth. And more, you are the murderer of Morgan Leighton, whom you most cruelly killed in the Cathcart Canyon, in Alameda County, some two months ago, and I now arrest you for that murder."

I took him to his tent to get his clothing before I took him away, he insisting all the time that I was mistaken and had got the wrong man. At the tent he picked out as his own a soldier's blue overcoat, a pair of gray and a pair of red blankets. Bringing the things out to the buggy, he went to the storekeeper for a final settlement.

I said, "George, if, as you say, you are not the man, there is no necessity for you to make a final settlement. If you are not the man I will return you here, pay you for your time, and all your expenses besides."

But George insisted upon full settlement. When that was done, I put a pair of handcuffs upon him, and placing him on the buggy seat, between Morehouse and myself, we started back to Los Angeles, McDonald going a short piece with us to show us the short-cut through the high mustard and also the crossing of the Los Angeles River. Arriving at the crossing, we thanked Mac for the kindness he had shown us, and letting the mustang team go, were soon fast bowling back to the City of the Angels.

We had ridden a mile, perhaps, when Newell, turning suddenly toward me, said, "Is your name Morse?"

"It is," I answered.

"I thought so," he replied, and then, bursting into tears, he said, "I am Joe Newell, the man you want. Great God, how I have suffered! I did not mean to kill the old man. I did not know he was dead. I don't care so much for myself. But my poor sister—it will be awful hard on her."

And then he broke out crying again. I really felt sorry for the fellow now that I had captured him. Pretty soon he became more calm and in a short time was in a condition to laugh and joke. Taking Newell to the Los Angeles County jail, I locked him up there. The next morning Morehouse started back overland with the team while I took Newell to San Francisco on the steamer.

Thus, after a long, tedious trip of forty-one days, we had accomplished our object. Forty-one days of hardship, anxiety, and suffering— a forty-one day trip never to be effaced from my memory. We had started out after a mere shadow, so to speak, for neither of us had ever seen Newell before and his description as given to us was not all accurate, and had at last caught the substance.

While absent on this pursuit I had destroyed by the earthquake of 1868 about $14,000 worth of property, and besides one of my dearest *friends, J. W. Josselyn, deputy treasurer of our county, was killed by the falling walls of the old rotten court house as they came crushing to the ground on that terrible 21st of October, 1868. Of these misfortunes I knew nothing for several weeks after they occurred, as I was out of the line of communication of any kind with the outside world, being most of the time in the mountain ranges of Southern California.*

I arrived safely home with Newell and in due time his trial came off [in March 1869]. Newell should have been hanged for that murder. Newell at large and not expected to be captured, they swore Newell murdered Morgan Leighton; but Newell captured and in the courtroom standing his trial was quite a different person. He was a bad, dangerous man and they did not swear quite so hard against him. They now swore that old man Leighton assaulted Newell first—struck at him with a club, so Newell's witnesses said and produced an immense oaken stick, the end of an old wagon tongue. The witnesses simply perjured themselves to save Newell. It was a well known fact, and was clearly proven, that Leighton had not been able to put his own coat on for over a year, he being crippled up with the rheumatism. Yet from the preponderance of testimony produced by Newell and his friends he was only found guilty of simple manslaughter and sentenced to the state prison for five years.

Most of the gang came to the bad. The curse of God seemed to be following them. Bill Powers afterward killed a man and was sent over for thirteen years. Al Wild was stricken stone blind and died a miserable death a few years after. Two or three of the gang died miserable drunkard's deaths; the balance scattered and were never heard of again.

A few months after Newell had been taken to prison some friend set fire to Leighton's house in the nighttime. Nothing but a few ashes were found the next morning, in the midst of which was the crisp and blackened body of poor old Mrs. Leighton. The fiends in human shape had taken their vengeance out on this poor old lady by burning her. I worked hard and diligently to find out who did this crime, and although I was morally certain in my own mind who the perpetrators were, yet I could never establish the fact by substantial proof. Whoever it was, they will not escape. There is one Judge before whom they will have to go and answer for their crimes and from whom there is nothing concealed.[9]

CHAPTER 9

A Mountain Manhunt

IT was one of the worst mass murders of nineteenth-century California. On the night of September 9, 1869, the isolated Medina store, near Bellota in the Sierra foothills east of Stockton, was held up and robbed. The storekeeper, Frank Medina, his clerk, Frank Mastraetti, and three visitors, Rosario Rodriguez, Loretto Robla, and Henry "Old Boss" Woodson, a black teamster, were found the next morning in a nearby ditch. Their hands had been tied behind their backs, and each had been shot in the head at close range. During the holdup one of the victims had evidently recognized the robbers, who then killed them all to prevent identification.

Word of the atrocity was quickly sent to Stockton. Henry L. McCoy, the crack Marysville policeman who had captured Manuel Rojas, happened to be in town. A month before, he had been temporarily laid off from the Marysville police and had come to Stockton looking for work. He volunteered to help hunt the killers and with San Joaquin County Deputy Sheriff A. R. Allard and two local rancheros, started in pursuit.

They learned that two Californios and a California Indian youth had been observed riding toward Medina's store shortly before the murders. Their tracks left the store and went southeast several miles to a spot where Medina's empty purse had been found. The posse followed these tracks in a circuitous route thirty miles to a Hispanic settlement known as Greasertown, near Burneyville, and now part of the town of Riverbank. One of the rancheros rode in alone and learned that the three horseman were Jesus Tejada, Ysidro (Isador) Padilla, and Antonio Garcia. Tejada and Padilla were native Californians; Garcia was an Indian. Padilla, who had lived both in Stockton and Marysville, was well known to McCoy and the rancheros. Learning that the three desperadoes had stopped at the jacal of Isador Padilla's cousin, the posse surrounded it, but their quarry had fled. They returned to Stockton empty-handed.

Like other Californians, Harry Morse was shocked by the brutal crime, calling it "one of the blackest pages in the criminal annals of the Golden State." Stockton newspapers lambasted the governor for offering a paltry $500 reward and called for vigorous efforts to track down the killers. The *Stockton Daily Independent*, pointing out that lawlessness reduced immigration and development in California, declared, "In many parts of Europe, the belief prevails at this day that the people in this state are a band of outlaws and that California is a land of blood and crime." Yet the hunt for the killers was eventually abandoned. Had not the victims been cultural and political minorities (two were Italian, two were Mexican, one was black), perhaps greater efforts would have been made to avenge their deaths. Six months passed, and the crime was all but forgotten. But not by Harry Morse.[1]

I kept up a constant inquiry among my numerous Mexican friends throughout the state as to the whereabouts of Tejada and Padilla. But none of them appeared to know, or if they did they took good care to keep the information from me. I exhausted all sorts of ingenious devices in that direction, but in every instance failed until, as luck would have it, chance threw the desired intelligence in my way. It happened in the following manner.

A valuable horse had been stolen from the eastern portion of my county, and in following the trail of the thief, it took me through Calaveras Valley and on in a southerly direction through the mountains to the Santa Clara Valley, and about ten miles south of the city of San Jose where I found the stolen animal and arrested the thief. It was dark when I arrived at the pueblo and too late for me to get home that night; so, placing my prisoner in the county jail, I went to the hotel and engaged a room for the night. After supper I lighted a cigar and started out for a stroll about town. I finally wandered down toward an old Spanish restaurant, or fonda española, situated nearly opposite the old Catholic church. Looking in at the eating house, I saw a large crowd of Mexicans seated around a table, playing cards.

I dropped in just to see if any of my old friends were there. The Mexicans were so deeply interested in their game that no one noticed my entrance. I quietly took a seat, and pulling my hat well down over my eyes, puffed away at my cigar and watched the players and the game. Directly behind me, at a small side table, sat two ill-looking Mexicans, also playing cards and talking together in a low tone. I had sat there perhaps ten

minutes, observing the faces of the men about me and listening to the jab-
ber of voices, when the name of Tejada came distinctly upon my ear from
one of the two men who were sitting behind me. In an instant I was all
attention. My back was toward them, but being quite near, I could hear
every word spoken by them. One of the men was telling his companion
that he had a few days before come from the New Idria quicksilver mines
and on his way out he had stopped at the house of a fellow countryman
named Jose Maria, who lived in a canyon at the head of Los Banos Creek
in Merced County and near the San Luis Rancho.

"Did you see any of the boys there?" inquired the other.

"Oh yes. Several," was the answer.

"Who did you see?" was the next question.

"Old Patrício Mancilla was there, and Jesus Tejada was also putting
up at Jose's house. Tejada told me he was keeping out of the way of the
sheriffs, but would not tell me what reason he had for doing so."

The last speaker also said that Tejada had been hurt by being thrown
from a bucking horse. He had sprained his foot very badly and was quite
lame, and he was getting over it and would soon be quite well again. His
foot was swollen so badly that he was obliged to cut his boot from the ankle
to the toes to enable him to wear it.

Not a single word spoken by these men escaped me. Many things were
talked about by them that were of importance to me thereafter. From further conversation between them, I learned that Tejada intended to stay at
Jose Maria's a month or more, and then leave the country forever, going
to Mexico. Presently a number of newcomers entered the fonda, and
looking around, some of them recognized me.

"Halloa, Morse!" cried one. "Come and take a drink with us, old fellow."

I arose and took a fresh cigar and then glanced toward the two men
whose conversation I had heard. Upon hearing my name called the attention of the whole crowd was attracted toward me, particularly that of
the two Mexicans who had sat behind me, as I was a well known character among them. They looked intently at my face, trying, doubtless, to
discover whether I had been listening to their conversation. I glanced
carelessly back at them but gave no outward sign that I had heard a single word they had spoken. After chatting a few moments, I bade them a
pleasant good night, and stepping out into the street, proceeded directly to
my hotel.

Entering my room, I took out a memorandum book and noted down
all that I had heard, being particular as to names and places. During my
official life I made it a rule to always jot down the current events of the

day and especially to make a note of things that I thought might at some future time be of use to me. Not daring to trust to memory alone in the civil duties of my office, I became habituated to noting down all circumstances of a criminal nature that took place under my own observation. This habit is a valuable one to an officer, for he is often called upon the witness stand in both civil and criminal cases, sometimes after a lapse of months and perhaps years, and unless he can refresh his memory he is likely to prove a very uncertain witness. Some lawyers will take advantage of his forgetfulness and upon a rigid cross-examination will endeavor to make it appear to the court and jury that the witness does not know what he is testifying about. Eventually the witness leaves the stand in confusion and angry with himself because he has forgotten more than half he originally knew, and is not exactly certain as to what he does remember about it.

On the morning following the events just described I took my prisoner to San Leandro and locked him up to await the result of the preliminary examination. After placing my man in the county jail I returned to my private office to arrange a plan for the capture of Tejada. The rendezvous of the gang, as before stated, was at the head of Los Banos Canyon, and about twelve miles south of the Pacheco Pass stage road where that highway enters the pass from the San Joaquin side of the inner Coast Range.

The Jose Maria, heretofore mentioned by me, was well known as a notorious desperado. It was a current report that he had brutally murdered his mistress in one of the northern counties. Whether this was true or not, it was known that he had hurriedly left that part of the state and settled in this rugged canyon and had drawn about him a crowd of as desperate cutthroats as could be found in any place. He was known far and wide as a tapadera, one who hides stolen property and shields thieves from pursuit—in other words, what is known as a "fence."

Jose Maria was very accommodating. When thieves stole cattle or horses and brought them to him he would secrete both until the hunt after them was over and then sell the stolen property, divide with the thieves, and then fit them out for another raid after plunder. Now, until I got to paying Señor Jose Maria frequent visits, he had a great big bonanza in this business. He did not relish my calls. They interfered with his plans. I called too often to suit him and he was anything but joyous upon my arrival in his camp. After vainly trying to bluff me, he finally gave it up in despair and moved away to Mexico, where I believe he now is.

The headquarters of this gang were about 140 miles from San Leandro, a good four days' trip. My first care was to procure an accurate description of Tejada. I wrote to parties in Stockton whom I supposed knew him well and in a few days received an answer with a description of him which was so totally at variance with the man that it was partially the cause of my having to make a second trip after him, beside useless expense. My description stated that he was five feet ten, pock marked, and forty years of age. He was neither, for when I found him he was six feet tall, twenty-eight years old, and not pock marked in the least.

Obtaining an old emigrant's wagon that had been used about town for years, I fitted it up for the trip, with blankets, and provisions. Calling to my assistance Lew Morehouse and my son [George], a mere lad of thirteen years, we left the little slumbering town at dawn of day. I being so well known throughout the country, I thought a disguise necessary and when I left home, so completely metamorphosed was I that my most intimate friend would not have known me.

Taking the old San Jose road as far as Castro Valley, we turned to the left, and crossing the little valley, were soon in the Hayward Pass leading to Livermore. Passing Livermore Valley, we emerged out of Corral Hollow canyon onto the great San Joaquin plain. Taking an easterly direction, we made direct for Graysonville, a small village on the banks of the San Joaquin River. Here we camped for the night. Being tired by our long day's journey, we rolled ourselves up in our blankets and were soon sound asleep. At daylight we were on the road again, long before the sleepy inhabitants of Graysonville were awake. A long, tedious, dusty, all day drive brought us to the old San Luis Rancho, arriving there at about seven o'clock in the evening. We were now only twelve miles from the rendezvous of Jose Maria's gang and it stood us in hand to use all due caution, as the slightest mistake on our part would spoil the whole business. We rested well that night and as it was not a very long drive to Jose's house, we did not start out til eight o'clock next morning.

We made direct for the mouth of the canyon leading to the robber camp. Driving slowly up the canyon, we passed many little huts occupied by members of the gang. Now and then a black, ugly-looking head would be thrust out of the doors and gaze intently at us for a moment and then be withdrawn, probably being satisfied that no sheriff's officer would be wandering in that part of the country, with evil intent toward them, in such an outlandish rig. We paid but little attention to them, but kept steadily on up the canyon, keeping a sharp lookout, however, for an old corral and a stone hut, situated just below the house of Jose Maria.

Passing along about half a mile, we came to the corral, and just beyond it, the stone hut. We drove on as though we were going to pass on up the canyon, and then suddenly halted. We were now just in front of Jose

Patrício Mancilla as he
appeared at the time
Sheriff Morse encountered
him. Courtesy of the San
Jose Historical Museum.

*Maria's house and where we expected to find Tejada. We were ready for
action and our nerves were strung up to the very utmost. Getting out of
the wagon, I walked up toward the house to reconnoitre the premises. I
found but one man there—old Patrício Mancilla—whom I knew to have
been a convict in the state prison. I spoke to him, asking for a drink of
water.*

*"Sí, señor," he replied to my request, and taking a tin cup from an old
table, he went to the bucket and brought me a drink of cool spring water.*

*Patrício did not recognize me, but I did him and knew that he was
wanted in Santa Clara County for a larceny committed there by him a
year or more before. But being on more important business, I did not think
it policy to molest him just then, as it would spoil the object that brought
me to the hut. I drew out some paper and tobacco and commenced to roll
up a cigarette, and at the same time tendered some to Patrício. He took it
and we both sat down and commenced to smoke and chat. I told him that
I was a sheep raiser and was looking for a suitable range for my stock, and
then invited him out to the wagon to get a drink of whiskey, hoping thereby
to get the old fellow's tongue loosened and thus get what information I
wanted out of him. I got two or three good nips into Mancilla and then told
him I thought I would camp there the night and would drive a little further up the creek, unhitch and get supper, at the same time inviting him to
visit us and join in a social chat and drink.*[2]

He replied, "All right," and pointed out a nice camping place near a spring of pure, cool water. We soon had our camp fixed up, and shortly after old Patrício came strolling toward us. I invited him to a seat, and again I tendered him some spirits. He took to it kindly and soon he began to talk more freely—inquired who we were and where we came from. I repeated the sheep raising story and added that I had a flock of 2,000 sheep near Antioch, Contra Costa County; feed was short there and I was looking out for a new range.

I expected that when the liquor got to work in the old villain's head that I could draw from him the information I desired, but a Mexican horse thief is mighty uncertain, as well as cunning. The old chap would talk about everything except what I wanted to talk about. Whenever I commenced to make inquiry as to who was living in the vicinity, the old ex-convict would turn the conversation in another direction. The drunker he got the more close-mouthed and cunning he became.

"Yes," he said in answer to a question, "there are plenty of people living in the mountains here—some Americans, but mostly Mexicans."

I wanted to draw him out as to names, so I said, "You have a rather singular name for a Mexican. Perhaps you are of Irish decent?"

The old chap burst out into a hearty laugh and said, "No, I am not the son of an Irishman. But why do you ask such a question?"

"You have an Irish name. Patrício, or Patrick, is Irish, ain't it?"

"No doubt it is," he answered.

"You have many curious names among your countrymen," I continued. "At least they seem so to us Americans. For instance, there are a great many named Jesus. I don't know of a single American by that name."

The old chap shut up like a clam as soon as I mentioned the name, and did not seem inclined to talk any more about his people. Finding I could get nothing from him, I concluded to let him go and take chances on events that might occur. Giving Patrício a parting drink, I told him we would sleep a few hours and that I would see him again before I left camp. I bade the old chap good afternoon, and he went back to Jose Maria's cabin. I was very much chagrined at my ignominious failure to get any information from Patrício, but the old fellow was too well trained.

We spread our blankets and were just preparing to lie down and rest when I heard the jingling of Mexican spurs, and glancing up, saw riding toward us a big, burly-looking Mexican. On his side was strapped the usual eight-inch Colt six-shooter and he kept prodding the mustang he was riding in the flank with the great Spanish spurs he had fastened to his heels. Riding straight toward us, he cast a suspicious glance at our little party, but a polite, "Buenos dias, señor," from me, and an invitation to alight and accept of our hospitality, in the shape of a swig at the bottle, brought to his repulsive features what was intended for a gracious smile, but it was a ghastly attempt, to say the least. Dismounting, he tied his mustang to a tree, came into our midst, and squatting near our campfire, took the proffered drink, and then rolling up a cigarito, lit it and sat some time without saying a word.

Suddenly he looked up and said, "What are you doing here?"

I repeated the sheep story to him, but he only frowned and did not seem to like the idea at all.

"I don't like sheep to come into these mountains," he said. "They spoil the feed for our horses. Besides, the ranges here are all taken up."

"Well," said I, "if that is the case, we will have to look somewhere else. But I was told sheep range was plentiful here, with no one to occupy it, and that is what brought us into these mountains."

"The range is all taken, I tell you," he replied, and he frowned at us again, while his hand wandered, seemingly unconsciously, back to the handle of his pistol, as though he would like to drive us out at once. The closest observer would never have noticed what was passing in my mind, but my feelings were not of the most cheerful nature while he was toying with the handle of his six-shooter. If he had attempted to draw his weapon, I should most certainly have gotten the first shot in on him, for I was prepared for any such emergency. Finally, I smoothed matters over and got another drink into him, and then commenced to talk about "la tierra mia," as he called it—Mexico. It seemed to please him. In a short time he got into a good humor and became quite communicative. He told us where we could find a good sheep range and ended up by inviting us, as he mounted his horse and left, to visit his camp and spend a few hours.

Our camping place was situated in a deep gorge in the mountains, the sides rising almost perpendicularly for hundreds of feet, with trails winding up and along their steep sides almost as far as the eye could reach, and were lost to view as they spread out in different directions among the lofty picachos. A dense growth of underbrush lined the mountains and canyons, with now and then a patch of oak and manzanita trees growing on the ragged and rocky points that projected out from from their steep and jagged sides. Immediately below us in the canyon, and from between two large granite rocks, ran a small stream of clear and sparkling water, pure and cool almost as ice itself.

It was a pretty site for a camp, and none could have been better selected for a robber's camp. Like the padres of old, these fellows seemed to have the knack of selecting the very best and prettiest places for their use and occupation. About twenty feet above us ran the main trail. It was well beaten and apparently led to the top of the highest peaks of the great mountains above us.

The trail was plainly visible from where we were for a mile or more, as it took its tortuous course up and around the steep cliffs and rocks, and over the little plateau and benches, and a man on horseback could be readily distinguished a mile away as he would have to make the turns in the trail as he rode over it. We waited patiently several hours, hoping that the rest of the gang would arrive in camp, and among them, Tejada. The sun commenced to throw its shadow on the eastern sides of the canyon and was fast sinking away into the western horizon. Night was approaching, and as no one came we concluded to hitch up and drive out of the camp and return in the morning, as we did not care to stay all night in such close proximity to a nest of cutthroats such as we knew infested this canyon. Our own lives might be in jeopardy, or at least the chance was great for us to lose our horses. My idea was to wait til near dark and then if the rest of the gang did not return, to drive down to the valley and camp in a secure and safe place and come back at early dawn and catch my man napping.

We had just come to the conclusion that it was time to vacate when, casting my eye toward the trail, I saw a man on horseback, followed by four others, making his way slowly down and around the various turns toward our camp. They were Mexicans, I knew, from the peculiar graceful motion of their bodies, made so from long practice on horseback. Morehouse and I gazed at them for a moment in silence and then turned and looked at each other. Here was the gang, sure enough, and rather more of them than we expected. Two already at the house and five coming down the trail, against Lew and I, not counting the boy, were great odds. However, we concluded to await events and see if something would turn in our favor, of which we could take advantage.

Down the trail they came, one behind the other. The musical jingle of their spurs could be distinctly heard as they came nearer and nearer. The last turn in the trail took them down into the bed of the creek just above us, and for a moment they were lost to our vision. Presently the leading man's head came into sight and in a second more the horse as well as the rider was in full view. He was a man about twenty-six years of age, tall and erect in his saddle, large piercing black eyes that seemed to cut through one like a knife. His nose was of the extreme Roman order, a regular hook, complexion a deep olive brown, the red on the cheek showing clearly through the transparent skin. In height he seemed fully six feet. He wore dark clothing and his sombrero was a black one, stiff-brimmed,

The notorious Jesus Tejada, captured by Sheriff Morse in 1870. From the collection of the San Luis Obispo County Historical Society and Museum.

and sat well back on his head, held on by a silken ribbon which was fastened at the sides and came down under his chin. He was armed with one of Colt's largest six-shooters. From the top of his boot leg there protruded the white ivory handle of a large knife. I took him all in at a glance, and as my eyes wandered still further down toward his feet I saw that his boot was slit from the ankle to the toe.

This man was Tejada to a certainty. My heart beat just a little faster as I recognized him from the description of the cut boot unconsciously given me by the two Mexicans at the Spanish fonda in San Jose. Tejada's face had a devil-may-care sort of look. He did not in the least, however, answer the description given me by the San Joaquin authorities, and this created a doubt in my mind and left me undecided just how to act.

My first idea was to cover him with my rifle and compel him to dismount and surrender himself. Then again it occurred to me that, as I was not certain it was Tejada, a mistake would spoil all. Besides, it was taking great and unnecessary risk, as no doubt the gang following so closely behind him would rally to his support and get him away from us, if not clean us out altogether. Thinking discretion the better part of valor, I changed my mind instantly and concluded to await further events. Tejada's horse was a fine-spirited specimen of the native mustang, and after glancing at us, Tejada rode quietly toward the hut where Mancilla was. Following close behind came Jose Maria himself, and after him the other three Mexicans. Taken together, they were as tough a looking crowd as one would wish to meet of a dark night and on a lonely road.

They all five dismounted at Jose Maria's hut and took the saddles from their horses, except Tejada. He appeared uneasy and as though he wanted to be off again. After they had all passed, Lew and I held a hurried consultation as to what was to be done. It was decided to hitch up the team, ready to start. My son was to occupy the front seat and drive down toward the house. Lew was to sit beside the boy, and when the horses were stopped opposite the door of Jose Maria's hut, he was to alight on the side away from the hut and appear to be fixing about the harness, but in reality to draw his pistol and be in readiness for immediate action. I was to sit in the tail end of the wagon with my Winchester rifle within easy reach and when the wagon stopped, if I saw a good opportunity, I was to cover Tejada with the rifle and compel him to hold up his hands, and then Lew was to step quickly to the front and handcuff him.

I told my boy the danger there was in the undertaking and asked him if he understood it. He replied that he did and was ready and willing to take the chances. I then directed him, in case it came to a fight and Lew and I were hurt or disabled in any way, to put the whip to the horses, drive them on a dead run down the canyon, and go to the San Luis Rancho for assistance. All this he agreed to do, and did not seem to have any fear as to the final result.

Being ready, Lew mounted to the seat beside the boy and I took my position in the end of the wagon, and we started for the house. My disguise was complete, for notwithstanding the fact that I was well—but not favorably—known to Jose Maria, he had so far failed to recognize me. I wore an old pair of ragged pants, a gray woolen shirt, and a great broad-brimmed hat that flopped about my ears like a dilapidated umbrella in a rainstorm. A pair of dark green goggles covered my eyes and the lower part of my face was covered by a long, shaggy beard. The disguise was necessary so that in case Tejada was not in camp it would not be known that I had been there, but they would imagine that we were what we represented ourselves to be— sheep-raisers in search of range.

We drove slowly down toward the house. My nerves, and no doubt Lew's and the boy's, were strung up to the highest pitch, not knowing what the final result might be. The wagon came to a halt directly in front of the thieves' den. The man I took for Tejada was standing beside his horse, bridle in hand, and as I looked sharply at him he attempted to put the bridle rein over the horse's neck, but in his anxiety he failed. His keen yet uneasy look was upon us all the time. He made a second attempt and again failed to get the rein over the horse's head. After the second failure he suddenly sat down upon the limb of an old tree just behind him. He was evidently very anxious to be on his horse and away.

I looked at him and hesitated. "He who hesitates is lost," they say, but in this particular case my hesitation saved us, for from what I afterward learned I am quite certain that had we attempted to arrest Tejada at that time we would never have gotten away alive. A bloody fight would have taken place, and they, outnumbering us four to one, must of necessity have had the best of it.

I took the situation in at a glance and made up my mind instantly what to do. Not much could possibly be lost by a little delay, while the chances were that all would be lost with too hasty action—perhaps our lives. I coolly slid down from the end of the wagon, and walking on by Tejada, went to the hut and asked for a drink of water, then turned back toward the Mexicans, talked a few moments with them, and bidding them "adios," jumped onto the wagon seat with Lew and the boy and told them to drive away.

I was much chagrined at my want of success— even felt as though I had acted cowardly about it. Still, there was a doubt about the man with the cut boot being Tejada, as the description given me of him was so different, and I at least felt reconciled for not attempting the arrest by giving the man the benefit of the doubt. As we drove away I explained my reasons to Lew for not attempting the arrest at that time. He coincided with me as to the great danger of the arrest and also as to there being a doubt on account of the variance in the description of the man.

With all our attempts to excuse ourselves, we did not feel exactly satisfied in our own minds as to our conduct in the matter. We imagined we had let a bird go, and might never succeed in catching it again. We were mortified and disgusted with ourselves, but we could not remedy it just then. All we could do now was to plan a new campaign against the enemy. We made our way home again, quite crestfallen but not discouraged

We camped that night at San Luis Rancho and at early dawn were on the homeward road, drove fifty miles, and camped in the brush on the banks of the San Joaquin. On the following night we reached San Leandro. I immediately wrote a letter to the Stockton authorities, telling them of their probable mistake in their description of Tejada, and sent them an accurate description of the man we had seen at Jose Maria's. Two days later an answer came, expressing regret at their unintentional blunder and adding that the man I described was the man Tejada, one of the Medina murderers.

I was now more than ever fully determined to capture the murderer, and to have no more mistake about it, I employed a Mexican who knew Tejada well to go to the camp and identify him positively and telegraph me from the stage station on the old Pacheco Pass road. My employee was a Mexican named Luis, of more than unusual intelligence. He had been in the employ of the government as mule-packer, spoke English well, and had served under General Crook during the [Paiute] Indian war in which that general operated. Luis had a grudge against Tejada and thus willingly undertook the hazardous job. Tejada had shot and badly wounded an uncle of his some years previous and this was his opportunity to be revenged upon him.

Luis, mounted on a good, stout mustang, his blanket strapped behind his saddle, and well armed, left for the robbers' camp the next morning after I had engaged him. I fixed up a telegram for him to send me in case Tejada was at the camp. I directed Luis to go by way of San Jose to Gilroy, and from there by way of the Quien Sabe Rancho over the inner Coast Range, striking the Los Banos high up so as to be apparently coming from the south when he struck Jose Maria's camp, and thus completely lull any suspicion. Bidding Luis good-by, and God-speed, he rode away and I quietly went about my usual official duties and anxiously awaited events. In about six days my telegram came to me, as follows: "The cattle are here. Come immediately. Luis."

My arrangements for an immediate start were perfected that day Luis left, so all I had to do was to start. Calling Lew to my assistance again, changing our clothes for others more suitable for such a trip, and hitching up my team of snug-built native horses onto a light spring buggy, we started.

It was 9 A.M. when we drove out of the little village of San Leandro. Crossing Livermore Valley, we struck Corral Hollow at 3 P.M. Passing down the canyon about six miles, we left the road and struck into the mountains with only a cattle trail to follow. We came out of the mountains onto the San Joaquin Valley at Arroyo del Puerto [Del Puerto Canyon, in Stanislaus County], and made directly for the river, arriving at the banks of that stream at 11 P.M., pretty tired. We had driven eighty-five miles since nine o'clock that morning.

Picketing out our horses, we wrapped ourselves in our blankets and lay down upon the sandy shore of the river and slept soundly til just as day was peeping. After coffee we were on the road again in the direction of the old San Luis Rancho, where we expected to meet Luis, our spy. We sighted the ranch buildings at noon and at 2 P.M. we drove up to the stable. Luis was there and we put up the team, got dinner, and then went into a room at the rancho house, taking Luis with us for consultation.

Luis stated that he had arrived at the robbers' camp on the sixth day after leaving us in San Leandro. He had stopped at their camp the night of his arrival. Tejada and six other Mexicans were in the camp. Tejada and three others slept under a large oak tree that grew near Jose Maria's hut. The latter, together with his woman, occupied the hut, while old Patrício Mancilla slept on the main trail, about fifty yards below where the others were sleeping, and acted as sort of sentinel to notify his companions in case any strange persons were to make their appearance suddenly in the night. A person going up the canyon in the dark would of necessity run right on top of old Patrício, and thus enable him to give the alarm to the others, and a chance for them to make their escape.

"The only way for you to get on to the gang," said Luis, "is for you to get quietly up to the old corral and then run past the old fellow before he is fairly awake."

Luis also stated that our first visit had alarmed Tejada, but our going away had quieted him and that he was now not at all suspicious.

It was arranged that we should retire early and get as much rest as possible, get up at one o'clock in the morning, have Luis drive us to the mouth of the canyon and leave us there. He was to return to the ranch, while we made our way up to Jose Maria's camp and attempt the arrest, doing as best we could under the circumstances. At one in the morning we were up and ready to start. It was a cold, dreary, and blustering morning. The wind swept down through the mountain pass, a perfect hurricane. The strong gust of wind tore through the telegraph wires that were strung along in front of the rancho and gave out sweet musical sounds, as of an aeolian harp.

"Whew," said Luis. "How the winds do blow."

We drove silently toward the canyon. Each one of us seemed to be lost in thought, the others thinking, no doubt (as I certainly was) about how the thing would end, and not knowing but that in a few hours one of us might not be in the land of the living.

As we drew near the place where Luis was to leave us, the late moon commenced to rise over the top of the eastern hills, throwing its silvery rays, making dark shadows across the little valleys, and making the surrounding country more discernible. Luis drew up at a bunch of willows near the canyon and we got ready to start on foot to our objective point. We bade Luis return to the rancho and to expect us there by noon, and if not, to summon assistance and come to our relief.

"God speed you, boys, and take good care of yourselves," said Luis as he drove away.

"Was that a cock crowing, Lew?" I said, as the strong shrill sound was borne toward us in the wind.

"Yes," he replied, "and we must be careful or the greasers' infernal dogs will alarm the camp as we go up. These fellows, although poor themselves, manage to keep a dog or two at each hut."

"You are right," I answered, "but we will circumvent them. We'll climb the mountain and pass along far above the huts, and come down to the camp through one of the little ravines running at right angles to the main canyon."

Up the steep mountain we started. A half hour's hard tugging brought us to the ridge. Turning to the left, we walked cautiously along for about two miles and until we got, as best I could judge, opposite the corral near Jose Maria's hut. The late moon was a grand thing for us; it enabled us to distinguish objects quite clearly.

We commenced to crawl carefully down the little ravine toward the corral. On each side of us was a dense growth of buckeye bushes and other trees. At each step the dry twigs and leaves would snap and crack under the pressure of our feet and make us almost hold our breath for fear that we would alarm the bandits so quietly slumbering below us. Now and then a flock of quail, frightened at our approach, would suddenly buzz from out of the brush, and as their swift wings beat the morning air it seemed to our excited minds as though a whole park of artillery had been set off. The sound seemed to echo and re-echo through the deep gorges. At every such flight we would stop and listen in breathless suspense for a moment, and hearing no further sound, we would move along again.

At last we reached the end of the ravine and emerged into the main canyon. Looking about, we discovered the old corral about fifty yards above us. Crawling on our hands and knees, we were soon alongside of it. Here for a few moments we rested and fixed between ourselves our plan *of attack. We were within a few hundred yards of the whole gang, and they were sound asleep, not suspecting for a moment that an enemy was so close upon them.*

Our first visit had made us familiar with the lay of the camp and we had no difficulty in locating things. From what Luis had told us, we knew that old Patrício was lying on the trail between us and the hut, and it was necessary to capture him before he could send the alarm to those who occupied it. Our plan was to run quickly by him and surprise the others in their sleep. I was to hold the gang under cover of my Winchester while Lew handcuffed Tejada. Then he was to march down the canyon with the prisoner while I covered the retreat.

All being in readiness, we sat and rested and waited for daylight to come. Soon the cocks commenced to crow, announcing the approach of day. As the time for action came a strange feeling of dread came over me, but I quickly shook it off and prepared for the forward movement. The faint streaks of day commenced to flash in the eastern sky, getting brighter and brighter each moment. In half an hour it was light enough to make all things visible. Peeping around the corral, we saw old Patrício rolled up in his blanket and fast asleep, snugly esconced in an edge of a buckeye bush that grew near the trail.

All being ready, we each stripped off the heavy overcoats we were wearing and laid them down beside the corral. Throwing a cartridge into my gun, we stepped from beside the corral into the trail and made directly for old Patrício. In a second we were beside him. He awoke with a start, sat up, rubbed his eyes, and looked at us. That is, he looked into the muzzle of a six-shooter. I stooped down and whispered into his ear that if he made the least noise we would blow the top of his head off, and told him that as long as he kept perfectly still he was safe, but the least alarm made by him to the others would be the signal for his death.

All he said was, "Bueno, señor," and fell back into his blankets again and covered up his head. We had captured the outpost, and now for the main army.

"Now for the house, Lew," I said. "Run, boy, run!"

And we did run, too. In a second more we were in the midst of the camp and got a cross-fire drop on them before they knew we were there. A quick, stern command from me for them to hold up their hands had a most magical effect, and brought every one of them into a sitting position, with each of them holding his hands high above his head. I told Tejada to get up and come to us. He seemed rather slow to obey, but a sharp, "Pronto! Pronto, Señor!" and at the same time pointing the rifle directly at his head, had the desired effect, and we soon had him handcuffed and on his way down the canyon. As Lew withdrew with the prisoner, I walked slowly backward until I got out of pistol range. Old Patrício still lay rolled up in his blankets as we went by him on our way out.

We recovered our coats at the corral and then, at a rapid gait, hurried on down the canyon with Tejada. In half an hour we were well clear of all danger and out of the canyon. We kept along the edge of the aliso that grew along the edge of the creek until we got to the main road and then struck out for the San Luis Rancho, where we had sent Luis with the wagon that morning. A walk of nine miles brought us to the ranch, where we found Luis anxiously awaiting us. There was quite a commotion among the rancheros when it became known who our prisoner was, and the crime he had committed, and a general curiosity to get a sight of him.

We left with our prisoner for home at eleven o'clock and camped on the banks of the San Joaquin that night. We camped on a sandy bar and prepared our supper. Lew stood watch till one o'clock and I relieved him and watched till daylight. I put a pair of heavy irons on Tejada to make him more secure and it was evident he did not like it from the frightful scowl that came over his face as I did so. We had collected quite a pile of driftwood for our campfire during the night, and as Tejada and I lay down to sleep he took occasion to reach out for and place beside him a large piece—evidently with intent to use it upon me, or both of us, in case he should catch us off our guard. I quietly removed it out of his reach, and handcuffing his right wrist to my left one, we both cuddled down to sleep.

At one o'clock Lew called me. I then took his place while he took mine, handcuff and all. The heavy leg irons would clank and ring as Tejada changed his position repeatedly during the night. This was about the only thing that broke the monotony of the long, silent, and dreary night watch. At daybreak we were on the road again and a drive of twenty miles brought us to Banta [near Tracy], a station on the line of the Central Pacific Railroad. There I took a train home with the prisoner and Lew drove the team. I then took Tejada to Stockton and delivered him to the authorities of San Joaquin County.[3]

As I have stated before, I knew that old Patrício Mancilla was a fugitive from justice, he having committed a burglary in Santa Clara County, for which a warrant had been issued for his arrest. About a week after the time that I had landed Tejada safely in jail, Nick R. Harris, who at the time was sheriff of Santa Clara County, and I concluded that we would make a flying trip after old Patrício.[4]

Harris and I, according to agreement, met at San Jose, took the train to Gilroy, and there hired a team and started for the San Luis Rancho again, distant from Gilroy thirty-seven miles. We arrived at the rancho at dusk the same day and put up for the night, as it was too late to operate that night. At three o'clock the next morning we were off for the camp, calculating to get there at daylight. We drove directly to the canyon where the hut was situated. It was full daylight when we arrived at Jose Maria's. As we drove up five men left the cabin and walked up the canyon and were lost sight of in the thick wood that grew on the banks of the ravine.

Stopping in front of the cabin door, I jumped out, and directing Harris to keep a sharp lookout on the outside, I entered to search the house, as Patricio was not one of the five who had left but a moment before. I went quickly into the hut but no sign of old Patricio could I find. Two Mexican women were there but nothing else human could I see. I searched the hut as I thought pretty thoroughly, but seemingly the man was not there. After searching a while I reported to Sheriff Harris my ill luck.

"Wait a few minutes, Nick," I said, "till I go and interview the chaps up the canyon, and at the same time you watch the surroundings of the cabin."

Walking up the canyon, I soon came upon the men who had previously left the cabin.

"Buenas dias, señores," I said to them. They answered my salutation politely.

"Do you know a man named Angel Castro?" I asked.

This was was only a pretense. None of them seemed to know such a man. I pretended to be certain that he was either with them or at the house. They contended that no such man was at either place.

"Yes, he is here," I said, "and you are trying to conceal him."

"No, señor, we are not."

"Are you sure," I asked, "that no one but yourselves are here—no other man?"

"No one but Patricio," they answered.

"Where is he? Let me see him," I said.

"He is at the house, or was a few moments ago, when we left him there."

I was now convinced that the old chap was hiding near by. Returning to where Harris was awaiting me, I told him that Pat was certainly close by and for him to tie the horses and assist me in the search. We entered the cabin and commenced the search anew. Looking under one of the bunks, I saw what appeared to be a mass of old rubbish—old bags, boots, and broken saddles. I reached under to move some of the things and the first thing I grasped was what seemed an old boot. I found that it contained a

*foot. Taking a firm hold, I gave it a stout pull. As I did so a smothered
sound of a voice called out, "Que quiere usted?"* [What do you want?]
   "I want you, Pat," I answered. "So come out—quickly, too!"
   *"Bueno," he responded, and he crawled out from among the rubbish
under the bed. Nick and I had a good laugh at his expense, he looked so
crestfallen. He looked at me in surprise for a moment and then exclaimed,
"Que, borreguero!"* [What, a sheepman!]
   *"I see you remember me, Patrício," I replied. "Have you found the
sheep range for me?"*
   *"El Diablo Morse," said the old chap, and added, "Always on hand
when least expected!"*
   *"Come, Mancilla, hurry up. Sheriff Harris wants to take you to San
Jose with him and we have no time to lose."*
   *We were soon homeward bound, reached Gilroy in time for the evening
train of that day, and had old Patrício safely incarcerated that same
evening at San Jose.*[5]

Sheriff Morse's capture of Jesus Tejada seemed to galvanize other
lawmen. Henry McCoy captured Isador Padilla in Marysville, and
Antonio Garcia was also picked up. Tejada, Padilla, and Garcia were
all indicted for murder. The court appointed David S. Terry, the famous dueling judge, to serve as attorney for Padilla and Tejada.
Isador Padilla was tried first, convicted of murder, and sentenced to
hang. A few weeks later, in June 1871, Tejada was also convicted and
sentenced to death. Terry appealed both cases to the California
Supreme Court, and in January 1872 Padilla's conviction was over-
turned because of a prejudicial jury instruction. The supreme court
also granted Tejada a new trial, but on April 10, 1872, he died of
syphilis in his Stockton jail cell. Padilla's retrial took place a month
later. As Morse explained, "During the long delay important witnesses moved away and could not be found. On the new trial he was
not convicted and thus escaped his just and merited punishment.[6]
   Isador Padilla and Antonio Garcia were freed from jail. Padilla's
narrow brush with the noose had no redeeming effect on him, for he
later joined the Tiburcio Vasquez gang. He next formed his own outlaw band, which included Harry Morse's old foe, Joaquin Olivera, as
well as such noted cutthroats as Ramon Ruiz and Antonio "Red Antone" Valacca. This band robbed stagecoaches and Chinese mining
camps until it was broken up in December 1875 by posses led by
Sheriff Tom Cunningham of San Joaquin County and Sheriff Ben K.

Thorn of Calaveras. Isador Padilla was sentenced to twenty years and died in San Quentin in 1877.[7]

Harry Morse had no legal obligation to search for the Medina killers. The crime, as well as the manhunt, took place far from his jurisdiction. But he could not sit idly by and allow the perpetrators of such butchery to escape justice. In that era many California sheriffs were reluctant to pursue criminals beyond their own counties. They were responsible for paying the costs of such manhunts themselves, with the hope that they might later be reimbursed by their county's board of supervisors. Thus Sheriff Morse paid all the expenses of the Tejada hunt from his own pocket. The governor had no authority to do anything in such cases except offer the usual state reward of $500. California had no state police, and Harry Morse, with increasing frequency, filled that void.

CHAPTER 10

A Duel to the Death: Juan Soto

AS the heavy iron door closed behind him, Tiburcio Vasquez stepped out of the Old Stone Cellblock. Exchanging his woolen stripes for civilian clothes, he walked out of San Quentin's front gate into the morning sunshine. It was June 4, 1870, a week after Harry Morse captured Jesus Tejada. Vasquez beat his way south to his old haunts in Santa Clara and Monterey counties. A few months later, on August 27, Juan Soto also completed his prison term and was released. The two compadres soon met up, and before long they were joined by Juan Soto's lifelong amigo, Bartolo Sepulveda.

Sepulveda, unlike Vasquez and Soto, had made an effort to settle down and live a responsible life. He had married Maria de los Angeles Alviso, the youngest daughter of the prominent ranchero Jose Maria Alviso, owner of Rancho Milpitas. The hacienda's main house was a two-story adobe, still standing, located on Piedmont Road near the corner of Calaveras Road. Now within the city limits of Milpitas, at that time it was about two miles east of town. Bartolo and his wife were given thirty-five acres of the rancho to farm. They lived in one of the four adobes on the rancho and raised five children.

By the late 1860s many Californios had been swindled out of their land. Others, because of ignorance of the American legal system, went into debt and lost their ranchos through legal judgments or foreclosure. Some Californios, however, through hard work, cautious business dealings, and good legal advice, managed to preserve their holdings as well as their social status. Among them were the Alvisos, as well as the Sunol, Bernal, Estudillo, and Peralta families of Alameda County. In 1871 the U.S. government confirmed almost five thousand acres of Rancho Milpitas to the heirs of Jose Maria Alviso. But the Alvisos' good fortune did not follow their errant son-in-law.[1]

Bartolo Sepulveda seems to have had mixed feelings about Anglos. When he was ten the forty-niners had descended on his pastoral

homeland in droves. He had seen his people reduced from the dominant social, political, and cultural force to an alien presence in their
own land. Yet Sepulveda was of genial disposition, and unlike Juan
Soto he was not filled with rage and hatred. Bartolo had many
friends in the Santa Clara Valley, and he socialized with Anglos and
Californios alike. However, he had a fondness for drinking and gambling that evidently did not sit well with his wife. When he was arrested
several times for cattle theft and jailed in San Jose, it was apparently
more than she or her proper family could take. About 1869 he and
his wife separated, and he began to wander. Bartolo drifted down to
Mexico, worked as a vaquero in Sonora, and returned to the Santa
Clara Valley in July 1870. He lived with friends and spent his spare
time playing billiards in the Auzerais House, a popular hotel in San
Jose. Bartolo took up with Juan Soto soon after the latter's release
from San Quentin, and Soto introduced him to Tiburcio Vasquez.[2]

In November 1870 Bartolo was jailed in San Jose on two charges
of cattle theft. His trial began on November 28, but a jury found
him not guilty. Two weeks later he and Juan Soto left the Santa
Clara Valley and rode across the Coast Range. They found work on
a hog ranch on the San Joaquin River near Modesto. Although both
of them were suspected of livestock theft and robbery, there were no
charges pending against them and neither was a fugitive at that time.[3]

Their movements are in stark conflict with the myth fostered by
Joseph Henry Jackson. In his popular book, *Bad Company,* Jackson
claimed that Juan Soto led an organized gang and that "Soto and his
men managed to stay hidden in the hills, making quick sorties to kill
and burn and rob, retreating to the dark canyons and the rough and
broken hills of the Coast Range." The belief that western bandit
gangs lived together in wilderness encampments and emerged only to
rob and kill is a common misconception. Like Vasquez, Procopio, and
other bandit chieftains, Soto worked as a vaquero and had no organized band. When moved by whim or financial need he would gather
a few men, make a raid, and then return to his honest vocation.[4]

On January 8 Sepulveda and Soto left the hog ranch and headed
home through the mountains, following the Arroyo Mocho into the
Livermore Valley. From here they turned south, passing the Foscalina
store in Sunol Valley in the early afternoon. The two riders continued to Mission San Jose, stopping at a store where they talked with
one Antonio, a friend of Soto's. Then they continued south several
miles to Agua Caliente (now called Warm Springs), where they dis-

mounted to take a drink at a saloon. Here they met Javier Higuera, a cousin of Bartolo's. They rode south to Milpitas, where Sepulveda stopped at a saloon and met Alexander Anderson, a respectable farmer. Anderson, who had known Sepulveda for many years, paid for the drinks and urged Bartolo to see his wife and reconcile with her. Sepulveda replied that "she could get along better without him than with him." Then he and Soto mounted up and left Milpitas without stopping at the Alviso adobe, where Bartolo's wife was living with their children.[5]

Since both Soto and Sepulveda had been born and raised near Rancho Milpitas and were well known in the area, few paid much attention to them as they passed through. The pair continued toward San Jose, arriving at five o'clock in the afternoon. The next day, January 10, 1871, Juan Soto and two compañeros rode from San Jose to the old Foscalina store in Sunol Valley, setting off an extraordinary series of events that would launch both the boldest exploit and the darkest deed of Harry Morse's life.

In the late 1860s George Foscalina had sold his store and trading post in Sunol Valley to Thomas Scott, a prominent local politician. Ever after the place was known as Scott's Store or Scott's Corners. Foscalina's old store was located on the east side of the old Stockton road; nearby was a cluster of small houses, a vineyard, and a corral. In mid-1871 Thomas Scott built a new store, a two-story affair, on the west side of the highway.[6]

At seven o'clock that evening Thomas Scott, his wife, and their two sons, Thomas, Jr., age twelve, and Winfield Scott, age eight, were warming themselves by the fire in the living quarters at the rear of the old store. Young Tom Scott was playing checkers with a Portuguese neighbor, Antone. With them were Scott's clerk, a thirty-five-year-old Italian named Otto Ludovisi, and a stranger, Cornelius Sullivan, who had stopped for the night. There was a knock at the front door of the store and Ludovisi unlocked and opened it. A Californio entered. He was a medium-sized man with a black beard and a wide-brimmed black hat. He purchased a bottle of whiskey and left. Ten minutes later there was another knock at the door. Once again Ludovisi opened it. This time the Californio and two others entered. All three had bandannas covering their lower faces.

Ludovisi, terrified, yelled, "Get out of here! Get out of here!"

The masked bandit shouted in response, "Say nothing! Say nothing!" Then he raised a six-shooter and fired. The ball tore into Ludovisi's chest. He fled into the back room, then fell dead on the floor.

Thomas Scott and the rest raced headlong out the back door. The bandits fired several shots after them, striking Sullivan in the left hand. Mrs. Scott, clutching her sons in the yard in front of the store, begged the outlaws, "For God's sake, don't shoot."

The three bandidos turned to looting the store, and Scott and the others fled to safety. Scott ran a mile to the Cosmopolitan Hotel in the village of Sunol, where he raised the alarm. His wife and boys escaped to Charles Hadsell's ranch house, a half mile across the valley. Hadsell immediately sent a telegraph message to Sheriff Morse in San Leandro, then raced to the scene with a band of his cowboys. Hadsell found that the robbers had fled, taking with them their paltry spoils: $65, several pairs of cashmere pantaloons, and a bundle of old clothes belonging to the stranger, Sullivan.[7]

The ground was soft and muddy and the murderers' boot tracks could easily be seen. Hadsell and his men followed the tracks two hundred yards through a gate into a newly plowed field. Next to a harrow they found the bottle of whiskey that had been bought at the store. Three horses had been tethered to the harrow, and the tracks showed that they had been led off by the men on foot. Hadsell closely examined the footprints and noted that one pair was from a very small boot, with the toes pointed inward. This was a characteristic of the Californio vaquero, as most spent their lives in the saddle and were exceedingly bowlegged and pigeon-toed.[8]

Deputy Sheriff Ralph Faville, who lived in Pleasanton, was on the scene within three hours of the murder. At daybreak, with his friend A. J. McDavid, a veteran hunter and tracker, plus several citizens, he followed the tracks south along what is now Calaveras Road some eight miles into the mountains to Calaveras Valley. From there the road dropped down the mountains to Milpitas where it met the Oakland–San Jose highway. In Calaveras Valley Faville was surprised to meet Nicholas R. Harris, sheriff of Santa Clara County, who happened to be there serving civil process papers. Faville told him of the murder, and Harris, who had just ridden up from San Jose, advised that he had not seen the killers on the road. Then Faville and his posse continued on the old trail out of the mountains, where it turned west, past the Alviso adobe to Milpitas. Here it connected with the main road to San Jose; the tracks they had followed now

Nick Harris, sheriff of
Santa Clara County. Photo-
graph taken about 1870.
Author's collection.

were obliterated by numerous tracks on the main road. Realizing
that the killers had made their escape, Faville and his posse turned
to ride north on the main road back to Scott's store.

By this time Sheriff Morse had arrived on the scene. He interviewed Thomas Scott and the other witnesses to the murder, but
they were only able to give him general descriptions of the masked
robbers. Morse carefully examined both the footprints and the horse
tracks. One animal was missing a shoe, one was unshod, and the
third was shod on the forefeet only. Knowing that the route Faville
had taken would bring him out of the mountains at Milpitas, Morse
mounted up and rode hard to intercept his deputy. At Milpitas he
found Faville and his posse. While the possemen returned to their
homes, Morse and Faville rode south to San Jose. There, with City
Marshal William Sexton and Officer J. M. "Mitch" Bellow, they
searched all the jacales, fandango houses, and brothels that badmen
were known to frequent. They were unable to find any trace of three
men matching the killers' descriptions.

The next day, January 12, Faville and Sheriff Harris searched the

New Almaden and Guadalupe quicksilver mines south of San Jose while Morse scoured the mountains east of the Santa Clara Valley. The lawmen all returned to San Jose that night, empty-handed. In the morning Faville and Constable John Haight set off to search the mountainous country surrounding the New Almaden Mine while Sheriffs Morse and Harris took the train south to Gilroy. From there they went by horseback over Pacheco Pass to the San Luis Rancho, then up into the mountains to search the headwaters of Los Banos Creek, where Morse had captured Jesus Tejada six months before. Unable to locate the murderers, they returned to San Jose. On January 14 Morse took the train home. He was exhausted but not discouraged.[9]

The sheriff returned to Sunol Valley to begin the manhunt all over again. With Ralph Faville and Lew Morehouse he retraced the bandits' tracks through Calaveras Valley, then down from the mountains and directly past the Alviso adobe, which Morse knew was the home of Bartolo Sepulveda's mother-in-law. Morse spoke with Javier Alviso, Bartolo's brother-in-law, who told the sheriff that someone had knocked down his fence and left a bundle of old clothes next to the creek, the Arroyo de los Coches. Morse examined the bundle, which matched the description of the one that had been stolen from Scott's store. He and his deputies rode back to Sunol, where Sullivan identified the clothes as those that had been stolen from him.

Harry Morse now began doing something he should have done days earlier. He and his deputies searched Sunol Valley and Mission San Jose for witnesses who may have seen anyone suspicious. Several persons reported that Juan Soto and Bartolo Sepulveda had been seen riding along the road through Sunol Valley toward Mission San Jose the day before the murder. This, coupled with the discovery of the stolen bundle, convinced Sheriff Morse that Sepulveda and Soto were two of the men who had slain Otto Ludovisi. On the morning of January 17 Morse boarded a train for San Jose and notified Sheriff Harris and the police to be on the lookout for the two bandidos. They began searching for the pair, and rumors quickly spread through San Jose's close-knit Hispanic community that Soto and Sepulveda were suspected of the murder at Scott's store.

Now Bartolo Sepulveda learned that he was a prime suspect in the killing. He kept out of sight and began making preparations to flee. Several months earlier Sepulveda had agreed to lease a parcel of his farmland to a man in San Jose. Now, to provide income for his

The notorious bandit
chieftain Juan Soto. He
was shot to death by
Sheriff Morse on May 10,
1871, in one of the classic
gun duels of the Old West.
Author's collection.

family, Bartolo and his wife quietly went to the office of Thomas
Bodley, a San Jose attorney, and signed the lease. Meanwhile Harry
Morse talked to one of Bartolo's brothers, who sent the sheriff on a
wild goose chase by telling him that Bartolo could be found at the
Rancho Milpitas. While Morse went north, Bartolo Sepulveda fled
south and disappeared.[10]

Sheriff Morse was under tremendous pressure to bring the killers to
justice. The murder at Scott's store had caused a public outrage. The
senseless violence seemed to epitomize the racial troubles between
Hispanics and Anglos. It became known, along with the Medina
butchery, the Golding murders in Corral Hollow, and the later "Tres
Pinos Tragedy," as one of the worst examples of bandido savagery.

During the next several months Morse made repeated rides into
the Coast Range, searching every outlaw haunt he knew. On one occasion he was absent from his home, without being heard from, for
five weeks. Although Virginia and his friends feared for his safety,
each time he returned home safe but empty-handed.

At the same time other murders kept Morse and local lawmen

busy. On January 16 a Briton, Henry Hiscock, while hunting in the foothills west of Pleasanton, was shot to death by Ramon Amador. The killer, a member of the prominent Amador family, had served a term in San Quentin for cattle theft. He murdered Hiscock to steal his rifle and shotgun. On March 26 another murder took place, this time in Cathcart Canyon. Bill Powers, Joe Newell's sidekick, stabbed to death Nels Larsen, a peaceable Norwegian. Both Powers and Amador were held in Morse's jail to await trial.[11]

Yet another problem for Harry Morse presented itself in the form of the notorious Procopio Bustamante. On March 1 he was released from San Quentin. He had been sentenced to nine years, but with "coppers," or credits for good behavior, he was discharged after serving seven and a half. Procopio headed straight for his old stomping grounds in the Livermore Valley. He made his headquarters at the fandango house and bordello run by Antonio Smith in Little Mexico and spent a month drinking, gambling, and whoring. It was not long before he returned to his old thieving habits.

On April 1 John Arnett, a rancher who lived between Pleasanton and Sunol, awoke to find one of his cows missing. The cow was heavy with calf and ready to give birth. Her tracks, coupled with those of two horses, led toward Livermore. Arnett asked his neighbor, A. J. McDavid, to help him trail the cow. McDavid tracked the animal a mile toward Livermore, then lost the trail. Arnett reported the theft to Ralph Faville, and the three spent the following day searching for the tracks in the fields between Pleasanton and Livermore. Finally they cut the trail and followed it to the jacal of the old tapadera Juan Camargo, who now lived north of Livermore. Near the jacal was a smoldering pile of rubbish containing the horns and entrails of a cow. Camargo was not at home, and the possemen searched his house. In a shed they found freshly butchered beef and an unborn calf with velvety hooves, hung up and skinned. In Camargo's stable they found the head and hooves of the cow, which Arnett immediately recognized as his missing animal.

Ralph Faville started off toward Livermore, and on the road he met Juan Carmago and arrested him without trouble. They questioned the badman, but he refuse to make any statement. Then Faville, Arnett, McDavid, and Deputy Sheriff J. M. Smith took Carmago to Pleasanton. Pleasanton then had no jail, so prisoners were kept under guard at the hotel. Here the two deputies held Camargo in irons so that he could be arraigned before the justice of the peace in the morning. That night a party of some fifty masked men entered the deputies' hotel room and seized Camargo. They locked the deputies in their room and took Camargo to the railroad bridge over the Arroyo Valle, just outside of town. A rope was draped around the outlaw's neck, and, as the *Alameda County Gazette* reported, he was "treated to a slight foretaste of his future doom." After being hoisted up several times, the gasping Camargo confessed that Procopio had brought the cow to his place. Camargo was then returned to the hotel and the two deputies were released.[12]

Juan Camargo later accused Arnett and McDavid of being the leaders of the mob. Whether Harry Morse's deputies, Faville and Smith, cooperated with the vigilantes is unknown. If they did, it would certainly have been without Morse's approval. In California during the 1860s and after, losing a prisoner to a lynch mob was the greatest affront to the professional lawman's authority and the most embarrassing incident that could befall him. Sheriffs like Tom Cunningham, Ben K. Thorn, and Doc Standley went to Herculean efforts to protect prisoners from lynchers and took great pride that they never lost a man to a mob. The existence of such vigilantism was considered to be a personal insult for two reasons. First, it showed that the community did not have sufficient faith in the sheriff's ability to put together a criminal case that would stand up in court and result in legal punishment. Second, and more important, it demonstrated that the vigilantes believed the sheriff was impotent to protect his prisoners. "No duty to retreat," the legal maxim that justified the western fighting man's stubborn refusal to back down from an enemy, applied equally to sheriffs who refused to back down from mob violence. These two considerations were often of greater significance to the western lawman than any abstract notion of justice or due process.[13]

John Arnett was concerned that the bandidos might retaliate against him. He kept a Henry rifle at hand and a watchdog outside at night. A week later, on the night of April 10, he was awakened by the baying of the watchdog. Seizing his rifle, he ran out in time to see two mounted thieves driving off a herd of his cattle. Arnett called out "Halt!" but the riders paid no attention. He opened fire, killing one of their horses. The horseman leaped onto the back of his compadre's saddle and they galloped off into the blackness.

Arnett raised a hue and cry and with his neighbors tracked the fleeing horse toward Livermore. There they met Sheriff Morse and

Ralph Faville, who immediately returned with Arnett to his ranch and carefully examined the dead horse, its brand, and its riding rig. Morse, Faville, and Deputy Smith rode to Little Mexico, made an unsuccessful search for suspects, and then headed for the Alisal. On the road they met the notorious Rafael Mirabel, compañero of Juan Soto. He had been released from San Quentin two years previous and was living in a jacal in the Arroyo Valle. Mirabel was on foot and claimed that his horse had been stolen from him during the night. Morse lodged him in jail in San Leandro but was soon forced to release the badman for lack of evidence. Sheriff Morse believed that the thieves had been Mirabel and Procopio.[14]

The Livermore Valley was much too hot for Procopio. He fled south to the Saucelito (Little Willows) Valley, located at the base of St. Mary's Peak, high in the Coast Range some twelve miles due south of Pacheco Pass. This was not far from the spot where Morse had captured Jesus Tejada and Patricio Mancilla. Not far from here Juan Soto's uncle, Lorenzo Soto, owned a small rancho. Nearby were adobe dwellings occupied by vaqueros and borregueros. There, far from the encroachment of Anglo civilization, they enjoyed a quiet, pastoral life. At the same time they often harbored bandidos and cattle thieves, who were frequently friends or family members and who could afford to pay in gold or silver for food and lodging. This area remains one of the most isolated in California. It is completely roadless, marked by towering peaks and deep canyons, accessible only by rough jeep trails.

The Saucelito Valley is a beautiful mountain meadow situated between the North and South forks of Los Banos Creek. Five adobes were located in or near the valley. At the northwest end of the valley, near the base of St. Mary's Peak, was a house owned by Juan Lopez and his wife, Carmela; two other small jacales stood nearby. Two miles south was the Alvarado adobe, built in 1860 by Juan Alvarado. Four miles south stood a long, narrow adobe, later known as the Storm Ranch. The Lopez, Alvarado, and Storm adobes are still standing.[15]

That spring there gathered in the Saucelito Valley one of the most dangerous outlaw congregations of the Far West: Tiburcio Vasquez, Juan Soto, and Procopio Bustamante. These were but the best-known bandidos present. Various other desperadoes drifted into the valley, including Bartolo Sepulveda, Pio Ochoa, and Ambrosio Gonzales, a highway robber and cattle thief who had escaped from

The Alvarado adobe as it looks today, protected by metal and wood roofing and siding. In 1871 it was the headquarters for outlaws Juan Soto, Tiburcio Vasquez, and Procopio Bustamante. Photo by author.

the Santa Cruz County jail. Procopio and Soto did not get along, and on May 9 Soto challenged Procopio to fight. Tiburcio Vasquez, who subsequently had his own falling out with Procopio, later told a newspaper reporter, "I was there. Soto made Procopio go down into his boots. If Procopio had not left like a coward Soto would have killed him."[16]

Vasquez and Procopio left the outlaw camp and rode out of the mountains to San Juan Bautista. It proved to be a fortuitous decision. The previous day, Harry Morse had received a telegram from his friend Nick Harris. The San Jose sheriff had heard rumors that Juan Soto was in the Saucelito Valley, high in the mountains south of Pacheco Pass, and was organizing a posse to hunt for him. Would Sheriff Morse like to join his posse?

Harry Morse did not even delay long enough to change his clothes but grabbed his Winchester saddle carbine and boarded the next train for San Jose. He found Sheriff Harris and Theodore C. "Sam" Winchell, a former constable and San Jose policeman, at the head of a six-man posse of local citizens, all well mounted and heavily armed. In an effort to avoid attention, the posse left San Jose in two groups.

Morse led one party south along the base of the foothills to Soap
Lake, while Sheriff Harris and the rest followed the main road to
Gilroy. From here they struck east into the Pacheco Pass. Both par-
ties joined up at the Mountain House, located at the summit.

None of the possemen had ever been to the Saucelito Valley, and
Morse and Harris had only a general idea of where it was located.
The lawmen rode south, and for two days they cautiously rode along
the mountain ridges, scouring the canyons and deep ravines and
sweeping the horizon with their field glasses. They saw nothing
alive save deer and white-tailed antelope. On the morning of May 10,
1871, while riding through a rocky canyon, they spotted a rider on
a mule ahead of them, spurring the animal in an effort to escape.
Morse and the others gave chase and managed to overtake their
quarry. The rider quickly dismounted, drew his pistol, and crouched
behind his mule to defend himself. Morse and Harris were surprised
to see that he was an Anglo, and after a brief parley they learned he
was a sheepherder rather than a bandit. He had mistaken the posse
for a roaming band of outlaws and had run for his life.

The sheepherder knew the Saucelito Valley well and told the lawmen that a large party of rough hombres had gathered there. He
agreed to pilot the posse to the valley, but only on the condition that
they would allow him to depart unseen by the outlaws, for they
would track him down and kill him if they learned that he had led
the lawmen to their lair. He guided Morse and the others along the
mountain ridges until they reached a saddle on the west side of St.
Mary's Peak from which they could look down on the Saucelito Valley Closest to them, at the northwest end of the valley, were the
Lopez house and rock corral, and near it, 500 yards distant, were two
other jacales. Two miles down the valley was the Alvarado adobe.
This, the sheepherder said, was the stronghold of the outlaws; the
three small adobes below were the homes of herders.

Morse and Harris quickly decided on a plan of action. They would
divide into three groups, swoop down on the three jacales, and capture their occupants. They would be placed under guard to keep
them from warning the bandits. Then the rest of the posse would
ride forward, raid the Alvarado adobe, and attempt to capture Juan
Soto and the entire band. Morse and Winchell set out to arrest the
occupants of the Lopez adobe while Harris and the others circled
around and headed toward the other jacales. Morse and Winchell
reached the corral without being discovered. A man was working
there. Morse dismounted and asked him in Spanish for a drink of

Rear view of the Lopez adobe, today known as the Pfeiffer adobe, scene of the gunfight between Harry Morse and Juan Soto. The Saucelito Valley is in the background. This was Morse's view when he first approached the site. The long wooden shed was built in later years. The pistol duel between Sheriff Morse and Juan Soto took place between the adobe and the rock corral. The large tree to the left of the shed was where Soto's horse was tied. Morse fired the fatal shot from a spot just to the right of the shed. Soto died in the meadow at the far left. Photo by author.

water. He responded courteously and invited them to follow him into the house. Morse and Winchell hitched their horses to the corral gate and followed the man through the corral and around to the opposite, or northern, side of the adobe. Morse wore a holstered six-gun; Winchell carried a double-barreled shotgun.

The Lopez adobe was a one-story house with a central room and two bedrooms along the side walls. A narrow covered porch ran along the front wall, on the north side, and also the east wall, on the left. Two doors opened into the front porch, and through one of them the officers entered into the main room. There Morse received the shock of his life. Several men and women were standing in the

Front view of the Lopez (Pfeiffer) adobe as it looks today. The second story was added in the 1880s. The door Morse entered to encounter Soto can be seen in the center of the first floor. Photo by author.

room. Three more sat at a table directly in front of him. One of them was Juan Soto. The sheriff recognized him immediately.

Unknown to Morse, Soto had just ridden down from the Alvarado house. He and the others had planned a fiesta and had butchered a beef. Soto had come to the little adobe for salt and onions for the barbecue and, according to one account, to visit several "seductive señoritas" there. Sheriff Morse had unwisely left his Winchester in its scabbard. He jerked his six-shooter and barked, "Manos arriba!"

Juan Soto did not move a muscle. Again Morse ordered him to put up his hands. Soto sat motionless, glaring with hatred at the lawman. A third time Morse gave the order, threatening him with instant death if he was not obeyed. Still Soto did not react.

With his left hand Morse yanked a pair of handcuffs from his gunbelt and passed them across his body to Winchell.

"Put them on him, Winchell," Morse ordered.

Winchell took the handcuffs but made no move toward Soto.

"Put them on him!" the sheriff snapped, angrily.

Paralyzed by fright, Winchell stood frozen.

"Then cover him with your shotgun while I do it!" Morse cried, fully realizing the danger.

Winchell took one last, long look at Juan Soto, then turned and fled out the door. At that, all hell broke loose. A "muscular Mexican Amazon" seized Morse's pistol arm, and a desperado grabbed his left.

"No tire en la casa!" they both shouted. ["Don't shoot in the house!"]

While Morse struggled violently to free himself, Soto leaped for cover behind one of his compadres. He was wearing a long blue soldier's overcoat, which was buttoned down to his knees. He began to tear the coat open to reach his two six-shooters on his belt, underneath. At the same time Morse freed his gun hand and took aim at Soto.

"I might have killed him then," Morse explained later, "by shooting through the man in front of him, who was much smaller than Soto, and my first impulse was to do so. And then the thought occurred to me, 'Why kill this poor devil, who may be innocent of any crime?' So I raised the pistol and fired over him at the head of Soto."

But Morse's aim was off, jarred by the pair who were grappling with him. The ball tore off Soto's hat and thudded harmlessly into the adobe wall behind. By now Juan Soto had pulled his coat back and seized a six-gun. Morse broke loose and jumped backward through the door before Soto could fire. Cursing violently, the huge bandit charged after the sheriff.

Morse sprang from the porch and raced around to the rear of the adobe, hoping to reach his rifle hanging from his saddle. But Soto was right behind him, and Morse realized he would be shot in the back before he could get to his horse. He spun around in time to see Juan Soto holding his pistol high over his head. Morse knew that Soto had a reputation as a dead shot and that his style of shooting was to raise his pistol straight up, then drop it suddenly down and fire the instant the weapon was level. Many gunmen used this technique in an effort to allow each fired percussion cap to fall from the cylinder so as not to jam the pistol. Sheriff Harris described what happened next:

I was in sight of the house, and about five hundred yards distant, when the first shot was fired. Sam Winchell first rushed out of the house, then Morse, followed closely (they were not more than fifteen feet apart) by Soto, who immediately fired

at Morse. I thought Morse was surely hit, for his body went al
most to the ground; but, quick as a flash, he sprang erect and
fired. Soto, advancing with a bound, brought his pistol down
to a level and fired again, and Morse going through the same
maneuver as before. This was continued for three or four—I
think four rounds, and I firmly believed Morse was hit every
time. The shots were fired in quick succession, Soto advancing
on Morse every time he fired, with a leap or bound of six or
eight feet, with pistol held above his head, landing on his feet,
his body erect, bringing his weapon down on a level with
Morse's breast, and then firing. After firing he never moved
until he re-cocked his pistol and was ready for another shot,
when, tiger-like, he would spring at Morse again. Soto fired
the first shot after they came out of the house and Morse returned every shot. There was about the same interval of time
between each shot, Morse firing while Soto was re-cocking his
pistol. Morse was retreating to his Henry rifle, and Soto was
pursuing until he received Morse's last shot, when he wavered
like he was hit, and then ran into the house.[17]

Incredibly, Morse had managed to drop to the ground each time
Soto fired, and the killer's bullet passed harmlessly over his head.
The sheriff's last shot had struck Soto's six-shooter underneath the
barrel as he was raising the weapon to cock it. The bullet wedged
against the cylinder, jamming the gun. The force drove the barrel violently into Soto's cheek, briefly stunning him, and he whirled
around and fled back to the adobe. Winchell had been standing next
to the corral and could easily have dropped Soto, but he was frozen
with fear. Now he managed to raise his shotgun and fire one barrel
at the running outlaw, but the buckshot missed its mark and
slammed into the rear wall of the adobe.

Morse ran at the top of his speed for his horse and jerked his rifle
from its scabbard. It was a Winchester 1866 saddle carbine, "Improved Henry's," and was the most advanced longarm available.
This was the first Winchester rifle manufactured, and although it
was an improved model of the older Henry rifle, it was still commonly called a "Henry."

Sheriff Harris was charging down the slope, his horse at a dead
run. Reaching the corral, he leaped from his mount, Spencer rifle in
hand, and sprinted to Morse's side. At the same instant two men
emerged at a run from the adobe and headed toward a lone horse

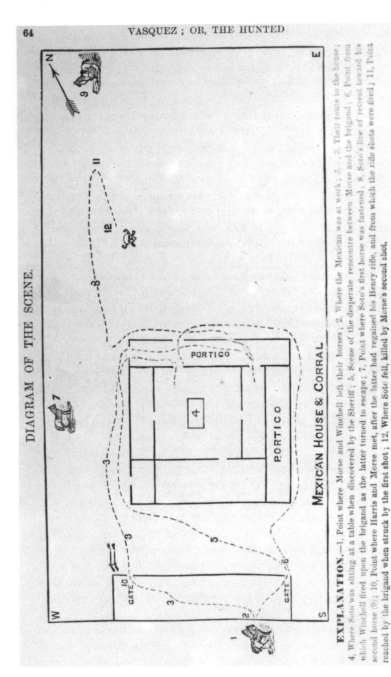

DIAGRAM OF THE SCENE.

MEXICAN HOUSE & CORRAL

EXPLANATION.—1, Point where Morse and Winchell left their horses ; 2, Where the Mexican was at work ; 3, , 3, Their route to the house ; 4, Where Soto was sitting at a table when discovered by the Sheriff ; 5, Scene of the desperate rencontre between Morse and the brigand ; 6, Point from which Winchell fired upon the brigand as the latter turned to escape ; 7, Point where Soto's first horse was fastened ; 8, Soto's line of retreat toward his second horse (9) ; 10, Point where Harris and Morse met, after the latter had regained his Henry rifle, and from which the rifle shots were fired ; 11, Point reached by the brigand when struck by the first shot ; 12, Where Soto fell, killed by Morse's second shot.

A diagram of the scene of Harry Morse's duel to the death with Juan Soto. Published in George Beer's book *Vasquez* (1875). Author's collection.

hitched to an oak tree forty yards west. One of them was wearing a long blue soldier's overcoat, and Nick Harris swung up his Spencer rifle and took dead aim at the man. Before he could fire Morse knocked up the barrel. In a matter of seconds inside the adobe Juan Soto had switched coats with a compadre, donned his hat, and seized three fresh revolvers. Fortunately for Soto's follower, Harry Morse had seen his ruse.

Soto, a five-shooter in each hand, rushed headlong at his horse, and Morse raised his rifle to kill the animal. But it had been spooked by the firing and broke away. Now the outlaw turned and raced to a second horse that stood saddled some two hundred yards north.

"For God's sake, Juan, throw down your pistols!" Morse pleaded. "There has been shooting enough!"

But Juan Soto paid no heed and continued running, followed by his compadre in the blue overcoat. The two outlaws were now one hundred fifty yards distant and virtually out of range. Morse quickly flipped up his gunsight, took careful aim, and squeezed the trigger. The .44-caliber bullet struck Soto with a sharp click and tore through his right shoulder. Badly wounded, the bandido gave up all hope of escape. He turned and charged toward the two sheriffs, a pistol in each fist and a third in his belt. Sheriff Harris fired at the advancing desperado but missed. Soto kept running directly toward the lawmen in a desperate effort to get into pistol range and kill his pursuers.

Harry Morse levered a round into his rifle's chamber and carefully drew a bead on the charging killer. At a range of more than one hundred yards he squeezed the trigger and the Winchester boomed. The heavy ball made a long, low arch and smacked into Juan Soto's forehead, just above the eyes. The impact tore off the top of the outlaw's head, and he toppled dead into the spring grass.

Morse searched the desperado's body and removed $80 in coin. This he gave to an old woman with instructions to bury the outlaw. Then Morse seized Soto's horse and pistols and pushed on to the bandit's stronghold at the Alvarado adobe. The posse searched all the adobes in the valley and rounded up every man they could find. Among them were Pio Ochoa, who was not wanted, and Ambrosio Gonzales, whom they identified as an escapee from the Santa Cruz jail. Morse was told that Procopio and Vasquez had left the camp and that the man in the soldier's overcoat was Bartolo Sepulveda. Then the posse headed back toward San Jose with Gonzales, arriving the next day.[18]

The rifle Sheriff Morse used to kill Juan Soto. It is a .44 caliber Winchester Model 1866, serial no. 13727, manufactured in 1866. The frame is inscribed, "Henry N. Morse, Sheriff Alameda Co." Author's collection.

News of the killing of Juan Soto was soon headline news throughout California and firmly planted Harry Morse in the public mind as the most famous manhunter on the West Coast. The *Alta California* said of Sheriff Morse,

> He has distinguished himself by one of the most daring and desperate acts that have ever been performed in the history of detective work on the Pacific Coast, and his own life has been preserved only by the manifestation of astonishing self-possession and presence of mind. It so happened that circumstances placed him in the focus of danger, out of reach of his companions, where he had to rely solely upon that steadfast courage and steadiness of nerve which have given him deserved celebrity among the foremost detective officers of the country. He had previously been through many perilous adventures among the more desperate characters of California, but we suppose the hand-to-hand and long continued conflict with the chief of the brigands was the most exciting and desperate of all.[19]

The gunfight between Harry Morse and Juan Soto was one of the most incredible in the history of the American West. Morse's ability to dodge Soto's gunfire at close range and his deadly marksmanship in hitting an armed, running opponent not once but twice at ranges of more than one hundred yards are without parallel in the annals of western gunfighting. It remains California's best-known and most celebrated lawman-outlaw gun duel and is considered by authorities on western gunfighting to be one of the classic shootouts of the Old West.

Harry Morse's victory over Juan Soto was no accident. He had spent years hunting and capturing wanted men. He had painstakingly trained himself in every skill he had used to overcome his foe: to recognize the faces and descriptions of wanted bandidos, to speak and understand their language, to win in hand-to-hand physical combat, to shoot straight with rifle and revolver, and most important, to think clearly and act quickly no matter how great the danger.

Sheriff Nick Harris, in writing his observations of that deadly encounter, provided Juan Soto's most fitting epitaph:

Soto was a perfect type of desperado, over six feet high, well proportioned, and quick as a cat, with a countenance the worst I ever saw in a human face. I never shall forget how he looked in that terrible encounter, as he emerged from the house, bareheaded, with long black hair streaming in the wind, his face covered with a full beard, dressed in a soldier coat, the skirts flying in a stiff breeze from his stalwart form, and he armed with two revolvers—and his murderous action, taken altogether, completely filled my mind's eye of a real desperado.[20]

CHAPTER 11

"Procopio, You're My Man"

HARRY Morse did not flinch from shooting a desperado who re-sisted arrest, but he had no stomach for hanging a man. On July 20, 1871, Ramon Amador was brought to trial before Judge Samuel Bell McKee for the murder of Henry Hiscock. His trial lasted but one day. Amador admitted that he killed Hiscock, but he told several conflicting stories about the crime. Now he claimed that he had slain Hiscock in self-defense. The evidence, however, showed that the victim had been shot in the back of the head. His body had been found face down with his pockets turned inside out. Hiscock's rifle and shotgun were missing and were found secreted in Amador's house near Pleasanton. The jury deliberated three hours before con-victing the ex-convict of first-degree murder.

Two days later Sheriff Morse brought the twenty-six-year-old pris-oner into Judge McKee's courtroom for sentencing. Amador was in-structed to stand, and the judge methodically recited the evidence against him. Amador, ashen-faced, stood silently as Judge McKee concluded,

> It is a sad thing to reflect upon that a man of your age should have been influenced by such moral depravity as to imbrue your hands in the blood of an innocent man for so slight a cause as a desire to possess yourself of his rifle. For a crime so great the law has but one penalty, and that is death. But the law is more lenient to you than you were to your victims. You shot him under circumstances which show that you did so without a word of caution or warning to him. You gave him no time to express a wish or breathe a prayer to Heaven. But the law gives you time to repent of the act, send for your priest, confess to him the sins of which you have been guilty, and make such preparations as you can to meet your God when you shall be swung from time to eternity. The sentence of the law is that

you be confined in the jail of the county until the 31st day of
August next, and upon that day, between the hours of ten o'clock
a.m. and twelve p.m., you be taken by the sheriff of the county
and hung by the neck until you are dead. And may God have
mercy on your soul.[1]

Amador's wife, sister, and two other family members were in the
courtroom, overcome with grief, and Morse allowed them to visit
the condemned man in the basement jail. Morse's friend George
Beers, a reporter for the *Alameda County Gazette*, was present and
wrote, "A wail of bitter anguish arose from the sorrowing women
and rang throughout the building."[2]

At that time the only punishment for first-degree murder was
death, unless the governor commuted the sentence to life in prison.
A petition for a reprieve was circulated by Amador's relatives, and
Harry Morse, who considered his forthcoming duty exceedingly
distasteful, agreed to sign it. Governor Henry H. Haight granted a
temporary reprieve so that he could look into the matter and postponed the execution until September 22. But on September 10 the
governor sent Morse a brief note: "Do not hold out to Ramon
Amador any hope of executive interference in his case. Upon an examination of the testimony I have not been able to see sufficient
cause for interposition."[3]

Up to this point Amador had accepted his sentence stoically, but
when Morse advised him that his last hope was gone, he went almost
mad with emotion. Alternately raging and weeping, he lashed out at
the judge, the officers, and his family, whom he refused to allow to
visit him. The night before his execution he calmed somewhat, and
Morse allowed George Beers and several other newspapermen to interview the condemned man through the wicket in his jail cell door.
Amador's demeanor immediately changed. Cursing at his jailers, he
shouted, "Morse has told everyone I am a desperado. I'm a son of a
bitch if I don't show them in the morning that I am one!" Forget-
ting that he had admitted from the beginning that he had slain Hiscock, Amador ranted, "I am going to hell in the morning, but by
God I never killed that man!" Referring to his term in San Quentin,
he complained, "Since I was in that God damned place across the
bay, everybody is down on me and I have no friends. That is a hell
of a law you have here for a poor man. Them God damned judges
don't care for a poor man." Then, weeping, he referred to Joe

Newell's partner, who had been convicted of second-degree murder and sentenced to prison: "Bill Powers killed a man because he tried to cheat him at cards, and they didn't hang him."[4]

In the morning all was ready for the hanging. Amador's grief-stricken mother came to see Morse at the courthouse. Sobbing uncontrollably, she clutched the sheriff and begged piteously for him to spare her son's life. This was more than Morse could stand. Commented one reporter who was present, "Though our sheriff is a bold, brave man, and has often faced death with unflinching nerves, the scene was almost too affecting for him."[5]

Morse went downstairs to the jail. The officers and newspapermen present now could find nothing but pity for the condemned killer, for he apologized profusely to them for his outburst the night before. "Excuse me for what I told you last night. I take every word back. I will die like a man!"

Sheriff Morse had arranged for the gallows to be erected at the rear of the courthouse, surrounded by a fence twenty feet high to keep out prying eyes. The scaffold had been brought out of storage, having been used in the county's last hanging in 1862. Morse had set up a rope, pulley, and sandbag system so that an unseen executioner, known only to him, would spring the trap by a rope pulled from a private room in the jail basement. The sheriff was required by law to have official witnesses at the hanging, and he received a great number of requests for invitations. Most of them he turned down. Whereas other sheriffs might have invited hundreds to a hanging, Morse wanted to avoid making it a spectacle. He invited but thirty witnesses, all of them peace officers, reporters, doctors, and friends of the prisoner. The latter included his uncle, Antonio Amador, a ranchero and elder member of the pioneer Californio family.

Shortly after eleven o'clock Morse and Ralph Faville entered Ramon Amador's cell, where he was praying with Father Nugent, the Catholic priest of San Leandro. Morse pinioned Amador's arms with leather straps, then led the way up the gallows steps. Amador almost fainted, and a chair was produced so he could sit down. Then Morse, his voice cracking with emotion, read the death warrant. Turning to the witnesses, he announced plaintively, "Gentlemen, there is nothing further left for me except to carry the sentence into effect."

Facing the prisoner, Morse said, "Ramon, stand up."

The sheriff led Amador onto the center of the trap. Then he and

Faville quickly strapped Amador's ankles, knees, and wrists. Morse adjusted the noose with the knot snug under the left ear, then dropped the black cap over the prisoner's head. Father Nugent pressed Amador's hand, whispered several words, and stepped back. Morse, after motioning Faville to stand clear of the trap, drew a handkerchief across his brow. At that signal the trap door was sprung and Amador plunged through it with a dull, heavy thud. The body twitched in convulsions at the end of the rope, and several spectators fainted in their tracks. The doctors came forward and monitored for signs of life. After five minutes the heart stopped beating. Thirty minutes later they pronounced Ramon Amador dead, and Morse cut the body down. It had been the most distasteful duty of his career. Commented the *Oakland Daily News,* "Sheriff Morse shrank from the unpleasant task, but feelings of duty overcame every other consideration."[6]

There was some truth in Ramon Amador's plea of injustice in Alameda County. In at least one prominent case a killer went free because of his wealth and political connections. In February 1871, in a quarrel over land, Frederick W. Clarke, the son of a wealthy San Francisco lawyer and landowner, shot and killed a squatter, Zelotus Reed. Although Reed had a bad reputation, he was unarmed and there was no justification for Clarke's killing him. Clarke claimed self-defense, but in the preliminary hearing a judge ruled that there was sufficient evidence to hold him for trial for murder. The grand jury, however, refused to indict him. This injustice created a public uproar, and the district attorney obtained a court order resubmitting the case to the grand jury. Clarke, represented by a battery of prominent lawyers, appealed to the California Supreme Court, which upheld the lower court's ruling. The lower court again ordered the case resubmitted to the grand jury, but Judge S. H. Dwinelle of San Francisco agreed to hear an appeal, even though he had no jurisdiction in the case. Dwinelle held the case for two years until public outrage finally forced him to make a ruling. He sent the case back to the Alameda County grand jury, which once again refused to indict Clarke. The killer was never punished. The public saw this case as a travesty of justice, and newspapers blamed judges and grand jurors who were influenced by the wealth and influence of Clarke's father.[7]

Unlike Ramon Amador, Juan Camargo had no complaints about the evenness of Anglo justice in Alameda County. On July 24 he had been tried for the theft of John Arnett's cow. Camargo had been in dicted as an accessory after the fact to grand larceny and Procopio had been charged with the actual theft. Camargo's confession, which had been strangled out of him, was not admissible in his trial. Today, modern case law excludes such illegally seized evidence from court. However, even in those early years, California courts had ruled that confessions obtained by threats, promises, or beatings were inherently unreliable and therefore inadmissible in court. The law at that time also provided that Camargo's possession of stolen property was not sufficient to convict him as an accessory. Camargo's lawyer argued that there was no evidence to show that he knew the cow was stolen, and the Anglo-dominated jury found him not guilty.[8]

That spring and summer Morse had made several trips into the mountains in search of Procopio Bustamante, Bartolo Sepulveda, and Tiburcio Vasquez. He soon realized the futility of such manhunts, for the bandits had many friends who were willing to harbor them and lie to the officers. So the sheriff hired Juan Soto's old compadre, Alfonso Burnham, to ride down to Monterey County and locate the outlaws. Almost sixty years later, at the age of ninety-three, Burnham wrote a fascinating account of his encounter with the gang. He related that it did not take him long to learn that Procopio, Vasquez, and other bandidos were in the habit of frequenting Sotoville, a small adobe settlement in Monterey County, now part of the city of Salinas.

Burnham rode to Sotoville and soon fell in with Vasquez, Procopio, and Francisco "Pancho" Barcenas. He had known them all in San Quentin, and he told the robbers that he had killed a man in Marin County and was a fugitive. They accepted him readily, and he spent a week with them in their camp at a sheepherder's place, fifteen miles distant. When Pancho Barcenas rode into Salinas for supplies, Burnham went along. Barcenas patronized one too many saloons in Salinas, allowing Burnham to slip away and send a letter to Morse describing the location of the camp and the desperadoes present. But Morse was away from his office for several days and did not receive the message in time. At the end of the week Procopio and Vasquez drew pistols over a woman. No blood was shed, but the outlaw band broke up. They divided their spoils and stolen horses equally, then Procopio rode south, taking the woman with him. Vasquez and Barcenas rode north toward Santa Cruz.[9]

Vasquez was aware that Morse was after him. He later gave his version of how he outwitted the Alameda lawman: "Sheriff Harry

Morse, desirous of capturing me, wrote to Tom McMahon, of San Juan Bautista, in Monterey County, who, through his relations with the Creole [native Californian] population of that region could best serve him, to inform himself without delay in regard to my whereabouts and to notify him [Morse] with all possible dispatch. Tom took measures to comply. This coming to my ears, I determined to teach Tom a lesson." Vasquez claimed that he held up and robbed McMahon, a prominent merchant, while he was on his way to Salinas, the county seat, to pay his taxes. In fact, this holdup took place under somewhat different circumstances. On August 5, 1871, Vasquez, with one gang member, robbed McMahon while he was on his way from Salinas to his home in San Juan Bautista. Vasquez relieved him of his pistol, watch, coat, and $50 in coin. According to the contemporary report published in the Monterey *Democrat*, McMahon recognized one of the bandits.[10]

A few days later, on August 10, Tiburcio Vasquez and two accomplices held up and robbed a stagecoach at Soap Lake (now San Felipe Lake) between Gilroy and Pacheco Pass. Sheriff Nick Harris made a lengthy manhunt for the bandits, whom he believed to be Tiburcio Vasquez, Procopio Bustamante, and Bartolo Sepulveda; he identified Pancho Barcenas and Pancho Galindo as two other members of the band. Vasquez later admitted that he had led the robbers and that his partners had been Barcenas and Narciso Rodriguez, a desperado from Santa Cruz.[11]

By this time lawmen from Santa Clara, Monterey, and Santa Cruz counties were busy hunting the outlaws. On the night of September 10 Vasquez and two companions shot up a bordello in Santa Cruz. When police officer Robert Liddell accosted them, the bandidos opened fire from horseback. Though wounded in the thigh, the officer shot back and and put a pistol ball through Tiburcio's torso. His compañeros helped the bandit leader to escape. Three days later Santa Cruz lawmen, on the alert for the gang, cornered Pancho Barcenas in a barn outside of town and shot him to death. Narciso Rodriguez was captured and sentenced to San Quentin for his role in the Soap Lake stage robbery.[12]

Vasquez's wound gradually healed. He later claimed that as soon as he was able to travel he went to Mexico, stayed three months, and then took a steamer to San Francisco. But he soon left the city. "Procopio was there then," recalled Vasquez. "I knew the officers wanted me, and San Francisco was no place for me to stay in."[13]

Thomas Procopio
Bustamante, better known
simply as Procopio. This
photograph was taken at
the time Sheriff Morse
captured him in 1872.
Author's collection.

But Procopio had no such concerns, for he was enjoying the pleasures of fast women in the brothels of Morton Street. In 1872 Procopio was more notorious than Vasquez, who would not achieve
statewide infamy until the following year. Numerous newspapers
had identified Procopio, perhaps erroneously, as the leader in the
bandit raids in Monterey and Santa Cruz counties. It was a measure
of his bravado that he would hide out in San Francisco under the
very noses of the police, who were on the lookout for him.

Today, in an effective disguise of its past, Morton Street is ironi-
cally named Maiden Lane. It is an alley, two blocks long, running
from Union Square across Grant Avenue to Kearny Street, lined
with upscale shops and fashionable galleries. But in 1872 it was one
of the most dangerous streets in San Francisco. Herbert Asbury has
described why Morton Street would be so attractive to a fugitive like
Procopio:

> The worst cribs in San Francisco were probably those which
> lined both sides of Morton Street. . . . These dens were occu-
> pied by women of all colors and nationalities; there were even

a few Chinese and Japanese girls. And not only were the Morton Street cribs the lowest in San Francisco's red light district; they were also the most popular, partly because of the great variety and extraordinary depravity of the women to be found there, and partly because the police seldom entered the street unless compelled to do so by a murder or serious shooting or stabbing affray. Ordinary fights and assaults were ignored.

Every night, and especially every Saturday night, this dismal bedlam of obscenity, lighted only by the red lamps above the doors of the cribs, was thronged by a tumultuous mob of half-drunken men, who stumbled from crib to crib, greedily inspecting the women as if they had been so many wild animals in cages. From the casement windows leaned the harlots, naked to the waist, adding their shrill cries of invitation to the uproar, while their pimps haggled with passing men and tried to drag them inside the dens.[14]

On February 9, 1872, Harry Morse received a telegraph message from Patrick Crowley, San Francisco's chief of police, advising that Procopio had been spotted in the city. This was the break he had hoped for. He and Lew Morehouse rushed to Oakland and caught the evening ferry. Morse carried in his pocket an arrest warrant charging Procopio with simple grand larceny. But as the boat slipped through the evening fog, it was a ten-year-old quadruple murder that was foremost on the sheriff's mind.

The two Alameda lawmen met up with Appleton W. Stone and Ben Bohen, both crack police detectives. They had been tipped, probably by a prostitute, that Procopio had been frequenting a brothel on Morton Street, several doors above Kearny. The officers kept the house under surveillance all night, but the outlaw failed to show up. Finally, at three o'clock the following afternoon, Morse learned that Procopio was inside the brothel, and had apparently been there all along.

A plan of attack was quickly decided on. Morehouse, Stone, and Bohen would enter the front door to make the arrest; Morse would cover the rear to prevent Procopio's escape. As Morse walked down an alley to the rear of the house he peered into a window and spotted the Corral Hollow murderer seated at a table, eating as he watched the front door. The sheriff slipped in the back door while Morehouse and the two detectives entered the front. Several of the prostitutes tried to block their entrance so Procopio could escape. The bandido, alerted by the commotion, rose from his chair. At the same time he started to draw his six-gun from his right pants pocket. In an instant Morse was behind him. With a single fluid motion he seized Procopio by the throat and clapped the muzzle of a cocked six-shooter to the desperado's right ear.

"Put up your hands, Procopio. You're my man," the sheriff said quietly.

Procopio had once boasted "that Morse should never take him." But now he took a long, sideways glance at the barrel of the sheriff's six-gun, then relaxed his grip on his own weapon. A moment later the other officers were upon him and he was disarmed and hand-cuffed. Sheriff Morse then pulled the arrest warrant from his pocket and read it to the bandido. Procopio asked Morse what he had been arrested for.

"For stealing John Arnett's cow," replied Morse.

"Only one cow?" the outlaw exclaimed.

"Yes," answered Morse.

"That's not much," Procopio responded.

Morse and Morehouse took the outlaw directly to the ferry and lodged him in jail in San Leandro the same evening. Procopio's capture proved a newspaper sensation. He was the most notorious bandido on the Pacific Coast at that time, because of his violent past and because he was Joaquin Murrieta's nephew. Newspapers throughout the state gave the capture prominent coverage and recounted Procopio's butchering of the Golding family in 1863. One detailed report that appeared in the *Alameda County Gazette* was picked up and reprinted in many East Coast newspapers.[15]

This account was spotted by Ned Buntline, one of the most prolific and most famous authors of dime novels. Buntline, whose true name was E. Z. C. Judson, knew a dramatic story when he saw one. Three years earlier he had "discovered" Buffalo Bill Cody and penned a popular but fictional story of his life that was published in *Street & Smith's New York Weekly*. It was Buntline who pursuaded Cody to become an actor, which led eventually to the formation of Buffalo Bill's Wild West Show. Buntline was always on the lookout for colorful westerners as subjects. He knew of Harry Morse by reputation, and apparently had met him at least once. In 1868 Buntline had made an extended visit to California, giving temperance lectures. He spoke to a large crowd in the courthouse in San Leandro and presumably met Morse there. Now he quickly wrote "Red Dick, The Tiger of California," which was published in *Street & Smith's New York Weekly* in serial form beginning in June 1872. This proved so popular that it was twice reprinted in dime novel form in 1890 and 1891. The hero of the story was Sheriff Morse; its villain, Procopio. Unlike Buffalo Bill, Morse was embarrassed by Buntline's attention and decried "the cheap novels in which he has been made to figure as a man who delighted in scenes of carnage and in desperate hand to hand conflicts."[16]

Procopio was brought to trial on April 25. His attorney moved for a change of venue to Santa Clara County on the grounds "that charges of all kinds of crimes have been published against him and the public mind is poisoned" and that "numerous false and garbled accounts of his life" published in the newspapers had made it impossible for him to get a fair trial in Alameda County. This motion was denied. In retrospect, Procopio's notoriety was so great it mattered little where he was tried.

The prime witness against him was Juan Camargo. The previous day Morse had lodged the tapadera in jail to make sure he was on hand to testify. Evidently the sheriff had a serious charge to hang over Camargo's head, for only the threat of state prison could have convinced him to testify against a man as dangerous as Procopio. Camargo admitted that Procopio and an unidentified man had brought the cow to his place and butchered it there the same night it had been stolen. Camargo was given a quarter of the cow as his share; Procopio took the rest away in a wagon. Camargo's wife confirmed her husband's story. John Arnett, A. J. McDavid, and Ralph Faville testified to tracking the cow and arresting Camargo.

Harry Morse was called as the prosecution's last witness. He described the arrest of Procopio and his brief conversation with him in the bordello. However, he also described a further conversation after he had taken Procopio outside: "Out on the street after we had gone a little ways, he asked, 'What did Camargo say?' I replied, 'Camargo says you stole the cow.' The defendant replied, 'By God, Morse, I did steal the cow. Camargo and his family were starving and I stole her to get them some meat. Camargo was with me.'"

This testimony by Harry Morse was almost certainly false. It defies belief that a seasoned ex-convict and desperado of Procopio's stripe would make such a voluntary statement incriminating himself. He had gone to great efforts to elude the many lawmen who were after him, and it was exceedingly unlikely that he would confess to one of them shortly after being captured without being offered any inducement, such as a plea bargain, in return.

Procopio took the stand on his own behalf. He vigorously denied making this confession to Morse and also denied that he had stolen a cow. He claimed to have spent that night in bed with a prostitute, Ygnacia Morales, in Antonio Smith's dance house. The girl next took the stand and provided Procopio an alibi, saying that he had slept with her the night of the theft, March 31, 1871, as well as the next two nights. However, on cross-examination, she admitted that she could not recall what dates she had slept with Procopio and that it may have been in a different month. Antonio Smith and his wife, Juana Uries, also testified that Procopio had spent three nights at their fandango house, but neither could recall the date.[17]

The trial lasted six hours. The jury deliberated only fifteen minutes before finding Procopio guilty of grand larceny. He was sentenced to seven years in San Quentin. The editor of the San Jose *Mercury* was not impressed with Harry Morse's accomplishment and sniffed, "Procopio, the desperado, has had his trial in Alameda County and been found guilty of stealing a cow. There is no doubt but this man has been guilty of all the crimes on the calendar, from petit larceny to murder, and it seems absurd that the only charge that could be made to stick against him should be that of stealing a $75 cow." To this the editor of the *Alameda County Gazette* responded that Procopio "has been convicted of every offense he has committed in this county. If the officers of other counties in which he has committed crimes will do their duty Mr. Procopio will end his days within the walls of San Quentin."[18]

But such was not to be Procopio's fate. With coppers for good behavior, he was discharged from San Quentin in 1877. Prior to his release Morse noted in his diary, "Juan Camargo told me that Felipe Valencia sent word to him that Procopio was going to kill him when he got out of prison." But Procopio wisely committed no crimes in Alameda County. Instead, he stole a band of cattle in Contra Costa County, sold them to crooked butchers in Martinez, and fled to the San Joaquin Valley. In November 1877 he led a five-man gang that rode into Grangeville in what is now Kings County, robbed a store, and stabbed a clerk. A month later he led a band of ten bandidos into Caliente in Kern County, robbing the hotel, express office, depot, and store. Five of the outlaws were captured and jailed in Bakersfield, but a mob lynched them all. On December 26 Procopio and his riders held up a store in Hanford. A posse tracked him to the Hispanic settlement at Poso Chane and surrounded him in a jacal. But the desperado shot his way out, killed a posse member, Sol Gladden, and escaped. Procopio fled to Mexico, where, in 1882, he shot and killed an actor in a brothel and was arrested and reportedly executed by firing squad. However, the next year he was reported at the head of a band of stock thieves operating along the border in Sonora and Baja California. Although California lawmen undertook several manhunts for him during the mid-1880s, he seems to have stayed mainly in Mexico, where he was slain about 1890.[19]

Alameda's sheriff had gone to great lengths to bring Procopio to justice. Self-righteous in his belief that the bandido was the personification of evil, Morse evidently felt justified in committing perjury to guarantee a conviction in court. In the decade that had passed since the murders of the Aaron Golding family, only he had consistently sought justice for the forgotten victims. Morse had cornered and shot Narciso Bojorques. His capture of Procopio completed his personal crusade to avenge the murders of those four helpless people who had been left butchered and burned in the lonely tules and scrub oak of Corral Hollow.

CHAPTER 12

"An Innocent Man":
Bartolo Sepulveda

HARRY Morse's efforts to bring California's worst outlaws to justice did not go unrewarded. In March 1872 the state legislature took the unusual step of passing Assembly Bill 334, An Act for the Relief of Henry N. Morse. The bill provided a $2,000 payment to reimburse the sheriff for his time and expense in tracking down Jesus Tejada and Juan Soto. In speeches praising Morse, the legislators recognized that he had pursued many outlaws far beyond the borders of Alameda County. Senator W. W. Pendergast declared, "I have no hesitation in saying that he has done more by his personal courage, coolness, skill and bravery to clear the state of a band of desperadoes and outlaws, certainly more than any other one man." Senator Edward Tompkins was even more effusive in his tribute:

> I do not believe there is a man in the state of California more widely or favorably known than Sheriff Morse of Alameda County. Under circumstances where other men shrink he has gone forward, until today he is the best known, and I think, generally conceded to be, the best sheriff in the state. The dangers he has encountered have become the subjects of romance on the other side of the continent.[1]

During 1872 and 1873 the most bitter political issue in Alameda County was the fight to move the county seat from San Leandro to Oakland. Unlike the bloody county seat wars of Kansas in the 1880s, this protracted dispute was resolved in the legislature, the California Supreme Court, and finally the ballot box. In 1873 the county's voters chose Oakland as the new seat of government. Construction of the new courthouse and jail in Oakland was completed the following year.[2]

This change made it necessary for Harry and Virginia Morse to move to Oakland as well. In the fall of 1873 they began construction

Virginia Morse and her buggy in front of the Morse home in Oakland, shortly after it was built in 1873. Courtesy Jack Reynolds.

of a fine new home on eleven acres in the Peralta Heights section of Oakland. The house, situated near the northeast corner of Newton and Hanover streets, was in the Victorian style and boasted fourteen rooms and a carriage house. This would be the Morses' home for the remainder of their lives.[3]

Their son George, now seventeen, had become increasingly unruly, and Morse had enrolled him as a cadet at McClure's California Military Academy in Oakland. The sheriff prized his own military experience and hoped that the academy would instill a measure of discipline in the boy. Such was not the case, for George Morse was expelled for insubordination. Not long after, on the night of September 20, 1873, a huge fire destroyed the academy. Its main building, armory, barns, and outbuildings were consumed in the inferno. Several weeks later it came to light that before the fire George Morse had told some former schoolmates that he intended to burn down the school; after the blaze he boasted that he had set it. Harry Morse was shocked when his son was arrested for arson. At the preliminary hearing in December, witnesses testified that the youth was a noto-

rious braggart and that his boasts were empty, but nonetheless the
judge held him to answer. Although the charges were apparently
dropped, Morse was thoroughly mortified by this incident.[4]

Since the murder at Scott's store, the sheriff had kept up a fruitless search for Bartolo Sepulveda. Morse was stunned when on
March 20, 1873, Sepulveda, after more than two years as a fugitive,
walked into his office and surrendered. He told Morse that he did
not commit the Ludovisi murder and declared that he was ready to
stand trial to prove his innocence. Both men profoundly misjudged
each other: Morse never doubted for an instant that Sepulveda was
guilty; Sepulveda did not imagine that Morse could put together a
case that would result in his conviction.

Sheriff Morse began painstaking preparations for the trial, which
was scheduled for the July term of court. Morse was greatly disappointed that his key witness, Thomas Scott, had left the state because
of a scandal that made newspaper headlines. The year before Scott
had seduced a young married schoolteacher, Mrs. L. M. Penwell.
When her husband learned of the affair, she shot herself to death in
an Oakland hotel room. Morse's friend George Beers, now a reporter for the *San Francisco Chronicle,* investigated and wrote a long,
sensational newspaper account of the affair. He dubbed Scott "the
wickedest man in Alameda County." The resulting scandal forced
Scott to flee to his home state of Tennessee.[5]

Despite this setback Morse gathered witnesses and meticulously
assembled a persuasive case, mainly of circumstantial evidence,
against Sepulveda. The outlaw's trial began in Judge McKee's packed
courtroom in Oakland on July 26, 1873. Sepulveda was represented
by Frank E. Spencer, the San Jose lawyer who had represented both
Juan Soto and Procopio. Spencer was assisted by his law partner,
James H. Lowe, and by an Oakland attorney, William Van Voorhies.
The prosecution was handled by A. A. Moore, district attorney of
Alameda County, and his deputy, Alfred Gibbons. Sepulveda's grief-
stricken wife, attired in black, attended each day of the trial.

The entire first day was taken up in selecting a jury. Then Moore
opened the prosecution's case. Cornelius Sullivan described the robbery and the bundle of clothes that was stolen from him but testified that he could not identify the bandits. Young Tom Scott, Jr.,
also related the robbery and killing of Otto Ludovisi. He said that
he thought Bartolo Sepulveda was the bandit who entered the store
just before the shooting but admitted that he was not certain.

Next Charles Hadsell took the stand. He described in detail the tracks of the horses and their riders. One boot print was quite broad, another had seven rows of nails in one sole, and the third was very small, with the side of the sole worn off, as if its wearer was pigcon-toed. Hadsell testified that he recognized this last track as that of Bartolo Sepulveda, who had worked for him as a vaquero in 1859 and 1860. But on cross-examination Hadsell's testimony was thrown into serious doubt, for he was forced to admit that he had not seen Sepulveda or his tracks for eleven years previous to the murder and that many Californios were bowlegged and walked pigeon-toed, owing to their habit of living in the saddle.

A Californio, Carlos Higuera, testified that he had seen Sepulveda and Juan Soto on the road two miles north of Scott's store a few days before the murder. A. J. McDavid and James Bonnell, who had helped Ralph Faville track the killers, both testified that they had examined the boots Sepulveda now wore and that they were the same that made the tracks at the crime scene. A young French sheep rancher, Bernard Bille, took the stand and recounted that on the morning of the fatal day three riders had stopped at his house, about halfway be-tween Scott's store and Calaveras Valley. They bought some bread and sugar, then rode on toward Scott's store. Bille pointed to Bar-tolo Sepulveda in the defendant's chair and identified him as one of the three horsemen. Bille, however, admitted on cross-examination that he did not know Sepulveda and had never seen him before the murder or since, until he identified him in court.

Next Ralph Faville and Sheriff Morse testified, slowly pulling the chain of evidence together. Faville described the tracks of the three horsemen and his trailing them to Bernard Bille's ranch house and then to Calaveras Valley. Both he and Morse stated that they had found the same tracks also leading from Bille's house to Scott's store. This, coupled with Bille's statement that Sepulveda was one of the three riders he had seen on the morning before the murder, was compelling evidence of Sepulveda's complicity in the crime.

Harry Morse now tightened the noose around Sepulveda's neck. He described finding the stolen bundle of clothes on the creek be-hind the house of Sepulveda's mother-in-law; he also testified that the footprints at the murder scene matched the outlaw's boots. Morse described for the jury his manhunts for Sepulveda as well as his killing of Juan Soto. Several other prosecution witnesses testified, including Javier and Anselmo Alviso, Sepulveda's brothers-in-law, who reported turning over the stolen bundle to Sheriff Morse.

Then District Attorney Moore produced his trump card. John

Bartolo Sepulveda, compadre of Juan Soto and Tiburcio Vasquez. He served more than ten years in San Quentin for a murder he did not commit. Courtesy of the San Jose Historical Museum.

Copp, a convicted forger, testified that he had become friendly with Sepulveda while they were in the county jail together several months earlier. Copp swore that Sepulveda had admitted to him that he had participated in the robbery and murder. Copp said that Sepulveda told him that Juan Soto and another man whom Sepulveda did not identify had been with him. According to Copp, he kept this information to himself and finally told Harry Morse about it when the sheriff was taking him to San Quentin. Copp declared that he had not been offered a pardon in exchange for his testimony and insisted that he had come forward "because his conscience affected him."[6]

Copp's testimony hit the defense like a bombshell. Sepulveda's lawyers did their best to impeach him, but Copp stuck to his story. Frank Spencer, undeterred, mustered his witnesses and forged ahead in his effort to save Sepulveda's neck. Six witnesses, all Hispanic, testified that they had seen Sepulveda in San Jose on the day of the murder. However, all of them were Sepulveda's friends or family members; none were independent witnesses. Sepulveda's sister, Luisa, also testified that she had bought her brother the boots that he was wearing in October 1872, long after the murder, and had sent them to him at Poso Chane while he was still a fugitive.

Finally Bartolo Sepulveda took the stand on his own behalf. He gave a long and detailed account of his comings and goings before and after the murder. He said that he had spent the past two years working as a vaquero and laborer at various places in California and Mexico. He admitted his close friendship with Juan Soto and that he had once provided a bail bond for Soto so he could get released from jail in San Jose. He described how he and Soto had left San Jose in December 1870 to work on the hog ranch near Modesto. He also confirmed the previous testimony that he and Soto had passed through Sunol Valley on their way home the day before the murder. He testified that he had left San Jose on January 20 or 21, 1871, to look for work and that he was then unaware that he was suspected of the Ludovisi killing. Sepulveda claimed that he had next seen Juan Soto at Soto's uncle's house in the Coast Range in March but denied having been with the bandido when Morse killed him on May 10.

In speaking of Juan Soto's death, Sepulveda stumbled badly on cross-examination. At first he stated that he had heard of Soto's death when he was riding from the Panoche mine back to San Jose. Later he contradicted himself and said that he had heard of the shootout after he had left San Jose and was on his way to the mines near Lone Pine in Inyo County. Further, even though he admitted that he had returned to San Jose for a few days in May 1871, he claimed he did not learn he was a wanted man until a year later. This statement seriously damaged his credibility, for numerous newspapers had reported in the fall of 1871 that he was wanted for killing Ludovisi, and others reported that he had taken part in the Soap Lake stage robbery. It was difficult to believe that he had not heard he was suspected of these crimes. In the end Sepulveda's testimony did more harm than good. His companionship with Juan Soto, who was widely believed to have been the leader of the robbers who killed Ludovisi, made a very bad impression on the jury. And his admitted presence with Soto at the crime scene the day before the killing was surely the most damaging part of his testimony.

Prosecution and defense argued the case to the jury for two days. Sepulveda's lawyers spoke eloquently for acquittal. Van Voorhies attacked Copp's credibility and pointed out the obvious: "It is preposterous that Sepulveda, who had come from a place of safety and demanded a trial, should make a confession of murder to a criminal who was on his way to the penitentiary, who could not help him in the least." Frank Spencer pointed out that had Sepulveda truly been guilty he never would have left the stolen bundle of clothes near his mother-in-law's house. The jury retired at four o'clock on August 2 and six hours later returned with their verdict: guilty of murder in the first degree. Judge McKee sentenced him to the only punishment the law allowed: death by hanging.[7]

Spencer moved for a new trial. Judge McKee was swayed by the fact that most of the evidence against Sepulveda was circumstantial. After agonizing over his decision for three months, McKee ordered a retrial. There were several delays, and finally Bartolo Sepulveda's new trial took place in June 1874. The result was the same: guilty of first-degree murder. However, the criminal code had changed. It now provided that the jurors could choose between death and life imprisonment. This jury sentenced Sepulveda to life in San Quentin.[8]

On August 5 Deputy Sheriff Fred Bryant, Morse's jailer, took Sepulveda to the Oakland city prison to await the afternoon ferry. Two other prisoners, Charles Edwards and Thomas Thornton, a pair of dangerous robbers, were also there waiting for Sheriff Morse to transport them to San Quentin. A newspaper reporter interviewed Sepulveda in the city prison and wrote, "He is very quiet, speaks but little, seems to have a kindly disposition, and appears to be very grateful for the kind treatment he has received while in jail."

Sepulveda was brought into the office of the police captain, Fred Tarbett, who said, "Well, Bartolo, you are going over for a long stay."

"Yes, they couldn't send me there longer," replied Sepulveda quietly. Puffing on a cigarette, he added, "There is one thing. I go there an innocent man."

"Let me give you one piece of advice," said Tarbett. "When you get over there, do everything the officers tell you to do. Put yourself on your very best behavior. Don't associate with disorderly characters. Do all you can to win the respect and goodwill of the officers and you will find that you will be well treated and you will be much better off."

At that, Fred Bryant remarked, "He is all right on that score, Captain. There is not a better behaved man in jail than Bartolo. He won't give them any trouble."[9]

That afternoon Sheriff Morse took the three prisoners, manacled together, to the ferry *Contra Costa* for the trip to San Francisco. From there a prison launch would take them north through the bay to San Quentin. On the ferry Edwards complained that his handcuffs were too tight, and Morse, seeing that the iron had cut into his wrist, loosened it a notch. Just as the ferry reached the Vallejo Street wharf, Edwards slipped his hand loose, leaped onto the dock, and fled into the crowd. Morse yanked his six-shooter but held his fire for fear of hitting a bystander. He stayed with the other two prisoners while several in the crowd pursued Edwards, but the robber escaped. This was the first and last prisoner that Harry Morse ever lost. *The Oakland Tribune* commented acridly, "Sheriff Morse needs a lesson occasionally, like the rest of us. He is not infallible. There was no sort of sense in his trying to escort a murderer and two highway robbers to San Quentin, without assistance. . . . The sheriff had too many irons in the fire."[10]

Bartolo Sepulveda followed Captain Tarbett's advice. He was a model prisoner at San Quentin and made many friends among the guards and the convicts. His wife and children worked tirelessly to secure a pardon from the governor, but to no avail. The years went by, and he despaired of ever being released. His pardon application in 1876 was turned down. Two legislative committees visited the prison in 1877 and 1879; to them Sepulveda pled his case, but no action was taken. Then early in 1882 Sepulveda met another lifer in the prison, William Donovan, and the two struck up a friendship. Hispanic and Anglo prisoners often did not congregate, and although Donovan and Sepulveda had been imprisoned together for years, the two had never met before. Donovan quickly realized that he had crucial information that might exonerate Sepulveda.

Donovan told Sepulveda and then declared in a signed statement that years earlier, on May 7, 1873, he had been sitting in front of the factory building in the prison yard when three new convicts who had just entered San Quentin approached him. They were John Copp, Wallace W. Rathbone, and a third man whose name he could not recall. Donovan said that he "asked Copp for what term of years he had been sentenced to the prison, that Copp told him, and said in conversation in reference to his case that . . . Copp could get out sooner if he would swear against a Mexican who was there in the Alameda County Jail charged with murder. That Sheriff Morse had offered him a pardon for so doing." Donovan told Copp, "Yes, I expect it is the California style, Morse wants you to swear that the Mexican confessed to you in jail." Copp then told Donovan that he would not do it. Donovan stated that he warned Copp "to not swear falsely in any event, that it might 'come home' to him when he least expected" and that "Copp said then he would not swear at all, leaving the inference that if he did not swear falsely he would not swear against the Mexican at all."[11]

Donovan stated that several months later Rathbone came to him and said that "John Copp had gone to Alameda County and had sworn falsely against the Mexican and that the latter had been convicted of murder." According to Donovan, he and Rathbone agreed to contact "the Mexican's" attorney in Alameda, but before they could learn his name "John Copp was returned to the prison and assigned 'a good billet'" and "Copp stood well now and was in a position to 'put a job' on them and they had concluded not to make any statement to send to the Mexican's attorney." Donovan did not know who "the Mexican" was and kept the matter to himself for almost nine years until he met Sepulveda and decided to help him.[12]

With this new evidence, Sepulveda's family began to circulate a petition for his pardon. When former sheriff Nick Harris was asked to sign it, he agreed and then went one step further: he sent Governor George Perkins a letter with an astounding admission. "I have no doubt of the innocence of [Sepulveda] of the crime for which he was convicted," Harris began.

> [On the evening of the murder] Bartolo Sepulveda came into the Sheriff's Office in the City of San Jose, and asked me for a permit to see his brother Miguel, who was in the County Jail very sick, and awaiting trial on an indictment for grand larceny. I saw that he was fully under the influence of liquor and refused his request, but he was persistent and detained me several minutes after the hour (5 o'clock) for closing the office. I locked the door and we both walked out in front of the Court House, where we met other parties and engaged in conversation that lasted twenty minutes so that when I parted with him it must have been as late as 5:30 P.M.

Harris pointed out that the robbery had begun at seven o'clock. And, he continued, "[With Sepulveda's] intoxicated condition when I parted with him and the bad conditions of the roads and the distance (about 30 miles) necessarily to be traveled on horseback, in an hour and a half or even two hours, I deem it almost or quite impossible for him to have participated in the murder." The former sheriff wrote that although he rode in the manhunt in the days following the crime, he never suspected Sepulveda.

Harris admitted, "I should have deemed it sufficient motive to volunteer my testimony, had not his character been notoriously bad." He added, "[Sepulveda] richly deserved the imprisonment for crimes that I know he is guilty of, but escaped conviction by perjury and subornations of perjury. But from reports of the officers at the prison, and from my own personal observations during several years past, I am convinced that a reformation has worked in his character."[13]

Now at last Sepulveda's family had compelling evidence of his innocence. They obtained letters to the governor from Judge McKee and the jurors who convicted him asking for his release, and many prominent citizens of Santa Clara County signed the petition. But the wheels of justice ground slowly. The State Board of Prison Directors looked into the case but took no action for more than two and a half years. There were several reasons for this. Nick Harris's statement did not give Sepulveda an ironclad alibi. The distance between the county jail in San Jose and Scott's store, via the Calaveras Road, was twenty miles, not thirty. An experienced vaquero like Sepulveda could ride that distance in an hour and a half. Indeed, Sepulveda's own testimony at the first trial indicated that he and Juan Soto had ridden leisurely from Scott's store to San Jose the day before the murder in less than two hours. Sepulveda was fully capable of leaving San Jose at 5:30 P.M. and reaching the murder scene by 7:00 P.M.

The statement by William Donovan was evidently given less weight by the board because he was a convicted felon. Nevertheless, it cast great doubt on the testimony of John Copp, for Donovan had nothing to gain by coming forward. On December 16, 1884, Nick Harris testified in person before the board, which finally recommended that Sepulveda be pardoned. He was released from San Quentin on January 22, 1885, having spent almost twelve years in jail and prison. Bartolo Sepulveda returned to his family a reformed man. He lived a full and useful life, working as a vaquero and horse breaker until old age. He died in San Jose in 1926 at the age of eighty-seven surrounded by loving children and grandchildren.[14]

In the final analysis, it seems evident that Bartolo Sepulveda was innocent of the murder at Scott's store. Although it is possible that he was present, it is most unlikely. The statements by Nick Harris show not only that Sepulveda was very intoxicated that day but also that he had little time to meet with the other two robbers, plan the crime, and travel to the scene. The statements by the convict John

Copp were especially unreliable and should have been disregarded by the jury.

One historian who studied this case concluded that Sheriff Morse "falsely accused Sepulveda of the crime and probably 'set him up' with John Copp." To accept this judgment, one must believe that Copp lied when he testified that Sepulveda had confessed to him but told the truth when he informed William Donovan that Harry Morse had persuaded him to "swear falsely" against Sepulveda. Since Copp was a twice-convicted thief, his credibility as a witness was very weak, and he is the only witness to accuse Morse of deliberately "framing" Sepulveda. And rather than Morse persuading the convict to testify, it is much more probable that Copp volunteered his testimony to the sheriff.[15]

To more fully evaluate Harry Morse's role in this unsavory affair it is necessary to consider the "jailhouse snitch" phenomenon. For John Copp was, in modern parlance as well as that of the 1870s, a jailhouse snitch. All jails and prisons have informants, but the most dangerous are those who fabricate confessions from criminal defendants in exchange for favors or reduced sentences. No reputable police detective or prosecuting attorney will use such testimony unless it is well corroborated by other witnesses or independent evidence. As an experienced lawman, Morse surely suspected that Copp's story was false. And Morse knew better than to offer a jailhouse snitch as a witness at trial. Yet he was so convinced of Sepulveda's guilt that he could not resist the temptation to use Copp's testimony to ensure a guilty verdict. By putting Copp on the stand, both Morse and District Attorney Moore were guilty of overzealousness as well as a reckless disregard for Sepulveda's civil rights. However, there is no reliable evidence that they deliberately "set up" Sepulveda or persuaded Copp to lie.[16]

It is clear that Harry Morse did not know that Sepulveda had been with Nick Harris at the jail prior to the murder. Harris confirmed this in an affidavit dated November 5, 1884: "I said nothing at that time to anyone of these facts." There is further evidence that Morse was unaware of Harris's alibi testimony. When Morse first identified Juan Soto and Bartolo Sepulveda as two of the killers, he also believed that the third man was Bartolo's brother, Miguel Sepulveda. Morse presented his evidence to the Alameda County grand jury, and all three were indicted for murder. However, as we have seen, Miguel Sepulveda was in jail in San Jose at the time of the killing and could not have participated. At some point the sheriff learned of this, and the indictment against Miguel Sepulveda was dismissed. Clearly Morse and his friend Nick Harris were not communicating very well during the weeks following the murder, or the Alameda lawman would have known that Miguel Sepulveda was in jail and that his brother had attempted to visit him there.[17]

The most obvious question is, why did Sepulveda fail to call Nick Harris as an alibi witness at his trial? The answer is that Sepulveda was so drunk he did not recall talking to Harris at the jail. As Harris stated, "Although I expected to be subpoenaed for the defendant Sepulveda, I was not. Why I was not subpoenaed I do not know, unless it was that Sepulveda was so far intoxicated on the evening of the 10th of January, 1871, that he forgot these facts." And if Sepulveda was that drunk, he could hardly have made the horseback ride necessary to place him at the murder scene.[18]

Who committed the robbery and murder at Scott's store? Juan Soto's leadership of the raid has never been directly questioned. However, in 1875 Sheriff John Adams of Santa Clara County, in an oblique reference to the Ludovisi killing, termed Soto "a daring and fearless robber but no murderer." Adams had his own ax to grind, for, as we will see, he disliked Morse and envied his superior reputation. His claim that the bandido was not capable of murder is difficult to reconcile with Soto's shooting at Deputy McElroy in 1867 and his desperate duel to the death in 1871.[19]

Thomas Scott's family always believed that the robbers were Juan Soto, Bartolo Sepulveda, and Tiburcio Vasquez. As Vasquez was the leader of so many bandit raids of the early 1870s, it is not unreasonable to include him as a prime suspect. In 1872 George Beers supplied a different theory. He wrote in the *San Francisco Chronicle* that Juan Soto and his companions had come to Scott's store "solely to kill Scott in revenge for an act of treachery toward one of their countrymen." Beers claimed that Otto Ludovisi resembled Scott and was gunned down by killers who mistook him for his employer. This theory lacks credibility, for the raid was clearly a robbery and not an assassination. Ludovisi was slain while shouting at the robbers to get out of the store, and the bandits also shot at Scott, Sullivan, and the neighbor, Antone, as they fled. No further effort was made to follow and kill them or the other witnesses.[20]

Bartolo Sepulveda no doubt deserved punishment for other crimes. But Alameda's sheriff had come within a hair's breadth of sending an innocent man to his death on the gallows. Frank Spencer later wrote that racism motivated the jury to convict Sepulveda: "At the time the people of Alameda County had a great prejudice against Native Californians, which showed itself where ever and when ever they were accused of crime."[21]

Whether one views the trials of Bartolo Sepulveda as a classic example of racial injustice, a case of mistaken identity, or a matter of overzealous law enforcement, one fact is plain: the arrest, prosecution, and conviction of Bartolo Sepulveda constitute the darkest chapter in Harry Morse's long career.

CHAPTER 13

Sixty Days in the Saddle

HARRY Morse's killing of Juan Soto, his capture of Procopio, and his conviction of Bartolo Sepulveda seem to have done little to quell the lawless spirit of Tiburcio Vasquez. In April 1872 he and several bandidos robbed the San Benito stage south of Hollister. Vasquez escaped, but one of the gang members, Jose Castro, was seized by vigilantes and lynched. In January 1873 Vasquez recruited a Chileno, Abdon Leiva, who became one of his most trusted followers. Vasquez, however, was more interested in Leiva's wife, Rosaria, and unwisely carried on a long, secret affair with her. Other robbers who rode with him included Vasquez's cousin, Teodoro Moreno, and a Frenchman, August DeBert. His lieutenant was Clodoveo Chavez, a twenty-two-year-old vaquero from San Juan Bautista. Vasquez never had an organized gang. He generally traveled about alone or with one or two compadres. When ready to make a raid he would recruit a few local men; the gang would disband after the crime was completed. Most members of his band followed honest occupations between raids.[1]

On February 26, 1873, Vasquez and five mounted brigands made a raid at Firebaugh's Ferry, robbing the store and an arriving stagecoach. On July 30 the gang held up and robbed the Twenty-one Mile House between San Jose and Gilroy. Tiburcio's bloodiest exploit took place on the August 26. Vasquez, Moreno, Chavez, Leiva, and Romulo Gonzales robbed a store and hotel in the hamlet of Tres Pinos (now Paicines), eleven miles south of Hollister. The bandits panicked and shot to death three innocent bystanders in what became known as the Tres Pinos Tragedy. A posse led by Santa Clara County Sheriff John H. Adams trailed the bandidos south to Los Angeles County, but after a brief gunfight in Rock Creek Canyon the outlaws escaped.

By this time Abdon Leiva had learned of his wife's unfaithfulness. He surrendered and offered to testify against Vasquez. Based on in-

195

The notorious Tiburcio Vasquez, pursued by Harry Morse in one of the Old West's longest manhunts. From a cabinet card taken by Bradley and Rulofson in San Francisco, May 27, 1874. Courtesy Robert G. McCubbin.

formation from Leiva, Teodoro Moreno was arrested and convicted of one of the Tres Pinos murders and sentenced to life imprisonment. The bandit chieftain was unfazed by these developments. He picked up a new gang member, Isador Padilla, who had barely escaped hanging for his part in the Medina murders. On November 10 Vasquez and his men held up the Jones store, near Millerton. The day after Christmas Vasquez made his boldest raid yet at Kingston in Fresno County. With ten desperadoes at his back, he plundered the town's two stores and hotel, tied up and robbed some thirty-five men, and escaped in a hail of lead.

These audacious bandit raids terrorized the citizens of central California and created a statewide uproar. It was clear that the uneven efforts of local lawmen to capture Vasquez were woefully inadequate. Local politicians who were willing to pay for manhunts often lacked the public funds to do so. Others refused to pay their sheriffs for out-of-county manhunts. California sorely lacked a state police force, such as the Texas Rangers, that could quickly put large posses in the field for long periods of time without fear of running out of money to pay for supplies and salaries. On January 2, 1874, legislators met in Sacramento with Governor Newton Booth and asked him to appoint a special posse to capture or kill Vasquez and his band. They introduced a bill in the legislature appropriating sufficient funds to finance such a manhunt. The legislature allocated $15,000 to bring Vasquez to justice. Of these funds, $5,000 were earmarked for the expenses of the posse; additionally, Governor Booth offered a reward for Vasquez: $2,000 dead, $3,000 alive. This was California's first state-funded police action since 1853 when the California Rangers were organized to track down Joaquin Murrieta and his band.[2]

Sheriff Adams of San Jose wanted to lead the posse, but Governor Booth had other ideas. He summoned Harry Morse to Sacramento and discussed with him at length the proposed manhunt for Vasquez. Booth's plan was for Morse to lead a band of thirty men south while smaller posses from the main group searched all the bandit hideouts from Alameda County to San Bernardino, with the goal of capturing or killing every desperado known to have associated with Vasquez. Morse was unhappy with this plan. He had rarely used a posse of more than a few men, and he knew that a huge posse would have great difficulty moving quickly and avoiding attention. Morse suggested a much smaller number, but finally he and the governor reached a compromise: he would take eight men, whom he would handpick.

Morse chose as his lieutenant Tom Cunningham, the energetic sheriff of San Joaquin County. At this time he had been sheriff just two years, but Cunningham would grow gray in public service and become one of the great lawmen of the Old West. Morse included his son George, plus a pair of friends who were always ready to aid him, Ralph Faville and A. J. McDavid. Also in the posse were two men who knew many of the bandidos: Harry Thomas, Fresno County deputy sheriff, and Ambrose Calderwood, former sheriff of Santa Cruz County. Morse allowed a reporter for the *San Francisco Chronicle*, A. B. "Boyd" Henderson, to accompany him, a decision he would come to regret.[3]

The sheriff rounded out his posse with its most colorful member, Ramon Romero, a forty-one-year-old Mexican who was an expert vaquero and a dangerous man in a fight. Romero had reportedly been a member of Joaquin Murrieta's band in the early 1850s. True or not, he knew all the mestenero trails in the San Joaquin Valley, the Coast Range, and along El Camino Viejo and La Vereda del Monte.

Ramon Romero, from his
San Quentin prison photo-
graph about 1886. Author's
collection.

Morse had known him since 1860 when he was noted in Oakland for
his skill with both guitar and Bowie knife. That year Romero stabbed
to death an American, John Doane, in a quarrel over a woman outside an Oakland fandango house. He was convicted of murder and
sentenced to hang, but the California Supreme Court reversed the
verdict. On retrial Romero was acquitted. In 1862, in Sacramento,
Romero stabbed to death another man in a fandango fight. This
time he served ten years in San Quentin for second-degree murder.
Despite Romero's violent record, Morse liked him immensely and
sorely needed a posseman who knew the bandidos' haunts. He
signed Romero on as guide at $5 per day.

   Harry Morse spent almost two months in preparation. He
planned to ride as soon as possible in the spring, as heavy winter rains
made streams impassable and flooded many parts of the San Joaquin
Valley. Also, it was necessary to wait until the grass was well up so the
horses would have plenty of feed. On March 9 Morse sent word for
his possemen to meet at Firebaugh's Ferry on the thirteenth. A re-
muda of horses, supplied free of charge by the Miller & Lux Ranch,
had been driven to Firebaugh's two weeks previous and fed on grain
to prepare them for the trip.

   A. J. McDavid's four-horse wagon was loaded with provisions,
cooking equipment, a tent, and a large magazine of rifle and pistol

cartridges. While he and George Morse drove the wagon south from Alameda County the others took the train to Lathrop, south of Stockton, where they were to meet Tom Cunningham. Vasquez had many friends in Stockton and Cunningham wished to avoid them. In Lathrop Morse searched in vain for his bald-headed friend among the many passengers waiting at the depot and adjacent restaurant.

When we arrived there no Cunningham was to be found. We were greatly disappointed, for besides being one of the finest bandit hunters in the West, Cunningham was a man of jovial spirits and happy disposition, well calculated to be of great service.

Greatly put out, I went to the telegraph office to ascertain the reason for his non-appearance. I had but written my telegram, "Party here; what's up?" and addressed it to Tom, when a gruff voice said, "Nothin'." I turned to find the worst-looking old tramp, with shocking red whiskers, deliberately reading my message. I was ready for a fight, and so was the tramp. Something, however, stepped in to save my skin, for as I looked closely at the fellow I recognized the twinkle of Cunningham's eye. His disguise was so perfect that his mother would not have known him.

Arriving at Berenda, we left the railroad and met the remainder of the party. Then we crossed the country and struck camp a little out of Cantua Canyon Romero, the Mexican, was sent out to interview the Mexican families about. Without exciting any suspicion regarding his mission, he soon learned that Vasquez had not been in that section of the country, but was expected in a few days.

In the middle of that week Cunningham and I rode to the house of a fellow named Culp. Being disguised, we passed without suspicion as to our identity until a singular chap appeared in the doorway. He was a lean, lank American, gayly rigged out with diamond shirt pin, felt hat, good clothes, and a Havana cigar pointing rakishly at his eye. He advanced knowingly and said, "I know what you fellers is on."

Considerably taken back, I replied with warmth, "What do you mean? We ain't on anything."

"Aw, that's too thin. You see, I'm on that lay meself." He pulled aside his coat and displayed a pair of handcuffs.

Disgusted, we turned away, rode back and returned to camp to hunt for a lookout where we could command a good view of the valley and catch early sight of approaching strangers.

About an hour afterward I was astonished to see Cunningham and Ramon mounted, riding like mad along the edge of the valley. Hastening

Tom Cunningham, sheriff
of San Joaquin County.
Cunningham rode with
Morse in the Vasquez
manhunt. Courtesy
R. Tod Ruse.

*to the wagon, I learned that the lanky American had just paid us a visit
without our knowledge, looked about, and hurried off.*

*Cunningham's suspicions having been aroused, he gave chase and cap-
tured the beauty. He was searched, and a letter containing this significant
remark found on him: "There is a party here in search of Vasquez. They
have a four-horse wagon and a greaser to interpret for them. They are the
biggest fools I ever saw, for Vasquez is a hundred miles from here."*

*We suspected the fellow of being some sort of robber, and that suspi-
cion turned out to be right. We discovered, after we had let him go, that
he was an ex-convict and in direct communication with Vasquez's gang.
When arrested by us he was on his way to a telegraph station, and within
a week the movements of the party would have been known to Vasquez.*[4]

Morse and his men spent the next two weeks searching Cantua
Canyon, Zapato Chino Creek, and Jacalitos Creek, the haunts of
bandidos since the days of Joaquin Murrieta. They discovered many
herds of stolen horses and cattle, but the thieves invariably fled into
the mountains at the posse's approach. The vaqueros and borre-

gueros they encountered were most untalkative, and if they gave any information at all it was usually false. Consequently the lawmen were kept busy running down many false leads and trails. Morse commented in a dispatch to Governor Booth, "It is going to be hard work to find Vasquez, he has so many friends among the Mexicans, they hide him and feed him, and lie to the officers."[5]

At the end of March Morse and his posse got on the trail of gang member Manuel Lopez, reported to have slain six men. They pursued him for several days through the Santa Lucia Mountains, suffering severely from cold and hunger, but their quarry managed to escape.[6]

Undaunted by their failure to capture Lopez, Morse and his possemen recrossed the Coast Range to Kettleman's Plains. They had now been in the saddle for twenty-seven days and had ridden more than one thousand miles. They had thoroughly searched all of Vasquez's known haunts, as well as the ranchos and jacales of the bandido's known and suspected friends from Monterey County in the north to Kern County in the south. They were able to obtain very little cooperation from the Californios and Mexicans, as Boyd Henderson later explained:

> Morse believed it would be an easy matter to find Vasquez if he could only induce the Mexican settlers in this region to disclose his lurking place. He therefore offered to them a reward of $1,000, in addition to the entire sum offered by the state, if they would simply furnish him information that would bring him in sight of Vasquez; but . . . there is a sort of glamour about the character and career of Vasquez in the eyes of the Mexican settlers and they all, with one accord, professed to have no knowledge of the bandit's whereabouts and declined to furnish any information concerning him. Vasquez's Mexican friends will not betray him, and his friends number most of the Mexicans in this region, who all admire the doughty robber in greater or less degree.[7]

Henderson hinted at how jealous lawmen deliberately undermined and hindered their work: "Morse represented himself and party as surveyors; and his identity, or the object of his inquiries and researchers, was not suspected until some of the up-country papers defeated the further success of his plan by announcing his presence in the lower counties, since which time he had been known wherever he appeared."[8]

Henderson also described how the bandidos and their sympathizers endeavored to recognize Sheriff Morse: "In almost every house in the horse-stealing communities, many of which we visited on our trip, may be found his photograph, which these people have obtained from a gallery in San Francisco where the negative was preserved."[9]

Morse became convinced that the elusive bandit chieftain was now somewhere south of the Tehachapi Mountains. On April 8 the lawmen started south, searching the country as they went, and reached the Tehachapis on April 12 after four days of hard riding. There the sheriff sent another report to Governor Booth in which he described some of the problems they encountered: "Have been in the saddle every day sleeping out from our wagon with only one blanket and about half the time without eating. Our greatest trouble is in getting fresh horses, every new lot of horses are grass fed and they don't stand our riding very long."[10]

Morse's hunch that Vasquez was in southern California was correct. Three days later, on April 15, Vasquez, his cousin, Francisco Cantua, alias Francisco Gomez, Isador Padilla, Clodoveo Chavez, and Lebrado Corona descended on the ranch of Alessandro Repetto, a wealthy Italian sheepman who lived some six miles northeast of Los Angeles, near the San Gabriel Mission. Repetto had but $80 in the ranch house, so Vasquez forced him to sign a bank order for $800 and ordered the sheepman's young nephew to bring it into a bank in town and return with the money. The boy, convinced his uncle would be slain if he did not obey, withdrew $500 at the bank. He was so nervous that suspicious bank officials notified Sheriff Billy Rowland, who soon elicited the whole story from the youth. Rowland quickly rounded up a posse, but he was able to obtain only mediocre livery horses. Vasquez, using a spyglass, spotted the lawmen approaching the Repetto ranch, and he and his compadres, all well mounted, easily outran their pursuers. So brazen was Vasquez that during the pursuit he and his band briefly stopped to rob four men in a wagon near the Arroyo Seco.

That same day Morse and his men were searching Rock Creek Canyon, where Sheriff Adams's posse had shot it out with the gang seven months earlier. They were in rough country and did not learn of the Repetto robbery until two days later. On April 21 Morse heard that Vasquez had been spotted the day before at the San Fernando Mission and that Sheriff Rowland was riding there with a posse. Morse and his men rode hard toward the San Fernando Valley but were stopped by a landslide in Little Tujunga Canyon and arrived too late. At a telegraph station Boyd Henderson filed a long dispatch that was published the next day in the *San Francisco Chronicle*. He unfairly blamed their plight on Sheriff Rowland: "We are unable to account for Sheriff Rowland's failure to promptly inform Morse last night of the presence of Vasquez at San Fernando. Had he sent us immediate notice and notified us of the impassibility of the canyon, if that fact was known to him, we could probably have taken such steps as would have insured the capture of Vasquez."[11]

Before entering Los Angeles County Morse's men had found that telegraph offices were virtually nonexistent and post offices almost as rare, making it impossible for Henderson to keep his editor advised of their progress. Now the manhunt brought them close to the telegraph line, and Harry Morse unwisely allowed Henderson to send several daily dispatches to the widely read *Chronicle*. They provided a ready means for Vasquez and his supporters to keep posted on the posse's movements. And this dispatch, publicly criticizing a popular local sheriff during an ongoing manhunt, was to prove a major blunder.

On April 24, at Petroliopolis, Henderson filed his last dispatch from Los Angeles County. It detailed the posse's movements and reflected their belief that Billy Rowland was not cooperating with them: "Our information as to the movements of Rowland have been meager, unfortunately. We have not received the details of his operations, which would have enabled us to guide our course so as to fully cover the points not reached by him."[12]

By this time Henderson's negative comments about Sheriff Rowland had been circulated in Los Angeles in late editions of *San Francisco Chronicle*. Rowland, clearly angered by the reports, assured the *Chronicle* that as soon as he learned of Vasquez's flight toward San Fernando he went directly to the Los Angeles telegraph office, but by then it was 11:00 P.M. and the office was closed. Sheriff Rowland's friend Ben Truman, editor of the *Los Angeles Star*, fired off his own potshot at Harry Morse:

Governor Booth, doubtless, did what he thought best in outfitting Sheriff Morse, whose courage and enterprise in such matters, we suppose, no man doubts, but we cannot help

thinking it would have been better to select some one familiar
with the lay of the land in this section instead of a gentlemen,
who, whatever may be his other qualifications, is an utter
stranger to the trails and defiles and passes which sometimes
puzzle even our oldest mountaineers.[13]

Henderson's dispatches created tremendous interest throughout
the state, but they rankled Sheriff Adams of San Jose. Angry over his
failure to lead the manhunt, Adams was undoubtedly the source of this
scathing criticism of Harry Morse, published in the San Jose *Mercury:*

> The correspondent of the *Chronicle* in the field has given some
> details of the route taken by Morse, etc. What we will add is that
> which could not come within the compass of his information:
> Morse had not been one week in the field before news was re-
> ceived in this city that his objects were known to Vasquez, who
> was on the alert and laughing in his sleeve at the bungling way
> in which his adversary "carried the war into Africa." At one
> time Morse and his party were engaged in "surveying" a tract
> of land near the Cantua Canyon, which everybody in that sec-
> tion of the country knew had been surveyed years before. The
> Sheriff's every movement was noticed by the bandit's spies . . .
> and consequently Vasquez had the advantage. At one time
> Morse camped out on the Zapato Chino Creek, and at the same
> time Vaquez and his band were camped but seven miles distant,
> and the two parties remained in these positions for several days.
> At another time Morse passed within one-fourth of a mile from
> Vasquez's camp, without knowing that he was so near the ob-
> ject of his search. The fact, however, was not unknown to
> Vasquez, who, with fleet horses and a fine stretch of country
> behind, was ready at a moment's notice to "git up and dust."
> When Morse went south, Vasquez went north, and vice versa.[14]

Harry Morse was in the saddle and in no position either to read
or to respond to such attacks. But the editor of the *San Francisco
Chronicle* made a brief and logical reply:

> All this may or may not be true. If true, why has not the ed-
> itor of the *Mercury,* or his informants, made the facts and the
> whereabouts of Vasquez known to Morse, and so aided in the

Captain John H. Adams,
sheriff of Santa Clara
County. Adams was a bitter
rival of Harry Morse.
Courtesy of the San Jose
Historical Museum.

capture of the bandit? Morse is making a great effort to bring
the outlaw to justice, and it is but a sorry spirit which can in-
cite nothing better than cavil at the method in which he has
proceeded. We fear that there is a little too much jealousy
among the sheriffs.[15]

Morse was greatly hamstrung during the hunt in Los Angeles
County. All the conditions that had made him a successful manhunter in the Bay Area counties were absent in the south. He and his
posse did not know the country and frequently got lost or took much
too long to reach their destination. They had no contacts among the
local Hispanics and consequently were unable to tell whether those
who did give them information were reliable or were intentionally
misleading them. They offered the entire state reward to anyone who
would listen, but Vasquez's popularity was widespread among the
rural Spanish-speaking people and there were no takers.

Sheriff Morse and his posse headed north for Fort Tejon, arriving there on April 27. They had been in the saddle continuously from sunup to sundown for six weeks. Not only were they exhausted, they were tremendously frustrated and beginning to despair of ever capturing Vasquez. More than ever it seemed as if they were chasing a wraith instead of a man. The sheriff was far from ready to give up, but most of his possemen had pressing business at home, and the hunt had already lasted longer then they had anticipated. Morse concluded that things were much too hot for the bandido in Los Angeles County and that he would be most likely to head north toward his old haunts in the Coast Range. The sheriff decided to make a slow trip home, searching again the coastal counties with the hope that his posse would cut Vasquez's trail on their way north.

The lawmen were preparing for the long ride back when Sheriff Morse received information at El Tejon that Vasquez was holed up in a small adobe near Nichols Canyon (in what is now West Hollywood) owned by a well-known character named Greek George, a native of Cyprus who had been brought to California in 1855 by General Edward F. Beale as a driver in the recently organized U.S. Army Camel Corps. His true name was George Caralambo, but he became an American citizen and took the name George Allen. Exactly how Morse obtained his information is something of a mystery, but it seems evident that Vasquez fell prey to his uncontrollable romantic urges.

There are several versions of how Tiburcio Vasquez was betrayed. One is that Vasquez seduced his niece, the daughter of Tiburcio's older brother, Francisco, an honest, hardworking miner who lived with his wife and children in Soledad Canyon. When the girl became pregnant, angry friends of the family turned the bandido in. Another account is that Greek George's sister-in-law, Modesta Lopez, betrayed Vasquez because of jealousy over another woman. Yet another version is simply that Greek George gave up Vasquez for a share of the reward.

At any rate, on April 27, while preparing to leave El Tejon, Morse received the information about Vasquez's hideout. He considered it to be reliable, but he had a difficult choice to make. Morse's friend George Beers explained: "He felt that if he were sheriff of Los Angeles County, he would not like to have an officer from a distant county come and effect the capture of Vasquez—about whom such a hue and cry had been raised—under his very nose; and he also thought it would be difficult if not impossible to move his whole party, now that its presence in the county was known to everybody."16

Accordingly, Morse boarded the evening stage for Los Angeles, 110 miles distant, arriving the following day. He knew that Vasquez's spies were keeping a close watch on Sheriff Rowland, so he went to the office of the Los Angeles Real Estate Agency and sent word for Rowland to meet him there. Rowland soon arrived and Morse laid his information before him, suggesting that a small party consisting of Morse and Cunningham plus Rowland and one of his deputies make a visit to Greek George's place and attempt the arrest. But Rowland dismissed Morse's information outright. As George Beers reported cryptically, "Rowland received the information and Morse's proposition with a quiet smile, and assured the Alameda County sheriff that his information was a 'sell.' He said he knew the party well, met him almost every day, and was confident he knew nothing about Vasquez."17

Harry Morse was keenly disappointed, but he trusted the sheriff's judgment. Morse knew that Rowland's mother was from a prominent Hispanic family, that the sheriff had many friends and contacts in the Californio community, and that he was certain to know which informants were reliable. By this time Morse had become used to disappointment, and he boarded the return stage for Fort Tejon. The Alameda lawman's desire to include his brother sheriff in the capture and his trust in that same officer proved to be one of the greatest miscalculations of his career.

Editor Ben Truman got wind of the sheriff's visit to Los Angeles and seized the opportunity to publish another slap at Morse in the *Star:* "We heard that there were two notorious persons in the city yesterday in disguise. Harry Morse, the man who is after Vasquez, and Tiburcio himself. But there was this difference in the disguises: no one knew Vasquez, while almost everyone knew Morse." The newspaperman, of course, did not explain why only he, not the officers, knew where Vasquez was. Truman's irresponsibility in making Morse's movements public was exceeded only by his inaccuracy, for it was later shown that the bandido had not been in the city at all.18

Morse arrived back at El Tejon on the morning of April 30. By this time his posse had received a tip that two men matching the descriptions of Vasquez and Chavez had left Los Angeles County and were headed for the New Idria mines. Morse, Cunningham, and the rest started north again. They trailed the two riders to Zapato Chino Creek, arriving on May 4. Here the lawmen split up into two groups. Morse took half the men to Poso Chane, where they were informed, incorrectly, that Vasquez had passed through four days earlier. They continued west over the mountains and up the San Benito River to New Idria. Cunningham and the others searched the Cantua Creek and Las Tres Piedras country, then crossed the mountains and joined Morse's men in New Idria on May 7.

From here the posse rode north through Carrisalito and Ortigalito canyons, searching as they went, and finally arrived at the San Luis Rancho on the night of May 10. They had used five relays of horses on their long ride north. Their mounts were as worn out as the riders. In the morning the manhunters headed for Banta in San Joaquin County, where they boarded a Central Pacific train on May 12 and enjoyed a fast and relaxing trip home.

No sooner had Morse arrived in Oakland than he immediately began planning a new hunt for Vasquez. He learned that several days earlier Governor Booth had issued a new reward proclamation for Vasquez: $6,000 dead, $8,000 alive. Sheriff Adams was organizing a rival posse in San Jose and the *San Francisco Chronicle* had assigned a reporter to accompany it. But just two days later telegraphic dispatches from Los Angeles reported the electrifying news that Tiburcio Vasquez had been captured near Los Angeles by a posse organized by Sheriff Rowland and that the bandit had been wounded while attempting to flee Greek George's house.

Morse, stunned, read the details in the San Francisco newspapers on May 15: Sheriff Rowland, acting on information from a confidential informant, had secretly organized a raid on Greek George's adobe. While Rowland remained in Los Angeles to throw Vasquez's spies off guard, a posse of local officers, including the reporter George Beers, quietly proceeded to Greek George's place and surrounded it. Vasquez jumped out a back window but was brought down by a load of buckshot. The posse also captured Lebrado Corona, and they brought the wounded bandit leader and his young compadre to the Los Angeles jail.

Harry Morse was astounded that the information he had provided Sheriff Rowland not only turned out to be accurate, but Rowland himself seemed to have taken full advantage of it. Whatever his suspicions were, he promptly penned a congratulatory letter to the Los Angeles sheriff:

Friend Rowland: Allow me to congratulate you on your success in the capture of Vasquez, and the masterly manner in which it was done. No one rejoices more than I do at your suc cess, although I should like to have been in at the last; yet my information led me to believe that he had started north toward the New Idria, and, of course, I immediately followed. Even after getting so far north as the Poso Chane, in Fresno County, I received what I thought was reliable information that he had passed through that place just four days ahead of my party. We spent ten days searching in and about the Cantua and New Idria country for him, but he not being in that vicinity, of course we could not find him. The boys of my party all join in sending their respects, and are (without wishing you any bad luck) only sorry that we were not fortunate enough to effect the capture of Vasquez. From what I have learned, I hardly believe that [name deleted] has been with Vasquez in your county. If there is anything that I can do to assist you in this part of the country, please call upon me; I will be ever ready to respond. Yours truly, Henry N. Morse.[19]

Did Sheriff Rowland deliberately deceive Morse? Did he discount Morse's information, wait until the Alameda sheriff was long gone, and then move in to grab the glory and the reward? Or did he honestly believe that Morse had been mistaken and take action only when he received new information that convinced him that Vasquez was indeed at Greek George's adobe? As a member of Sheriff Rowland's posse, George Beers was in a position to know the facts firsthand. Beers, in his account of the meeting between Morse and Rowland, strongly implied that he mistrusted the Los Angeles sheriff's motives. Beers's further comments, written only a year after the capture, imply that Rowland may have used Morse's information to negotiate a deal with the informant:

Subsequent events warrant the belief that the information brought one hundred and ten miles from Fort Tejon to Los Angeles . . . by Henry Morse to Billy Rowland was correct, notwithstanding the opinion of the latter at the time to the contrary, and that the increased reward led to negotiations with Rowland by the same parties, which led to his betrayal into our hands. Be that as it may, it would be manifestly improper to publish the real facts of the betrayal even if the writer had them at his command.[70]

Billy Rowland in 1874.
The sheriff of Los Angeles
County, Rowland double-
crossed Harry Morse in
order to capture Tiburcio
Vasquez. Courtesy Jack
Reynolds.

Billy Rowland had the motive to deceive Harry Morse. Having been publicly criticized and embarrassed by an interloping sheriff from a distant county, Rowland surely felt no loyalty to Morse. Persuasive evidence that the Los Angeles sheriff double-crossed Morse came from Rowland himself. He later revealed that two weeks before the Vasquez capture he heard that Vasquez had been hiding out near Greek George's place. Rowland sent a posseman, D. K. Smith, to keep watch, and after two weeks Smith reported to Rowland that Vasquez was indeed at Greek George's. One need only remember that Harry Morse met Rowland in Los Angeles on April 28 and that Rowland sent his posse out to seize Vasquez on the night of May 13, two weeks later. The conclusion is inescapable that Rowland acted on Morse's information, first sending Smith to keep an eye on Greek George's place and then negotiating with Greek George to turn in Vasquez for a share of the reward.[21]

Although Sheriff Rowland and his men garnered the glory and the reward, it is clear that it was Harry Morse's painstaking and exhausting legwork that was ultimately responsible for the bandit chieftain's capture. Morse's posse forced Vasquez out of his usual haunts in the Coast Range to Los Angeles County, and Morse's information

led to Vasquez's arrest. But Vasquez announced a different opinion
of Morse's effectiveness. In a jail interview the day after his capture,
he laughed about the sheriff's efforts to find him, saying, "I knew
every move Morse made. I have been around his camp night after
night, and could have killed him on numerous occasions if I wanted
to. So, too, with Cunningham, of San Joaquin. Neither of them
were very smart. Rowland is the one I've been looking out for. He's
taken more risks than any of them."[22]

But Vasquez was a notorious liar who, like many professional
criminals, survived by selfish manipulation of other people. His
transparent sycophancy, in heaping praise on his jailer, Rowland, got
him no favors, and on May 23 he was loaded onto a steamer and
brought north to stand trial for the Tres Pinos murders. Lodged in
jail at San Francisco, he was paid a visit by Harry Morse. The agile
bandido now praised Morse and denied his previous boasts. Wrote
George Beers, "Vasquez most emphatically denied the report that
had appeared in a newspaper . . . that he had full knowledge of
Morse's movements, and had been around his camp nights, and admitted that the first knowledge he had of the Morse party was
through the newspapers after the Repetto robbery."[23]

Harry Morse's own evaluation of the manhunt, along with his
criticism of Sheriff Adams, appears in his report to Governor Booth.
It read in part:

> It is not necessary for me to go into a detailed account of
> our hunt, as Vasquez is now in custody. Sufficient is it for me
> to say that we did 61 days hard work in the saddle, part of the
> time in the night, through the darkness, and part of the time
> through heavy rains, never resting but always on the go. We
> rode 2,720 miles, searching the southern part of the state from
> the San Joaquin River to the sea coast, and although we did not
> succeed in getting our man, yet we did the state a good service
> in this. We broke up many dens of reputed murderers and
> thieves in places where officers had never ventured to go be-
> fore. I regret one thing very much. It is this, that officers in the
> upper part of the state, to wit, Santa Clara, should have a feel-
> ing of jealousy toward myself and party, and make known my
> whereabouts and plans through the public prints, and thereby
> making it more difficult for us to do our work properly. Too

much praise cannot be bestowed upon Sheriff Rowland and party for the very able manner in which they carried out their plans, and effected the capture of Vasquez.

One thing I think is quite certain and that is this. We deserve credit for the thoroughness of our search. Had we not been out, Vasquez would still have been at liberty. At least Vasquez told me so himself. He told me the only thing that kept him about Los Angeles was the fear of meeting my party, he thinking that I was still in the southern part of the state.

It is a good deal like hunting a needle in a hay stack, this hunting a man in the mountains. The only way is to do as was done in the present case, to wit, purchase the information that will lead you to the whereabouts of the party sought, the rest is easy.[24]

The trial of Tiburcio Vasquez took place in San Jose in January 1875 and lasted but four days. He was convicted of one of the murders at Tres Pinos and sentenced to death. After his attorneys made an unsuccessful appeal to the California Supreme Court, his execution was scheduled for March 19, 1875.

On the fateful day Harry Morse journeyed by train to San Jose. He found the jail yard packed with three hundred spectators, each of whom had been issued an invitation card. Among them were a small horde of newspapermen, many of them from Eastern cities, as well as several dozen peace officers from around the state. Sheriff Adams put aside his personal feelings long enough to invite Morse onto the gallows, along with former sheriff Nick Harris and several other lawmen. Undersheriff Theodore C. Winchell, who had failed Morse during the gun duel with Juan Soto, fastened leather straps around the outlaw's body at the elbows, wrists, knees, and ankles, then draped the noose around his neck and placed a long white shroud over his shoulders.

His bearing on the scaffold was remarkable. He did not wince nor flicker an eyelash. Perhaps because he had eluded the dark angel so many times he was willing to meet her at last. He swung quietly out into eternity and died almost instantly. His calmness was a surprise to the officers, who thought, as he had eluded capture so long, he must be a cowardly dog and would die as one.

I stood at Vasquez's side an instant before he dropped through the trap and heard the very last words he spoke. "Pronto! Pronto!" he said, meaning "Quick! Quick!" Evidently his nerve was failing him and he feared he would give way.

The subsequent rites were solemn and most impressive. Day after day the corpse was carried to the little church in Santa Clara to be blessed, and in the evening great crowds of people thronged the house where the bandit lay in state. Finally it was interred, the sister of Vasquez following his guilty corpse to its resting place, giving full tide to all her grief.[25]

Thus Tiburcio Vasquez passed from history into legend. By the time of his death he had become, next to Joaquin Murrieta and Juan N. Cortina of Texas, the most famous Hispanic outlaw of the American West. Over the years his legend grew, and to many disenfranchised Hispanics he became a folk hero who had exacted revenge against the conquering Anglo and had died a martyr.

The historical Vasquez was colorful in the extreme, and his life was filled with episodes of high drama. But there was little nobility and heroism in his life. Vasquez was a lifelong criminal and confidence man who preyed on women, victimized persons who could not defend themselves, and took part in a number of cold-blooded murders. It is a great irony that Tiburcio Vasquez remains a folk hero in California while such real Hispanic heroes as the Los Angeles sheriffs Tomas Sanchez and Martin Aguirre are completely forgotten.[26]

CHAPTER 14

Pistols and Politics

HARRY Morse now set his sights on Tiburcio Vasquez's lieutenant, Clodoveo Chavez. Governor Booth had offered a $2,000 reward for the young bandido after the Tres Pinos Tragedy. When Vasquez was convicted of murder, a letter entitled "Notice to the Town of Hollister" was dropped into the Wells Fargo letter box in Hollister. Written in Spanish and purportedly signed by Chavez, it threatened, "If . . . Vasquez does not get his sentence appeased, then you will have to suffer as in the time of Joaquin Murrieta—the just with the unjust alike will be reached by my revenge."[1]

The sheriff believed that Chavez was in the Coast Range, east of Hollister. He wrote to Tom McMahon of Hollister, who had aided him with information about Vasquez several years before. McMahon confirmed that Chavez was in the mountains. Morse met with Governor Booth in San Francisco to discuss plans for a manhunt. On February 10, 1875, he outlined his plans in a letter to the governor:

> Sheriff Cunningham, Harry Thomas, and myself will make a vigorous hunt for him next month. We will go in light marching order, and take the chances of living off the country as we find it. I would say that if there is about $500 in the Vasquez fund that could be put at our disposal, I can only say that it would be used judiciously, and if there is no money we will pay our own expenses. We propose to ride a month at least. Money we don't want without it comes from the State. I have offered the entire reward to several parties whom I know could tell Chavez's whereabouts if they would. We would be satisfied with the honor of capturing the rascal. . . . It does seem to me that the officers of the counties through which Chavez runs, and in which he stops for weeks at a time, ought to be able to capture him.[2]

On February 7, Clodoveo Chavez, leading several bandidos, robbed a store and stole five horses on the South Fork of the Kern River in the Sierra Nevada in Kern County. Chavez returned to Hollister on March 19, the day Vasquez was hanged. That night he walked boldly down the main street, visiting several saloons, talking with old friends, and tearfully mourning the death of his chieftain. Sheriff B. F. Ross was out of town to attend the hanging, and by the time a posse of citizens was organized, Chavez had vanished. Riding furiously, the bandido rejoined his band in Kern County, crossed the Sierra, and on March 24 held up the Little Lake stage station south of the Cerro Gordo mining district. Three days later Chavez and his bunch, some eight in all, held up another stage station on the Panamint Road.

Harry Morse believed that Chavez would again return to his old haunts in the Coast Range. On April 12, with Sheriff Cunningham and Harry Thomas, he went to Firebaugh's Ferry, ready for a long manhunt. There they were to meet an informant who could lead them to the bandit leader. The lawmen spent three frustrating days in camp waiting for their guide to appear. In his diary Morse noted that he had heard a "rumor that Sheriff Adams with a party of 8 men were scouting the mountains for Chavez." In his diary entry of April 15 Morse wrote, "It is very dull laying around camp, and our patience is almost exhausted. . . . Our man, that is the man who was to lead us into Chavez's camp, came in about 2 o'clock. He is a fraud, don't know a thing of his own knowledge. All hearsay. We are disgusted. Will make a raid on California Ranch and Las Juntas in the morning."[3]

Sheriff Morse returned to Oakland empty-handed. He never captured Clodoveo Chavez. After a spree of daring robberies, Chavez fled to Arizona. On a ranch near Yuma he was recognized by Luis Raggio; they had been boyhood enemies in San Juan Bautista. On November 25, 1875, Raggio and two companions attempted to arrest Chavez. The outlaw tried to run but was brought down by a fatal load of buckshot. Like Joaquin Murrieta, Chavez's head was cut off and placed in a container of alcohol. It was brought to California for identification, and the $2,000 reward was paid to Raggio and his partners.[4]

The sheriff's failure to capture Chavez was not his only disappointment that year. For the previous fifteen years Republicans had outnumbered Democrats in Alameda County. Six times Morse had easily won reelection, but not without critical opposition. Prior to the election in 1871, the *Oakland Daily Transcript*, a new Democratic newspaper, had accused him of killing outlaws for political gain. Its editor, John Scott, who held an intense dislike for the popular sheriff, wrote that the lawman could win reelection by furnishing "a few dozen desperadoes' corpses to the coroner between this date and the day of the election." Added the editor, "He is on the warpath, and the crack of his rifle, accompanied by the despairing shriek of some dying Greaser, may soon be expected. All's fair in politics." If anything, such outrageously unfair sentiments won Harry Morse sympathy and even more popular support.[5]

Morse faced more criticism during the 1873 campaign. Editor Scott revived the old charges that the sheriff had been a shoulderstriker during the war and discounted his reputation as a lawman:

> It doesn't require a very extraordinary person, when backed by a faithful friend and sustained by the strong arm of the law, to capture surprised and terrified guilt. Morse always succeeded, under these circumstances, and although the faithful friends have not always been conspicuously paraded as prominent actors in the thrilling adventures and desperate rencontres, they have invariably been there. The newspaper writers could only see the central figure of these brilliant exploits. Morse has become a hero. . . . But the numerous years that have rolled into the past since Morse was first elected, have made material change in the aspect of affairs. The desperadoes who formerly struck terror to the heart of the lone settlers in Livermore have been captured or intimidated. The valleys that then were howling wildernesses are now the garden spots of the county. Villages have sprung up, and order reigns where chaos held command. . . . It is therefore no longer necessary that the chief law officer should be renowned for his personal prowess, or that he should promulgate the law's edicts through the muzzle of a Henry rifle.[6]

Harry Morse was stung by this criticism, so much so that he took no part in the manhunt for the Vasquez band following the Tres Pinos Tragedy on August 26, just before election day. The *Alameda County Gazette* commented, "Our Sheriff Morse, would, ere this, have taken the war trail, but that his motives might be misconstrued, and that he was desirous of making political capital on the eve of an election."[7]

At that time the principal issue of California politics was opposition to the monopolies held by railroad, land, water, and utility companies. Between 1870 and 1910 the Central Pacific and Southern Pacific Railroad companies were the single most powerful political force in the state. Newton Booth, a Republican, was elected governor in 1871 on an antimonopoly platform. The Republican party was under the influence of the railroad, and dissatisfied members, under Governor Booth, formed the People's Independent party in 1873. This party had the support of farmers and some Democrats, and its platform included destroying the power of monopolies, regulating railroad fares and shipping fees, and building a state irrigation system.[8]

At the Republican party's county convention that year, Sheriff Morse was challenged for the nomination by Ellis Haynes. Failing to get the nomination, Haynes became the Independent party's candidate for sheriff. In the election on September 3, 1873, the Republicans elected their whole county ticket except for two offices; Morse was reelected by a comfortable margin. However, the formation of the Independent party would become a significant political problem for Morse and other Republican officeholders.[9]

During the next two years the county's population increased by about ten thousand and there were many new Democrats and Independents. In the campaign of 1875 Morse was supported by most of the county's newspapers: the *Alameda County Gazette* and the *Oakland Daily News*, plus the recently established *Oakland Tribune* and Livermore *Enterprise*. However, his old friend Lew Morehouse, the popular constable of San Leandro, was chosen by the Independents as their candidate for sheriff. The Democratic candidate was Thomas O'Neil, a wood and coal dealer. In the election on September 1 Morse polled 2,091 votes, O'Neil 2,080, Morehouse 1,242. Morse had squeaked by O'Neil with a majority of just 11 votes. Lew Morehouse's candidacy siphoned off much of the sheriff's support, for many of the constable's votes came from those who otherwise would have voted for Morse.[10]

O'Neil and his attorney appeared before the county board of supervisors and demanded a recount. District Attorney A. A. Moore advised the board that it had no authority to count ballots, and O'Neil's request was denied. He then filed a lawsuit against Morse, contesting the election and alleging misconduct by the elections board in counting the ballots. The case was heard before Judge Stephen G. Nye on October 25. The votes had been recounted, and Judge Nye ruled that Morse actually had a majority of thirty-eight votes. Although he had won, it had been a hair's breadth, and the sheriff began to realize that he could lose the next election.[11]

Harry Morse soon faced a political problem of another sort. His income had consisted of fees for performing the official duties of his office: thirty cents per mile for necessary travel in criminal cases and in serving subpoenas and arrest warrants; fifty cents per mile for transporting prisoners to the state prison; $2 for each arrest; and fifty cents for each subpoena served. These fees provided Morse with a very handsome income. For example, in the fiscal year 1874–75, the fees of his office totaled $11,070.62. From such fees his undersheriff and deputy each earned $1,800 annually; his jailer's salary was $900 per year. Subtracting costs for travel and feed for his horses, Morse netted some $6,000 per year.[12]

This wage was exceedingly generous, and it mirrored the income earned by other sheriffs in the state. Reacting to public concern over such high pay, the legislature began to enact laws fixing elected officials' salaries. In 1874 the salary of the Alameda County sheriff was set at $4,500 per year; his undersheriff and deputy received $1,500, and his jailer $780. Under the new law the sheriff was to receive no fees or mileage, only his salary.[13]

Needless to say, Alameda's sheriff was not happy about this reduction in income. He submitted to the board of supervisors a livery bill of $2,555 for the fiscal year 1875–76. Morse charged the county $5 per day for use of his team and buggy and $2 per day for his saddle horse and riding rig. These charges were plainly exorbitant; the county could have purchased outright the horses and equipment for far less than what Morse billed for a single year. The new salary law made no provision for reimbursement for these expenses and the board summarily rejected the bill.

Sheriff Morse was outraged. He threatened a lawsuit, then fired off a complaint to the board of supervisors: "I can see no reason why I should be at this expense any more than I should for rent, stationery, or any other article that is furnished to me at the expense of the county to enable me to do my official work. . . . The expense of furnishing horses, travelling fees, etc. amount to nearly one-half of my salary, and all comes out of my own individual pocket." But this latter claim was somewhat disingenuous; after all, the amount he demanded was more than his undersheriff and jailer combined earned in annual salary.[14]

Harry Morse did sue the county, alleging that he was entitled not only to the $2,555 livery bill but also to recovery of all mileage fees that had been paid to him by civil litigants, which under the former law he had been allowed to keep. This sum for the years 1874 through 1876 was almost $8,000. Judge Samuel Bell McKee ruled that there were no legal grounds for Morse's lawsuit and threw the case out of court. Morse appealed to the California Supreme Court, which upheld Judge McKee and ruled that Morse had no lawful claim to the money. In the end, however, Morse was vindicated, for such expenses were eventually borne by the government. This was only fair, for Morse's situation was analogous to a modern police department requiring its officers to purchase and maintain their own patrol cars.[15]

Morse's natural frugality, coupled with his sheriff's income and reward money, had made him financially secure. The destruction of his flour mill in the earthquake did not deter him from investing in other enterprises. He lent money to associates and acquaintances, usually requiring an interest-bearing note. He purchased one thousand acres of grazing land in the mountains south of Pleasanton and leased them to local stockmen. A lover of horseflesh, he bought and raised thoroughbreds. He did not race them, however, limited his gambling to friendly bets on political races.

Despite his parsimony Morse was loyal to his friends and family, and he could be generous. He made interest-free loans to friends in need. He employed his wife's cousin, Ella S. Viers, as housekeeper for many years. She was very close to both Virginia and Harry and became an influential member of the household, which later was to cause jealousy among the Morse children. Another of Virginia's cousins, young Jesse Viers, worked as a jailer. His friend Peter Borein served faithfully as undersheriff until 1874, when he was elected county auditor. Morse replaced him with his old comrade and former business partner, Jeremiah Tyrrel. In 1875 he appointed his friend William S. Harlow, a reporter for the *Oakland Daily News*, deputy sheriff. Morse's choice was a good one: Harlow served for more than twenty years under many sheriffs. He became an authority on sheriff's law and procedures and in 1884 wrote the definitive work on the topic, *Harlow on Sheriffs and Constables.*[16]

Stage robber Charlie Pratt,
captured by Sheriff Morse
in Oakland, June 3, 1876.
Author's collection.

When not preoccupied with politics, the sheriff continued to de-
vote as much time as he could to catching bandits. In January 1876
three notorious ex-convicts, Charlie Pratt, Old Jim Smith, and Texas
George Wilson, pulled two stagecoach robberies in the Sierra Nevada
foothills of Amador and El Dorado counties. Smith and Wilson were
quickly tracked down, but Charlie Pratt managed to elude capture.
Morse knew Pratt well. The badman had served five terms in San
Quentin; on three of those occasions Morse had transported him to
the prison.

On June 3, 1876, Sheriff Morse attended the auction sale of a
house on Twelfth Street in Oakland. A large crowd was present, and
as the auctioneer began, a half-drunk spectator called out a series of
mock bids. As the bidding proceeded the man continued to annoy
the auctioneer, much to the amusement of the crowd. Morse thought
the jokester's voice sounded familiar. Elbowing through the throng,
he came face to face with the swaying form of Charlie Pratt. Before
the stage robber knew what happened Morse had clapped him in
irons. The sheriff delivered Pratt to a grateful Jim Hume, Wells

Fargo's chief detective, who saw to it that the highwayman was sent across the bay for twelve years.[17]

Joe Newell had been released from San Quentin in 1873 and returned to his old haunts in Alameda County. In 1875 he stabbed a man in Livermore and again was let off with light punishment—just nine months in prison. Harry Morse took him to San Quentin, but it was not the last he would see of Joe Newell.

Newell came back to my county and commenced a regular life of dissipation among the thieves and lewd women at a place called "Mexico," about a mile north of Livermore. His murder of old man Leighton, his cutting of the man at Livermore, and his two terms in the state prison had made people afraid of him, and he got the name of being a bad, bold, and desperate man, ready and willing to do most any crime in the calendar.

It got to be quite dangerous to be out at night, especially in the vicinity of Mexico. Men were continually being knocked down and robbed. I myself had a very narrow escape one night. It was raining, and I was walking alone from Livermore down toward Mexico. I was in search of some witnesses who were wanted at the courthouse the next day in a trial for grand larceny. Just as I was passing the old bull pen near the dance houses, from my side view I saw a bright flash, heard the report of a pistol, and a bullet whizzed past my head. Pulling my own weapon, I started on the dead run back toward where I had seen the flash. When I got there, I found Newell and another ex-convict named Hays. I asked who fired the shot and at the same time I thrust my pistol right under Newell's nose. They both denied it.

"You lie, you scoundrel," I said. Seizing Newell by the throat, I threw him violently to the ground, and then fell on him with both knees into the pit of his stomach. Hays in the meantime skipped out. I gave Newell a good lambasting before I got through with him, and then preached him a good moral lecture on the uncertainties of life for men of his character. Newell was always good to me after that night.

A few months after the event just related, Newell got out on one of his usual sprees and started out to capture Mexico. It did not take him long to do it. The first place he struck was in the southern portion of Mexico, a dance house kept by one quite as bad as Newell himself, a Mexican named Pio Ochoa. Newell picked a quarrel with Ochoa, threatened to shoot him, and drew his pistol to carry out his threat. Too late, Joe, your time had come.

A quick, nervous movement of the Mexican's hands, a flash, a loud

ringing report, and a bullet went crashing through the brain of the mur-
derer, Newell. He dropped dead on the floor, his pistol still grasped in his
hand. He never moved after being shot. Thus the light of this notorious
desperado was put out at last, and by one of his own kind, too. [18]

In addition to running his fandango house, Pio Ochoa was, next
to Juan Camargo, the principal tapadera in the Livermore Valley. Although he had been present in the Saucelito Valley when Morse
killed Juan Soto, Ochoa was careful to avoid conflict with lawmen.
Ochoa and Camargo acted as middlemen, inducing thieves to steal
cattle, then selling them to dishonest ranchers and crooked butchers in Livermore and Pleasanton. On November 26, 1876, Stanislaus
Cibrian and Henry Welch, both from old ranchero families of Contra Costa County, stole twenty-five head of choice Durham cattle
from the ranch of William Rice near Walnut Creek. They drove
them south and sold eight head to Herman Barthold, a corrupt
butcher in Livermore.

Pio Ochoa was impressed with this brazen theft, and when Cibrian visited his fandango house, Ochoa offered to buy all the cattle he
could steal. On the night of December 29 Cibrian returned to Rice's
ranch with Trinidad Mesa and Jose Ruiz, an ex-convict, and made off
with another twenty-five head. They drove the animals to Livermore
and herded them into Barthold's corral. The butcher bought only
two steers. Ruiz then offered the cattle to Ochoa, who agreed to
purchase them. For several weeks the thieves moved the cattle from
one pasture to another in the valley and finally drove them up the
Arroyo Valle to a secluded spot in the mountains. [19]

In the meantime William Rice had searched energetically for his
herd. Believing that the cattle had been driven into Santa Clara
County, he notified Sheriff Nick Harris. On January 12, 1877, after
a four-day search in the mountains south of Livermore, Harris and
Rice located the missing herd in the Arroyo Valle. An Indian, Juan
Palmos, had been left in charge by Ochoa and did not know the herd
was stolen. He told Harris that the animals were Ochoa's. Sheriff
Harris rode into Livermore and quickly arrested Pio Ochoa, Juan Camargo and Jose Ruiz.

At the preliminary hearing Ochoa was held to answer on a charge
of grand larceny, but both Camargo and Ruiz were released for lack
of evidence. Sheriff Morse was unhappy with this result. He suspected Stanislaus Cibrian in the affair and with the assistance of
Captain Appleton W. Stone, arrested the cattle thief in a San Fran-

cisco saloon on February 13. Cibrian made a full confession, implicating Jose Ruiz, whom Morse picked up. Ruiz too confessed, giving Morse full details of Pio Ochoa's role. In May all three were sentenced to lenient terms of two years each in San Quentin.[20]

By now Morse had made a very difficult decision. He had been keenly disappointed in his loss of salary and the burden of paying all the expenses of manhunting from his own pocket. But more significant, his narrow victory in the last election showed him that his political strength had greatly weakened. Morse was too proud to risk defeat at the polls and decided not to seek reelection. Instead he threw all his support behind Jerry Tyrrel, and in the September 1877 election his undersheriff was victorious. Tyrrel would serve two terms as sheriff of Alameda County.

Harry Morse's last day in office was March 3, 1878. The day before, in a simple ceremony, Jerry Tyrrel called Morse into a rear office in the courthouse. Present were Deputy Sheriff Harlow, Special Deputy Fred Bryant, Jailer Jesse Viers, and Assistant Jailer Frank Miller. They presented Morse with a magnificent cane, the staff made of rock-hard mesquite, the head wrought of solid gold and suitably inscribed, set with large polished gold quartz stones. Such canes were very expensive and highly prized, for jewelry made of gold quartz, known as "the California gem," was the mark of a successful California gentleman. Following the presentation, champagne and toasts flowed generously.[21]

For Harry Morse it surely was an emotional, bittersweet moment. Like many pioneers, he fully recognized that his part in the making of a new community in the Far West had been something special and significant. And during his years in office he had been acutely aware of the critical and historic role he was playing in the settling of the West. Now he surely realized that an era was coming to an end. When Morse had first been chosen sheriff, much of his bailiwick was a sparsely populated frontier where communication was poor and law enforcement was lax. Now, the countryside was crisscrossed with good roads, railroad tracks, and telegraph lines. Farms and ranches, towns and cities, had sprouted everywhere. Alameda County's population, more than fifty thousand by 1878, had more than tripled.

That year, 1878, was the thirtieth anniversary of the discovery of the gold at Sutter's Mill. California had seen three decades of rapid growth and progress, accompanied by the gradual disappearance of its frontier conditions. In stark contrast many other parts of the

West were still a wild frontier, marked by isolation and lawlessness. More people lived in Alameda County than in the entire Arizona Territory; the population of the city of Oakland was greater than that of Wyoming. There were still no railroads through Arizona, New Mexico, Montana, or Wyoming. The great longhorn drives north from Texas to the rowdy Kansas cowtowns were still under way. The U.S. Army's campaigns against the Bannock, Cheyenne, Ute, and Apache were still in the future. In New Mexico, the Lincoln County War had just begun, and few had ever heard of young Henry McCarty, alias Billy the Kid. Jesse James was still pillaging the middle border states; it would be four years before he was slain by Bob Ford. And it would not be until 1881 that Wyatt Earp and his brothers would shoot it out near the O.K. Corral in Tombstone, Arizona Territory. These events were a far cry from the relative tranquillity that Alameda County, as well as much of the state, now enjoyed.

During his fourteen years in office Harry Morse had made hundreds of arrests, many of dangerous outlaws. Most men in rural California in the 1860s and 1870s carried firearms, and most of those he arrested, even for minor offenses, had been armed. That Morse killed but two of them is testament to his ethic of taking men alive.

The sheriff had become a legendary figure, not because of boasting or posturing, but because his real exploits had established him as one of those heroic fighting men so admired by the public in that age. As a result Morse had received a great deal of favorable publicity. He had cultivated journalist friends and had supplied accounts of his exploits to the newspapers. He had not done so to hunt glory but for pragmatic political reasons: to make the public aware that he was doing his job and, by the resulting popularity, to ensure his reelection. Morse was one of very few real frontier lawmen who was made the subject of a dime novel. But he was embarrassed by Ned Buntline's literary attentions. Like most cosmopolitan Californians, Morse laughed at what he called "the blood-curdling, improbable hogwash dished up by the cheap story writers" and "the rot published in the flash story papers and the dime novels about 'Old Sleuth' and such characters."[22]

In an era when official corruption was common, his office was never tainted by financial scandal. To ensure the public's confidence in his honesty, Morse had made it his custom to keep his books open to any citizen who wished to inspect them. His fiscal integrity, however, had been tempered by several cases of dishonest law enforcement. Although he had enforced the law without fear or favor, his dealings with the Hispanic community result in mixed judgment. He had brought to justice men who had murdered Hispanics and stolen livestock from Californios. But the sheriff's fairness had sometimes been mitigated by his overzealousness. Although he undoubtedly committed perjury to ensure that Procopio would be convicted, the latter's subsequent bloody history tended to justify what Morse had done. This was not true of his prosecution of Bartolo Sepulveda. Morse, by taking advantage of his popularity and credibility with jurors, had presented highly unreliable evidence that came close to sending an innocent man to the gallows. The memory of that injustice would haunt Morse for more than twenty years and would lead him to redeem himself in another sensational murder case.

These failings aside, Harry Morse had made a vital contribution to the growth and development of California. He had broken up the bands of stock thieves and highway robbers that had plagued the central part of the state. He had brought to justice many of the worst outlaws west of the Sierra Nevada. No longer would bandidos descend from the Coast Range to murder and pillage with impunity. No longer would the names of Narciso Bojorques, Juan Soto, Tiburcio Vasquez, or scores of other desperadoes strike terror to the public heart. In large measure Harry Morse had brought law to the Contra Costa.[23]

CHAPTER 15

The Morse Detective Agency

HARRY Morse's first act on leaving office was to entrain for the East Coast to visit old friends and family. It was his first visit home in thirty years. On his return he was asked by the directors of the Oakland Bank of Savings to investigate a year-old fraud. A swindler had forged a deed to property in Oakland, used it as security to obtain a $4,000 loan from the bank, and then vanished with the money. Other detectives had long since given up when the former sheriff took over the case. Using the forger's description and aliases, Morse trailed him through Sierra, Placer, and Butte counties before collaring his man in Stockton. He proved to be Wright LeRoy, a crooked lawyer. LeRoy was convicted and served five years in San Quentin. Soon after his release he swindled and then murdered Nicholas Skerritt, a wealthy San Francisco merchant. LeRoy was hanged in the San Francisco County jail in 1885.[1]

Morse's success in the LeRoy case made him realize that there was a market for his services. In July he founded a detective agency, with offices in San Francisco and Oakland. His assistant and Oakland office manager was twenty-three-year-old Alfred B. Lawson. A former printer and newspaperman in Oakland, Lawson worked for Morse for several years, then formed his own agency. He became one of the most successful private detectives in California and later moved to Los Angeles. Morse's longest and most loyal employee would be Jules J. Callundan, whom he hired as a sixteen-year-old office boy in 1881. By 1888 Callundan was Morse's captain and general manager; eventually he became an equal partner in the business.[2]

In 1882 Morse saw a need for private policing in San Francisco, and he added a night patrol function to his agency. He hired a dozen patrolmen and renamed his business Harry N. Morse's Detective Agency and Patrol System. Modeled after Pinkerton's Protective Police Patrol in Chicago, it provided uniformed officers who were supervised by a captain, a lieutenant, and two sergeants. Morse

226

Badges of the Morse Detective Agency. Left, a patrolman's star, and right, a sterling silver detective's star, both circa 1890. Center is a bejeweled gold shield bearing Morse's watchdog logo and inscribed on the reverse, "Presented to Capt. J. J. Callundan by the members of Morse's patrol, Jan. 12, 1889." Author's collection.

established two six-hour night watches between 6:00 P.M. and 6:00 A.M. Each man worked just six hours so that he was always alert. Merchants in San Francisco and Oakland paid a monthly fee for protection from burglary, theft, and fire. Morse's venture thrived, and before long his agency was the largest and most important on the West Coast. By 1888 he employed sixty men, including plainclothes detectives and uniformed private policemen.

But Harry Morse was not San Francisco's first private detective. A number of private sleuths operated in San Francisco in the 1860s and 1870s. Some, such as Jake Chappell and Jim Boyce, were former police detectives under Captain Isaiah W. Lees. Dan Gay and Bob Harrison had been crack Sacramento police detectives before opening their San Francisco agency. Wells Fargo & Company also had its own express detectives. In 1873 James B. Hume, former sheriff of El Dorado County, was hired as chief special officer, a position he held until his death in 1904. Prior to 1873 several of Isaiah Lees's men, including Henry Johnson and Leonard Noyes, did detective work for Wells Fargo on a case-by-case basis.[3]

Americans of the nineteenth century had mixed feelings about detectives, alternately marveling at their exploits and viewing them with distrust. The reasons for this ambivalence were rooted in the origin of policing in medieval England. Britons then were expected to enforce the law themselves, through the "hue and cry" and service on the night watch. The seventeenth century saw the rise of a class of professional police, the "thief takers," who developed close ties to the criminal underworld. Some were former thieves themselves. They ferreted out burglars and tracked down highwaymen for the standing rewards. The thief takers soon branched out into more profitable work, including entrapping young men into committing highway robbery, then arresting them to secure the rewards. They also recovered stolen property and charged the victim a fee that was divided between the thief taker and the thief. This was the dismal lineage of the American detective.[4]

During the 1840s and 1850s the first modern police departments sprang up in the United States. The first police detective bureaus were organized in the 1850s. Police and detective work grew in fits and starts, partly because policing was new and few men knew how to do it and partly because Americans feared the dangers of a police state. Former police detectives soon began to perform private detective work. In 1855 Allan Pinkerton founded what would soon become the principal such enterprise in the country, the Pinkerton National Detective Agency. The Pinkertons established a reputation for honesty and integrity that was repeatedly tarnished by violent strikebreaking activity. But many private detectives of the nineteenth century were shady and disreputable. They were often depicted in popular fiction as marvelous masters of disguise who unraveled mysteries through guile and trickery and in the newspapers as porch-climbing peepers who dogged philandering spouses.[5]

By the late 1850s San Francisco had one of the most modern and professional police departments in the nation. Its detective bureau was headed by Captain Isaiah Lees, one of the greatest sleuths of the nineteenth century. Appointed to the department in 1853, he was made captain of detectives three years later and held this position until 1897 when he became chief of police. A giant in the history of American law enforcement, Lees managed to stay in office so long due to his consummate skill both in criminal investigations and in negotiating the labyrinth of San Francisco politics. Over the years he carefully trained a loyal cadre of highly capable police detectives, most of whom served under him for decades. Lees blurred the line between public and private investigative work and often assigned on-duty detectives to work on civil cases and other private investigations on behalf of businesses, banks, merchants, and lawyers. Fees and rewards were paid to Lees, who shared them with his detectives. He was a close friend of William A. Pinkerton, who with his brother Robert ran the Pinkerton agency after their father's death Lees and his men did much work for the Pinkertons in San Francisco, so much that the Pinkertons did not find it necessary to open an office in the city until 1896. It was inevitable that a rivalry between Lees and Morse soon sprang up. As one San Francisco newspaperman observed, "Lees has no love . . . for Harry Morse, whom he dislikes with the hatred of a Digger Indian."[6]

Harry Morse was well aware of the disreputable nature of many private detective agencies. He took great pride in the fact that when he was sheriff no taint of corruption or fiscal dishonesty had ever tarnished him or his deputies. He set the same standard for his new business. Advertisements for his agency noted that Morse "employs only those as detectives who have established reputations for integrity." Morse refused to handle divorce cases or to work for rewards: "In the estimation of the agency the working for a reward for the detection of crime is no less despicable than the crime itself. No man, or set of men, can faithfully and justly pursue an investigation under the stimulus of what in effect is a bribe." Morse also rejected the ancient "thief taker" approach to detective work: "It has heretofore been held as the leading canon of detective practice that 'a thief only can catch a thief.' Thieves have been employed by detectives and have been allowed to commit crimes [and] . . . share with them their ill-gotten gains." Morse declared that his agency "employs no stool pigeons or thieves to furnish it with information or brains, but works out its difficult cases unaided by such disreputable practice." In such advertisements, however, Morse neglected to point out that when he was sheriff he had collected numerous rewards and had successfully used criminal informants many times. And in practice, Morse's stated standards were to prove quite flexible if enough money was at stake.[7]

From the start Morse engaged in a wide variety of detective work, from investigating murder cases to tracking down defaulting bank clerks. He was regularly hired by merchants to spy on employees suspected of dishonesty, particularly bookkeepers and cashiers. Morse would assign one or two operatives to "pipe" the man to determine whether he might be gambling, drinking, chasing fast women, or otherwise living beyond his means. The operatives' reports to Morse contained no names so as to protect the privacy of those being in-

Members of Morse's Patrol, circa 1900. Author's collection.

vestigated. Morse explained that "there are a great many men in San Francisco who are being looked after in this manner, for a good purpose." Today, civil libertarians would denounce such invasions of privacy. But in Morse's day such spying by private detectives was common and was justified on the theory that whatever was good for business was good for the country.[8]

In September 1878, with his friend Captain Stone of the San Francisco police, Harry Morse captured James Johnson, alias John Wilson, an escaped convict from the Oregon state prison who had shot a youth to death after robbing a pawn shop in Portland. Two weeks later Morse was hunting a "check raiser" who altered a $19.75 check to $9,000, passed it at the Pacific Bank in San Francisco, and vanished with the cash. The following month Morse and A. B. Lawson investigated the case of A. W. Fiske, a traveling salesman who had absconded with $1,700 worth of cigars in 1876. Fiske had supposedly committed suicide, but Morse learned that he was alive and well in the East. When the cigar thief made a surreptitious visit to Oakland, Lawson nabbed him.[9]

After 1880 Morse became increasingly identified with San Francisco instead of Oakland. Although he continued to live in Oakland, he maintained his principal office in San Francisco and crossed the bay by ferry to work each day. San Francisco of the 1870s and 1880s was a burgeoning metropolis of almost schizophrenic milieu. Its port and its geographic location had helped make it the commercial, industrial, political, cultural, and educational hub of the West Coast. The city was wealthy, literate, and cosmopolitan. It was the West's center of art, theater, literature, music, and architecture. San Francisco was, at different times, home to such luminaries as Mark Twain and Robert Louis Stevenson, Henry George, Lotta Crabtree, Edwin Booth, and Albert Bierstadt. The great magnates of mining, shipping, banking, and railroading built opulent mansions on Nob Hill. Spectacular vistas, a mild climate, and the proximity to the great natural wonders of the Golden State made San Francisco a popular stopping place for travelers and tourists.

San Francisco's post–Civil War history has been so rich in culture and romance that this has all but eclipsed the darker side of the city's past. Any portrait of San Francisco then as an idyllic, genteel community ignores the reality of a seething urban center burdened by crime, labor unrest, and corrupt machine politics, home to more than two thousand saloons and hundreds of brothels, parlor houses, cribs, gambling halls, and fandango houses. The city's population had exploded from 20,000 in 1850 to 234,000 in 1880. Politics in the 1880s were controlled by the party bosses: Martin Kelly (Republican) and Chris Buckley (Democrat). Though both were corrupt, San Francisco's politicians were relatively honest when compared to the excesses of the bosses in the cities of the East.[10]

In 1879 Harry Morse got a firsthand look at crooked San Francisco politics when he was called on to investigate what became known as the Dupont Street Frauds. It was his first big case as a private detective, and before he was done he would implicate San Francisco's mayor, Andrew J. Bryant, who was mired chin deep in municipal corruption. The case began inauspiciously enough on March 15, 1879, when the attorneys for David Hunter, who owned property on Dupont Street, asked Morse to look into the suspicious circumstances regarding a warrant for $10,932 that had been issued to their client by the city treasurer. Hunter had learned that his warrant had already been cashed, but he had never been paid the money. Harry Morse and one of his operatives, P. E. Davis, began an intensive investigation.

Morse soon uncovered a byzantine scheme involving manipulations and thefts of money from a fund set up to widen Dupont Street. At that time Dupont Street ran from Market Street north, past the cribs of Morton Street, and straight uphill to Chinatown.

Today it is called Grant Avenue and is one of the city's principal retail shopping streets. The four blocks from Market Street to Bush Street are quite wide and lined with fashionable shops. At Bush, Grant Street enters Chinatown through a green gate decorated with dragons, a famous tourist attraction. Beyond the gate, Grant Street is still a narrow alley. The story of how the four blocks from Market to Bush were widened forms the basis of one of the most significant municipal scandals of late nineteenth-century San Francisco.

During the gold rush San Francisco had been a prototypical boomtown and had sprung up quickly with little thought given to planning for urban congestion. Eventually it became clear that some downtown streets were too narrow. The legislature authorized the widening of Montgomery Avenue, Kearny Street, and Dupont Street. The last project was in 1876 when the Dupont Street Commission was formed to oversee the Dupont Street work. The commissioners were Mayor Andrew J. Bryant, City Auditor George F. Maynard, and City Surveyor William P. Humphreys. Two of Mayor Bryant's cronies, Henry S. Tibbey, secretary of the Board of Public Works, and William M. Pierson, former state senator, were chosen as secretary and attorney for the board, respectively.[11]

Dupont Street was to be widened by chopping off thirty feet of frontage from each lot on the west side of the street. West-side property owners were to be compensated for the loss in value to their lots. Funds for this compensation and for the construction work would be raised by selling bonds. The money needed to pay off the bonds would be raised by increasing the tax assessments on the property owners on the east side of the street, for their property would be worth more due to the improved street. The Dupont Street commissioners hired real estate appraisers to fix a value for each property owner whose lot was to be reduced in size. This procedure was quite common for such municipal improvements. However, Harry Morse soon discovered, there was more to the plan than met the eye.

On March 17, 1879, Morse and Davis visited the city hall. After carefully examining the books of the San Francisco treasurer they found that Hunter's warrant had already been cashed. Five warrants totaling $65,000 had been issued in duplicate, signed by both Tibbey and Mayor Bryant. Each had been paid twice. Morse immediately recognized that Tibbey had embezzled the money by forging the duplicate warrants and cashing them. By cosigning the warrants, Mayor Bryant was guilty at worst of complicity and at best of gross negligence in allowing the warrants to be issued twice. Morse and Davis went to Tibbey's office to examine his books, but Mayor Bryant, who had just learned of Morse's investigation, rushed in and took Tibbey into a private office. Tibbey soon emerged alone and told the detectives that his books were at the county clerk's office, which was then closed. Early the next morning Davis asked the county clerk for the books but was told that Mayor Bryant had taken them away that morning. Morse and Davis attempted all day to get access to the books, but Bryant claimed that he was examining them himself. Finally Morse called in Captain Stone, who took Tibbey into custody.[12]

Mayor Bryant brought in Captain Isaiah Lees, who had been out of town, to conduct an investigation. Bryant then announced to the newspapers that he had discovered the frauds himself. Morse's response was swift. He gave reporters a statement from the city treasurer that confirmed that he and not Bryant had uncovered the theft. Morse commented acridly, "It is strange that Mayor Bryant should have the courage to claim the credit of the discovery when, had he done his duty properly, the infamous robbery could not have been done at all."[13]

Captain Lees conducted a two-day interrogation of Henry Tibbey before Mayor Bryant, Deputy City Treasurer William F. Cassebahm, the Dupont Street commissioners, and the commission's attorney, Pierson. Despite repeated requests by Morse and Davis to examine the books, Captain Lees refused. Lees's investigation was directed solely at the conduct of Tibbey. He made no effort to inquire how Tibbey could have embezzled the funds without Bryant's knowledge, as the latter had cosigned all of the fraudulent warrants, or that of the other commissioners, who were responsible for approving all warrants and other payments. The impropriety of the mayor and his fellow commissioners investigating themselves was obvious to Morse, and he suspected a coverup. A letter to the San Francisco *Bulletin,* signed "An Interested Citizen" and written by the detective or at his behest, decried the "effort being made at present to cover up . . . the full extent of the frauds. . . . [T]he whole matter is rotten from top to bottom. . . . Mr. Morse has been again put off from an examination of the books of the secretary of the Dupont Street Commission, which are now in the possession of Captain Lees. . . . Is there not great impropriety in the Commissioners investigating themselves . . . ?"[14]

Despite such criticism, Lees carefully directed the focus of his investigation away from Mayor Bryant. Lees, a master politician as well as a master sleuth, was not about to expose his own mayor to civil or criminal charges. He continued to investigate Henry Tibbey with his usual energy and skill and insisted that the case was a run-of-the-mill embezzlement. Tibbey had been secretary of the Montgomery Avenue Commission from 1872 to 1874, and Lees's examination of that commission's books revealed that Tibbey had embezzled $112,000 the same way he had stolen the Dupont Street funds. Lees traced all the stolen monies to Tibbey's private bank account.[15]

The evidence gathered by Morse and Lees was presented to the grand jury, which indicted Tibbey for forgery. The grand jury also made its own inspection of the books and accounts of the San Francisco treasurer. Not surprisingly, they found lax bookkeeping and a $20,000 shortage. The following day the treasurer's deputy, William Cassebahm (who had helped interrogate Tibbey), sat down at his kitchen table, wrote out a full confession, and shot himself in the head. He died instantly.[16]

Eventually Harry Morse gained access to the Dupont Street books, but by then he had greatly widened his investigation. Morse learned that Thomas Blythe, an eccentric but shrewd multimillionaire, had suspected wrongdoing when he was assessed some $97,000 against his property on the east side of the street. The real estate appraisers appointed by the commission, headed by Richard Ivers, another of the mayor's cronies, had decided that a total payment of more than $700,000 for loss of frontage was required. Blythe recognized that his neighbors across the street were entitled to much less money for two reasons: the frontage that was cut off held only ramshackle old buildings and the values of those lots actually increased due to the wider, improved street. While other property owners had meekly accepted the Dupont Street Commission's edicts, Blythe hired appraisers and lawyers to contest his assessment and issued an ultimatum to Mayor Bryant: "Let others do as they please; no stealing from me. Reduce my assessment to $39,653 . . . not as favor, but as a right, or you shall not be permitted to go on."[17]

Mayor Bryant had been extremely worried that Blythe's contest would open the commission to closer scrutiny, and he saw to it that Blythe's assessment was reduced exactly as the millionaire had demanded. Morse now learned the reason for the mayor's concern. Bryant himself owned a small lot on the east side of the street, at the corner of Dupont and Morton streets. One of the men who worked on Blythe's case had commented to Bryant that "it would come pretty hard on him [Bryant] to be assessed to pay damages awarded to the west side of the street." To this the mayor made an unguarded

Andrew J. Bryant, the
corrupt mayor of San
Francisco. Morse exposed
his involvement in the
Dupont Street Frauds in
1879. Author's collection.

reply, admitting that he had a gross conflict of interest: "Oh, that is
all right. I have an interest on the west side of the street also."[18]

Digging further, Morse and his assistant, Davis, discovered that
Richard Ivers had pressured the owner of a large west-side lot to sell
to him under the threat of getting a very low appraisal. Another of
the appraisers, C. H. Reynolds, had acted as broker and received a
large commission. The purchase price was secured by Ivers's note,
which had been endorsed by none other than Andrew J. Bryant.
Thus Ivers and the mayor owned the lot jointly. Then Ivers appraised
his own lot and naturally gave to himself and his partner, Mayor
Bryant, the largest proportionate award of any frontage on Dupont
Street: $38,000 for a strip of their lot and $4,296 for a ramshackle
frame building. Morse learned that the actual value of this part of the
property was not more than $17,000. Ivers and Bryant, by forcing
the taxpayers to buy their frontage at a grossly inflated price, had
made a $25,000 profit.[19]

Morse discovered that Ivers and Bryant were not the only crooks involved in the scheme. The commission's attorney, Pierson, while serving as state senator in 1876, had been bribed to push the Dupont Street bill through the legislature. Once the commission was formed, he was paid for his services from commission funds and Bryant appointed him attorney for the Dupont Street Commission at a generous salary. The detective learned that several other legislators had been paid $21,000 in bribes for their support of the bill.[20]

Morse concluded that of the $1 million set aside for the purchase of Dupont Street frontage, only $300,000 had been paid legitimately. The balance had been doled out for exaggerated loss of frontage or for bribes or had been embezzled by Tibbey. Including the money stolen by Tibbey from the Montgomery Avenue fund, the loss to the taxpayers was more than $800,000, a staggering sum for that era.[21]

Henry Tibbey now faced criminal prosecution and a long prison term. To save his neck, he appeared before the grand jury in July and gave a detailed confession. He described how legislators had been bribed, how Bryant and Ivers had illegally profited, and even how attorneys representing property owners who objected to their assessments had been bribed to drop their clients' objections. To avoid an indictment, Mayor Bryant and his friends brought heavy pressure to bear on the grand jurors. In the end, eleven of the twelve grand jurors voted to indict Bryant for fraud. One juror held out, but that was enough. Bryant escaped prosecution.[22]

Henry Tibbey's confession was published in full by the San Francisco newspapers. This disclosure, coupled with the discoveries of Harry Morse, implicated a number of preeminent San Francisco financiers in the scandal. Among those who had also made illegal profits from the Dupont Street fund were James Phelan, W. S. Hobart, Charles Sutro, and John P. Jones. It was evident that if Tibbey went to trial, prominent men would be embarrassed, if not charged with crime. Tibbey's lawyers asked the court to throw out his indictment on technical grounds, and the prosecution against him was eventually dismissed.[23]

Morse urged that a lawsuit be filed against Mayor Bryant to force him to repay the lost money. But Bryant did not have the kind of fortune necessary to repay the vast sums that had been misappropriated and he was not sued. Instead, a group of the east-side property owners filed a lawsuit against the city tax collector to prevent him from collecting the taxes assessed on them to pay the Dupont Street bonds. They claimed that the tax had been levied on them by fraud and therefore they had been unconstitutionally denied due process of law. The case dragged through the courts for years, and in 1887 the California Supreme Court ruled against them. The court held that they should have objected to the fraudulent assessments before the bonds were issued and the street work was done. They could not sit back and allow their property to be improved and then sue to avoid paying for the improvements. The court agreed that the Dupont Street Commission was guilty of fraud but ruled that this did not excuse the east-side owners from paying their share of the tax. They appealed to the U.S. Supreme Court, which in 1891 also ruled against them.[24]

The Dupont Street Frauds had provided the background for the first of many clashes between Harry Morse and Isaiah Lees. The irony of Lees interrogating Tibbey in front of five corrupt officials was not lost on Morse, who was far from impressed with the captain's skill in protecting Mayor Bryant. In turn, Lees and Chief Crowley were not happy with the close relationship between Morse and Appleton Stone. A detective for years, Stone had become captain in charge of the city prison in 1878 but was still considered a detective. It was no coincidence that after 1880 Stone was allowed to do less and less detective work, and he was buried in the city prison until his retirement in 1895.

Andrew Bryant's political career had been seriously damaged. He did not run for reelection and lived only a few more years. In 1882 he died mysteriously, either falling or jumping from a ferry into San Francisco Bay. Harry Morse paid little heed, for he was already deep into a new investigation of corruption, one that would uncover extensive graft in the U.S. Customs service and would uncloak a crooked member of the federal judiciary. Newspapers would dub it the Harkins Opium Ring.[25]

San Francisco was the largest port on the West Coast and the principal entry point for goods imported from Asia. Heavy customs duties were levied on silk, tobacco, and opium. Smuggling of these items, particularly opium, was common. The possession of opium was then legal, as was smoking the drug. The collector of customs in San Francisco was charged with preventing smuggling, and he had a force of twenty-five day inspectors, seventeen night inspectors, and various bargemen, boarding officers, and weighers. Many other types of crime were common on the embarcadero, and the police department had its own harbor police to patrol the waterfront and the bay.[26]

Problems in San Francisco's customshouse surfaced on January 3, 1882, when harbor police observed a small boat stealthily leave the *City of Tokio,* a Pacific Mail Company steamship. They seized the boat, arrested all hands, and recovered three thousand pounds of opium valued at $36,000. Those arrested were John Hennessey, purser of the *Tokio,* Joseph Goetz, William McDermott, two brothers, James and Henry Kennedy, and a Chinese, Ah Yue Wye. In a hearing before U.S. Circuit Court Commissioner Joseph F. O'Beirne, Hennessey was released for lack of evidence and bail for the rest was set up at $10,000 each. Much to the surprise of court officials, all the arrested men posted cash bail instead of a bond. James Harkins, a wealthy Watsonville landowner and retired Pacific Mail steward, provided the bail for James Kennedy and McDermott. The ability of the five arrested smugglers to come up with $50,000 cash was the topic of considerable talk in the federal courthouse. San Francisco's collector of customs, Eugene Sullivan, reported this suspicious affair to Charles Folger, Secretary of the Treasury, in Washington, D.C. Secretary Folger directed Joseph F. Evans to investigate.[27]

Evans was an energetic and trustworthy special agent of the Treasury Department and he attacked his task with a vengeance. He found that customs revenues had declined during the previous few years and suspected that $5 million in opium had been smuggled through the port without payment of duty. Evans believed that Jim Harkins had something to do with the smuggling, but he had no evidence. He obtained permission to retain Harry Morse and one of his operatives, John Gamage, to work on the case. "Mr. Morse's reputation as a detective is the best in the State," Evans assured Secretary Folger. "He was long sheriff, knows almost person in the city, and is . . . thoroughly honest." The government offered to pay only $6 per day each to the two detectives, which was less than Morse's usual fee. However, as Evans explained, "the possibility of gaining reputation by success led them to accept these terms."[28]

Harry Morse insisted that he work in complete secrecy, and only a select few in the Treasury Department knew of his employment. He and Gamage started by "piping" Harkins, the Kennedy brothers, Goetz, and the other smugglers to and from their favorite saloons and haunts downtown and on the waterfront. They also kept a close watch on the Pacific Mail wharf. After five months of painstaking investigation, Morse and Gamage uncovered a mass of evidence. They learned that James Harkins was the head of a well-organized opium ring and observed numerous U.S. Customs officers hobnobbing with the smugglers. Three of them, Lee Matthews, Tom Rogers, and John Hicks, were in daily contact with the members of the ring. The detectives were surprised to find Colonel Henry P. Finnegass, a U.S. Secret Service agent, drinking in saloons with several of the gang. Finnegass, a veteran federal lawman, was responsible for investigating counterfeiting and smuggling. They put a tail on Finnegass and found him to be thoroughly mixed up with the smugglers. Morse learned that another deputy U.S. marshal, named Favor, was also a member of the ring.[29]

Morse and Gamage next visited Watsonville and discovered that Harkins, in spite of the modest income he had earned as a ship's steward, was worth $300,000 and owned several large ranches in Santa Cruz and Monterey counties. He was a heavy drinker and when in his cups had boasted of his smuggling activities to several neighbors and business associates. Harkins admitted to them that he had been a smuggler for fifteen years. The detectives learned that Harkins and the other smugglers had close ties to politicians such as state senators Tim McCarthy and W. J. Hill. Harkins had enough political clout to get friends appointed as U.S. Customs officers in San Francisco. As Morse reported to Evans, "Many of the ring and those indirectly interested in the smuggling business are local politicians and ward strikers."[30]

In the meanwhile a preliminary hearing of the arrested smugglers was held before U.S. Commissioner O'Beirne. The U.S. commissioner was a federal magistrate who assisted the federal judges by handling criminal arraignments, preliminary hearings, and certain civil cases. Despite proof of the smugglers' guilt, O'Beirne ruled that there was not enough evidence and dismissed the charges against them. Special agent Evans was shocked by O'Beirne's action and asked the attorney general's office in Washington to investigate. Lorenzo Sawyer, the U.S. Circuit Court judge in San Francisco, had secured O'Beirne's appointment as a magistrate and had full faith in his integrity. He threw his support behind O'Beirne, and the commissioner was cleared of any misconduct. However, Judge Sawyer apparently believed that O'Beirne had used poor judgment, for he relieved him from hearing any further criminal cases.[31]

Morse and Evans found the investigation an uphill fight from the beginning. The power of the opium ring seemed to be boundless. The detectives met with interference at every step, from crooked cus-

Detective Harry Morse
in 1885. Courtesy Jack
Reynolds.

toms officers, local politicians, and the corrupt lawmen, Finnegass
and Favor. For example, the detectives learned that when plans were
made to arrest several of the crew of the *City of Tokio* on smuggling
charges on that ship's return to San Francisco, Finnegass and Favor
tried to warn the smugglers beforehand. Later it was found that the
three thousand pounds of smuggled opium, which had been stored
in the seizure room of the customshouse, had disappeared and been
replaced with lampblack and other worthless material. The con-
nivance of corrupt customs men was obvious. Evans reported to
Secretary Folger, "Captain Morse states that this is the most difficult
case he ever had, that the persons employed are so mixed up in local
politics as to almost defy exposure."[32]

With evidence gathered by Morse and Gamage, Special Agent
Evans saw to it that Hicks, Matthews, and Rogers were fired from
the customs service on suspicion of smuggling. Some seventeen
other crooked customs officers, as well as Deputy U.S. Marshal
Favor, were also removed from their jobs. Jim Harkins, fearful that
Evans would put his smuggling ring out of business, caused false
charges of misconduct and bribery to be made to Treasury Secretary
Folger. After a full hearing in San Francisco, Evans was not only ex-

onerated but commended for his efficiency. Foiled here, members of the ring filed another set of trumped-up charges before the federal grand jury. Once again Evans was cleared and commended for his good work.[33]

By making cautious inquiries in Santa Cruz County, Morse learned that while the smuggling case was pending before O'Beirne, the commissioner had visited Watsonville. He had been a guest at the home of Harkins's brother-in-law, William Gaffey, who was also a member of the ring. O'Beirne had also visited Harkins's ranch. One of the Kennedy brothers had been there at the same time. Morse discovered that John Hicks, the crooked customs officer, was Gaffey's brother-in-law. Morse reported to Evans that "Gaffey was a scoundrel in every sense. . . . Gaffey and Hicks while pretending to be true friends of Harkins would betray him for coin."[34]

By early 1883 Gaffey and Harkins had a falling-out over an old debt. Gaffey was a prominent citizen, made affluent by smuggling. By threatening him with public exposure and by offering to reinstate John Hicks to his customs job, Morse and Evans got them to agree to testify against Harkins. They told the detectives that during O'Beirne's visit to Watsonville, Harkins had given the magistrate a $1,200 bribe to dismiss the case against the smugglers. At the Bank of Watsonville the detectives found a $1,200 certificate of deposit that had been paid from Harkins to O'Beirne on June 19, 1882. After a yearlong investigation, Morse and Gamage had finally cracked the case. In July 1883 Jim Harkins and Commissioner O'Beirne were both indicted for bribery. Harry Morse and U.S. Marshal Moses M. Drew placed Harkins under arrest in Watsonville and returned him to San Francisco. Morse believed that he could get Harkins to confess, but the old smuggler was confident that he could escape punishment. He told newspapermen that he was the victim of a "job" put up by Evans "for political capital."[35]

Harkins and O'Beirne were tried in August before Judge Ogden Hoffman of the U.S. District Court. They denied the charges of bribery, and both claimed that the $1,200 payment had been a loan to O'Beirne. Both Gaffey and Hicks testified for the government. Harkins's lawyer, W. H. L. Barnes, a fiery orator, argued that his client was innocent and had been framed by "Morse and Company, the suborners of perjury." The jury, unsure of whom to believe, could not reach a verdict. Six voted to convict, six to acquit. Judge Hoffman declared a mistrial.[36]

Although Morse was hugely disappointed by the verdict, he was enraged by the charge Barnes made against him. Said Morse later, "I sent Mr. Barnes a letter that was exceedingly peppery, and such as no man of honor and courage would have allowed to pass unnoticed, but he, not being cut after such a pattern, never made any reply."[37]

Despite the failure to get a conviction, the work of Morse, Gamage, and Evans had completely exposed and broken the Harkins Opium Ring. Customs duties collected at the port doubled over the amount collected in previous years, a clear indication of how widespread smuggling had been. Secret Service Agent Finnegass, by exercising his political connections, managed to hang on until 1888 when he was replaced by Morse's old friend, Nick Harris.

Government prosecutors, fearful of an acquittal, were in no hurry to retry Harkins and O'Beirne. Finally, after a delay of four years, Judge Hoffman ordered the case to trial. By now Jim Harkins was fifty-eight, publicly disgraced, and his health was broken by heavy drinking. Edward O'Beirne had been removed from his position as U.S. commissioner and had not been able to find steady employment since. Wracked with guilt, he confessed to the U.S. attorney, and in exchange for a promise to dismiss the charges he agreed to testify against Harkins. On November 10, 1887, O'Beirne took the stand and told a stunned Judge Hoffman that he had committed perjury in the former trial and admitted that he had accepted a $1,200 bribe from Harkins. The trial lasted but two days. The jury convicted Harkins of bribery and recommended him "to the extreme mercy of the court" due to his ill health. Judge Hoffman sentenced Harkins to a year in prison and a $2,400 fine. This sentence was exceedingly lenient considering the gravity of his crimes. However, judicial custom and practice would not allow Judge Hoffman to levy a severe sentence on Harkins when O'Beirne, who was equally guilty, escaped punishment.[38]

In the end, Harry Morse had been fully vindicated. He told a reporter:

> It is a source of great gratification to me to know that poor O'Beirne, whom I always regarded as a good-natured fellow, not prone to evil of his own motion, and only the cat's paw of others, has by his confession set me right and proved to this community that every act of mine in the opium ring business was done in good faith and with the sole object of furnishing

the government with the facts in the case, and nothing but the facts.[39]

The Dupont Street Frauds and the Harkins Opium Ring cases, both involving corruption at the highest levels of government in San Francisco, were two of the most significant exposés of graft in nineteenth-century California. Harry Morse's success in each case went a long way to establish him as the foremost private detective on the Pacific Coast. His handling of these cases secured his reputation for integrity and hard work and did much to instill public confidence in his fledgling detective agency. These cases also marked a turning point in his career, for they demonstrated his willingness and ability to investigate increasingly more complex and politically charged crimes.[40]

CHAPTER 16

Black Bart

ON a crisp November evening in 1883, on a busy sidewalk in downtown San Francisco, Harry Morse put the arm on a well-dressed, graying, distinguished-looking gentleman named Charles Bolton. Bolton's true name was Charles E. Boles, but for six years he had been known to Californians as Black Bart, the Poet Highwayman. Black Bart today retains his distinction as one of the most colorful and romantic brigands of the Old West and as the most prolific stage robber in American history. Morse's capture of Black Bart, the result of simple but painstaking detective work, firmly secured his reputation as one of America's great detectives.

Black Bart remains something of an enigmatic figure, a gentleman bandit who repeatedly thwarted Wells Fargo and never harmed a soul but who abandoned his wife and family for a career "on the road" and vanished completely on his release from San Quentin. He was born about 1829 in Norfolk County, England, probably in the tiny village of Shelfanger, one of seven sons and three daughters of John and Maria Bowles. The following year his father brought the family across the Atlantic, settling on a farm near Alexandria Bay, Jefferson County, New York, where Charles grew to manhood. Young Boles, as his family now spelled the name, was popular and well regarded, as a childhood friend later recalled: "Charley, as we usually called him, received a common school education, and when grown up became better known than any other young man in this section on account of excelling in athletic sports, and was probably for his weight the best collar-and-elbow wrestler in Jefferson County. He was a young man of excellent habits and greatly esteemed and respected by all who knew him."[1]

Young Boles despised farming and was quick to join the gold rush, traveling overland with his brother David in 1850. In the fall they met up with another brother, James, at Union Bar, and the three worked the placers for a year and then returned home, arriving in January 1852. But Charley was stricken with gold fever, and three months later he, David, and another brother, Robert, secured passage around the Horn to San Francisco. This trip ended disastrously for the brothers, for both David and Robert took sick on the trip out; David died in San Francisco on their arrival in July, and Robert died in the mines soon after.

In 1854 Boles returned east, married Mary E. Johnson, and settled in Decatur, Illinois. He joined the Union Army in 1862 and served with bravery and distinction, being severely wounded in combat in 1864. He returned to his unit and fought at Vicksburg, Chattanooga, and Atlanta and was promoted to the rank of lieutenant by war's end. But the courage and honor he displayed during the war soon gave way to a darker spirit. Boles returned home, sold his farm, and moved his wife and three daughters, Ida, Eva, and Lillian, to Oregon, Illinois. After fathering a son, Arian, in 1865, he departed for the mines in Montana, promising to send for his family soon. They never saw him again.

Boles drifted through Montana, Idaho, and Utah and finally returned to California. From time to time he sent letters to his wife, promising to come home, but he never did, and Mary Boles raised her children in poverty, eking out a living by taking in sewing. By 1875 Charles Boles had landed in San Francisco, where he became known as a gentlemanly and well-to-do mining man. It would be eight years before the secret of his "wealth" would be discovered. While living in San Francisco, according to Wells Fargo's Chief Detective James B. Hume, Boles "made but few close friends, and those of first-class respectability, [was] neat and tidy in dress, highly respectable in appearance, and extremely proper and polite in behavior, chaste in language, eschewed profanity, and has never been known to gamble, other than buying pools on horse races and speculating in mining stocks."[2]

Black Bart's debut performance as a road agent took place on July 26, 1875, as driver John Shine, the springs of his stagecoach creaking loudly, urged his team up Funk Hill, four miles from Copperopolis in Calaveras County. Shine was startled when a ghostly apparition suddenly sprang into the middle of the road. Clad in a dirty linen duster, a white flour sack mask, and boots covered with large socks, the figure leveled a double-barreled shotgun and intoned, "Please throw down the box."

As Shine reached for the Wells Fargo box the highwayman cried, "If he dares to shoot, give him a solid volley, boys!"

Glancing toward the roadside brush, Shine saw what appeared to be a half-dozen rifle barrels aimed at him from the rocks and undergrowth. He tossed down the box, and a panicky woman passenger followed suit and threw her purse out the coach window. The bandit handed it back to her, saying gallantly, "Keep it, madam. I don't need your money. I only want Wells Fargo's." At the robber's order Shine drove his stage forward a short distance, and seeing the bandit vanish into the manzanita brush, he ran back to the scene to recover the express box. Only now did he realize that the "rifle barrels" were instead wooden sticks, expertly fastened by the highwayman to simulate a well-armed band of confederates.[3]

The gentlemanly brigand struck next five months later when he halted the San Juan–Marysville stage and again in June 1876 when he robbed a stagecoach north of Yreka. It was more than a year until he was heard from again. On August 3, 1877, following a holdup of a stagecoach on a picturesque, windswept bluff overlooking the Pacific Ocean, between Fort Ross and the mouth of the Russian River, an old waybill was discovered inside the shattered express box left behind by the robber. On the back of the waybill was scrawled one of the most famous bits of verse in the annals of American crime:

I've labored long and hard for bread
For honor and for riches,
But on my corns too long you've tred
You fine-haired sons of bitches.

It was signed, "Black Bart, the Po8." A brief postscript followed: "Driver, give my respects to our friend, the other driver; but I really had a notion to hang my old disguise hat on his weather eye. Respectfully, B.B."

Another year passed before Black Bart appeared again. On July 25, 1878, he stopped the coach from Quincy to Oroville and took $379 from the Wells Fargo box. The next day lawmen reached the scene and in the broken chest found a second piece of doggerel:

Here I lay me down to sleep
To wait the coming morrow,
Perhaps success, perhaps defeat,
And everlasting sorrow.
I've labored long and hard for bread

For honor and for riches,
But on my corns too long you've tred
You fine-haired sons of bitches.
Let come what will, I'll try it on,
My condition can't be worse,
And if there's money in that box,
'Tis munny in my purse.

—Black Bart, the Po8.

Although the humorous highwayman never left behind any further verse, he was known ever more as Black Bart. He continued to stop stages and rifle Wells Fargo boxes with monotonous regularity. His trademarks were the linen duster, the flour sack mask, a shotgun he never fired, and the deep-voiced command, "Throw down the box." Although Wells Fargo's Jim Hume flooded northern California with reward posters, lawmen were unable to catch him. Bart robbed four coaches in 1878, three in 1879, four in 1880, and five in 1881. He plagued stage routes from Sonora in the Southern Mines to the Oregon border and from the Sierra Nevada west to the Pacific Coast. Between holdups he lived quietly as mining man Charles Bolton in a series of San Francisco rooming houses. When he needed a "raise" he would tell friends that he had to visit one of his mines, and then he would vanish for a few weeks to plunder another coach.

In 1879 Boles resided at the Commercial Hotel at the corner of Montgomery and Pacific streets. So confident was he of his disguise that he often ate breakfast with San Francisco police detectives at the New York Bakery, a Kearny Street restaurant. One day a sneak thief stole his overcoat from the reading room of the Commercial Hotel and Boles had the gall to report the theft to the police. Detective Edward Byram recovered the coat from a fence on December 18, 1879, and returned it to Mr. Bolton. Byram and the other detectives were greatly embarrassed by this affair four years later, when Bolton's identity was revealed.[4]

Black Bart chose his targets carefully. He wisely avoided any coach with a shotgun messenger or express guard. He broke this rule but once, on July 13, 1882, when he tried to stop the southbound stage from LaPorte to Marysville. The coach carried $18,000 in bullion, as well as Wells Fargo's crack messenger, George M. Hackett. Two blasts from Hackett's sawed-off shotgun sent Black Bart fleeing for

Charles E. Boles, better known as Black Bart. America's greatest stage-coach robber, he was cap-tured by Harry Morse in 1883. Author's collection.

safety and left a deep scar on the robber's forehead where it was creased by a lone buckshot.[5]

After the poetic bandit's twenty-seventh holdup on June 23, 1883, near Jackson in the Sierra Nevada foothills, Jim Hume decided that he needed a man full time on the Black Bart case. And he needed the best man he could get. But Harry Morse had no better luck than any of the many officers and detectives who hoped to garner the laurels and the rewards for the elusive road agent. Because Black Bart managed to disappear so completely, Morse suspected that he made his headquarters in San Francisco, where he could live anonymously. Four months later California lawmen finally got their first break in the eight-year hunt for Black Bart.

On November 3, 1883, Reason E. McConnell was at the ribbons of the Sonora-Milton stage on Funk Hill, site of the first Black Bart holdup in 1875. With him was a nineteen-year-old friend, Jimmy Rolleri, and in the express safe, bolted to the stage floor, was $4,200 in gold bullion. Young Rolleri had been out hunting, and Henry rifle in hand, he had hitched a ride up the hill with McConnell. The coach was moving so slowly that the youth jumped down to see what game he could rustle up as he took a shortcut around the hill.

Near the summit McConnell was startled by the same duster-clad, shotgun-wielding brigand who had startled twenty-seven other "whips" before him. In short order the road agent blocked the rear wheels, forced McConnell to unhitch his team and run them up the hill, and then set to work on the safe with a sledgehammer. Meanwhile McConnell spotted Jimmy Rolleri crossing the hill and waved him over. Snatching the boy's rifle, he drew a bead on Bart, who was crawling out of the coach, a sack of plunder in one hand and an express package in the other. McConnell pulled the trigger and missed, then fired a second shot and missed again.

"Here, let me shoot," Rolleri told the driver. "I'll get him and I won't kill him, either."[6]

Jimmy snapped a quick shot at the fleeing robber and Black Bart stumbled, dropping the papers, but he continued on and vanished into the chaparral with his booty. Calaveras County Sheriff Ben K. Thorn and Wells Fargo Detective John N. Thacker were soon on the scene, hunting feverishly for evidence and witnesses. They found an old hunter named Martin who before the robbery had spoken with a suspicious stranger who matched Black Bart's description. And within a few days Harry Morse was busy at work on the case.

Last June [1883] *I was employed by Wells, Fargo & Co. to go to Calaveras County to see if I could get any clue to the person who had been robbing the stages. He had been plundering the company's treasure boxes on the stages for years and as yet there had been no clue whatever obtained. I spent three or four days there making investigations and came back and reported to the company my idea about the matter. A consultation was held between Captain J. B. Hume, detectives Charles Aull and J. N. Thacker, in the employ of the express company, and Sheriff Ben Thorn of Calaveras County, who determined upon a plan for capturing the man. Once we thought we had a clue to him but it proved to be a mistake. We have all been diligently at work at it ever since the matter was placed in the hands of Hume, Thacker, and myself. We often consulted and compared notes and at length concluded that we would have to wait until another robbery had been committed by him, and then with any clue we might obtain, act quickly.*

We did not have to wait very long for the opportunity. On the 3rd [of

November 1883] *the robbery of the Sonora and Milton stage was com-*
mitted near Copperopolis. We fixed upon a plan by which we could get the
man when he came to town. Thacker started immediately for the scene
of the robbery with Sheriff Thorn and made diligent search for the robber,
but failed to obtain any other clue than the things they found there, which
he had left behind him in his hurry to get away from the stage driver, who
was shooting at him. Among the articles he left in his hiding place behind
the rocks by the roadside were a hat, three pairs of cuffs, an opera glass
case and a silk crepe handkerchief with the mark "F.X.O.7." on it.

On being notified of this, Mr. Hume telegraphed to Thacker and Thorn
to send the thing down to the office in San Francisco, which was done.
Hume took the hat and opera glass case to see if he could have them iden-
tified, placing the handkerchief in my hands, with instructions to find the
owner of the mark, if possible. This was on Wednesday following the rob-
bery, which was committed on Saturday. On his way down to San Fran-
cisco detective Thacker gave the mark to an officer who had been stationed
at Lathrop by [San Francisco Police] *Chief Crowley, telling him all about*
the case. I left all other business and devoted myself exclusively to this.

I knew I had a job before me, as there were ninety-one laundries in the
city. After diligent search I was, on Monday afternoon, the 12th, re-
warded by finding on the books of a laundry agency at No. 316 Bush
Street, kept by a Mr. [Thomas C.] *Ware, the identical mark. The hand-*
kerchief had been left there three times—the first time on Saturday, Au-
gust 11th. I found also on inquiring that the washing belonged to one C.E.
Bolton. I made the most cautious inquiries at the laundry and found that
he was well known there. The laundryman said Bolton was a mining man
who often visited his mines, although he [Ware] *did not know where they*
were situated. Sometimes he would be gone a week or two and sometimes
a month. I assumed as a pretext that I wanted to consult with him on some
mining matter, and not being certain that he was the Bolton I was look-
ing for, I wished he would describe him. The laundryman did so and re-
marked that he had left the office but a few minutes before, and would be
around again next morning if not that evening. I also learned that he
roomed at No. 37 Second Street, room 40.

I at once placed a close watch on this house, with instructions to keep
a close eye and see if any person went in or out, and if anyone was seen
to send word immediately to me, taking care in the meantime not to lose
sight of him. I then returned to the laundry office and while I was talking
to Mr. Ware, Bolton came walking up the street toward us. Ware re-
marked, "Why, here comes Bolton now. I'll introduce you to him."

This was about five o'clock in the afternoon, just two hours after I got his name from the laundryman. I knew at once from the descriptions I had received that he was the man. He was elegantly dressed and came sauntering along carrying a little cane. He wore a natty little derby hat, a diamond pin, a large diamond ring on his little finger, and a heavy gold watch and chain. He was about five feet, eight inches in height, straight as an arrow, broad shouldered, with deep sunken, bright blue eyes, high cheek bones, and a large, handsome grey mustache and imperial; the rest of his face was shaven clean. One would have taken him for a gentleman who had made a fortune and was enjoying it, rather than a highwayman. He looked anything but a stage robber. He was quick in his movements and had muscular and symmetrical lines.

Ware introduced me to him by the name of Hamilton, that being the name I gave him. I shook hands with Bolton and asked him if he was Mr. Bolton, the mining man. He said, "Yes, I am."

I then told him that I had a matter of importance relating to some mines which I wished to consult him about, and asked him if he would spare a few minutes with me. He said "Certainly," and we walked together down Bush to Montgomery Street, then to California and Sansome, bringing up at Wells, Fargo & Co.'s office. We went upstairs to the superintendent's office. I introduced him to Mr. Hume, who requested him to be seated, saying that he wished to have a little talk with him. Mr. Hume commenced by inquiring about his business. Bolton said he was a mining man. Mr. Hume asked him where his mine was situated. He said in Nevada, on the California line. On being closely pressed he was unable to give either the name of the mine or the exact locality. He then began to get a little excited, and great drops of perspiration stood out on his forehead and nose. Said he, "I am a gentleman and don't know who you are. I want to know what all this inquiry is about."

Mr. Hume told him that if he would answer his questions satisfactorily he would tell him his reasons for asking them. I will state here that when Black Bart committed the robbery he dropped a package that had a blood stain on it, and while we were in Mr. Hume's office I noticed that on Bolton's right hand there was a piece of skin knocked off, about the size of a ten-cent piece. I drew Mr. Hume's attention to this and he asked Bolton how it occurred. He replied that he struck his hand against a car while he was getting off the train at Truckee. He was asked a great many questions, many of which he could not, and others he would not, answer, and at length grew indignant. He said it was the first time in his life that his character had ever been called into question; that he was a gentleman and that he would refuse to answer any more questions.

Mr. Hume then sent to the City Prison for Captain [Appleton] Stone, and upon his arrival a hack was summoned and Captain Stone, Mr. Hume, Black Bart, and myself proceeded to Bart's room at No. 37 Second Street, leaving Detective Thacker and Captain John Curtin of Morse's Agency at Wells Fargo's to await our return. This was about eight o'clock in the evening. The interview at Mr. Hume's office lasted about three hours. Bolton said he was 47 years of age [he was actually 54] and a native of Jefferson County, New York.[7]

On arriving at the room, we immediately proceeded to search for evidence. We found a large trunk, two valises, three or four suits of clothes, among them a suit answering the description of that worn by the man who robbed the stage near Copperopolis. In one of the pockets I found another handkerchief bearing the same mark as that found at the scene of the robbery, and perfumed with evidently the same perfume. Upon opening the trunk we found a lot of shirts, cuffs, and collars, all having the same laundry mark, and also a letter, written by Bolton, the writing in which corresponded with the handwriting of the doggerel written by the robber on one of the express company's waybills and left on the treasure box, and would leave no doubt in the mind of anyone that they were written by the same person.

On being spoken to about the marks on the handkerchief found at the scene of the last robbery, he said, "I am not the only one whose things bear this mark. Others have their washing done at the same place. Somebody may have stolen the handkerchief from me, or I may have lost it and someone else found it."

We told him that the handkerchief was found at the spot where the stage was robbed, whereupon he asked with an air of offended dignity, "Do you take me for a stage robber? I never harmed anybody in all my life, and this is the first time that my character has ever been brought into question."

Usually he spoke with calmness and with a pleasant smile, though his voice was low and a little hollow, as if he had affection of the throat or chest. There was also found a flyleaf of a Bible, on which was some writing in lead pencil, rather indistinct and portions quite illegible. As near as could be deciphered the writing was: "This precious Bible is presented to Charles E. Boles, First Sergeant, Company B, 116th Illinois Volunteer Infantry, by his wife as a New Year's gift. God gives us hearts to which His . . . faith to believe. Decatur, Illinois, 1865."

His wife's name was signed to the writing. We told Black Bart that he was suspected of having committed the stage robbery on the third of this month, and we took him from his room to the City Prison. Next morning

Captain Stone and Mr. Hume started with him on the 7:30 boat for Stockton enroute for San Andreas. At Clinton Station, Alameda County, Mr. Thacker and I met them. Mr. Hume returned from there to San Francisco, having business which called him to Bakersfield, and Captain Stone, Mr. Thacker, and I proceeded with the prisoner to Stockton. In the meantime we had telegraphed to Sheriff Thorn of Calaveras County to meet us at Stockton and bring down with him "Old Martin," the hunter, who had seen a man, supposed to be the robber, twice in the vicinity of where the robbery was committed, and about a week before it occurred, and once had a talk with him. The object was to see whether he could identify the prisoner as the man.

Black Bart seemed full of fun all the way going up and showed no disposition to attempt an escape. He was not ironed. When we got off the train at the Stockton depot and were met by Sheriff Thorn and Martin, the hunter, the latter's eyes fell immediately on Black Bart, and he exclaimed, even before he saw the officers, "That's the man, that's him!" identifying him in a crowd of more than a hundred people who had gathered there to see the noted prisoner. Bart was at once taken to a photographer's to have his picture taken. At first he strongly objected, saying that we had no right to do it, and he had done nothing; but finally he submitted and sat quietly, and a good picture was obtained. When the photographer turned the camera on him as he sat in the chair, he asked with a laugh, "Will that thing go off? I would like to go off myself."

From the photographer's he was taken to the Stockton jail and locked up for the night. On the following morning we went to Milton, Calaveras County. Here we met the driver of the stage that was robbed on the 3rd. He came up and spoke to the prisoner but said he could not identify him, as the robber was disguised in flour sacks, but the voice was the same. Bart seemed unconcerned and kept up his jokes. The great crowd that had assembled attracted his attention and he said, "The whole town has turned out to meet me. I guess they'll know me when they see me again."

At Milton we took a team and drove over to San Andreas—twenty-two miles. The whole population of the town—men, women, and children—had turned out, and it was amusing to hear the remarks as they mistook the natty looking prisoner for an officer and some one of us for the culprit. It was agreed that we would start the next morning for the scene of the robbery to look for further evidence, and that before we went we would have another interview with Bart. I was selected to interview him.

At seven o'clock in the evening he was taken into the jailer's room and I was left alone with him. I had written down all the facts we had gath-

ered in connection with the case. These I carefully read to him, explain-
ing what bearing they would have at the trial. He would often break off
and go into other subjects. He would give graphic descriptions of his experience in battle and how he was wounded. Then he would branch off
into Bible matters, in which he seemed well posted. He thought that
Moses had a great deal of pluck to reprove the Lord for his harsh dealing
with the children of Israel on different occasions. I would bring him back
to the right subject again, and for five hours and a half I talked with him,
ending the interview at 12:30 in the morning. During the interview, Bart
said, "I don't admit that I committed this robbery, but what benefit would
it be to the man who did, to acknowledge it?"

I called his attention to the fact that if the case went to trial it would
show what sort of a man he had been, and how he had committed
numerous robberies, and it would naturally prejudice his case, while if he
made restitution of the property and should go into court, and plead
guilty, it would save the county the great expense of a trial and would, no
doubt, be taken into consideration by the court and effect a mitigation of
his sentence. Bart then said, "Suppose the man that did commit the robbery should do this. Would it not be possible for him to get clear altogether?"

I said that would be impossible, but if it went to trial and it would be
shown that he had committed all these robberies, the chances were strongly
in favor of his being sentenced for life. Bart then said, "I want you to understand that I'm not going to San Quentin. I'll die first! These men may
all come up and testify just as you say. Men are apt to commit perjury and
courts are apt to be prejudiced, and whether a man is guilty or not, he has
to suffer the consequences."

He told of a stage robbery where a man was arrested for the offense.
The witnesses all swore against him. "I know of my own knowledge," said
he, "that he didn't do it. I wonder whatever became of him?"

At the end of the interview I called Captain Stone and Sheriff Thorn
in, and after talking together with him for a few minutes he suddenly said,
"Well, let us go after it."

We then got a team and at one o'clock started out of San Andreas. The
night was cold and clear and the moon was shining brightly and we had
a ride of twenty-four miles through the foothills and mountains, over deep
gulches, canyons, etc. He told interesting stories all the way. He said it was
a great relief to him, for there had been a great strain on his mind, and this
was the first time he had had the opportunity to tell anybody about this
thing.[8]

Morse and fellow lawmen celebrate the capture of Black Bart, 1883. *Left to right:* Tom Cunningham, Appleton W. Stone, Ben K. Thorn, John N. Thacker, and Harry Morse. Cunningham and Stone were two of Morse's closest friends; Morse and Thorn became bitter enemies in a very public quarrel over the Black Bart rewards. Courtesy Jack Reynolds.

Boles guided Morse, Thorn, and Stone to a hollow log where he had concealed the loot, about $4,000 in gold amalgam. He told his captors that after fleeing the robbery scene he walked almost one hundred miles to Sacramento where he shaved his beard, leaving only a mustache and imperial. He then took the overland train for Reno, finally returning to San Francisco a few days later.

Morse and his fellow lawmen returned the highwayman to his jail cell in San Andreas. Morse lost no time in sending a telegram to Leonard F. Rowell, division superintendent of Wells Fargo in San Francisco: "Black Bart throws up the sponge. Stone, Thorn, and myself have recovered all the stolen treasure. Inform Thacker."

Captain Isaiah Lees was greatly humiliated by the fact that Black Bart had been living for years under his very nose; the newspapers poked fun at the police unmercifully. The detective captain was angry that Morse had brought his old friend Appleton Stone out from obscurity in the city prison to share in the laurels. From then on Lees and Morse would be lifelong rivals, even outright enemies.

Two days later, on November 17, 1884, Bart appeared in court in San Andreas, pled guilty to a single charge of robbery, and was sentenced to a remarkably brief term of six years in San Quentin. With time credits for good behavior, he would be released in a little more than four years. The newspapers were quick to charge that Bart had made a deal with the officers and had received a short sentence in exchange for turning over the stolen gold. Morse, Hume, and Thorn denied the charge vehemently, but in retrospect it seems self-evident that Charles Boles had negotiated, in modern parlance, a plea bargain.

The *San Francisco Examiner* was particularly harsh in its criticism of Harry Morse and the other lawmen involved in the case. Its reporter mocked Morse, sarcastically referring to the "luminous spot on a soiled handkerchief, which was Harry Morse's pillar of fire by night and cloud of dust by day, leading him, after almost superhuman trials, to the presence of Black Bart." He questioned Morse's accounts of the arrest, referring to them as "beautifully garnished romances" and concluded that an informant had led Morse to Black Bart: "It looks as though the only feat of detective skill exhibited in the capture of Black Bart was an agreement to turn over to an informant a portion of the reward." The *Examiner* even questioned whether Boles was Black Bart:

Whether the Charles Bolton who was sentenced yesterday is Black Bart remains to be proved. If he is, the law has been tampered with. . . . A term of six years in prison—really about four and a half under the Goodwin Act—as a punishment for ten years' depredations is a mockery of law. The only tenable explanation of such a miscarriage of justice is that Bart's prosecutors made a bargain with him whereby he received a light sentence, and they the $4,000 which he had hid in the woods near Copperopolis.[9]

This attack brought a characteristic reply from Harry Morse:

To the Editor of the *Examiner*—Sir: In your article of Sunday you do an act of injustice. . . . No one could have been more astonished than Captain Stone and myself were when we read the accounts, as written in the daily papers, of the affair, and it was a mystery to us who could have given such a contorted statement to the press. As far as I am concerned, I make no pretension to great detective ability in the Black Bart case. A robbery was committed; a handkerchief was left behind by the robber, upon which was a laundry mark; the laundry was found whose mark it was; the name of the party whose laundry mark it was was obtained; he was well known and was easily found and taken into custody. Now, any man with ordinary common sense could have done that. The robber's room was searched, in which sufficient evidence was found to warrant a conviction. Bart was taken to the vicinity of the robbery and identified by several men who saw him in the immediate scene of the robbery. All the evidence was written out and read to him. He saw at once that the chain of evidence was complete against him, and like a sensible man, he confessed.

The simple facts above stated are true. No informer gave him away for a consideration. No inducements were held out to him to make him confess. He was simply told that a confession and restitution of the property stolen would likely be taken into consideration by the court and go in mitigation of sentence; that the Court, if he pleaded guilty, could not take judicial notice of the fact that he had committed other robberies. No bargain of any kind or promises were made to Black Bart. He made the confession of his own free will and accord. He was told that the confession of robberies made prior to October, 1880, were outlawed [i.e., the statute of limitations had expired, preventing prosecution for such crimes]; and as no indictment was found against him for them, he could not be convicted of them upon his own statement that he did them. He talked freely about them and acknowledged many of them. He also acknowledged writing the Black Bart poetry, and quoted some that he had written and intended to leave at the scene of his last robbery on the 3rd instant, but on account of the shooting at him he had to beat a hasty retreat, and so failed to leave it. His handwriting found in his room was identical with that of the poetry written on the company's waybill. He stated to me that he had taken the name Black Bart from Caxton's story of "Summerfield." . . .

If Bart denied his identity as Black Bart to the judge and stated that this was his first robbery, his object in so doing must have been to get a light sentence. I earnestly request that you publish this plain statement of facts. Captain Stone, Sheriff Thorn, nor myself have certainly done nothing to throw the glamour of romance about the arrest of this man Bart, and therefore you do us all an injustice when you attempt to hold us up to ridicule.[10]

Sheriff Thorn was not particularly impressed with Morse's effort to defend his good name. Ben Thorn, next to Tom Cunningham, was California's most famous sheriff of the 1880s and 1890s, and he was unhappy that most of the laurels for the capture of Black Bart fell on Harry Morse's shoulders. He was even more unhappy when he learned that Morse had put in a claim for the entire reward. Unlike Morse, who when sheriff had been scrupulously honest, Sheriff Thorn had become quite wealthy through imaginative manipulation of Calaveras County tax receipts. He was like Morse, however, in that he was never shy about claiming any rewards for the outlaws he captured, and Black Bart was no exception. The two officers' greed for the reward money led to a bitter war of words, which Morse decidedly got the worst of in the end.[11]

Wells Fargo officials paid the bulk of $800 reward to Harry Morse and Ben Thorn. This left unresolved the state reward of $300. Morse wrote to the Calaveras County clerk and inquired whether Sheriff Thorn claimed the state reward, and if so, on what grounds. The clerk turned the letter over to an outraged Thorn, who denounced Morse's inquiry as "a mean, cowardly, unmannerly stab at myself, and unworthy of anyone making any claims to decency."[12]

Morse fired back a blunt response: "If you are entitled to any part of the state reward, you are entitled to the whole of it. But what you did to entitle you to any part of it, I am at a loss to understand. If any person outside of myself should have the reward, John N. Thacker is that person." Morse then claimed sarcastically that he would send Thorn the entire reward, less his expenses, and concluded, "I would advise you to give it to Thacker, as he is entitled to it and not yourself."[13]

Sheriff Thorn responded with both barrels. In what the newspapers described as "sixteen sheets of good legal cap," he began relatively mildly by terming Morse's letter "one which no gentleman, would ever write. To say that it is impudent, insolent, malicious and malignant but partially designates it. It is false in every detail, and under any other circumstances would have been ignored by me as the scurrilous exhalation of an illiterate and pusillanimous brain." Warming to his task, Thorn reminded Morse of his promise to deliver the state reward to him. "Notwithstanding your profuse assurances that I would receive the entire state reward, some considerable time has elapsed . . . . and it has not been forthcoming. It is hardly possible that the expense incurred in collecting it absorbed the entire amount."

Thorn declared that it was really Captain Stone who deserved the reward. "Who took B.B. into custody and escorted him to the Station House? Who escorted him to San Andreas if not the man who arrested him, Captain Stone?" Finally the sheriff delivered his coup de grace. Referring to a conversation between the lawmen as they rode from San Andreas to recover the stolen gold, he suggested that Morse had been unfaithful to his wife. Thorn reminded Morse about a "fair enchantress, of whose accomplishments, talents, and literary attainments you dilated with so much enthusiasm upon the occasion of our famous ride out of San Andreas."[14]

Morse wisely let the matter drop, for the *San Francisco Examiner* gleefully reported the embarrassing details of the dispute. Its reporter concluded, "It is not on record that Mr. Morse recovered from the effects of this literary walloping sufficiently to take his pen in hand to let Mr. Thorn know he was alive."[15]

Black Bart dropped from the public eye and quietly served out his term as a model prisoner in San Quentin. He was released in January 1888, and for a few weeks detectives piped him in San Francisco and then through the San Joaquin Valley to Visalia, where he disappeared in February. In a letter written to his wife in Hannibal, Missouri, he complained about the detectives who were shadowing him but boasted, "I have made no effort to avoid them or anyone else yet—but when I do Mr. Detective will find his hands full to keep track of me."[16]

The slippery stage robber was soon back on the front pages. Following three holdups on isolated stage roads by a lone bandit in July and November 1888, Jim Hume announced that Black Bart was the prime suspect. Although every lawman on the West Coast was on the lookout for him, he had vanished completely. A reporter for the *Examiner* who buttonholed Harry Morse asked for his opinion of the road agent's whereabouts. The detective was uncharacteristically tight-lipped, and when the newsman insisted, "Where do you think he is?" Morse replied cryptically, "If he is trying to do right I think he should be left alone."[17]

Even Bart's family never saw him again. His wife, Mary Boles, referred to herself as a widow and died in Hannibal, Missouri, in 1896. Over the years many persons have tried to determine what became of her errant husband, but modern historical sleuths have had no better luck than their detective counterparts of one hundred years ago. The fate of Charles Boles, alias Black Bart, the Po8, remains one of the enduring mysteries of the Old West.[18]

CHAPTER 17

Personal Troubles

CALIFORNIA had a long tradition of vigilantism. During the gold rush government was minimal, law enforcement was uneven, and men were expected to solve their own problems. As a result, extra-legal justice had been socially and politically acceptable and lynchings were common. In 1855, for example, there were forty-seven lynchings in the state and only nine legal hangings. As formal government became established and as Californians became increasingly more cosmopolitan, they slowly shed the rough ethics of frontier society. By the 1880s there were on average no more than three lynchings per year statewide.[1]

Thus the public was shocked when newspapers reported on their front pages the apparent lynching of seventy-year-old Dr. A. W. Powers in San Benito County on September 18, 1885. The buckshot-riddled body of Powers had been found hanging from a tree limb in Bear Valley, thirty miles south of Hollister. A cardboard sign, "Vigilantes 150," was pinned to his shirt. Harry Morse remembered Powers well. Twenty-one years earlier he had evicted the doctor from his squatter's claim near San Leandro. Morse read in the newspapers that Powers had been up to his old tricks in San Benito County. Although he practiced medicine, he was primarily a rancher, and was just as troublesome in Bear Valley as he had been in Morse's old bailiwick. Powers had quarreled frequently with his neighbors, mostly over title to land, and had been suspected of shooting and poisoning their stock. A month before he died the crops of a neighbor, John Prewett, had been destroyed in an arson fire, and Prewett had accused Dr. Powers of the crime.[2]

Powers was a widower, but he had a daughter, Mrs. Samuel Bonner, who lived in Oregon. She came promptly to San Benito County, determined to see the killers brought to justice. Local lawmen lacked the ability to conduct a proper investigation. A group of civic boosters, concerned about the image of their community, raised a fund to hire private detectives to investigate the crime. They turned the money over to Mrs. Bonner, who immediately retained the Morse Detective Agency. Harry Morse knew that he faced a daunting task, for inquiries into lynchings were traditionally unpopular and rarely undertaken. He assigned his two best men, A. B. Lawson and Jerome Deasy, and they arrived in Hollister early in October.

By this time an autopsy had revealed that Dr. Powers had died from the gunshot wounds and that his body had been hanged after death. The footprints of six different men had been found at the crime scene. It developed that Dr. Powers had boasted he had evidence that would convict John Prewett of obtaining government land by false representations. After the fire Prewett had sent written invitations to a meeting of settlers in Bear Valley to discuss ways of driving Powers out of the county. Three such meetings took place; sixteen men attended the last one, two days before the doctor's death. Detective Deasy examined the cardboard "Vigilantes 150" sign. From markings on it he determined that it had been torn from a corset box that came from Freud & Co., a San Francisco clothing store. Morse's operatives learned that the only corset Freud & Co. had sent to San Benito County had been shipped to the sister of Isaac Slavin in Bear Valley. The writing on the sign matched that on Prewett's invitations.

John Prewett and his brother-in-law, Andrew Irwin, were arrested and charged with killing Dr. Powers. Soon they were joined in jail by sixteen of their neighbors who had attended the meetings. All were charged with conspiring to murder the doctor. But there was little evidence against any of them until detectives Deasy and Lawson managed to obtain a full confession from young Dick Alexander. The youth revealed that Prewett had called for a fourth meeting on September 17 at a deserted cabin. While on the way to the meeting Prewett and Irwin unexpectedly encountered Dr. Powers on the road. Prewett raised his shotgun and blew Powers out of the saddle with a load of buckshot. As Powers lay writhing on the ground, Prewett shot him in the back, then dragged the corpse into the brush. At the meeting Prewett told Alexander and the other five men present what he had done. They all agreed to return to the scene, where they hanged Powers's body to a tree limb to make it appear that he had been lynched by a vigilance committee. Isaac Slavin then wrote out the "Vigilantes 150" sign and pinned it to the dead man's shirt. Those present took a solemn oath never to reveal what had happened, on pain of death.[3]

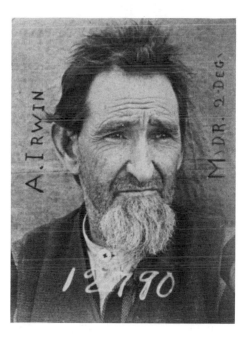

San Quentin prison photograph of Andrew Irwin, one of the killers of Dr. A. W. Powers. Courtesy California State Archives.

In December all the arrested men were released on bail except Prewett and Irwin, who were held in jail pending trial. Prewett's trial began in February 1886. The charges against the other conspirators were dismissed two weeks later when they agreed to testify against Prewett. But when they were placed on the witness stand they refused to talk. Although two were fined $500 each for contempt of court, they had taken their vow of silence seriously.

Prewett's defense was lame in the extreme. During his preliminary hearing he had denied any involvement in the murder. Now he admitted that he had committed perjury at the hearing and confessed that he had killed Dr. Powers. However, he claimed that Powers had drawn a pistol and challenged him to a duel and that he had fired in self-defense. As Morse commented, "The story of self-defense told by Prewett is a silly, weak fabrication." Dr. Powers did not carry a gun. Despite the clear evidence of Prewett's guilt, the jury, after deliberating for four days, could not agree on a verdict. A mistrial was declared.

Dr. Powers had been very unpopular. Too, Prewett and Irwin had many friends and relatives in the county and it was difficult to find jurors who did not sympathize with them. Prewett's retrial began in June, but it was impossible to find twelve jurors in the county who had not already made up their minds about the case. A second mistrial was declared. Prewett's case was then transferred to Monterey County, where the new trial began in March 1888. This trial also ended in a hung jury. In November 1887 Andrew Irwin was placed on trial. He was convicted of second-degree murder and sentenced to life imprisonment. However, an appeal was brought to the California Supreme Court, which found that the trial judge had erred in allowing several neighbors to testify that Dr. Powers had told them that Prewett, Irwin, and others were holding secret meetings and planning to shoot him from ambush. The court ruled that these statements were hearsay and thus inadmissible evidence and that Irwin was entitled to a new trial. Irwin was released after serving a year in San Quentin. San Benito County taxpayers were unhappy about these expensive trials, and the district attorney gave up trying to prosecute the two murderers.[4]

Harry Morse had feared such a result. Before the trials he wrote in the *California Police Record* that "the co-defendants . . . who have already been admitted to bail . . . are now roaming about San Benito County" and were "trying to intimidate witnesses and fix jurors." Morse questioned whether there was any "sense of right and justice among the majority of the people in San Benito County" and declared, "The body of the poor old murdered doctor lies rotting in his grave. Let us see if the jury is honest enough and has the nerve to do right and send his murderers to their just doom—the scaffold."[5]

Despite Morse's pessimism, his long experience dealing with criminals had never made him hardened or cynical. He retained a certain idealism and believed strongly in the rule of law. It was this faith in the courts that caused him to be outraged at such a gross miscarriage of justice. For Dr. Powers had unquestionably been shot from ambush and not in a fair fight. Despite the failure to convict the killers, Morse could take credit for his agency's leading role in one of the few serious efforts to prosecute a lynch mob in the West during the 1880s.

Much of Morse's work involved run-of-the-mill civil cases. An important exception was the lawsuit over the estate of Thomas Blythe, the eccentric millionaire who had figured so prominently in the Dupont Street Frauds. Blythe's death in San Francisco in 1883 set the stage for one of California's biggest and most protracted heirship cases. Blythe's real name was Thomas Williams, and he had come to

California from England in 1849. As was the custom in gold rush days, few questions were asked about his background. He worked as a peddler and by 1851 had saved $300, enough to purchase a city block, bounded by Market, Geary, and Dupont (Grant) streets. The rents made him wealthy, and he wisely held on to his property. The downtown soon expanded to encompass Blythe's block, and its value inflated to $4 million at the time of his death. Blythe also purchased 75,000 acres of land in San Diego County and a million acres in Mexico. Despite a fortune valued at $6 million Blythe lived frugally in a San Francisco lodging house crowded with dogs, birds, and cats.

Blythe's weakness was beautiful women, and he romanced many in California and abroad. In 1873 he seduced twenty-year-old Julia Perry in London, and their brief affair produced a daughter, Florence Blythe. The millionaire publicly acknowledged her as his child and regularly sent money to London for her care and education. At the time Blythe died he was living with Alice Dickason, whom one newspaperman described as "a woman of some education, somewhat shady reputation, and a leaning for art and high-proof stimulants." Blythe left no will, and Dickason claimed the entire estate by way of an alleged verbal marriage contract. Florence Blythe's mother, however, hired the finest lawyers in San Francisco. They in turn retained Harry Morse to do all the necessary investigative work to prove that she was entitled to inherit the estate.

Morse had his work cut out for him. More than two hundred claimants alleged in court that they were heirs of Blythe and thus entitled to share in his estate. Morse and the lawyers had to prove that Florence was Blythe's daughter and at the same time disprove the claims of the spurious heirs. After years of preparation and bitter legal wrangling, the trial finally began in San Francisco probate court in 1889. It lasted almost a year, and some 350 witnesses testified. Florence Blythe showed plainly that she was the natural daughter of Thomas Blythe. Numerous witnesses testified that Blythe had proudly admitted that she was his daughter; many loving letters from father to daughter were produced. Alice Dickason was unable to prove that she was Blythe's widow. Under California law an illegitimate child is entitled to inherit from the parent, and the judge awarded Florence Blythe the entire estate. So bitter was this legal fight that numerous appeals were then brought to the California Supreme Court, which issued seven decisions in the case, the last in

1895. After twelve years of litigation, Florence Blythe's right to inherit the estate was fully upheld.[6]

Harry Morse had always been interested in journalism and had counted reporters like George Beers among his closest friends. A natural storyteller, he still enjoyed regaling his children and friends with yarns of his adventures. In an effort to publicize his detective agency, he wrote a number of detailed accounts of his exploits for the San Francisco newspapers. These proved very popular, and as a result he began publishing a weekly newspaper, *Morse's Merchant Patrol*, which first appeared in August 1885. Morse soon changed its name to the *California Police Record*, which by 1886 became the *San Francisco Saturday Mercury*. In the early 1890s he published a monthly, the *Police Record*. Although these publications primarily served to advertise his detective agency, they contained an entertaining mixture of crime news, poetry, editorials, and reminiscences by Morse and other detectives.[7]

Further favorable publicity came from his friend Charles Howard Shinn, a noted journalist and naturalist. Shinn, born in 1852, had grown up in Alameda County where, like many other boys, he had idolized the dashing sheriff. As an adult Shinn saw in Harry Morse's career the grist for a dramatic story. Morse allowed the writer to read his voluminous scrapbooks, and from them Shinn wrote a short article about Morse for the San Francisco *Call* and a long biographical sketch for the New York *Sun*, both published in 1890. Morse was so pleased by this latter effort that he had a San Francisco printer publish it as a thirty-two-page pamphlet, entitled *Graphic Description of Pacific Coast Outlaws*. Its covers contained advertisements for Morse's detective agency, and Morse distributed copies free to prospective clients.[8]

Morse's business was lucrative, and he was becoming wealthy. He now had enough money to pursue the dream that had brought him to California in the first place. Morse had learned a great deal about mining as a youth, and now in his middle age he came down with a virulent attack of gold fever. He became interested in the Gold Park mining region located in the Shoshone Mountains about thirty miles southwest of Austin, Nevada. Gold had been discovered in 1880 and the mining camp of Gold Park sprang up. Two years later Harry Morse opened the Gold Park Trading Company, which sold mining supplies. He began to speculate in local mining claims and eventually took over the Star of the West, Arctic, San Francisco, and Irene mines. Morse later purchased an interest in the Holbrooke Mine near Grass Valley, California, a half interest in a claim in the Applegate District in Jackson County, Oregon, and a quarter interest in another mine in the Rosario Mining District in the state of Sinaloa, Mexico. Although Morse loved speculating in mining property, they were a drain on his finances. He had trouble finding reliable men to run them, and he never struck paydirt.[9]

Morse's newfound willingness to gamble on risky mining properties revealed a renewed restlessness of spirit that seems to have seized him in his middle age. As a result, during the 1880s Harry and Virginia Morse began to experience marital problems. By 1885 they had been married for thirty years and had numerous grandchildren. Ten years earlier their son George had married Kitty Hicks of Watsonville who bore him three children. Emma Morse had married Mathew de la Montanya in 1877, and the couple had four children. Annie Morse married Stewart MacMullan, and they had one son. While Virginia devoted herself to her grandchildren, her husband appears to have had trouble envisioning himself as grandfather. To him, grandchildren seemed to be a constant reminder of advancing age. He had always seen himself as a young, vigorous man and had been proud of his athletic physique. As sheriff he had tipped the scales at a muscular 155 pounds, but now he was decidedly paunchy, and his weight exceeded 200 pounds. When Morse was sheriff he had often been in the saddle and away from home, but now most of his work was done in San Francisco, supervising his operatives. Although he had more time to spend at home with his family, Morse appears to have had trouble adjusting to a more domestic lifestyle. This restlessness was different from that which had plagued his youth, for it manifested itself in a fascination with risky mining ventures and attractive women. Harry Morse had, in modern parlance, a midlife crisis.

Virginia Morse certainly knew that Sheriff Thorn had publicly accused her husband of infidelity a year before. The newspaper account of Thorn's charges surely caused her deep humiliation. Others were aware that Morse had a roving eye, as illustrated by a facetious letter found in one of Detective Jim Hume's scrapbooks. Written on Wells Fargo's letterhead in about 1885, it purports to be a report from Morse to Captain Charles Aull at San Quentin prison. Morse and Hume had had a falling out after the Black Bart case. The letter, in the handwriting of Hume's wife, Lida, a noted wag, mocks Morse, his detective skills, and his penchant for telling colorful sto-

ries about California badmen. More significant, it refers to his interest in champagne, women with red hair, and "chambermaids at
the Traveller's Glory," a colloquial euphemism for a brothel. The letter suggests that Morse's infidelity was a source of humor to Hume
and his wife.[10]

Virginia Morse sought refuge from her marital woes by immersing herself in volunteer work with several charitable organizations in
Oakland. Her pain was compounded by troubled relations with her
father. In 1885 Judge Heslep died alone and forgotten in his law office on Kearny Street at the age of seventy-eight. The judge had mel-
lowed little over the years, and his orneriness had left him with few
friends. Virginia and her surviving brother and sister had been estranged from him for many years. The newspapers reported that a
long letter to Harry Morse was found on his desk. In it, the old man
pleaded with Morse to help him reconcile with his children. Virginia
evidently had never forgiven him for divorcing her mother.[11]

More trouble would come from the Morses' only surviving son,
George. As Morse once said, his son was "subject to paroxysms of
rage and violence," and as a consequence George and his wife divorced after about five years of marriage. In 1882 he married Annie
Nightingill, the widow of an Oakland newspaperman. George Morse
was a plumber, and in the mid-1880s, while working in a well, a box
of tools fell on him, striking his head and aggravating his old injury.
His behavior became increasingly erratic and violent. He mistreated
and beat Annie. On one occasion he thrashed his stepson for forty-
five minutes with a harness tug. The youth was laid up for a week
with injuries.

The years of living in the shadow of a famous lawman seemed to
have profoundly affected the younger Morse. He developed a misplaced fascination with guns and a desire to be known as a dangerous man. George Morse also suffered from paranoid delusions that
he was being cheated in all his business dealings. He threatened to
kill various supposed enemies. In 1888 he and his wife publicly accused W. E. Dargie, owner of the *Oakland Tribune* and a friend of
Harry Morse, of swindling them out of an ownership share of the
newspaper. The charges proved to be totally false. In July 1889
George got into a boundary dispute with his next-door neighbor and
also a contract dispute with a builder whom he had hired to con-
struct a new home. George accused the builder of trying to cheat
him and threatened to shoot him. When he threatened to kill his

neighbor too, he was arrested on a charge of insanity. The resulting
public hearing in Oakland, before a packed courtroom with news
papermen jotting down every salacious detail, proved to be the most
embarrassing experience in Harry Morse's life.

For two days a parade of witnesses testified against Harry Morse's
son before a special panel of one judge and two doctors. It came out
that George owned a small arsenal of firearms and had turned his
barn into a fortress, complete with gun ports drilled through the
walls. He was in the habit of firing potshots from the barn at night.
He had been seen beating his wife and stepson. Some witnesses
stated that although George was eccentric and suffered from delusions, he was not insane. Others reported that he was a braggart and
a coward and that his threats were empty. A neighbor testified that
once when a small poodle had chased George, he climbed onto a
fence and remained there for three hours. Harry Morse was subpoenaed and testified that his son was mentally unsound but he did not
believe him to be insane. Said Morse, "He has a mania for carrying
weapons. . . . I have had nothing to do with him for many years. It
is three or four years since I have spoken to him."

For his part, George Morse had told witnesses that "his father was
not fit to live and that he would shoot him on first sight" and that
he was "the only man in the world that his father feared." George,
testifying on his own behalf, denied any wrongdoing. He claimed
that his father "had not been doing just right by his mother." He implied that his parents were separated and said that his mother was
then residing in Livermore. George admitted, however, that he had
not seen his mother in a year.

Virginia's cousin, Ella Viers, the family housekeeper, was called to
the stand and testified that at her brother Walter's home near Livermore, George had fired four shots at her. She said that she simply
walked up to him, took his gun away, and brought him home. George's
version was entirely different. He claimed that while he and his mother
were visiting the Viers home he heard a cry inside the house and
rushed inside. He found his mother extremely upset, and she told him
that Walter Viers had tried to rape her. George said that he went after
Viers, and when the two grappled, Viers tried to cut him with a
knife. George drew his pistol and opened fire, putting Viers to flight.

Annie Morse and her son denied that George had ever beaten
them, but the panel ruled unanimously that they were lying to protect him. Loath to send the younger Morse to the state insane asy-

lum, the panel ruled that he was sane but suffered from delusions. They released him on his promise to cause no more trouble. To Harry Morse's utter dismay, the newspapers had a field day with this story and devoted columns to it. George and Annie Morse eventually divorced. Still later George obtained more newspaper notoriety by claiming that he had taken part in revolutions in Guatemala and boasting of killing men in battle. Whether these yarns were true or mere delusions is unknown. But for Harry and Virginia Morse, the greatest pain caused by their wayward son was still years away.[12]

Despite episodes of infidelity, Morse remained loyal to his wife. They seem to have patched up their differences, for in their later years they were constant companions and their marriage lasted until Virginia's death. Loyalty was one of Harry Morse's strong points, and it was this attribute that led to a long struggle to aid his old amigo and posseman, Ramon Romero. Following the Vasquez hunt, Romero had returned to herding cattle in Contra Costa County. In 1877 he stabbed Jose Arrayo to death near Walnut Creek. Romero first reported that he had been protecting Arrayo's wife from an abusive husband, then claimed that Arrayo had fallen on his own knife. But blood was found on Romero's knife and clothes, and it developed that he had been having an affair with the woman. There was nothing Morse could do for him. Ramon was convicted of first-degree murder. This was the third man he had slain over a woman and the fourth time he had been tried for murder. The judge sentenced him to life imprisonment.[13]

By 1889 Morse and Sheriff Cunningham believed that Romero had been punished enough. They began a nine-year effort to secure a pardon for the errant vaquero. The two lawmen lobbied the governor and the state board of prison directors on behalf of Romero. Morse wrote to the governor, "I have known Romero nearly thirty years and he was in no sense what might be called a bad man." Morse stressed Romero's exemplary conduct in prison and insisted "that the service that he rendered the State in the hunt for Vasquez is entitled to some recognition by the people of California, for, to my certain knowledge, his action in that matter caused him many bitter enemies among people of his own nativity, and which caused him much trouble thereafter." He assured the governor that "the fires of his youth are sufficiently quenched so that the cause of trouble . . . will not occur to him again, by reason of his age and his long term of imprisonment."[14]

Telephone 1488

9/12/889
W????

San Francisco, September 12, 1889.

Hon. R. W. Waterman,

    Governor State of California,

Dear Sir:-

    There is a poor devil of a Mexican named Ramon Romero, now
serving a life sentence in San Quentin for murder, who has not a
dollar or a friend on earth. During the Vasquez hunt he did the
State good service, that is, he was with Sheriff Cunningham, of
SanJoaquin, and myself in the hunt after that bandit, and did
excellent work.

    Sheriff Cunningham and I desire to have his sentence com-
muted to twenty years and he to leave the State forever. He has
already served twelve years and I believe has been a good prisoner.

    Your printed rules relating to pardon proceedings say that a
copy of the notice must "be published in a daily paper for thirty
days in some daily paper published close by." Would it be sufficient to publish notice in the Oakland daily, or can the publication of notice be waived? Will you kindly answer this and
oblige,

                         Yours respectfully,

                         H. N. Morse

*There is a weekly but no daily paper
published in Contra Costa Co.*

One of Harry Morse's letters to the governor seeking clemency for his old
posseman, Ramon Romero. Courtesy California State Archives.

Their efforts were repeatedly rebuffed, however. California governors in the past had come under political fire for "gross abuses of the pardoning power" and had become reluctant to commute the sentences of convicted killers. Undaunted, Morse and Cunningham enlisted the support of Warden W. E. Hale of San Quentin and four justices of the California Supreme Court. Year after year the two lawmen never missed an opportunity to bring up Romero's case with anyone who could help. After nine years of lobbying three different governors, Romero's sentence was finally commuted by Governor James H. Budd in 1898. On his release from San Quentin, Warden Hale wrote the governor, "A happier man does not exist than Ramon." Interviewed by reporters, the old vaquero was exuberant. "I thank God I am free, and I thank Sheriff Cunningham and Mr. Morse. If I have five million dollars I would give it all to them and not think it enough for what they have done for me."[15]

Tom Cunningham had arranged for Ramon Romero to live in Stockton, and there he lived out his life in peace. In 1901 every prominent elected official in San Joaquin County signed a petition to the governor seeking to restore his citizenship, which had been automatically revoked when he was convicted. The request was promptly granted.[16]

Harry Morse's friendship with Ramon Romero throws light on his attitudes toward Hispanics. The compassion and loyalty that he displayed in helping to free his old posseman from prison were not the attitudes of a racist. Nonetheless, by modern standards Morse would be considered a bigot, as evidenced by his repeated use of the pejorative term "greaser." But when judged in light of the mores of his era, he was far more open-minded than most Californians. Morse had a deep respect for and understanding of the language, customs, and culture of the Spanish-speaking people. He counted numerous Hispanics as friends; his personal attorney for many years was a Californio, R. M. F. Soto. It was bandidos that he disliked, not Hispanics. Harry Morse judged men by their deeds, not by the color of their skin.

CHAPTER 18

The Crime of the Century

HARRY Morse often claimed that he did not work for rewards and that he only employed men of sterling character. Money, however, was one of the driving influences of Morse's life, and he did not always practice what he preached. In 1893 he departed from his rule in a very public way. Wells Fargo and the Southern Pacific Railroad Company had placed a $10,000 price on the heads of Chris Evans and John Sontag, at that time the two most wanted and most dangerous outlaws on the Pacific Coast. Morse decided that he would hire the toughest manhunters he could find and make a try for the reward.

Chris Evans was a popular forty-five-year-old farmer and father of seven from Visalia. John Sontag, thirty, was a former Southern Pacific brakeman who harbored an intense hatred for the railroad, which he claimed had mistreated him. Between 1889 and 1892 they held up and robbed four trains in California and two more in the Midwest. There was no hard evidence against them until after the last holdup, when two lawmen went to the Evans farm near Visalia to question the pair. A gunfight erupted in which both officers were wounded, and Evans and Sontag fled in a buggy. That night they slipped back to the Evans place to obtain supplies of food, clothing, guns, and ammunition. But lawmen were watching the farm, and in a second gun battle a deputy sheriff was slain. Evans and Sontag escaped into the mountains, and one of California's biggest and most sensational manhunts began.

Lured by the large reward, scores of regular peace officers, Southern Pacific detectives, and private bounty hunters flocked into the Sierra Nevada in Fresno and Tulare counties. For ten months the two fugitives eluded posses in the mountains, aided by Evans's many friends and by settlers who despised the Southern Pacific. The railroad company was thoroughly resented by many Californians for its unscrupulous business methods and its corrupt influence over state

273

politics. On one occasion Evans and Sontag ambushed a pursuing posse and killed two more lawmen. Such violence quickly eroded their folk hero status, and public opinion eventually turned against them.

Harry Morse fully recognized how dangerous the two outlaws were. He recruited two men who were just as dangerous as their prey. One was Tom Burns, an ex-convict from Visalia who had known Chris Evans for years. Burns was a gunfighter and sported a fast-draw "swivel rig," in which a Colt revolver swung from a slotted plate on his gunbelt. It could be fired from the hip by simply tilting the weapon up and pulling the trigger. Morse's other man was Sam Black of San Diego. A veteran of the Civil War, he had long been a lawman in Texas where he had killed several desperadoes.

In October 1892 Black rented a small cabin just outside of Camp Badger in the Sierra Nevada in northeastern Tulare County. Evans and Sontag had often been spotted in the area, where friends supplied and supported them. Black was later joined by Tom Burns, and the two posed as laborers, cutting wood and hauling lumber. They quietly picked up information and rumors about the fugitives and sent regular reports to Morse in San Francisco. For months neither was suspected, but in May 1893 Evans and Sontag sent word to Black by a local rancher that he must leave the mountains or they would kill him. Black ignored the warning.

Ten days later, on the night of May 26, Black and Burns, after playing cards at the hotel in Camp Badger, walked back to their cabin. As they approached it, Evans and Sontag, crouched behind a woodpile, opened up a barrage of fire, first with shotguns and then with Winchesters and six-shooters. Black dropped, with ten buckshot in his legs, left hand, and hip. Burns, exercising prudence over valor, raced back to the hotel while Black crawled into the cabin for his Winchester. As rifle balls splintered the walls, he returned the fire and the outlaws fled into the darkness.[1]

Sam Black was out of the manhunt, but Tom Burns was not. A few days later, on June 2, U.S. Marshal George E. Gard recruited Burns and two veteran lawmen, Hiram Rapelje and Fred Jackson, to help him run down the outlaws. After nine days of hunting they had a stroke of luck. The little posse was resting inside a vacant cabin near Stone Corral, fifteen miles north of Visalia. Suddenly they spotted two heavily armed men approaching on foot. A violent gun battle with shotguns and rifles erupted. Jackson was wounded in the leg so

Reliving his horseback days, Morse posed for this photograph near Nevada City in 1897. Author's collection.

severely it later had to be amputated. But Evans and Sontag were badly shot up and captured. Sontag soon died of his wounds. Evans recovered, was convicted of murder, and then escaped jail and eluded a huge dragnet. He was finally recaptured in 1894 and served seventeen years in prison for murder.

Harry Morse was so pleased with Tom Burns's work that he called him to San Francisco and gave him a magnificent presentation rifle. Burns drifted into Arizona where he ran up a bad record. He took part in several shooting and cutting scrapes and was finally slain by a young cowboy in 1901. Sam Black did not fare much better. He killed a man in a fight in San Diego and was convicted of manslaughter. Sentenced to San Quentin, he died in prison of natural causes in 1902.[2]

At the same time that Morse's men were hunting Evans and Sontag, another Morse operative, W. R. McFarlane, was in Fresno investigating the mysterious murder of Louis McWhirter. An attorney and journalist, McWhirter had been shot to death in his backyard, apparently by an assassin, on the night of August 29, 1892. A $25,000 reward had been offered for the arrest and conviction of the killer, and many private detectives flocked to Fresno. None of them had any luck. The newspapers called the McWhirter murder "one of the remarkable mysteries of the decade," and the case threatened to push the Evans-Sontag manhunt off the front pages.[3]

McFarlane and another San Francisco detective, C. J. Stilwell, managed to uncover a web of circumstantial evidence implicating Richard S. Heath, a barroom politician, in the killing. Heath and McWhirter had been political enemies. In July 1892 Heath and a journalist friend of McWhirter's, J. E. Baker, had a fistfight in which Heath was badly beaten. Heath later displayed a pistol in a Fresno saloon and promised he would kill Baker, who lived in McWhirter's home. The detectives believed that in the dark, Heath had mistaken Baker for McWhirter. Heath and a friend, Frederick Polley, had been seen in the vicinity of McWhirter's house shortly before he was slain. A pistol with the letter "H" carved on the grip was found next to the body. The detectives dug up a witness who produced a mask and a handkerchief bearing Heath's initials that were supposedly found the morning after McWhirter died.

Based on this rather flimsy evidence, a warrant was issued charging Heath and Polley with murder. On March 13, 1893, Jules Callundan arrested Heath in San Francisco. He was returned to Fresno to stand trial. However, many believed that Heath was innocent and that McWhirter had shot himself. The dead man's law practice had failed, his property was heavily mortgaged, he had spent all of his wife's money, and he had been drinking heavily. He had taken out $60,000 in life insurance prior to his death, but the insurance companies refused to pay on the grounds that McWhirter had committed suicide. It also turned out that Detective Stilwell had been hired by the *San Francisco Examiner*, which was out to scoop its competition by "solving" the case. John Curtin, a former Pinkerton detective who had worked for Morse and now ran his own San Francisco agency, was highly critical of Morse's men and Stilwell. "It's an outrage to arrest Heath. He was suspected at the time of the murder and my man had him under surveillance for several days, but the suspicious circumstances were exploded at an early day. . . . [I]t was a clear case of suicide and this new story has been devised, I think, in order to secure the insurance money for Mrs. McWhirter."[4]

In Heath's trial his lawyers claimed that the private detectives had deliberately framed him. They argued that if Heath was convicted, the detectives would receive the $25,000 reward and McWhirter's widow would receive the insurance funds. By this time Morse had distanced his agency from the case and Stilwell and the *Examiner* bore the brunt of the criticism. There was enough evidence to convince eleven jurors that Heath was guilty; one man held out for acquittal. Heath was retried, and the new jury also hung, with ten men voting to convict. Polley's trial also ended in a hung jury. The two men were released, and the McWhirter murder mystery was never solved.[5]

Harry Morse had never lost his passion for politics. Although still a loyal Republican, by the 1890s he had become disenchanted with the Republican party's control over Alameda County affairs. A party machine, the so-called courthouse ring, was firmly entrenched in power through the influence of the Southern Pacific. In 1894 local reformers chose Morse as a nonpartisan candidate for sheriff to campaign against the ring's candidate, Louis Schaffer. However, the reformist People's party also fielded a candidate, C. B. White. In the election on November 6, White won, with 6,281 votes. Schaffer came in a close second, and the Democratic candidate was third. The former sheriff, in what was surely a severe blow to his ego, finished a distant fourth with just 1,969 votes, only 10 percent of the total cast. Despite his poor showing at the polls, he was not discouraged, and would seek political office again.[6]

Five months later Harry Morse became embroiled in the so-called Crime of the Century, the case of William Henry Theodore Durrant, who was accused of the sex killings of Blanche Lamont and Minnie Williams. This was by far the most sensational murder case of nineteenth-century San Francisco, and it pitted the West Coast's foremost private detective against its foremost police detective.

Blanche Lamont was a pretty, churchgoing student of twenty-one. On the afternoon of April 3, 1895, while on her way home from school, she disappeared. Nine days later Minnie Williams, an attractive nineteen-year-old, left home to attend a youth group meeting of the Emanuel Baptist Church on Bartlett Street in San Francisco's Mission District. She was never seen alive again. The next day, ladies decorating the church for Easter services entered a small storage room in search of spare Bibles. Instead they made a blood curdling discovery: the partly nude body of Minnie Williams. She had been gagged, stabbed, mutilated, and raped.

VOTE FOR

HARRY N. MORSE

NON-PARTISAN NOMINEE FOR

SHERIFF

OF ALAMEDA COUNTY.

Election November 6th, 1894.

Harry Morse tried to regain the sheriff's post in 1894. He did poorly at the polls. Courtesy Jack Reynolds.

The following day, police detectives made a systematic search of the entire church. Breaking the lock on the door to the unused belfry, they climbed the stairs and found Blanche Lamont laid out on the belfry floor. She lay peacefully on her back, her head supported by two small blocks of wood and her hands folded neatly on her breast. She had been strangled to death, her body stripped naked. Her clothes and schoolbooks were found stuffed into the walls and rafters. She had been dead about two weeks. The body had decomposed too much to determine whether she had been raped.[7]

To say that this double murder created an uproar is a gross understatement. In that era crimes against women were far less common than today. Most murders took place in quarrels between ruffians and in domestic disputes. Murder of an innocent person was enough to shock and outrage the public; murder of an innocent woman was far worse. A serial sex murder was beyond comprehension.

Police detectives attacked the case with a vengeance. They quickly discovered that Blanche Lamont had last been seen entering the church with twenty-four-year-old Theo Durrant. Quiet and respectable, young Durrant was the church librarian, assistant superintendent of the Sunday school, a student at Cooper Medical College in San Francisco, and a member of the Signal Corps of the California National Guard. Both young women belonged to the Emanuel Baptist Church and had been friendly with Durrant. Police detectives learned that soon after Durrant had been observed entering the church with Blanche, the organist saw him come down from the belfry, pale, sick, and disheveled. Additionally, they found that in medical schools, bodies were laid out in the dissecting room in the same manner as Blanche Lamont's body in the belfry. After Blanche had disappeared, Durrant had spread a rumor that she had "gone astray" and become a prostitute. Police searched his parents' home, and in Durrant's coat pocket they found Minnie Williams's purse. On April 15 Theo Durrant was arrested for murder. Lynch mobs gathered at the city prison and howled for his neck.

Durrant insisted that he was innocent, but Isaiah Lees and his men quickly dug up an overwhelming mass of circumstantial evidence against him. Durrant's character had been so sterling that his closest friends and family refused to believe him capable of such monstrous crimes. His commanding officer in the National Guard, General John H. Dickinson, a prominent attorney, volunteered to defend him. Dickinson persuaded Eugene Deuprey, one of the finest trial lawyers in San Francisco, to act as lead counsel. The newspapers quickly convicted Durrant in print, labeling him "the Beast in the Belfry" and his case "the Crime of the Century."

Durrant's lawyers needed a good investigator to assist in his defense and called on Harry Morse. Explained Jules Callundan, "Captain Morse was not inclined to touch the case at first. He spent a week looking into it. When he became convinced that the young man was not guilty he went in as a matter of business and justice."[8]

Durrant's parents were of very modest means and could ill afford the services of attorneys and detectives. Thus Harry Morse agreed to work for free. Morse's decision to help defend Durrant was a courageous one. He did not need the publicity, for his patrol and detective business was lucrative. His clients, mostly businessmen, bankers, mining companies, and merchants, had no desire to be linked to one of the defenders of San Francisco's most infamous woman killer. But for Morse, the decision was a moral and ethical one. "I worked on the case without a cent of pay because I believed the man not guilty," he explained. "The only time I ever saw him break down and cry was when his attorneys went at him rough-shod to tell us the truth. It was then that he wept and swore by the Bible and his mother that he was the victim of circumstances and that he had no part in the crime." Morse told another reporter, "I am convinced that no one man committed both of these murders. The Lamont murder and the Williams murder were committed in different ways. Both were brutal enough, but the Williams case was more blood-thirsty that the other."[9]

Perhaps, too, Morse recalled another murder case twenty-two years earlier. Then, as now, the victim had been wholly blameless, the crime vicious, and the public outraged. That case had also been a cir-cumstantial one, and the accused, like Durrant, had consistently as-serted his innocence. Perhaps the shadow of Bartolo Sepulveda loomed large in Morse's mind. Perhaps his conscience compelled him to be-lieve Durrant, to labor gratuitously in his behalf, and to try to save him from the gallows.

San Francisco's major daily newspapers, the *Call, Examiner, Chronicle*, and *Bulletin,* embroiled in an ongoing circulation war, de-voted tons of ink and pulp to the story. Every aspect of the case, in-cluding wild speculation, rumor, and innuendo, was covered in detail. In defiance of a court order, a local theater company produced a play, "The Crime of the Century," which dramatized the case. The au-thor, producer, and cast were arrested for contempt of court.

The newspapers played up the rivalry between Morse and Isaiah Lees. Said the *Chronicle,* "The ancient feud between Captain Lees and Detective Harry Morse has been reopened and intensified." Jules Callundan tried to play down the rivalry: "These stories about a feud between Captain Morse and Captain Lees are all rot and nonsense. They do not glare at each other, nor crouch down like lions ready to spring at each other's necks. . . . Whatever Captain Morse may think of some of the police methods he has none but the kindliest feelings for the men on the force. This is not a contest for supremacy."[10]

Durrant's trial for the murder of Blanche Lamont began on July 23, 1895. Huge crowds fought to get into city hall to watch. Se-lecting a jury took more that a month; some 1,400 potential jurors were examined. Most were excused on hardship and employment grounds; others were rejected for having formed opinions of Dur-rant's guilt. There had been so much pretrial publicity that there were few San Franciscans who believed Durrant innocent. Finally a

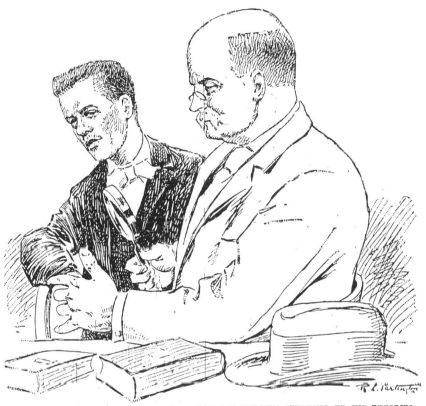

DETECTIVE HARRY MORSE IN A CHARACTERISTIC POSITION STUDYING UP HIS THEORIES

Theo Durrant and Harry Morse as depicted in the San Francisco *Call*, July 30, 1895. Author's collection.

jury was chosen and testimony began. Harry Morse sat at the counsel table with Dickinson, Deuprey, and Durrant. Across from them was the prosecution team: District Attorney William Barnes, his assistant, Edgar Peixotto, and Captain Lees. A reporter described the scene in court: "Several detective officers are always near the Captain's elbow, ready at a moment's notice to jump into hacks and hunt down a possible witness. Harry Morse, the sleuth of the defense, sits opposite Captain Lees and quietly bites the ends of his closely cropped moustache as he follows the testimony. Lees and Morse, rivals and almost open foes, are the two pilots of the case."[11]

Testimony in the trial lasted more than two months. Some fifty witnesses were called by the prosecution. Blanche Lamont's final day was reconstructed in detail for the jury, and a chain of evidence linking Durrant to the crime was methodically forged. A woman who lived across the street from Blanche's school testified that at about two o'clock on the afternoon of April 3 she had seen a young man matching Theo Durrant's description waiting in front of the schoolhouse. At three o'clock he met Blanche Lamont and another girl outside, then the three boarded a streetcar. Blanche's schoolmate, Minnie Edwards, testified that it was she who had boarded the car with Blanche and Durrant. Blanche was carrying her schoolbooks with her. Two other classmates testified that they also saw her sitting in the streetcar with Durrant.

Elizabeth Crossett, who had known Durrant for four years, swore that she saw him and a girl matching Blanche's description leaving a Valencia Street car and walking toward Bartlett Street. The time was between 3:30 and 3:45 P.M. An attorney, Martin Quinlan, testified that he knew Durrant well and at about 4:15 P.M. saw the couple walking up Bartlett Street toward the Emanuel Baptist Church. A woman who lived across the street from the church, Caroline Leake, testified that she attended the church and knew both Theo Durrant and Blanche Lamont. At about 4:20 P.M. she saw Durrant and a young lady whom she thought was Blanche enter the church. George King, the church organist, testified that he entered the church at five o'clock. A few minutes later he observed Durrant's suspicious descent from the belfry, sick and disheveled.

A pawnbroker testified that Durrant offered to sell him a ring that was later identified as Blanche's. Prior to Durrant's arrest, this ring had been mailed by an unknown person to Blanche's aunt. Following the girl's disappearance, Durrant had called on her aunt and offered to help search for her. He told the aunt and one of classmates that he had received information that Blanche had run away from home to a brothel.

Durrant's defense was a weak one, but his attorneys and Harry Morse did the best they could. He denied having been with Blanche Lamont on the afternoon of April 3 and claimed an alibi. He produced notes from a medical school lecture he said he had attended during those crucial afternoon hours. But one of his classmates testified that while on a visit to Durrant in the city prison, Durrant had told him he had no notes so he could establish an alibi. The class roster for that lecture was produced, and it bore Theo Durrant's name. However, it was proved that students commonly answered "present" on behalf of their classmates so they would not be marked absent.[12]

Harry Morse worked busily to round up character witnesses for Durrant. He also dug up nine witnesses who testified that the attorney, Martin Quinlan, was a "police court shyster" and bore a bad reputation for truth and honesty. Dickinson and Deuprey did all they could do to discredit the memory of each witness who had seen Durrant and Blanche Lamont together, and Durrant took the stand himself to proclaim his innocence. But in the end the chain of circumstantial evidence against him proved overwhelming. The case was submitted to the jury on November 2. The jurors deliberated just twenty minutes before returning a verdict of guilty of first-degree murder. While Durrant's mother shrieked and clutched her son, the courtroom exploded into cheers.

Harry Morse was philosophical, telling a reporter, "Well, I suppose we ought to be glad that they have not hanged us. I really believe that there are some people who would have liked to have hanged us because we defended him. I do not think he is guilty, though I confess this morning I thought he would be convicted. The jury surprised me. I thought they would be out longer than they were. Well, one side had to lose. We made a good fight and did the best we could."[13]

Theo Durrant was sentenced to death. After appeals to the California Supreme Court and the U.S. Supreme Court failed, he was hanged on the gallows at San Quentin in 1898. Durrant was so loathed that no funeral parlor in San Francisco would accept the body, and it had to be shipped to Los Angeles for cremation.

Durrant's last words were, "I am innocent." However, in later years police officers told of damning evidence against him that was not admissible in his trial. Durant had made "disgraceful propositions" to other young girls and had been a regular patron of brothels on the Barbary Coast. Otto Heyneman, clerk to Isaiah Lees, wrote that prostitutes had submitted photographs taken of Durrant "in all sorts of disgusting poses." In 1910 police Captain Thomas S. Duke reported that he had "a photograph of Durrant at a picnic when he was only sixteen years of age, and the position in which he posed proves conclusively that he was a degenerate even as a child."[14]

Although Harry Morse's faith in the innocence of Theo Durrant was certainly misplaced, his willingness to defend the reviled killer, and without recompense, demonstrated both moral courage and devotion to justice. With nothing to gain and much to lose, Morse's role in the Crime of the Century was one of the high points of his career.

CHAPTER 19

Rival Detectives

HARRY Morse and Isaiah Lees had much in common. They shared the same career, the same political party, and the same background. Each was a forty-niner; their old homes on the East Coast had been but twenty miles apart. They both had mined briefly as young men and had worked as sailors and laborers before becoming lawmen. Both were members of the Masonic fraternity. It is ironic that they never developed a close friendship. In many ways, San Francisco was not big enough for two master detectives with large egos and competing interests. Thus Harry Morse and Isaiah Lees frequently clashed.

Morse's son-in-law, Mathew de la Montanya, was chief deputy city treasurer in San Francisco in 1898. De la Montanya's close friend and boss was the city treasurer, Augustus C. Widber. Late in March 1898 de la Montanya became suspicious that his treasurer friend and boss was embezzling city funds. He contacted Morse, who sent Detective Jerome Deasy to investigate. Deasy and de la Montanya confronted Widber, who admitted stealing $76,000 but promised to return all the money by the next day. Instead, Widber skipped town and headed for his ranch in Contra Costa County. De la Montanya immediately notified his father-in-law, who sent Jules Callundan in pursuit. Callundan and Constable Palmer of Walnut Creek arrested Widber at his ranch and started back to the San Francisco ferry.

In the meantime Isaiah Lees, now chief of police, had learned belatedly of the theft and sent two of his detectives to Walnut Creek to find Widber. But Callundan already had the treasurer in custody, and together they returned to the city. At the ferry Lees met them and took custody of the defaulter from Callundan. The San Francisco *Call*, never missing a chance to stir up the rivalry between Morse and Lees, headlined its story of the arrest, "Lees Grabs Some More Greatness." The *Call* made much of the fact that Morse had bested Lees and reported, "When the desk sergeant asked for the names of

Isaiah W. Lees of the San
Francisco Police. The
rivalry between Lees and
Morse lasted more than
twenty years. Courtesy
William B. Secrest.

the arresting officers the Nero of the Police Department promptly
replied, 'Chief Lees and Detective Wren.'" Wren, declared the *Call*
acridly, "shared with the Chief the glory of a capture with which
they had nothing whatever to do. But of such is the record of the
Chief as a thief taker."[1]

Such criticism of Isaiah Lees were hardly fair, but it helped sell
newspapers. A year later Lees was busy searching for an Australian
confidence man named Howard who had swindled a Colorado millionaire. A reporter for the *San Francisco Examiner* called on Harry
Morse for his opinion of Lees's efforts. Morse disclaimed any interest in working up the case himself but, with biting sarcasm, commented, "If the Chief should ask me to get Howard for him I would
do so. I think it is the duty of every citizen to assist Chief Lees when
he is grievously in need of assistance. At any time the Chief has a big
case he cannot handle my services are at his disposal."[2]

The rivalry between Morse and Lees was aggravated by a long-
standing tension between Morse's patrolmen and the San Francisco
police "patrol specials." The latter were sworn police officers who
wore the uniform of the regular city police. They were appointed by

the police commission to patrol certain beats but were paid by merchants, not by the city. Morse's men provided major competition to the patrol specials. As early as 1884 Morse accused a patrol special named James Wigmore of neglect of duty and of insulting his men at every opportunity. Wigmore's character was indeed bad; when he shot and killed an innocent citizen, he was arrested for manslaughter. Over the years Morse charged that other special officers assaulted his men in an effort to drive them off their beats. The specials in turn accused Morse's men of misrepresentation. In 1898 a lawyer for the specials charged, "Only recently several of Harry Morse's men canvassed the downtown beats, and by claiming that they had the powers of a special officer, took away a portion of the business belonging to the special on the beat." The patrol specials attempted to secure passage of an ordinance limiting Morse's ability to compete with them. The effort failed, and Morse's patrol continued to prosper.[3]

In 1896 San Franciscans had elected a reform mayor, the wealthy financier James D. Phelan. Among the reforms Phelan intended was a change in the administration of the police department. Since the days of the Vigilance Committee of 1856 the department had been continuously controlled by a small, close-knit cadre of highly professional lawmen, principally Isaiah W. Lees and Chiefs Martin Burke, Henry H. Ellis, and Patrick J. Crowley, the latter police chief for twenty-five years. Under these men the department had garnered a national reputation for efficiency and professionalism. And despite individual examples of crooked officers and cases of police corruption in Chinatown, the San Francisco police remained relatively scandal-free throughout the nineteenth century.

The professional officers in charge of the rank and file, which by the 1890s included numerous policemen with long service records of twenty to forty years, maintained strict control over the department. Local political meddling was kept at a minimum due to an 1878 legislative act that provided that a nonpartisan panel of state district court judges appointed the San Francisco Police Commission. And it was the police commission, not the mayor or the board of supervisors, that appointed the chief of police. Thus local politicians had little control over the police department. From 1856 to 1900 only seven men held the chief's office, ensuring a high degree of stability and a continuity of professionalism.[4]

Mayor Phelan rightly saw a great weakness in the city charter, which vested scant power in the mayor and made him essentially a figurehead. At the same time, Phelan, a Democrat, sought an opportunity to seize control of the police department from its two Republican leaders, Chief Crowley and Captain Lees. He successfully sponsored a bill that took effect in 1900 and that adopted a new charter for San Francisco. It placed central control in the hands of the mayor, who now had authority to appoint the members of all city commissions, including the police commission. The new charter provided for elections that November, and Phelan eagerly sought a second term. But to secure the support of San Francisco's leading Democratic newspaper, the *Examiner,* Phelan struck a deal with the devil.

William Randolph Hearst's *Examiner* had built up the city's largest circulation through heavy doses of cheap sensationalism, or, as it came to be known, yellow journalism. By 1895 Hearst had moved to New York and left the paper in charge of his editor, Andrew M. Lawrence. Harry Morse knew Andy Lawrence well and, like many San Franciscans, considered him a thorough scoundrel. Morse and Lawrence became embroiled in a struggle for control of the San Francisco Police Department. Morse's uncharacteristic decision to align himself with a man like Andy Lawrence would prove a serious error in judgement.

Generally known as "Long Green" because of his ability to turn a shady dollar, Andy Lawrence was ruthless, unscrupulous, and well connected to the highly influential Hearst family. Lawrence began his career as a reporter for the *Examiner* in 1884, when he was twenty-three. In 1886 he was handpicked by U.S. Senator George Hearst (father of William Randolph Hearst) as a candidate for the state assembly and served one term. In 1891 Lawrence was publicly accused on the assembly floor of attempting to extort $10,000 from a widow who had asked his help in passing a bill. Despite later accusations of blackmail while he was an *Examiner* reporter, in 1895 Lawrence was made the paper's managing editor. By 1896 Long Green had made so many enemies that he found it prudent to retain as a bodyguard the noted gunfighter Wyatt Earp, who was then living in San Francisco.[5]

Today, in popular myth, Wyatt Earp is known as one of the greatest lawmen of the Old West, but in fact he was primarily an itinerant frontier gambler. His entire law enforcement career in Kansas and Arizona spanned only a few years. He was capable of great bravery, but most of his gunfighting was the result of personal quarrels rather than legitimate law enforcement. Wyatt Earp is now famous for his part in the street gunfight near the O.K. Corral in Tombstone, Arizona Territory, in 1881. But when Earp moved to San Francisco in 1892 he was generally unknown to respectable citizens. He ran a string of horses at the local racetracks and was popular and very well known among the saloon and sporting crowd.[6]

Harry Morse also knew Earp, but only one of their meetings is recorded. From time to time Morse was hired by landlords to eject gamblers from their property, and on one occasion, in 1896, he apparently ran off several of Earp's associates. Earp accosted Morse on a San Francisco street and upbraided the detective for harassing his gambler friends. Morse simply advised Earp to tend to his own business, and the gunfighter wisely let the matter drop.[7]

Wyatt Earp reached a pinnacle of notoriety in San Francisco on December 2, 1896, when Andy Lawrence managed to have him appointed referee of the heavyweight boxing championship match between Bob Fitzsimmons and Tom Sharkey. In one of the most controversial decisions of American prizefighting, Earp called a foul on Fitzsimmons and awarded the title and $10,000 prize to Sharkey. Earp and Lawrence were accused of conspiring to throw the fight, and the weight of evidence suggests that Earp, at least, did so.[8]

In 1899 Andy Lawrence and Mayor Phelan struck a simple deal: Lawrence promised to throw his paper's support behind Phelan, and the mayor, once reelected, would fire Chief Lees and allow Long Green to handpick a new police commission, chief of police, and chief of detectives. With the police department under Lawrence's control, the *Examiner* would be able to scoop every paper in the city and effectively control access to much of San Francisco's news. For in those years little of note, whether social, political, or commercial, took place in the city that escaped the watchful eyes and ears of its police.

The city charter was to take effect January 8, 1900. Three days before this police Detective Ed Byram made the following entry in his daily journal:

Heard that Jules Callundan, Superintendent of Harry Morse's Patrol System, had been appointed on the Force as a Patrolman. A fine job is put up by Andy Lawrence and the *Examiner* to make Esola Chief of Police [and] Callundan Captain of Detectives. Throw out all of the old detectives. Then Harry Morse would control the Force, and what a squeezing the town

would get from the *Examiner* gang. . . . Later Callundan came
into the Bank of California and I had a talk with him. He gave
me a yarn about better pay and a chance of promotion with the
other men. He told it nice.[9]

Fred Esola was a young police lieutenant and a protégé of Lawrence.
Although he was a likeable man, he was poorly educated and as a
youth had hobnobbed with several juvenile thieves. Esola had worked
on Lawrence's assembly campaign in 1886 and served as Long
Green's bodyguard. As a reward for his loyalty Lawrence got him
hired as a guard at San Quentin. When Esola was forced to resign for
insubordination, Lawrence had him appointed to the San Francisco
Police Department in 1892. Due to his political connections, Esola
rose rapidly through the ranks, making lieutenant in the record time
of three years.

Fred Esola was so far removed in terms of character and experience from the men who had served as police chief during the previous forty years that news of his candidacy stunned John D. Spreckels,
wealthy owner of the *Call*. He began an investigation and on January 13 broke the story in the *Call* with a headline that proclaimed:
"Conspiracy to Betray the City to Criminals." Spreckels charged
that the new police commissioners had been appointed on the condition that they name Esola as chief of police and Jules Callundan as
chief of detectives. The police department would then be used as "an
engine of blackmail," and gambling and prostitution would be allowed to flourish. Reportedly, the first step had been the appointment of Callundan as a lowly patrolman, preparatory to elevating him
to chief of detectives. The *Call* referred to Morse's assistant as "Jules
J. Callundan, alias Worthington" and charged that he was "a thief,
defaulter, and fugitive from justice of the employer he had robbed."
Declared the *Call* in an accompanying editorial, "If Callundan be appointed chief of detectives San Francisco will be wide open to all the
avenues that lead to corruption, degradation, vice, villainy, prostitution and crime."[10]

Harry Morse rushed to Callundan's defense, telling an *Examiner*
reporter, "There is absolutely not a word of truth in these charges.
Mr. Callundan began working for me when he was a boy, eighteen
years ago, and he has been with me ever since. I can go away and
leave my affairs in his hands with perfect trust. I know him to be
honest, because I have proved him."[11]

Harry Morse, left, and Jules Callundan in Morse's San Francisco office, December 1, 1898. Author's collection.

However, Spreckels was a man of integrity, as well as wealth and influence, and his charges soon caught the attention of Fremont Older, muckraking publisher of the *Bulletin,* and Michael H. DeYoung, owner of the *Chronicle.* Now they jumped on the *Call*'s bandwagon, and all three newspapers aligned themselves against the *Examiner,* Esola, and Callundan. The *Chronicle* repeated the charge that "Mayor Phelan, previous to the election, bargained in consideration of certain newspaper support . . . to turn over the Police Department of this city to the paper promising its support. There is no doubt that such an act is a felony." The paper's editorial writer called it "a scandal more serious than any which has for many years come to light.[12]

The charges against Jules Callundan were quickly forgotten as the *Call, Bulletin,* and *Chronicle* turned their attention to Fred Esola. For two weeks they raked him over the coals, devoting pages to his less than sterling background and his close connection to Long Green Lawrence. Fremont Older brought formal charges against Esola before the police commission, forcing an open hearing on the issue of his fitness to hold public office. The police commission's hearing, which lasted three days, proved a sensation. Evidence was produced that Esola had been mixed up in a burglary as a boy, that he had once used the name "Harrington" as an alias, and that while he was supposed to have been on duty as a police officer he had made a number of extended trips to the East as a guest of Andy Lawrence. Isaiah Lees, never one to miss a chance to butt heads with Harry Morse, came in and testified that Esola had neglected his duty, was generally incompetent, and had been promoted and retained in the department solely through the influence of Andy Lawrence. Evidence of Long Green's influence was also made clear. First, it was proved that on January 7 Lawrence had brought Lieutenant Esola into the mayor's office in city hall to meet Mayor Phelan and the members of the police commission; Lawrence wanted the commissioners to meet the new candidate for police chief. But when Lieutenant Esola took the stand on his own behalf, he stumbled badly. In his eagerness to conceal the fact that Lawrence was behind his candidacy, Esola told the flabbergasted commissioners that he could not recall his meeting with them and Mayor Phelan just two weeks before.[13]

Harry Morse worked energetically to counter the evidence against Esola. Reported the *Bulletin,* "In the corridor private detective Harry Morse marshalled Esola's witnesses and displayed an unholy activity, part of the price which is to buy the preferment of Jules Callundan." When a key witness against Esola, Al Meador, disappeared, the *Bulletin* pointed the finger at the detectives: "No time had been lost by Morse and Callundan in making away with persons who knew anything detrimental to Esola." Called to the stand, Morse testified that he had been asked by Andy Lawrence to interview Al Meador and ascertain the truth of a statement Meador had given. Morse stated that he did not know where Meador was and flatly denied spiriting the witness away.[14]

In the end the police commissioners rejected the charges against Esola. However, the tremendous negative newspaper publicity had completely derailed Long Green's effort to have Esola and Callundan appointed. The drama came to an end on February 14, when Esola withdrew his name and the commission selected Mayor Phelan's secretary, William P. Sullivan, to serve as chief of police. Isaiah Lees was retired on pension. Jules Callundan, who had been granted a leave of absence "to settle his affairs with Morse," was ordered to be measured for his uniform and to report for patrol duty. He promptly handed in his patrolman's star. "Callundan had no appetite for patrol duty for even a fortnight," snorted the *Bulletin*. At the same time an angry Phelan removed one commissioner, William J. Biggy, who had refused to vote for Esola. Biggy quickly confirmed to Spreckels and Older that their charges had been true: Phelan had allowed Lawrence to appoint all four members of the commission and Long Green had personally selected Esola as chief.[15]

Nonetheless, the *Call*'s charges that Lawrence, Esola, and Callundan intended to turn San Francisco over to criminals were a gross exaggeration. Long Green's motives were much less Machiavellian than portrayed by the *Call:* he merely wanted to win San Francisco's bitter newspaper circulation war by controlling the police department, which in turn would have allowed him to control access to the news.

Neither Fred Esola nor Jules Callundan was the evildoer the *Call* had painted. Both were merely ambitious young men; Callundan was competent, and Esola was not. Harry Morse, however, should have known better than to have gotten himself mixed up with Andy Lawrence. Clearly he recognized the great advantage in having Callundan appointed chief of detectives. Morse faced substantial competition from the increasing number of private detectives in San Francisco, and the Pinkertons, having opened a San Francisco office in 1896, were now competing directly with him. With Callundan in charge of the police detective bureau, Morse would have had ready access to all the influence, business contacts, and investigative information of the entire police department. The competitive advantage would have been of incalculable benefit to him. Last but not least, it would have been a final victory over Isaiah Lees. Instead Morse ended up with a raft of negative newspaper reports. His involvement in this disreputable affair was a serious blunder, and the bad press he garnered tarnished his hard-won reputation for honesty and fairness.[16]

With Isaiah Lees gone from the police department, Morse no doubt believed that their long rivalry was over. Yet in 1901 Lees came back from retirement for one more bout with his old opponent. For several years Morse's patrol had guarded the bullion shipments of the Selby Smelting Company, which operated the largest gold refinery on the West Coast. Raw gold—dust, nuggets, and bars—was shipped to the company's San Francisco office where it was assayed and melted. The metal, in rough bars, was then shipped across the bay to the company's smelting works located midway between Rodeo and

Harry Morse in 1901.
Author's collection.

Crockett on the Contra Costa shore. There it was smelted into fine gold for jewelry and the minting of coins.

On August 5, 1901, a large shipment of gold bars, worth $400,000, was brought from San Francisco and unloaded at the smelter's wharf. From there it was carried a short distance by wagon to the smelting works and locked in a large, iron walk-in safe. Fifty men worked around the clock in the smelter in full view of the vault. At five o'clock the next morning the night watchman opened the safe to remove several bars. Instead of gold piled up like cordwood, he saw a gaping hole in the vault's iron floor, red pepper sprinkled around the hole, and most of the gold bars gone. "My God!" he yelled. "The safe has been robbed!"

A workman dropped down into the hole and found that a short tunnel had been dug under the building. A trapdoor from the tunnel opened near the outside wall, and a trail of red pepper led through an adjacent railroad tunnel to the shore of the bay. There a pile of gunny sacks had been left by the water; inside were two gold bars worth $16,000. Thirty-seven bars of gold, some weighing as much as eighty-five pounds, with a total value of $283,000, were missing.[17]

News of the burglary created a newspaper sensation in both the United States and Europe. "It is the largest theft of gold bullion known in this country," reported the *San Francisco Chronicle*. The company president, A. J. Ralston, offered a $25,000 reward for information leading to the arrest of the perpetrators and recovery of the gold bullion. This extremely large reward caused a horde of detectives to converge on the crime scene.[18]

Harry Morse, with two of his men, and Richard R. Veale, sheriff of Contra Costa County, were the first on the scene, arriving several hours after the theft was discovered. Morse quickly focused his investigation on John Winters, a former Selby employee who had a cabin on the hill above the smelter. Said Morse later, "Within thirty minutes after I landed I learned that John Winters had been acting in a very suspicious manner and had been seen four times in the vicinity of the works, dodging about and trying to escape observation. I learned that he lived alone in a cabin on the hill and I concluded that he must know something about the robbery."[19]

Morse and Sheriff Veale forced an entrance into Winters's cabin. Morse found an electric light and battery, splattered with mud that matched the mud in the tunnel. He also discovered a revolver with the same type of mud caked on the cylinder, an iron shovel, and cloth and nails of the same type used in making the trapdoor of the tunnel. Morse and the sheriff marked the electric battery with their initials. Veale then stored all the evidence in the Selby vault. Morse also noticed several letters written to Winters, but with uncharacteristic carelessness, he did not bother to read them.

Morse left his two operatives to watch the cabin for Winters's return, then returned to San Francisco on a tip that the suspect was there. The next morning he reported to A. J. Ralston that John Winters had been involved in the burglary. By this time Isaiah Lees and W. B. Sayers of the Pinkerton National Detective Agency had arrived at the Selby smelting works. Lees claimed to have been hired by the Selby company and not by the Pinkertons. His actions in the case illustrated the tangled relations between the Pinkertons and the San Francisco police. Lees brought with him several San Francisco police detectives, who, in time-honored fashion, were allowed to do private investigations while on duty.

Sheriff Veale innocently turned over to Lees all the evidence he and

Morse had found. Lees and his men searched Winters's cabin, read the letters Morse had unwisely ignored, and found that one had been written by a girl in San Rafael. At her home the detectives located John Winters and arrested him. Instead of turning their prisoner over to Sheriff Veale, in whose county the crime had occurred, Lees brought him to San Francisco and placed him in the custody of his friend John Seymour, captain of detectives. Lees also turned over to Seymour all the items of evidence. A huge reward was at stake, and the old thief catcher was not about to let Veale and Morse have the first crack at "sweating" Winters into revealing the location of the missing gold.

Sheriff Veale was puzzled when he learned that Isaiah Lees had taken Winters to San Francisco. He crossed the bay and visited police headquarters, only to find that Winters was gone. He had confessed, and Lees, Seymour, and the other detectives had just left by tugboat for the smelting works. Winters told them how he had spent two months digging the tunnel alone at night and how he had drilled through the vault floor. He pointed out where he had made fourteen trips from the tunnel to a nearby wharf with the bars in gunny sacks. He had sprinkled red pepper to confuse bloodhounds and had dropped the gold bars into six feet of water. Divers recovered all of the stolen bullion.[20]

Harry Morse was furious that Lees and the San Francisco detectives had taken over the case and that Sheriff Veale had turned the evidence over to them. Morse told newspapermen that he was the first to report to Ralston that Winters was the thief: "Up to that time I did not know that any other detectives were employed in the case. They got ahold of the man before we did and that is all there is to the case. We did the preliminary work and Lees got in and shut us out. I had all the evidence before anyone else was in the case." Further, Morse disclaimed any interest in the big reward: "I am not making any claim for the reward. I do not know that I shall try to get any part of it. I am not going to make any fuss over the reward, that's a moral certainty."

Isaiah Lees quickly responded, telling a reporter, "I never saw Detective Morse in all the course of the investigation. I don't know who got the articles that were found in Winters's cabin. Why do you want to stir these things up and make trouble? We had fixed on Winters and secured the articles in his cabin before Morse knew anything about him."[21]

Lees, however, was wrong. A reporter who examined the evidence at the San Francisco police headquarters noted that the electric battery plainly bore the marks "H.N.M." and "R.R.V." Harry Morse was so angered by Lees's comments that he forgot all about his promise not to claim the reward. The next day, August 12, he submitted a lengthy letter to the Selby Smelting Company, describing his investigation and claiming the entire reward on behalf of himself, Sheriff Veale, and Peter Donaldson, a smelter worker who had told him about Winters's suspicious actions. Said Morse to a newspaperman, "The plain truth is that while we are entitled to the credit of discovering the criminal, Lees is trying to gobble the whole thing. He wants all the credit and all the reward. Veale was too easy when he surrendered that evidence."[22]

A response came quickly from an infuriated Lees: "The statement is false. I do not desire the reward, and am not an applicant for it, and when Morse said that he lied, and you can quote my word if you want to do so." Lees, however, refused to state that he did not expect to receive part of the reward; he only said that he had not put in a claim for it. He added, "I never saw Morse in this case and never had anything to do with him. If he has evidence that will convict that man Winters, let him produce it and go on with the trial. Why doesn't he do something, instead of talking about it?"[23]

The reward squabble was settled a month later when A. J. Ralston announced that the $25,000 would be split among Morse, Lees, Donaldson, the San Francisco police detectives, and Sheriff Veale and his deputy. Only the Pinkertons, who had a strict policy of not accepting rewards, refused to accept any of the money. Harry Morse had once again demonstrated his willingness to ignore his own "no rewards" policy if there was enough money at stake.[24]

From his jail cell John Winters basked in his newfound notoriety. Reporters, impressed with his bravado and the ingenuity of his crime, flocked to see him. He regaled them with claims that he was to receive $50,000 from the Selby company for showing where he had hidden the gold. But Ralston denied that such a deal had been made. Winters pled guilty and served only seven years in prison, which suggests that he received leniency in return for his cooperation.[25]

On December 21, 1902, Isaiah Lees died in San Francisco at the age of seventy-two. Never again would Harry Morse face competition from such an able foe.

CHAPTER 20

The Mysterious Death of
Mrs. Leland Stanford

IN January 1901 delegates to the Republican municipal convention in Oakland nominated Harry Morse as their candidate for mayor, calling him "a man of courage, character, integrity and executive ability and of unswerving devotion to public duty." Flattered by the offer and eager to clean up an inept city administration, Morse impulsively accepted. He received immediate support, one newspaper editorializing that "the delegates could not have elected a better or a stronger man." Morse soon realized, however, that he lacked the time to run both his detective business and the city government. He withdrew his name from nomination.[1]

The old lawman still harbored political ambitions. Late that year he sought appointment as the U.S. marshal for the Northern District of California. Morse's bid was backed by numerous influential supporters. His petitions for the appointment included the signatures of five justices of the California Supreme Court and all the superior court judges of Alameda County. President Theodore Roosevelt instead named John Shine, a former stage line owner, to the post.[2]

Now approaching seventy, Morse suffered from occasional bouts with sciatica and rheumatism but otherwise remained robust. Virginia's health, however, was starting to fail, and Harry spent more time with her and his grandchildren, most of whom were now grown. He was ecstatic in 1904 when his granddaughter, Ethel de la Montanya Newell, had a baby girl, Aileen. He was now a great-grandfather. Writing to a friend, Morse crowed, "I tell you Joe, it's a great baby and there is no rubbing it out. In fact I don't suppose there ever was or will be such another baby. You know how that is?"[3]

Morse's son, George, was still estranged from his parents. In the spring of 1904 he drifted into Yuba County and got work on a fruit ranch near Marysville. Still erratic and ill-tempered, he habitually carried a .38 Smith & Wesson. He told the ranch owner that his name was George Mosse but admitted that was not his true name. In

298

July a fourteen-year-old boy from Alameda, Claude Hankins, was sent by his family to the ranch to work. Hankins was a thief and a troublemaker, and his family believed that hard work on an isolated ranch would be good for him. However, he and George Morse immediately clashed. Morse verbally abused the boy, who in turn was unruly and refused to work. When Hankins let the workhorses run off, Morse tried to horsewhip him and threatened to "cut his head off." On the evening of July 19, after milking the cows, George walked back to the ranch house. As he passed Hankins the youth drew Morse's pistol, which he had taken from the house, and fired. The bullet struck Morse in the back of the head, killing him.

Young Hankins was quickly arrested and confessed to the crime. He admitted taking $60 from the body to pay his way back to Alameda. As the victim had no known family, he was buried in a pauper's grave in Marysville. The San Francisco and Oakland newspapers gave prominent coverage to the boyish killer and his crime. They mentioned that the dead man, George Mosse, possessed letters written to him by Ella Viers of Oakland. Harry Morse read the newspaper accounts and the sickening reality jolted him to his core: "George Mosse" was his own son.[4]

Virginia was overcome with grief. Her failing health suffered a blow from which she did not recover. Harry paid for the body to be exhumed and shipped to Oakland. After a private service in the family home, the Morses' son was laid to rest in the family plot. Claude Hankins was convicted of second-degree murder and, despite his youth, was sentenced to fourteen years in San Quentin.[5]

The hopes and dreams that Harry Morse had once harbored for his son had long since been dashed. He had tried years before to bury any feelings he once held for his wayward son. Now he was seized with anguish, deepened by the recognition that at least some of George's problems had been caused by his own failures as a parent. His son had acquired all the attributes that Morse found most undesirable in a man. Unstable, violent, and a bully, George Morse had become the very antithesis of his father. It was the saddest irony of Harry Morse's life.

While Virginia was confined to her sickbed, Harry buried his grief by immersing himself in the fight against political corruption. At that time San Francisco was controlled by the corrupt political boss Abe Ruef and graft was unchecked. Corruption, while not so blatant in Alameda County, had become a persistent problem. The

Republican machine, backed by the Southern Pacific, continued to control county politics, and it fleeced the taxpayers through exorbitant purchases of county supplies at inflated rates and by unnecessary civic "improvements." The excess funds were "raked off" and distributed to ring members and their cronies. Morse, outraged at the political and moral decay, took up the banner of the "good government" movement, which aimed to wipe out corruption. He was nominated as both Democratic and Independent candidate for the county board of supervisors. Although the Democratic party was anathema to Morse, he hated corruption even more. He accepted the party's nomination. Morse's opponent was H. D. Rowe, the incumbent member of the Republican ring. Morse ran a strong campaign and published detailed flyers that carefully described the methods by which the ring fleeced the county's taxpayers. Although a political reform movement was brewing in California, it would not take a strong hold of the populace for several years. Most citizens still blindly cast their votes for their party's candidate regardless of the evidence of corruption. In the election on November 8, 1904, Morse was soundly defeated, polling 1,857 votes to Rowe's 3,975.[6]

Despite his opposition to the Southern Pacific's political power, Morse had maintained business relations with the railroad giant. He had once lobbied the Southern Pacific to take over its detective and policing operations. Although he had been unsuccessful, he was nonetheless held in high regard by railroad attorneys and by the family of Leland Stanford, one of the founders of the Southern Pacific. Thus in 1905 Morse was called on to investigate the mysterious death of Mrs. Leland Stanford. The aging detective played a major role in investigating her supposed murder. It was Morse's last big case and proved to be one of the most controversial of his long career.[7]

Jane Lathrop Stanford was one of the wealthiest and most prominent women in the nation. A great philanthropist, she was the widow of Leland Stanford. As one of the "Big Four," Stanford, with Charles Crocker, Mark Hopkins, and Collis P. Huntington, built the Central Pacific and Southern Pacific railroads. He served as governor of California and later as U.S. senator. In 1887 Leland Stanford and his wife founded Stanford University near Palo Alto. After her husband's death in 1893, Jane Stanford took an active role in the university's growth and in 1901 donated much of her vast estate, some $28 million, to the university.[8]

On January 14, 1905, Mrs. Stanford, while preparing to retire for the night at her Nob Hill home in San Francisco, took a drink from a bottle of Poland Springs mineral water. It tasted very bitter, and she summoned her maid, Elizabeth Richmond, who gave her several glasses of salt water to induce vomiting. A suspicious Jane Stanford had the mineral water sent out for chemical analysis. A week later, the chemist advised that the water contained a fatal dose of strychnine. Mrs. Stanford, greatly upset, reported this to Dr. David Starr Jordan, president of Stanford University, and her attorney, Mountford Wilson. They immediately retained Harry Morse to investigate.

Morse assigned Jules Callundan and several of his best operatives to work on the case. They carefully questioned all the household servants at the Nob Hill mansion. Then they checked every pharmacy from San Francisco to San Jose and determined that none of the servants had recently purchased strychnine. However, they neglected to have any of the other medicines in the Stanford home analyzed or destroyed. Morse and Callundan soon focused on the maid, Elizabeth Richmond, as the most likely suspect. David Starr Jordan recalled years later:

> Mr. Callundan found that a maid temporarily employed by Mrs. Stanford, an Englishwoman forty-five to fifty years of age, named Richmond, was subject to periodic attacks of mania, that the chief subjects of her conversation with her associates turned on her experiences in the houses of the English aristocracy, with numerous anecdotes of those members of high society who had died from poisoning.
>
> I reached the conclusion that no one else could be under suspicion for the affair in San Francisco. Meeting Callundan at Placerville some time after he told me that this phase of the mystery was fully solved. The poison was put into the Poland Water in an insane freak. Meanwhile, as nothing could be absolutely proved, nothing was done in her case.[9]

On January 27 Elizabeth Richmond was forced to resign her position. Morse's detectives piped the maid for several weeks thereafter but could obtain no further evidence against her. Mrs. Stanford was shocked that someone would try to kill her. Fearing for her safety, she fled the Nob Hill mansion to her estate in Palo Alto. Her doctor and her attorney suggested that she take an ocean voyage to Hawaii for her health as well as her personal safety. On February 15 she left San Francisco by steamer, accompanied by Bertha Berner, her trusted secretary for twenty years, and her maid, May Hunt. They arrived in Honolulu on February 21.

Morse tried to keep the poisoning incident secret, but word of his investigation soon spread. On February 19 the *San Francisco Chronicle* broke the story. The details of the *Chronicle's* report were correct, except it erroneously identified the private detectives as Pinkertons. Mountford Wilson, when questioned by reporters, refused to comment. David Starr Jordan, however, denied that there had been any attempt at poisoning. Said Jordan, "Mrs. Stanford's present trip to Honolulu was taken for the purpose of recuperating from a severe cold and attack of tonsilitis."[10]

Morse and Callundan also denied the poisoning reports. They told the *Call* that "the matter was closed as far as they were concerned and that the report that they suspected anyone of an attempt to injure Mrs. Stanford or had been shadowing anyone in connection with the matter was absolutely false." Callundan declared, "From all the facts that I have in hand from over two weeks' investigation of the case, I would stake my good right eye against a dollar that no attempt was made to poison Mrs. Stanford. I do not believe that there was any intention to poison anyone."[11]

By this time the detectives, attorney Wilson, and Dr. Jordan were in possession of a written report from the chemist, Louis Falkenau, dated January 31, 1905, which showed that the Poland water contained a fatal dose of strychnine. The false public statements of Morse, Callundan, and Jordan were made in an effort to hush up the affair and thus avoid any scandal or embarrassment to Mrs. Stanford.[12]

Jane Stanford and her two servants took lodging at the Moana Hotel at Waikiki. On February 28 they took a sightseeing trip by buggy. Mrs. Stanford ate a very large picnic lunch and then returned to the hotel. That night she complained of an upset stomach, and before retiring to bed she took a cascara capsule (a laxative) and a glass of water mixed with a spoonful of bicarbonate of soda. The bicarbonate of soda came from an open bottle that had been brought from the medicine cabinet in her San Francisco mansion.[13]

Soon after, at eleven o'clock, Bertha Berner was awakened by cries from Mrs. Stanford's room. "Bertha, May. I am so sick." The two servants rushed out and found Mrs. Stanford clinging to the bedroom doorway. "Bertha, run for the doctor!" she ordered. Miss

Jane Stanford posed for this snapshot in front of a friend's San Francisco home the day before she embarked on her ill-fated trip to Honolulu. Author's collection.

Berner sent the elevator boy after Dr. F. H. Humphris, the hotel physician, then assisted Mrs. Stanford to a chair in her room. "I have no control of my body," she gasped. "I think I am poisoned again."

Miss Berner tried to get her to drink a glass of warm water, but she said, "I can't drink it. My jaws are set."

The secretary massaged her jaws until she could open them, then gave her six glasses of warm water to induce vomiting. Dr. Humphris quickly arrived, and Mrs. Stanford told him, "Doctor, I think I have been poisoned."

She was in great agony and was convulsing. Between convulsions she gasped, "This is the second time they have tried it. They tried it last January and I came here to avoid them."[14]

The doctor gave her an injection to relieve the spasms. Another physician, Harvey Murray, rushed into the room, but a few seconds later a final, heaving convulsion wracked Jane Stanford's body. "Oh God, forgive me my sins!" she cried. "This is a horrible death to die!"

Then she collapsed in the chair, dead. An autopsy showed traces of strychnine in her intestines but not in her stomach. An inquest into her death was held March 6 through 8 at the Moana Hotel. Bertha Berner and May Hunt testified in detail about the earlier poisoning attempt. Four doctors testified that Mrs. Stanford's symptoms as well as the postmortem condition of her body—clenched hands, stiff jaw, turned-in toes, and absence of blood clotting— were consistent with death by strychnine poisoning. Two chemists testified that the bottle of bicarbonate of soda contained a small quantity, one-half grain, of strychnine. The cascara capsule was found to contain a small medicinal amount of the poison. In that era tiny amounts of strychnine were commonly used in some laxatives and heart medicines.

One of the chemists, Dr. Edmund Shorey, testified that strychnine was a usual ingredient in cascara capsules; although a cascara capsule did not hold a fatal dose of strychnine, it contained enough to produce the positive test result of Mrs. Stanford's organs. The four medical doctors testified that it was not unusual that no poison was found in the stomach. A small amount of strychnine was fatal, and since the human body is two-thirds liquid, the poison would disperse very quickly throughout the body. The tiny amount of strychnine contained in the bicarbonate of soda Mrs. Stanford consumed, coupled with the strychnine in the cascara tablet, was enough to kill an elderly woman. The coroner's jury ruled that Jane Stanford had died "from strychnine poisoning, said strychnine having been introduced into a bottle of bicarbonate of soda with felonious intent by a person or persons to this jury unknown."[15]

News of Mrs. Stanford's death created a sensation on the mainland. For three weeks San Francisco newspapers blanketed their front pages with the story. Harry Morse was stunned by the news. No longer bothering to deny the first poisoning incident, he told a reporter, "We have redoubled our efforts since the news of her death, and last night I hardly slept at all, I got to thinking so much about it." He added, "There evidently is some connection between Mrs. Stanford's illness here and her death in Honolulu. If her death there was caused by poison it was put in here and we must find out where it came from."[16]

Morse and Joseph Burnett, captain of detectives of the San Francisco police, assumed control of an intensive investigation. Newspapers engaged in a frenzy of speculation that one or another of the nine servants in the Nob Hill mansion was guilty of murder. Morse, Callundan, Burnett, and several police detectives reinterviewed all the Stanford servants but focused on Elizabeth Richmond, who was repeatedly grilled at police headquarters. She steadfastly denied any complicity.

David Starr Jordan and Timothy Hopkins, a trustee of Stanford University, left for Honolulu on March 4, ostensibly to bring Mrs. Stanford's body home. They were accompanied by Jules Callundan and a veteran police detective, Harry Reynolds. Neither Jordan nor Hopkins could bring himself to believe that Jane Stanford had been murdered. Their public comments foreshadowed a bitter public controversy. Before leaving, Dr. Jordan said to a reporter, "What a horrible thought it is that such a great, good woman should meet her death by rat poison." Hopkins added, "It is hard to bring oneself to think that Mrs. Stanford was murdered, but in the light of recent developments such must be the accepted fact."[17]

During the voyage, Jordan seems to have become increasingly aware of the devastating effect the murder of Mrs. Stanford would have on the struggling university. He had labored tirelessly to make Stanford University one of the most prestigious in the nation. Now it seemed that the Stanford name, and the university along with it, was becoming embroiled in a scandal of epic proportions, one that would forever attach murder, mystery, and intrigue to it and jeopardize the success of the university. Acutely conscious of the rigid social propriety and fear of scandal so pervasive in that era, Dr. Jordan was determined to learn whether there might be a less infamous explanation for Jane Stanford's death.

They arrived in Honolulu on March 10, two days after the inquest was completed. A correspondent for the San Francisco *Call* boarded their steamer in the harbor for an interview. Instead of expressing a desire that the mystery be solved or that the culprit who contaminated Mrs. Stanford's tonics be identified, Jordan and Hopkins continued to express disbelief that their patroness had been murdered. Said Hopkins, "Both Dr. Jordan and myself have been earnestly hoping during the voyage that by the time we should arrive at Honolulu the news would have been cabled to the world that poisoning was not the cause of Mrs. Stanford's death. Now that the coroner's jury has decided that her death resulted from strychnine administered with purpose of murder our hopes are blasted."[18]

Callundan and Reynolds set out to interview all the witnesses in Honolulu, as well as the doctors who had testified at the inquest. Jordan hired E. C. Waterhouse, a Honolulu physician, to conduct a separate inquiry. Callundan soon concluded that Mrs. Stanford had died of natural causes. On March 15 Jordan and Hopkins released the findings of his investigation. They announced, "Mrs. Stanford's death was not due to strychnine poisoning nor to intentional wrongdoing on the part of any one." They asserted that "there was no evidence that any of the characteristic symptoms of strychnine poisoning were present" and that her death was caused by "her advanced age, the unaccustomed exertion, a surfeit of unsuitable food, and the unusual exposure on the picnic party of the day in question. These conditions were perhaps somewhat aggravated by the presence of strychnine and other drugs in a medicinal capsule, and possibly also by the presence of strychnine contained in a dose of bicarbonate of soda." They speculated that the strychnine was placed in the soda due to "an error of a pharmacist" and that the tampered soda "was prepared for tonic purposes."[19]

Callundan's findings were supported by Dr. Waterhouse, who concluded that Mrs. Stanford had died from myocarditis or angina pectoris—heart disease. However, this was in direct contradiction to the opinion of the Honolulu doctors, four of whom testified that they had attended the autopsy and that there was no evidence of heart disease. They issued a new report endeavoring to refute Jordan's theory, point by point. The San Francisco newspapers blanketed their pages with details of the dispute.[20]

Dr. Jordan's solution to this dilemma was to have Mrs. Stanford's heart examined by several physicians on the staff of Cooper Medical College in San Francisco. These doctors found that the aorta had been ruptured and that death had been caused by "chronic myocarditis—chronic disease of the heart muscles resulting from partial obstruction of the blood vessels of the heart."[21]

Dr. Jordan did not receive the report from Dr. Waterhouse until early April; the Cooper Medical College report was not available until May. Neither was ever publicly released. Apparently the representatives of Mrs. Stanford's estate and the university trustees believed that to release the reports at that late date would only renew the controversy. They simply wanted the whole matter to die out. The one fact that Dr. Jordan could not explain was the presence of strychnine in the bicarbonate of soda in Honolulu. Surprisingly, in a series of private letters, Jordan claimed that there had not been any strychnine in the soda water when Mrs. Stanford drank it. He accused Dr. Humphris and Dr. F. R. Day of adding the poison themselves to "bolster up" their diagnosis of death by poison. Understandably, Jordan never made these libelous charges public, for he had no evidence whatsoever to back them up.[22]

Officially, Jane Stanford's death remains a murder. However, over time, David Starr Jordan's theory became almost universally accepted. Encyclopedias and reference works such as *Who Was Who* all relate that Jane Stanford died of heart failure. Over the years the evidence that supported death by poisoning was all but forgotten. To this day Stanford University publications assert that Jane Stanford died from heart disease.[23]

The circumstances of Jane Stanford's death were exceedingly suspicious. Poison was placed in the Poland Water in San Francisco; poison again appeared in the bicarbonate of soda in Hawaii. These two facts rule out Dr. Jordan's claim that strychnine had been mistakenly added by a pharmacist. It is undisputed that there was poison in the bicarbonate of soda, that Mrs. Stanford consumed the poisoned soda water, and that she died quickly after. By the same token, reputable doctors from the prominent Cooper Medical College found evidence of heart disease that was apparently missed or ignored by the Honolulu doctors.

It seems evident that a member of the Nob Hill household, perhaps Elizabeth Richmond, placed strychnine in the Poland water and the bicarbonate of soda at the same time. After the first incident no one purged Mrs. Stanford's medicine cabinet, and the poisoned soda was foolishly taken to Honolulu. After grilling Elizabeth Richmond repeatedly, Harry Morse allowed her to return to England. No one was ever arrested or charged in the death of Mrs. Stanford.

In the hope that modern medicine might throw light on the mystery, I enlisted the aid of Boyd G. Stephens, M.D., San Francisco's chief medical examiner and coroner and one of the nation's leading forensic pathologists. Dr. Stephens reviewed the autopsy report, coroner's inquest transcript, doctor's reports, and witness statements. Although he found the circumstances of her death "highly suspicious," he reported, "I do not know whether Mrs. Stanford died of strychnine poisoning or other findings. . . . A heart attack could not be ruled out." In defense of the Honolulu doctors, he pointed out, "Since strychnine poisoning was very common in the time period . . . the physicians were very familiar with it; whereas, now strychnine poisoning is quite uncommon in the Americas." Dr. Stephens concluded:

I do not believe that there is sufficient evidence to conclusively prove that the death is due to strychnine poisoning only. Conversely, given the documented circumstances of strychnine being present in the San Francisco analysis and the color test in the Hawaiian analysis, I do not believe that strychnine poisoning can be totally eliminated as being the cause of death. . . . The symptoms that are related during Mrs. Stanford's last day have some features that are not consistent with strychnine poisoning. . . . Many of the symptoms exhibited by Mrs. Stanford could be due to a central nervous system process such as a stroke.[24]

Thus the cause of Jane Stanford's death remains an open question. At the height of the investigation Harry Morse told a newspaper reporter, "This whole business is an amazing mystery to me." With evidence pointing to both poisoning and natural causes, the death of Mrs. Leland Stanford will undoubtedly forever remain an enigma.[25]

CHAPTER 21

End of an Era

JUST before dawn on April 18, 1906, a massive earthquake ripped through northern California. San Francisco bore its brunt. Thousands of homes and buildings were reduced to rubble, and in the three-day inferno that followed, much of the city was destroyed. Three thousand people perished. Although Morse's home in Oakland was untouched, his San Francisco office was consumed in the fire, and with it all of his business records. Morse, like most San Franciscans, was thoroughly shaken, both physically and psychologically. He had neither the energy nor the desire to rebuild. The next day he transferred to Jules Callundan a one-half interest in his detective agency on Callundan's promise to pay him half of the profits. Harry Morse retired from active duty as a private detective.[1]

Virginia's health had been steadily declining, and on May 23, 1907, she died quietly in bed at the Morse home. Morse was despondent after her death, and his daughters and grandchildren did all they could to ease his grief. After months of mourning Morse decided that a trip to Europe would lift his spirits. He invited two of his grandchildren, Harry de la Montanya and Blanche Kenna, and they departed in October. Morse found the trip exciting and thoroughly revitalizing, particularly the ocean voyage from New York to Liverpool. He was flooded with sixty-year-old memories of his boyhood before the mast on that very trade route. The trip lasted more than two months, and the trio visited England, France, and Germany. Despite his age and frequent sciatic pain, Morse walked everywhere. A consummate tourist, he took in everything from the Tower of London to the Royal Art Gallery in Berlin.[2]

On his return home Morse again took up the battle against municipal corruption. As one of Oakland's oldest pioneers, he had a passionate love for his community and a deep concern for its welfare. Having spent most of his adult life fighting crime, it galled him that his beloved city and county were in the hands of crooked politicians.

Four generations of
the Morse family in
1905. Harry Morse
holds his great-grand-
daughter, Aileen
Newell. His grand-
daughter, Ethel
Newell, is seated next
to him. Standing is his
daughter, Emma de la
Montanya. Author's
collection.

After the 1906 earthquake and fire San Franciscans set out to rebuild their city. Their efforts included dismantling the corrupt machine led by political boss Abe Ruef and Mayor Eugene Schmitz,
both of whom were prosecuted for extortion. Ruef was sent to San
Quentin, and political reform became the order of the day.

Even before that, in 1905, Harry Morse had helped organize the
Committee of One Hundred, a group of prominent Alameda
County men opposed to the corrupt, railroad-dominated machine in
Alameda County. Morse became its chairman, and under his direction
the committee brought a number of lawsuits against the board of supervisors and members of the ring. He bombarded Governor George
Pardee with letters, railing against corruption: "Governor, the people of Alameda are being looted from Hades to Halifax. So greedy
are this gang of villainous, hermaphroditic grafters who now infest
our county that they stoop so low as to steal ten cents on a mileage
bill." However, Pardee, a Republican elected with railroad support,
was in no position to assist Morse.[3]

Throughout 1908 Morse repeatedly brought public charges of
malfeasance against city and county politicians. He claimed that cor-

porate interests were controlling the city of Oakland, that streets and water lines were unsafe and not maintained, and that the board of supervisors had misappropriated county road funds. These charges were similar to those that had been proven true in San Francisco. Morse demanded that the district attorney prosecute the latter charge. When that official failed to act, Morse brought a taxpayer's lawsuit against the board of supervisors. The chairman, John Mitchell, a Southern Pacific henchman, was forced to retire when it developed that he had submitted fraudulent mileage bills to the county.[4]

In the end, Harry Morse and his fellow reformers claimed victory. In 1910 progressive Republicans nominated Hiram Johnson for governor. Johnson, who had gained fame as a prosecutor in the San Francisco graft trials, ran on a promise "to kick the Southern Pacific Railroad out of politics." Johnson was elected, as were many progressives in the legislature, and soon the railroad's corrupting influence was a thing of the past.

Morse assumed that long after his death his patrol and detective agency would be run by Jules Callundan. But in March 1911 Callundan suddenly died of complications from diabetes. The old detective was shocked, for Callundan had been only forty-seven. With his characteristic fairness, he moved promptly to provide security for Callundan's wife. Following the funeral Morse wrote out a contract confirming that the widow was now half owner of the agency. The business was then conducted by Callundan's nephew, William Ruwe, and Harry de la Montanya.[5]

In June Morse was delighted that he had lived long enough to attend the fiftieth anniversary celebration of the founding of the Oakland Guard. The former captain, his old friend Jerry Tyrrel, and ten others were the only survivors of the original 125 men who had enlisted during the Civil War. The company had remained in existence until it was absorbed by the California National Guard in 1879.

The years had taken most of the men who had figured so prominently in his life. George Swain had died suddenly of natural causes in 1873, still holding office as deputy sheriff and constable. John H. Adams, defeated for sheriff of Santa Clara County by Nick Harris in 1876, was murdered two years later by Mexican bandits while serving as a deputy U.S. marshal in Arizona. George Beers had died of drink and insanity in 1892. A. B. Lawson had opened a detective agency in Los Angeles and prospered. In 1895 he was shot to death in his office by a fellow detective in a dispute over a train robbery reward. Tom Cunningham retired as sheriff in 1899; the following year he dropped dead of a heart attack. Peter Borein had died in 1901, Nick Harris the following year, and Appleton Stone in 1904. Increasingly Morse was plagued by rheumatism, but his health remained robust. However, in November he suffered a sudden stroke at his home. Bedridden with paralysis, he was cared for by his daughters and a trained nurse. The old lawman put up a tough fight, and at first he rallied. He lingered for two months but then slowly began to fail. On the night of January 11, 1912, Harry Morse died peacefully in bed. Had he lived another forty-two days he would have been seventy-seven years old. Newspapers eulogized him as "one of California's famous pioneers" and "one of the bravest, most daring spirits of the early days."[6]

Morse left an estate that was first estimated at $500,000. But his mining properties had lost much of their value, and the real worth of the estate was closer to $100,000. His will was a model of fairness and loyalty. He made generous provisions for each of his family and left his share of the detective agency to Harry de la Montanya. He gave a half interest in his Oregon mine to the miner who worked the claim for him. To Ella Viers he left $3,000 and a stipend of $50 per month for the rest of her life "on account of the long faithful services and friendship to my family."[7]

The funeral was held the afternoon of January 13 at the Morse home. Relatives, friends, fellow pioneers, police officers, politicians, lawyers, merchants, newspaperman, and uniformed members of the Morse Patrol flocked to the big house near Lake Merritt, in somber recognition that the passing of the old peace officer marked the end of an era. The crowd was so large that many had to stand outside while the services were held in the home. His old friend Charles Reed of the Oakland Guard delivered the eulogy. Calling him "the bravest and best of men," Reed paid tribute to an old soldier and lawman. "In the death of Captain H. N. Morse we have lost from our ranks one of our ablest commanders, best of comrades, and truest of friends, whose patriotism and devotion to our country's flag was excelled by no one. . . . As a public official Captain Morse had few equals and no superiors in our state."[8]

The funeral procession slowly wended its way through the city streets and up the hills to Mountain View Cemetery, high above Oakland. There, in a family plot with spectacular views of San Francisco and the bay, he was buried with full military honors. Veterans of the Oakland Guard were pallbearers, and a detail from the National Guard fired a salute over the grave. He rested next to Virginia and all of their loved ones: the children who had gone before them, his parents and his brother, Virginia's mother and brother. Forty years before, Harry Morse had picked out and purchased the plot. It was where he wanted to rest, overlooking his home and surrounded by the oak-studded hills he loved so dearly.

Morse's grave was showered with garlands of wildflowers and eucalyptus, symbolic of his rugged life in the saddle, in the mountains. Then, one by one, the mourners drifted away.

A bitter January wind moaned as it drifted down the hills and through the lonely scrub oaks.

The dusk brought a sad stillness.

And there was peace.

Notes

CHAPTER 1

1. J. M. Guinn, *History of the State of California and Biographical Record of Oakland and Environs* (1907), 300; J. E. Reynolds, ed., *Graphic Description of Pacific Coast Outlaws* (1958), 87–90; *Oakland Tribune,* March 2, 1878; clipping ca. 1899, Emma de la Montanya, Scrapbook. For the *Panama*'s voyage, see Theodore Messerve, "The Log of a 49er," *Overland Monthly,* July–December 1914.

2. Theodore Messerve. "The Log of a 49er," *Overland Monthly,* October 1914, 6.

3. *Oakland Tribune,* October 28, 1962.

4. Ibid., November 21, 1896.

5. *San Francisco Chronicle,* undated clipping in author's collection; Reynolds, *Graphic Description of Pacific Coast Outlaws,* 90.

6. *San Francisco Chronicle,* undated clipping in author's collection.

7. An insightful examination of the bachelor culture of the 1850s and its connection to bare knuckle boxing is Elliot J. Gorn, *The Manly Art: Bare-Knuckle Prize Fighting in America* (1986), esp. chap. 4.

8. Harry N. Morse, "Reminiscences of Criminal Life in the Golden State," undated newspaper clipping in Harry N. Morse, Scrapbook, author's collection.

9. Ralph P. Bieber, *Southern Trails to California in 1849* (1937), 353–86.

10. *Alta California,* January 21, 22, 1855; *A History of Tuolumne County* (1882), 153–60, 385–86.

11. Guinn, *History of the State of California,* 303; Reynolds, *Graphic Description of Pacific Coast Outlaws,* 93; *Records of the Families of California Pioneers* (1940), 7:341–44.

12. *Alta California,* September 9, 1856, August 21, 1885; *Stockton Daily Independent,* July 20, 1863; John Myers Myers, *San Francisco's Reign of Terror* (1966), 209, 228–29.

13. *Oakland Tribune,* March 30, 1901.

14. Dudley Ross, *Devil On Horseback* (1975), 129–32; John Boessenecker, "Pio Linares: Californio Bandido," *The Californians* (November–December 1987): 40.

15. Hubert Howe Bancroft, *History of California* (1888), 7: 215; John Boessenecker, *Badge and Buckshot: Lawlessness in Old California* (1988), 15.

16. San Francisco *Call*, February 24, 1878.

CHAPTER 2

1. William Halley, *Centennial Year Book of Alameda County* (1876), 153–54; California State Archives, Muster Roll, Oakland Guard.

2. Halley, *Centennial Year Book of Alameda County*, 176; *Alameda County Gazette*, August 8, September 5, 1863.

3. *Oakland Daily Transcript*, March 9, 1873.

4. Harold G. Davidson, *Edward Borein, Cowboy Artist* (1974), 23.

5. In Mexican California class lines were well defined, with rancheros and those of Spanish extraction at the top, those of mixed Spanish-Indian blood, or mestizos, at a lower level, and Indians at the bottom. Prior to the American occupation the term Californio applied to the elite, propertied ranchero class. During the gold rush the term came to be applied by Anglos to all native-born, Spanish-speaking Californians, regardless of class or degree of Indian blood, so as to distinguish them from Mexican and Chileno immigrants. It is in this latter and broader sense that I use the term here.

6. *California Police Record*, October 1, 1885, author's collection. The Old Stockton House was located near the present intersection of First Street and Interstate 580 in Livermore.

7. *California Police Record*, October 1, 1885, author's collection.

8. Frank F. Latta, *Joaquin Murrieta and His Horse Gangs* (1980), 177–79, 631–36. Latta was firmly convinced that Joaquin Murrieta was not slain by the California Rangers in Cantua Canyon, Fresno County, on July 25, 1853, but instead escaped and was wounded by lawmen a few days later, and made it back to his Niles Canyon rancho to be buried under the adobe floor. This scenario is most unlikely for the following reasons. After the gunfight with Rangers led by Captain Harry Love, Murrieta's head was cut off and publicly displayed throughout the northern and southern mines. The head was identified by numerous persons who knew Murrieta and also by various victims of his bandit raids. In addition, Jose Ochoa, a gang member who had been captured by the Rangers at the Cantua Creek fight, confessed in justice court in Mariposa that the head was that of Joaquin Mu-

rrieta. Latta's theory was further weakened in 1986 when the foundation of the old adobe in Niles Canyon was located and excavated. No grave was found. See William B. Secrest, "Who Died at Cantua Creek?" *Real West Special* (Spring 1985): 20–25; and *San Francisco Chronicle*, July 26, 31, 1986.

9. Esther Boulton Black, *Rancho Cucamonga and Dona Merced* (1975). 69–80; Benjamin Hayes to Cave Coutts, December 10, 1862, and Robert Carlisle to Cave Coutts, March 8, 1863, in Huntington Library, San Marino, California.

10. *Stockton Daily Independent*, February 2, 1863; *Alta California*, April 6, 1863.

11. In his diary Morse identified Quarte as "Quarto [Cuarto] Prieto," a nickname that means "quarter dark" or "quadroon." His given name is unknown. Not a few Californios and Mexicans were of mulatto blood.

12. *California Police Record*, October 1, 1885, author's collection.

13. *History of Washington Township*, 2d ed. (1950), 95; Halley, *Centennial Year Book of Alameda County*, 179, 186–87; *Alameda County Gazette*, January 23, 1864.

14. Robert Greenwood, ed., *The California Outlaw* (1960), 14. This is a well-annotated edition of George Beers, *Vasquez; or, the Hunted Bandits of the San Joaquin* (1875). Vasquez gave his date of birth as August 14, 1835; at various times he also claimed to have been born in 1837, 1838, and 1839.

15. Baptismal records, Mission Santa Clara, nos. 7731 (Francisco Soto) and 10578 (Juan Bautista Soto), University of Santa Clara Archives; Census Population Schedules (1860), Gilroy Township, Santa Clara County, 249. George Beers claimed that Juan Soto met Vasquez about 1855; he has the pair taking part in various criminal adventures before 1857. See Greenwood, *The California Outlaw*, 142–61. Juan Soto's involvement is fictitious, for he was less than eleven years old at that time. Daniel Murphy was one of the sons of Martin Murphy, a leader of the Steven-Murphy party of immigrants that pioneered the Truckee route over the Sierra Nevada in 1844. By his death in 1882 Murphy was one of the largest stock growers in America.

16. San Francisco *Post*, May 28, 1887.

17. Ibid.; San Jose *Mercury*, May 11 and 18, 1865; *People v. Francisco Salazar, Jesus Sanchez and Juan Soto*, County Court, case no. 1081, Santa Clara County Clerk.

18. *Report of the Directors of the State Prison* (1856), 46; Clare V. McKanna, "The Nameless Ones: The Ethnic Experience in San Quentin, 1851–1880," *Pacific Historian* 31, no. 1 (Spring 1987): 24, and "Crime and Punishment: The Hispanic Experience in San Quentin, 1851–1880," *Southern California Quarterly* 72, no. 1 (Spring 1990): 3.

19. D. S. Richardson, "Duels to the Death," *Overland Monthly* (August 1888), 129–30.

20. Joseph Henry Jackson, *Bad Company* (1949), 251.

21. Horace Bell, *Reminiscences of a Ranger* (1927), 100; Leonard Pitt, *The Decline of the Californios* (1966), 256.

22. Pedro Castillo and Albert Camarillo, *Furia y Muerte: Los Bandidos Chicanos* (1973), 2. For a discussion of the weaknesses of the social bandit concept, see John Boessenecker, "Social Banditry's Righteous Rebels v. Common Criminals," *The Californians* (November–December 1987): 36–37; Mark Dugan and John Boessenecker, *The Grey Fox: The True Story of Bill Miner, Last of the Old-Time Bandits* (1992), 205–11; and Clare V. McKanna, "Banditry in California, 1850–1880: Myth and Reality," in San Diego Corral of the Westerners, *Brand Book Number Eight*, 1987, 45–46.

CHAPTER 3

1. *Alameda County Gazette,* August 8, 1863, September 3, 1875.

2. "Charles G. Reed Tells of Oakland's Infant Days," undated clipping ca. 1906, in Emma de la Montanya, Scrapbook, author's collection.

3. *Oakland Daily Transcript,* March 9, 1873.

4. *Oakland Daily News,* March 12, 1873.

5. "Charles G. Reed Tells of Oakland's Infant Days."

6. Edgar J. Hinkel and William E. McCann, *Oakland 1852–1938* (1939), 2:549.

7. *San Francisco Chronicle,* June 20, 1911, January 12, 1912; undated Oakland newspaper clipping, "Old Guard to Celebrate at Annual Reunion and Banquet," in Morse, Scrapbook, author's collection.

8. *San Francisco Chronicle,* February 25, 1872.

9. Richardson, "Duels to the Death," 131; Reynolds, *Graphic Description of Pacific Coast Outlaws,* 56; Greenwood, *The California Outlaw,* 218, Jackson, *Bad Company,* 254–59.

10. Halley, *Centennial Year Book of Alameda County,* 189; Henry N. Morse, Sheriff's fee book, 2–144, and *California Police Record,* October 1, 1885, both in author's collection. Of the county's Civil War period newspapers, only the *Gazette*'s issues still exist.

11. Frank Richard Prassel, *The Western Peace Officer* (1972), 24–30; Lawrence M. Friedman, *Crime and Punishment in American History* (1993), 67–71; Kevin J. Mullen, "Founding the San Francisco Police Department," *Pacific Historian,* 27, no. 3 (Fall 1983): 45–46.

12. Harry N. Morse, "Aberisto Marquis," handwritten manuscript, 43–44, author's collection.

13. Jacob Wright Harlan, *California From '46 to '88* (1888), 221–26; Henry N. Morse, Sheriff's fee book, 79.

14. Halley, *Centennial Year Book of Alameda County*, 524–25.

15. *Alameda County Gazette*, October 28, November 4, 1865.

16. Ibid., November 25, 1865, September 28, 1867, May 18, 1871; J. P. Munro-Fraser, *History of Alameda County, California* (1883 [reprint, 1969]), 343.

17. *Alameda County Gazette*, July 8, 1865.

18. *California Police Record*, October 1, 1885; Halley, *Centennial Year Book of Alameda County*, 519.

19. San Francisco *Bulletin*, January 6, 1873; *San Francisco Chronicle*, October 2, 1898.

20. Harry N. Morse, Diary, May 1866, author's collection.

21. Frank F. Latta, in *Joaquin Murrieta and His Horse Gangs*, 99, reports that Caravantes had been a member of Murrieta's band in the early 1850s.

22. *Oakland Daily News*, July 17, 1866; *Alameda County Gazette*, July 21, 1866; *Stockton Daily Independent*, October 11, 1866. For Caravantes, see California State Archives, San Quentin Inmate Register, convict no. 3380.

23. *Oakland Daily News*, August 27 and 29, 1866.

24. *California Police Record*, October 1, 1885.

25. *Alameda County Gazette*, September 29, 1866.

CHAPTER 4

1. *California Police Record*, October 1, 1885.

2. *Alameda County Gazette*, September 8, 1866.

3. This account appeared in the *California Police Record*, October 1, 10, and 17, 1885.

4. Ibid., October 17, 1885; *Alameda County Gazette*, February 9, 1867.

CHAPTER 5

1. *Alameda County Gazette*, October 13, 1866.

2. *California Police Record*, October 1, 1885, author's collection.

3. Presentación and Abelino were the sons of Agustín Bernal, prominent ranchero and owner of the Rancho El Valle de San José in the Livermore Valley.

4. *San Francisco Chronicle*, October 2, 1898. This account has been edited slightly to reduce its length. George Foscalina's name, which Morse omitted to protect his reputation, has been added for narrative clarity. This story differs somewhat from a handwritten manuscript by Morse entitled "Aberisto Marquis" in the author's collection. There, Morse identified the two thieves as Jesus Cruz and Aberisto Marquis, identified Foscalina by name, and gives a different version of the capture. Whether the Juan Robles of this story and Aberisto Marquis are the same man is unclear. According to Morse's sheriff fee book, he arrested Marquis on November 10, 1866. San Quentin records show he was sentenced to two years for grand larceny.

5. *Alameda County Gazette*, June 22, 1867.

CHAPTER 6

1. The conclusions in this paragraph are my own and are based on my examination of the facts in several hundred criminal cases involving Hispanic defendants in nineteenth-century California. For data on sentencing fairness, see Clare V. McKanna, "Ethnics and San Quentin Prison Registers: A Comment on Methodology," *Journal of Social History, Carnegie-Mellon University* 18, no. 3 (1985): 477–82. An insightful scholarly study of criminal justice in Alameda County is Lawrence M. Friedman and Robert V. Percival, *The Roots of Justice: Crime and Punishment in Alameda County, California, 1870–1910* (1981). Researched partly from Oakland police records, it deals primarily with crime in the city of Oakland after 1880, and thus the title is overbroad. The authors did not examine Hispanic banditry in rural Alameda County, and their work contains no mention of Harry Morse.

2. *Alameda County Gazette*, December 15 and 22, 1866.

3. Ibid., June 1, 1867.

4. *Oakland Daily News*, June 1, 1867; *Alameda County Gazette*, June 1, 1867; Munro-Fraser, *History of Alameda County*, 344. For a discussion of the legal doctrine of "no duty to retreat" on the American frontier, see Richard Maxwell Brown, *No Duty to Retreat: Violence and Values in American History and Society* (1991).

5. *Alameda County Gazette*, July 4, 1868; June 5, 1869; May 25, July 27, and September 23, 1871.

6. Ibid., February 2, 1867.

7. Ibid., March 9 and 30, 1867.

8. Ibid., July 27, 1867; *Oakland Daily News*, July 24, 1867.

9. *Oakland Daily News,* July 24, 1867; *Alameda County Gazette,* July 27, 1867.

10. *Oakland Daily News,* August 12, 1867.

11. Boessenecker, *Badge and Buckshot,* 138–40, 152–55.

12. *Oakland Daily News,* August 12, 1867; *Alameda County Gazette,* August 27, October 5, 1867; Boessenecker, *Badge and Buckshot,* 110–12.

13. *Alameda County Gazette,* August 24, 1867; Halley, *Centennial Year Book of Alameda County,* 236.

14. Marysville *Daily Appeal,* September 18 and 21, 1867; *Alameda County Gazette,* September 28, 1867, May 18, 1871.

15. *California Police Gazette,* October 26, 1867; *Alameda County Gazette,* March 21, 1868; Munro-Fraser, *History of Alameda County,* p. 348.

16. *Alameda County Gazette,* November 9, 1867, February 29, 1872; *Oakland Daily News,* November 4, 1867; Richardson, *Duels to the Death,* 132–33; California State Archives, Stephen G. Nye to Governor Frederick F. Low, October 9, 1867, Governor's Offers of Rewards.

17. *Oakland Daily News,* December 16, 1867; *Alameda County Gazette,* December 17, 1867; *San Francisco Chronicle,* February 25, 1872.

CHAPTER 7

1. Harry N. Morse's personal genealogical documents, author's collection.

2. Oakland *Times,* July 16, 1889; Oakland *Enquirer,* July 16, 1889.

3. *Oakland Tribune* clipping, dated 1879, in Morse, Scrapbook. Author's collection.

4. "Charles Reed Tells of Oakland's Early Days," undated clipping in Emma de la Montanya, Scrapbook, author's collection.

5. *Oakland Daily Transcript,* April 30, 1873.

6. *Alameda County Gazette,* February 8, 1872.

7. Ibid., August 11, 18, and 25, 1870.

8. *Oakland Daily Transcript,* March 12, 1873.

9. San Jose *Mercury,* November 28, 1867; Santa Clara County Clerk, *People v. Juan Soto and Pancho Galindo,* County Court, case nos. 1311 and 1312; California State Archives, San Quentin Prison Inmate Register no. 3692 (Alberto Salazar), no. 3693 (Juan Soto), no. 3694 (Rafael Mirabel).

10. Santa Clara County Clerk, *People v. Juan Soto,* County Court, case no. 1304; and *People v. Pancho Galindo and Juan Soto,* County Court, case no. 1311. San Quentin Prison Inmate Register, no. 3977 (Francisco Galindo), no. 3983 (Juan Soto).

11. Massachusetts State Library to author, November 19, 1993; Frank Soule, John H. Gihon, and James Nisbet, *The Annals of San Francisco* (1855 [reprint, 1966]), 44; *Alta California,* January 12, 1859.

12. Burnham entered San Quentin as Fred Welch on April 6, 1868.

13. This account was published in Morse's *Pacific Monthly,* June 1886, 25–26. It has been edited to reduce its length and to include Burnham's true name, which Morse deleted to protect his reputation. For Burnham's criminal record, see San Quentin Prison Inmate Register, convict no. 2600 and 3196; and Harry N. Morse, Diary, 1874, in author's collection. Burnham had fully reformed by the time Morse wrote this account, and Morse evidently forgot that he had arrested him, under his alias Federico (Fred) Welch, and Ricardo Alviso for horse theft in 1878. See San Francisco *Bulletin,* January 15, 1878; Oakland *Times,* January 15, 1878.

14. *Oakland Daily News,* March 6, 1868; *Alameda County Gazette,* March 7 and 21, 1868.

15. Ferol Egan, *Frémont: Explorer for a Restless Nation* (1977), 355–56; Bancroft, *History of California,* 5:171–74.

16. Nevada City *Democrat,* March 18, 1857; Pitt, *The Decline of the Californios,* 101–3, 172–73; Mildred B. Hoover, Hero G. Rensch, and Ethel Rensch, *Historic Spots in California,* 3d ed. (1966), 443–44.

17. San Jose *Telegraph,* March 8, 1855; San Jose *Semi-Weekly Tribune,* May 9, 1855.

18. Annie L. Morrison and John H. Hayden, *History of San Luis Obispo County and Environs* (1917), 82.

19. *Alameda County Gazette,* May 30, 1868.

20. Morrison and Hayden, *History of San Luis Obispo County,* 82–83; San Luis Obispo *Pioneer,* May 9, 16, and 30, 1868; *Alameda County Gazette,* 30 May 1868.

21. *Alameda County Gazette,* September 18, 1869.

22. Ibid., October 30, 1869.

23. Ibid., August 14, 1869.

24. Ibid., March 6 and 20, 1869.

25. Ibid., March 20, 1869.

26. Ibid., March 27, 1869.

CHAPTER 8

1. *Alameda County Gazette,* September 26, October 3, 1868; *California Police Record,* November 14, 1885.

2. The San Luis Rancho is now covered by the San Luis Reservoir.

3. Hawthorn Station was a stagecoach stop on the Butterfield stage route, located about one and a half miles southeast of the present town of San Joaquin.

4. The Twenty-five Rancho was located near the present community of Hub on the southern boundary of Fresno County.

5. Fountain Springs was another stage stop on the old Butterfield route.

6. Kernville is now covered by Lake Isabella.

7. Fort Tejon was established in 1854 and abandoned by the army in 1864.

8. The correct name was the Los Angeles and San Pedro Railroad, connecting the city with the port at San Pedro. Construction had begun at Wilmington a month earlier, on September 19, 1868.

9. This account appeared in serial form in the *California Police Record*, November–December 1885. It has been edited substantially to reduce its great length by eliminating some extraneous material and long diversions by Morse into the history of the places he visited on the manhunt. The fire that killed Annie Leighton took place on September 29, 1869.

CHAPTER 9

1. *Stockton Daily Independent,* December 11, 13, 14, 15, and 16, 1869; San Joaquin County Clerk, Stockton, *Inquest upon Frank Medina and Four Others,* December 10, 1869.

2. Mancilla and three other prisoners had dug their way out of the Santa Clara County jail in August 1869. He had been at large ever since. San Jose *Daily Independent,* January 17, 1871.

3. Morse returned to Oakland with Tejada on May 27, 1870, and took him to Stockton on June 3. Alameda County Sheriff's Department, Daily Record of Current Events, 1870–1876, 6–7.

4. Here Morse's memory was incorrect, for the capture of Mancilla took place more than six months later, on January 13, 1871, during the manhunt for the murderers of Otto Ludovisi. San Jose *Daily Independent,* January 18, 1871; San Francisco *Bulletin,* January 20, 1871.

5. This account, which has been edited to reduce its length, appeared in the *California Police Record,* October 24 and 31, November 7, 1885.

6. *Stockton Daily Independent,* February 7, June 13, 1871, April 10, May 23, 1872; *People v. Ysidore Pudillia* [*sic*], 43 Cal. 535 (1872).

7. Boessenecker, *Badge and Buckshot,* 110-12.

CHAPTER 10

1. Phyllis Filiberti Butler, *The Valley of Santa Clara* (1981), 58–59.

2. During his trial for murder Sepulveda testified in detail about his comings and goings with Juan Soto. See *Oakland Daily News*, July 31, 1873.

3. Santa Clara *Argus*, November 19 and 26, December 3, 1870.

4. Jackson, *Bad Company*, 260.

5. The movements of Soto and Sepulveda were described by numerous witnesses in Sepulveda's murder trial. See *Oakland Daily News*, July 29, 30, and 31, August 1 and 2, 1873.

6. This two-story building remained standing longer than any of the other structures and was razed about 1959 so that Highway 680 could be constructed. Local historians believed incorrectly that the two-story 1871 store was the scene of Sheriff Morse's shooting of Narciso Bojorques and of the Otto Ludovisi murder, but it had not yet been built. See *San Francisco Chronicle*, November 10, 1872, which contains an interview with Thomas Scott by George Beers. Scott served one term in the state assembly (1863–65) and one term as a member of the board of supervisors of Alameda County (1869–71).

7. *Oakland Daily Transcript*, January 12 and 17, 1871; San Jose *Daily Independent*, January 13, 1871.

8. *Oakland Daily News*, July 29, 1873; *Alta California*, August 3, 1873.

9. It was on this hunt that Morse and Harris captured Patricio Mancilla, described in the previous chapter. San Jose *Daily Independent*, January 18, 1871; *Alameda County Gazette*, January 18, 1871.

10. According to his own testimony, Sepulveda left San Jose on January 20 or 21, 1871. The lease was signed on January 17, 1871. *Oakland Daily News*, July 31, 1873.

11. *Alameda County Gazette*, February 2, March 30, 1871. The year 1871 was a banner one for homicides in Alameda County. In addition to Ludovisi, Larsen, and Hiscock, three more men were slain in quarrels. At that time the county's population was approximately 26,000. This works out to an annual rate of 23 homicides per 100,000 population, more than double the current national homicide rate of 11 per 100,000.

12. *Alameda County Gazette*, April 13, 1871.

13. See Brown, *No Duty to Retreat*, 3–37.

14. *Alameda County Gazette*, April 13, 1871.

15. By 1883 the Lopez adobe was owned by an American, John Stub-

bles; later it became, and still is, the headquarters of the Pfeiffer Cattle Company. See Hoover, Rensch, and Rensch, *Historic Spots in California,* 204; and Peter C. Frusetta, *Quicksilver Country: California's New Idria Mining District* (1990), 20–21, 71.

16. San Jose *Daily Patriot,* May 19 and 28, 1874. Vasquez later told various reporters that he never met Juan Soto, that he first met Procopio at the house of Abelardo Salazar in San Juan Bautista in 1871, and that he only knew Procopio slightly. This is untrue, for Vasquez, Procopio, and Soto all met while in San Quentin during the 1860s and spent years in confinement together. Vasquez gave numerous interviews to reporters after his capture, and they contain many such false statements.

17. Greenwood, *The California Outlaw,* 172.

18. The Morse-Soto gunfight has been recounted many times by many writers with varying degrees of accuracy. The most correct accounts are *Alameda County Gazette,* May 18, 1871; *Oakland Daily News,* May 13, 1871; San Jose *Daily Patriot,* May 12, 1871; Richardson, "Duels to the Death," 134–39; Reynolds, *Graphic Description of Pacific Coast Outlaws,* 68–75; and Greenwood, *The California Outlaw,* 168–73. The most widely read but least accurate version appears in Jackson, *Bad Company,* 259–66.

19. *Alta California,* May 14, 1871.

20. Greenwood, *The California Outlaw,* 172–73.

CHAPTER 11

1. *Alameda County Gazette,* July 27, 1871; *Oakland Daily Transcript,* July 28, 1871.

2. *Alameda County Gazette,* July 27, 1871.

3. Ibid., September 23, 1871.

4. *Oakland Daily News,* September 23, 1871.

5. Ibid.

6. Ibid.; *Alameda County Gazette,* September 23, 1871; *Oakland Daily Transcript,* September 23, 1871.

7. Halley, *Centennial Year Book of Alameda County,* 314–18; Munro-Fraser, *History of Alameda County,* 356–57; *Alameda County Gazette,* January 23, 1873; *Oakland Tribune,* July 3, 1874.

8. *Alameda County Gazette,* July 27, 1871; *People v. Jonas Rodundo* [Tomas Redondo] 44 Cal. 538 (1872). For the law regarding illegal confessions, see *People v. Soto* 49 Cal. 467 (1874),

9. Alonzo M. Burnham [sic], "I Knew Vasquez," Touring Topics 22, no. 7 (July 1930): 60–61, 71. Burnham appears to have worked for Morse as a private detective in the 1890s. He died a respected man in San Francisco on July 17, 1936, at the age of 97. See California State Library, Register of Deaths, 1936; San Francisco Examiner, July 21, 1936; Edward Byram, San Francisco Police Journals, 1892, author's collection.

10. San Francisco Chronicle, May 18, 1874; Monterey Democrat, August 12, 1871. Vasquez made many such contradictory statements regarding his exploits. In another interview he claimed that McMahon paid gang member Abelardo Salazar $300 to turn him in but denied that he had ever tried to "get even" with McMahon.

11. San Jose Daily Patriot, July 25, 1874; San Francisco Bulletin, August 19, 1871.

12. San Francisco Bulletin, September 15, 1871. Several authors have written incorrectly that Harry Morse was involved in this manhunt and that he took part in these gunfights. See, for example, Harry S. Drago, Road Agents and Train Robbers (New York: Dodd, Mead, 1973), 33; and Jay Robert Nash, Encyclopedia of Western Lawmen and Outlaws (New York: Paragon House, 1992), 308.

13. San Jose Daily Patriot, July 25, 1874.

14. Herbert Asbury, The Barbary Coast (1933), 258.

15. Alameda County Gazette, February 15, 1872; Oakland Daily Transcript, February 12, 1872; Oakland Daily News, February 12, 1872; San Francisco Bulletin, February 12, 1872; San Francisco Call, February 11, 1872; San Francisco Chronicle, February 11, 1872; People v. Rodundo [sic] 44 Cal. 538 (1872).

16. Reynolds, Graphic Description of Pacific Coast Outlaws, 49. A well-researched biography of Ned Buntline is Jay Monaghan, The Great Rascal (1951). For his courthouse lecture in San Leandro, see the Alameda Democrat, August 29, 1868.

17. Oakland Daily News, April 26, 1872; Alameda County Gazette, May 2, 1872; San Francisco Call, April 26, 1872; California State Archives, People v. Rodundo [sic], California Supreme Court, case no. 8783. The redoubtable Frank Spencer handled Procopio's unsuccessful appeal.

18. Alameda County Gazette, May 2, 1872.

19. Harry N. Morse, Diary, February 1, 1877; Alta California, January 14, 1878; William B. Secrest, "Riders With Vasquez," Real West (October 1986): 22–23. Secrest's Dangerous Trails: Five Desperadoes of the Old West Coast (1995) deals with Procopio's career in much greater detail than is set forth here.

CHAPTER 12

1. *Oakland Tribune,* March 2, 1878; *Alameda County Gazette,* March 14, 1872; *Oakland Daily News,* March 15, 1872.

2. Munro-Fraser, *History of Alameda County,* 244-59; Halley, *Centennial Year Book of Alameda County,* 328-35, 350-64. For the Wichita County, Stevens County, Garfield County, and Gray County wars in Kansas, see Robert K. DeArment, *Bat Masterson: The Man and the Legend* (1979), 301-5.

3. *Oakland Daily News,* September 29, 1873; *Oakland Tribune,* February 13, 1957. Its later address was 411 Lester Street. The home was razed in 1957 to make way for an apartment building.

4. *Alameda County Gazette,* September 27, December 6, 1873; *Oakland Daily News,* December 2, 1873.

5. *San Francisco Chronicle,* November 10, 1872; *Alameda County Gazette,* November 14, 1872.

6. *Oakland Daily News,* July 30, 1873.

7. The testimony in Sepulveda's trial appears in detail in the *Oakland Daily News,* July 29, 30, and 31, August 1 and 2, 1873, and the *Alta California,* August 3, 1873.

8. *Oakland Daily Transcript,* November 15, 1873; *Oakland Tribune,* July 3, 1874; *Oakland Daily News,* July 3, 1874.

9. *Oakland Daily News,* August 6, 1874.

10. *Oakland Tribune,* August 6, 1874; *Alameda County Gazette,* August 8, 1874; San Francisco *Bulletin,* August 6, 1874.

11. California State Archives, Governors Pardon Papers, Pardon File of Bartolo Sepulveda, Affidavit of William Donovan.

12. Ibid.

13. California State Archives, Governors Pardon Papers, Pardon File of Bartolo Sepulveda, Affidavit of N. R. Harris, March 10, 1882.

14. *Alta California,* December 18, 1884; San Quentin Prison Inmate Register, convict no. 6097; Bartolome Sepulveda, author's interview, San Jose, California, July 29, 1988. Mr. Sepulveda is the great-grandson of Bartolo Sepulveda.

15. Clare V McKanna, "The Case of Bartolo Sepulveda: Mistaken Identity or Doctored Evidence?" *Pacific Historian* 27, no. 3 (Fall 1983): 5-23.

16. For an examination of the jailhouse snitch phenomenon, as well as the 1988 Los Angeles jailhouse informant scandal, see Martin Berg, "Snitch," *California Lawyer* (November 1991): 51-55, 97; and Mark Thompson, "The Truth About the Lies," *California Lawyer* (February 1989): 15-16.

17. Governors Pardon Papers, Pardon File of Bartolo Sepulveda, Affidavit of N. R. Harris, November 5, 1884.

18. Ibid.

19. Eugene T. Sawyer, *Life and Career of Tiburcio Vasquez* (1944), 11. Eugene Sawyer was a San Jose newspaperman; his book was first published in 1875. It is based on information provided to him by Sheriff Adams. Frank F. Latta claimed that Soto and Procopio once robbed and killed an oil drilling crew in Kern County. See Frank F. Latta, *Black Gold in the Joaquin* (1949), 55–61. No verification of this story has yet been found in the contemporary press.

20. Winfield Scott to Mrs. A. Py, November 5, 1930, in California State University Library, Hayward; *San Francisco Chronicle*, November 10, 1872.

21. Governors Pardon Papers, Pardon File of Bartolo Sepulveda, Frank E. Spencer to Governor George Stoneman, no date.

CHAPTER 13

1. Clodoveo Chavez's first name is rarely spelled correctly by chroniclers; the most common misspelling is Cleovaro.

2. *Oakland Daily News,* January 5, 1874; Greenwood, *The California Outlaw,* 221–22.

3. Greenwood. *The California Outlaw,* 222–23. For Tom Cunningham, see Boessenecker, *Badge and Buckshot,* Chap. 5. Boyd Henderson had made a reputation as a correspondent for the New York *Herald* in 1872 when he spent several weeks with the Lowry outlaw band in North Carolina. See W. McKee Evans, *To Die Game: The Story of the Lowry Band, Indian Guerrillas of Reconstruction* (1971), 209–10.

4. San Francisco *Bulletin,* August 13, 1905.

5. California State Archives, Harry N. Morse to Governor Newton Booth, March 21, 1874.

6. *San Francisco Chronicle,* May 18, 1874.

7. Ibid.

8. Ibid.

9. Ibid., May 15, 1874.

10. California State Archives, H. N. Morse to Newton Booth, April 12, 1874.

11. *San Francisco Chronicle,* April 23, 1874.

12. Ibid., April 25, 1874.

13. *Los Angeles Star,* April 28, 1874.

14. Quoted in the *San Francisco Chronicle,* April 26, 1874.

15. *San Francisco Chronicle,* April 26, 1874.

16. Greenwood, *The California Outlaw,* 257.

17. Ibid.

18. Los Angeles *Star,* May 1, 1874.

19. *San Francisco Chronicle,* May 16, 1874.

20. Greenwood, *The California Outlaw,* 259.

21. Janet Powell and Dan Powell, *La Puente Valley, Past and Present* (1937), 79–80.

22. *San Francisco Chronicle,* May 16, 1874.

23. Greenwood, *The California Outlaw,* 271.

24. Ibid., 42–43.

25. San Francisco *Bulletin,* August 13, 1905.

26. Tomás Sanchez took a leading role in breaking up the Juan Flores gang in 1857 and was elected sheriff in 1859. Martin Aguirre spent his entire adult life as a lawman, serving as deputy sheriff and constable in Los Angeles for many years. He was sheriff from 1888 to 1890 and warden of San Quentin from 1899 to 1902.

CHAPTER 14

1. Greenwood, *The California Outlaw,* 282–83, *Alameda County Gazette,* January 30, 1875.

2. California State Archives, Harry N. Morse to Newton Booth, February 10, 1875.

3. Morse, Diary, 1874–1875, author's collection.

4. San Diego *Union,* December 8, 1875; William B. Secrest, "The Return of Chavez," *True West* (January–February 1978): 6–12.

5. *Oakland Daily Transcript,* September 2, 1871.

6. Ibid., March 9, 1873.

7. *Alameda County Gazette,* September 6, 1873.

8. Bancroft, *History of California,* 2: 364–65; Munro-Fraser, *History of Alameda County,* 261.

9. *Alameda County Gazette,* August 2, and 30, 1873.

10. Halley, *Centennial Year Book of Alameda County,* 415; *Alameda County Gazette,* July 30, August 14, September 3, 1875; *Oakland Daily News,* July 28, 1875; *Oakland Tribune,* July 30, August 3 and 5, 1875.

11. *Alameda County Gazette,* September 10 and 17, October 29, 1875.

12. Ibid., December 27, 1873; Harry N. Morse, sheriff's fee book, 1864–1867, author's collection.

13. *Oakland Tribune*, July 30, 1875.

14. San Francisco *Call*, April 7, 1876.

15. California State Archives, California Supreme Court Records, *Henry N. Morse v. Alameda County*, case no. 5892; *Morse v. Alameda County* 2 Cal. Legal Record 256 (1879).

16. Harold G. Davidson, *Edward Borein, Cowboy Artist* (1974), 22–23; San Francisco *Call*, November 3, 1895.

17. *Oakland Tribune*, June 5, 1876; *Oakland Daily News*, June 5, 1876; Boessenecker, *Badge and Buckshot*, 53–55.

18. *California Police Record*, November 28, 1885.

19. Morse, Diary, 1876–77. The detailed confessions of Ruiz and Cibrian are contained therein.

20. *Oakland Daily Transcript*, January 26, February 2, 13, and 17, April 20, 1877; *Oakland Tribune*, February 16, 1877; *Contra Costa Gazette*, March 3, 1877; San Quentin Prison Inmate Register, convict nos. 7566 (Pio Ochoa), 7568 (Jose Ruiz), and 7569 (Stanislaus Sibrian [*sic*]).

21. Oakland *Times*, March 5, 1878; *Oakland Tribune*, March 2, 1878; Hayward *Weekly Journal*, March 9, 1878.

22. *San Francisco Examiner*, February 4, 1886.

23. In Richard Maxwell Brown's view, Harry Morse fits his concept of the "incorporation gunfighter." Brown has identified a principal source of frontier violence as "the Western Civil War of Incorporation," a conflict in which urban, industrial, and corporate forces "incorporated" rural America and the West in the nineteenth century. Brown's "incorporation gunfighter" was a political conservative and a Republican who supported property rights and eliminated opposition to productive settlement of the land. Brown would argue that outlaws like Tiburcio Vasquez and Juan Soto fit his model of the "resistance gunfighters," those men who opposed expansive settlement in the West and battled the incorporation gunfighters. See Brown, *No Duty to Retreat*, 39–47.

CHAPTER 15

1. *San Francisco Chronicle*, May 19, 1878; *Alta California*, May 19, 1878; Thomas S. Duke, *Celebrated Criminal Cases of America* (1910), 70–74. It is worth noting that anti–death penalty advocates often quote the late Clinton Duffy, celebrity warden of San Quentin and prison reformer, who claimed that no man of money or social position was ever executed in California. However, the cases of Wright LeRoy, an attorney, and Troy Dye, pub-

lic administrator of Sacramento County, who was hanged for murder in 1879, illustrate that Duffy perhaps should have stuck to penology and stayed away from history.

2. Oakland *Mirror*, July 27, 1878; Boessenecker, *Badge and Buckshot*, 194-95; Morse, Scrapbook, containing various clippings on Jules Callundan.

3. On the advent of Morse's patrol, see the San Francisco *Call*, November 2, 1882. On James B. Hume, the authoritative biography is Richard Dillon, *Wells Fargo Detective* (1969).

4. Frank Morn, *The Eye that Never Sleeps: A History of the Pinkerton National Detective Agency* (1982), 1-14; Lawrence M. Friedman, *Crime and Punishment in American History* (1993), 203-8.

5. Friedman, *Crime and Punishment in American History*, 67-71; James D. Horan, *The Pinkertons: The Detective Dynasty that Made History* (1967), 22-50.

6. San Francisco *Call*, January 5, 1900. The journals of San Francisco police detective Edward Byram, covering in great detail his daily activities from 1876 to 1908, provide many examples of private detective work performed by on-duty officers, including Pinkerton cases. On the professionalism of the San Francisco police, see Philip J. Ethington, "Vigilantes and the Police: The Creation of a Professional Police Bureaucracy in San Francisco, 1847-1900," *Journal of Social History*, 21 (Winter 1987):197-227.

7. *Pacific Monthly*, June 1886, 1.

8. Reynolds, *Graphic Description of Pacific Coast Outlaws*, 98.

9. *San Francisco Chronicle*, September 10 and 28, 1878; *Alta California*, October 15, 1878.

10. On San Francisco politics during this period, see William Issel and Robert W. Cherny, *San Francisco, 1865-1932: Politics, Power, and Urban Development* (1986), and William A. Bullough, *The Blind Boss and His City: Christopher Augustine Buckley and Nineteenth-Century San Francisco* (1979).

11. Harry N. Morse, *Report of Harry N. Morse on Dupont Street Frauds* (1879), 10-11.

12. San Francisco *Bulletin*, March 20, 21, and 26, 1879; San Francisco *Call*, March 20, 21, and 22, 1879; *Alta California*, March 20 and 21, 1879; Morse, *Dupont Street Frauds*, 27-30.

13. San Francisco *Bulletin*, March 24 and 26, 1879; *Alta California*, March 23, 1879.

14. I. W. Lees, *Full and Complete Statement of the Forgeries and Frauds of H. S. Tibbey* (1879), 3-59; San Francisco *Bulletin*, March 22, 23, and 26, April 1, 1879.

15. Lees, *Full and Complete Statement*, iii–iv; San Francisco *Call*, May 1, 1879.

16. San Francisco *Bulletin*, April 29 and 30, 1879.

17. San Francisco *Call*, July 15, 1879; Morse, *Dupont Street Frauds*, 8–9.

18. Morse, *Dupont Street Frauds*, 35.

19. San Francisco *Real Estate Circular*, March, April, May 1879; San Francisco *Bulletin*, April 3, 4, and 5, May 5, 1879; San Francisco *Call*, April 12, May 5, 1879.

20. San Francisco *Call*, July 15, 16, and 19, 1879.

21. Morse, *Dupont Street Frauds*, 8–9. Morse may have been charitable, for the San Francisco Grand Jury found that only $200,000 were legitimate. San Francisco *Bulletin*, May 5, 1879.

22. San Francisco *Bulletin*, July 14 and 31, 1879; San Francisco *Call*, July 14, 15, and 16, 1879.

23. San Francisco *Bulletin*, July 30 and 31, August 14, 1879; *People v. Tibbey* 57 Cal. 153 (1880); California State Archives, California Supreme Court Records, 1880, *People v. Tibbey*.

24. *Lent v. Tillson* 72 Cal. 404 (1887); *Lent v. Tillson* 11 S.Ct. 825, 140 U.S. 316 (1891).

25. William Heintz, *San Francisco's Mayors* (1975), 108.

26. San Francisco *Bulletin*, October 29, 1872.

27. *San Francisco Chronicle*, July 19, 1883; San Francisco *Call*, May 29, July 19, August 2 and 3, 1883.

28. National Archives, Record Group 36, U.S. Customs Service, Special Agents Reports and Correspondence, J. F. Evans to Charles J. Folger, April 14, 1882; Evans to Folger, September 23, 1882.

29. National Archives, Record Group 36, U.S. Customs Service, Special Agents Reports and Correspondence, H. N. Morse and John Gamage to J. F. Evans, September 18, 1882; J. F. Evans to H. N. Morse and John Gamage, September 23, 1883.

30. H. N. Morse and John Gamage to J. F. Evans, September 18, 1882.

31. National Archives, Record Group 36, U.S. Customs Service, Special Agents Reports and Correspondence, J. F. Evans to Charles Folger, November 24, 1882 and March 29, 1883.

32. Evans to Folger, September 23, 1882; *San Francisco Examiner*, November 11, 1887.

33. Morse and Gamage to Evans, November 20, 1882; *San Francisco Chronicle*, July 19, 1883; San Francisco *Call*, July 19, 1883.

34. Morse and Gamage to Evans, November 20, 1882.

35. Morse and Gamage to Evans, November 12, 1882, March 1, 1883; San Francisco *Call*, May 29, 1883.

36 San Francisco *Call*, August 2, 3, 4, 7, and 9, 1883.

37. *San Francisco Examiner*, November 12, 1887.

38. Evans to Folger, July 21, 1883; *San Francisco Examiner*, November 11, 12, 15, and 17, 1887. Ogden Hoffman served as U.S. District Court Judge in San Francisco from 1851 to 1891. For an examination of his life and the federal judicial system in California, see Christian G. Fritz, *Federal Justice in California: The Court of Ogden Hoffman* (1991). For examples of lenient punishment meted out by Hoffman in smuggling cases, see pp. 219–22.

39. *San Francisco Examiner*, November 12, 1887.

40. Historians interested in political corruption in San Francisco have generally focused on the 1856 Committee of Vigilance and the Abe Ruef graft prosecution. This is the first effort to reexamine and recount the Dupont Street Frauds and the Harkins Opium Ring cases.

CHAPTER 16

1. San Francisco *Weekly Chronicle*, January 10, 1884.

2. James B. Hume and John N. Thacker, *Robbers Record* (1885), 92.

3. Dillon, *Wells Fargo Detective*, 169–70; Ralph Moody, *Stagecoach West* (1967), 309–11; William Collins and Bruce Levene, *Black Bart: The True Story of the West's Most Famous Stagecoach Robber* (1992), 19–22.

4. Edward Byram, Journals, 2:250, author's collection.

5. John Boessenecker, "George Hackett: Terror to Road Agents," *Old West* (Fall 1987):15–17.

6. Dillon, *Wells Fargo Detective*, 174–76; Collins and Levene, *Black Bart*, 138–41.

7. John Curtin had been a Pinkerton detective in the Midwest. He moved to San Francisco in 1881, worked briefly for Morse, and then operated his own agency until his death in 1902.

8. San Francisco *Call*, November 17, 1883.

9. *San Francisco Examiner*, November 17, 1883.

10. Ibid., November 18, 1883.

11. For Ben Thorn's fiscal dishonesty, see Boessenecker, *Badge and Buckshot*, 68–69, 72.

12. *San Francisco Examiner*, December 10, 1888. For the exact division of the reward, see Collins and Levene, *Black Bart*, 175–76.

13. *San Francisco Examiner,* December 10, 1888.

14. Ben K. Thorn to Harry N. Morse, dated 1884, copy in author's collection.

15. *San Francisco Examiner,* December 10, 1888.

16. *San Francisco Examiner,* December 11, 1888.

17. Ibid., November 28, 1888.

18. The story of Black Bart has been told many times, although this chapter is the first effort to tell Harry Morse's full story. The best accounts are Dillon, *Wells Fargo Detective;* Jackson, *Bad Company;* Collins and Levene, *Black Bart;* and a recent, well-researched contribution by George Hoeper, *Black Bart: Boulevardier Bandit* (1995).

CHAPTER 17

1. Bancroft, *History of California,* 7:215; Boessenecker, *Badge and Buckshot,* 15, 266.

2. San Francisco *Call,* September 19 and 20, 1885; Duke, *Celebrated Criminal Cases of America,* 272.

3. Duke, *Celebrated Criminal Cases of America,* 273–74; Morse Scrapbook, undated clippings; *People v. Irwin* 77 Cal. 494 (1888); San Francisco *Call,* October 22, November 8 and 14, 1885.

4. *People v. Irwin* 77 Cal. 494 (1888); Duke, *Celebrated Criminal Cases of America,* 274–75; San Francisco *Call,* March 6, 7, and 11, 1886; handwritten statement of John Prewett, 1885, Philip Hudner collection.

5. Morse, Scrapbook. Undated news clippings from the *California Police Record.*

6. *San Francisco Chronicle,* December 1, 1892; *Blythe v. Ayers* 96 Cal. 532 (1892). On the Blythe estate, see also 102 Cal. 254 (1893), 105 Cal. 357 (1894), 108 Cal. 124 (1895), 110 Cal. 226 (1895), 110 Cal. 229 (1895), 110 Cal. 231 (1895).

7. San Francisco *Call,* August 11, 1885; Reynolds, *Graphic Description of Pacific Coast Outlaws,* 28–29; *California Police Record, San Francisco Saturday Mercury,* and *Police Record,* sample copies in author's collection.

8. San Francisco *Call,* May 25, 1890; New York *Sun,* September 14, 1890; Charles Howard Shinn, *Graphic Description of Pacific Coast Outlaws* (ca. 1890). The latter book is now very rare. Shinn wrote it with the usual journalist's haste, as evidenced by many errors of fact, misspellings of names, and incorrect dates. It was reprinted in 1958 by Westernlore Press and ably edited by J. E. (Jack) Reynolds. For Charles Howard Shinn, see Reynolds, ed.,

Graphic Description of Pacific Coast Outlaws, 21–24, and Joseph Henry Jackson's introduction to Charles Howard Shinn, *Mining Camps* (1948), x–xxi.

9. T. J. Jones, *Report on the Gold Park Group of Mines,* May 29, 1900; H. N. Morse to Joseph Miller, October 23, 1903, April 7 and 18, 1904; *Estate of Henry N. Morse,* Last Will and Testament, December 28, 1910, and Inventory and Appraisement, April 23, 1912, all in author's collection; Guinn, *History of the State of California and Biographical Record,* 303.

10. Wells Fargo Bank History Department, San Francisco, "Harry N. Morse" to Captain Charles Aull, ca. 1885.

11. San Francisco *Bulletin,* August 21, 1885; *San Francisco Examiner,* August 20, 1885; San Francisco *Call,* August 20, 1885.

12. *Oakland Tribune,* November 3, 1888; July 15 and 16, 1889; Oakland *Times,* July 16 and 17, 1889; Oakland *Enquirer,* July 16, 1889; San Francisco *Call,* July 14, 1889.

13. *Contra Costa Gazette,* March 10 and 17, November 24, December 1, 1877.

14. H. N. Morse to Governor R. W. Waterman, September 12, 1889; H. N. Morse to M. D. Boruck, December 15, 1890; H. N. Morse and Thomas Cunningham to Governor James H. Budd, December 1, 1897. These and numerous other letters are contained in the Governors Pardon Papers, California State Archives, Ramon Romero pardon file.

15. Morse, Scrapbook, undated newspaper clippings; *San Francisco Examiner* May 18, 1897, June 2, 1898.

16. Ramon Romero pardon file, restoration of citizenship documents.

CHAPTER 18

1. San Francisco *Call,* May 28 and 29, June 4, 1893.

2. The two principal accounts of Evans and Sontag are C. B. Glasscock, *Bandits and the Southern Pacific* (1929), and Wallace Smith, *Prodigal Sons* (1951). Both books contain many errors and omissions. The latter account, although written by a professional historian, is heavily biased in favor of the outlaws. Neither author was aware of the role of the Morse Detective Agency in the manhunt.

3. *San Francisco Examiner,* March 14, 1893.

4. *San Francisco Chronicle,* March 15, 1893.

5. *San Francisco Examiner,* March 14, 15, and 16, June 29, 1893; April 15, 1894; *San Francisco Chronicle,* March 15 and 17, 1893; Fresno *Republican,* March 14 and 15, 1893; Paul E. Vandor, *History of Fresno County*

(1919), 38–379; Charles W. Clough and William B. Secrest, Jr., *Fresno County: The Pioneer Years* (1984), 242.

6. *San Francisco Examiner,* November 3, 1894; *Oakland Tribune,* November 8, 1894.

7. On the Durrant case, see Joseph Henry Jackson, ed., *San Francisco Murders* (1947). A more complete account is Joseph Henry Jackson and Lenore Glen Offord, *The Girl in the Belfry* (1957). Strangely, the authors do not mention the important role Harry Morse played in the Durrant case. Jackson, who greatly admired Morse and made him the hero of *Bad Company,* died while working on *The Girl in the Belfry* and it was completed by Offord. Evidently neither she nor Jackson was aware of Morse's involvement in the case.

8. *San Francisco Chronicle,* July 29, 1895.

9. Ibid., November 2, 1895; *San Francisco Examiner,* November 2, 1895. Modern forensic psychiatrists might well agree with Morse's analysis. Serial killers generally do not change their method of murder so drastically within such a short time. The rituals they engage in when killing, such as strangling, stabbing, or mutilation, are usually quite similar in each crime. The different ways the two girls were killed suggest that there might have been two killers. However, that does not mean that Durrant was innocent, only that he may have had an accomplice. And no evidence of an accomplice was ever uncovered.

10. *San Francisco Chronicle,* July 26, 29, 1895.

11. *San Francisco Examiner,* September 29, 1895.

12. A summary of the trial testimony appears in *People v. Durrant* 116 Cal. 179, 201–7 (1897). The testimony appears in great detail in Edgar Peixotto, *Report of the Trial of William Henry Theodore Durrant* (1899).

13. *San Francisco Examiner,* November 2, 1895.

14. William B. Secrest, "The Beast in the Belfry," *True West* (November 1986):18; Duke, *Celebrated Criminal Cases of America,* 122. A recurring story is that the real killer of the two girls was the Reverend George Gibson, pastor of the Emanuel Baptist Church. In 1897 an ex-convict living in a soldier's home in Colorado claimed to have seen Reverend Gibson carrying the dead body of Blanche Lamont up the belfry stairs. He later retracted his story. In April 1900 a mentally ill preacher committed to a San Mateo sanitarium made a deathbed statement claiming that he had been pastor of the church and had murdered the two girls. Absurd as it was, the story was repeated for years and even appeared in 1913 in a book published in London. See *San Francisco Chronicle,* May 28, 1897, July 30, 1916; Jackson and Offord, *The Girl in the Belfry,* 185–86.

CHAPTER 19

1. San Francisco *Call*, April 29, 1898; *San Francisco Chronicle*, September 24, 1898.

2. For Morse's comments on the Howard case, see *San Francisco Examiner*, September 2, 1899.

3. For the rivalry between Morse's agency and the patrol specials, see *Alta California*, May 29, 1884, and San Francisco *Call*, January 25, 1898. It is noteworthy that Morse's patrolmen did not take part in the major labor confrontations of the 1890s. The Pinkertons were active strikebreakers during this period and garnered a great deal of bad publicity for their anti-labor work. Perhaps Morse, as a former workingman himself, sympathized with organized labor. During the great San Francisco strike of 1901, a bloody gun battle erupted between private watchmen and strikers; nine men were wounded. The special officers were not Morse's men, however, but those of his former employee and competitor, John Curtin. See *San Francisco Chronicle*, September 30, 1901.

4. Conventional wisdom holds that all large municipal police departments of the nineteenth century were incompetent and corrupt. The San Francisco police, to the contrary, employed one of the finest detective forces in the nation, and the department made early and extensive use of criminal photographs, criminal arrest and identification records, written crime reports, and police telegraph and telephone. Although corruption existed among both detectives and patrolmen, it never appears to have been institutionalized, for there was a consistent effort by the chiefs to root out crooked officers. The newspapers reported numerous examples of policemen who were fired from the force for accepting bribes and for shaking down gamblers and prostitutes. See Ethington, "Vigilantes and the Police"; Edward Byram, Journals, 1876–1908. William B. Secrest has kindly allowed me to read his 500-page manuscript of the life of Isaiah Lees, as well as his voluminous files containing daily newspaper reports of police activity in San Francisco from 1853 to 1900, from which these conclusions are also drawn.

5. San Francisco *Call*, February 25, 1898; Morse, Scrapbook, miscellaneous undated clippings. Lawrence's hiring of Wyatt Earp foreshadowed his later penchant for keeping armed thugs on his payroll. In 1903 Hearst sent Lawrence to Chicago where he ran the *Chicago Examiner* and built up an even worse record, including using hired gunmen to win circulation wars. Some of Long Green's gunmen proved the nucleus for Chicago's notorious bootlegging gangs of the 1920s. See Ferdinand Lundberg, *Imperial Hearst* (1939), 149ff., and W. A. Swanberg, *Citizen Hearst* (1961), 270–71.

6. Wyatt Earp did not become a nationally famous figure until the publication in 1931 of a part-fact, part-fiction biography, *Wyatt Earp, Frontier Marshal*, by Stuart N. Lake.

7. Earp described this encounter to his secretary, John Flood; it took place not long before the Sharkey-Fitzsimmons fight. Interview, John D. Gilchriese, February 20, 1993.

8. The most detailed account is Jack DeMattos, *The Earp Decision* (1989), which contains a compilation of contemporary newspaper accounts, of the match and its aftermath.

9. Bryam, Journals, 13:287–88.

10. San Francisco *Call*, January 13, 1900.

11. *San Francisco Examiner*, January 14, 1900.

12. *San Francisco Chronicle*, January 17, 1900. A few years later Older and Spreckels's brother, Rudolph, would become leaders in the great San Francisco graft prosecutions involving political boss Abe Ruef and Mayor Eugene Schmitz.

13. *Call*, *Examiner*, *Chronicle*, and *Bulletin*, January 17, 18, 19, and 20, 1900.

14. San Francisco *Bulletin*, January 19 and 20, 1900; *San Francisco Examiner*, January 20, 1900.

15. San Francisco *Bulletin*, February 14, 1900. Biggy was appointed chief of police in 1907 and died under mysterious circumstances the following year.

16. The *Call*, *Examiner*, *Bulletin*, and *Chronicle* gave extended coverage to this affair in numerous issues during January and February, 1900. For Andy Lawrence's later career, see Lundberg, *Imperial Hearst*, and Swanberg, *Citizen Hearst*. Fred Esola's political connections kept him in good stead, for he became an early member of the FBI and in 1924 President Calvin Coolidge appointed him U.S. marshal of northern California. The Lawrence-Esola affair was one of the low points in the political career of James D. Phelan; it is not mentioned in his biography, *Legacy of a Native Son*, by James P. Walsh and Timothy J. O'Keefe (1993).

17. *San Francisco Chronicle*, August 7, 1901; Duke, *Great Criminal Cases of America*, 291–92; Dick Boyer, "The Famous Selby Gold Robbery of 1901," *Crockett Signal* (January 1990):9.

18. *San Francisco Chronicle*, August 7, 12, and 14, 1901.

19. Ibid., August 11, 1901.

20. Ibid., August 10, 1901.

21. Ibid., August 11, 1901.

22. Ibid., August 13, 1901.

23. Ibid.
24. San Francisco *Call*, September 13, 1901.
25. *San Francisco Chronicle*, August 14, 1901; Duke, *Celebrated Criminal Cases of America*, 292. The account of the Selby Smelter robbery in Pete Fanning's *Great Crimes of the West* (1929), 36–54, is wholly fictitious.

CHAPTER 20

1. *Oakland Tribune*, January 25, 1901; Morse, Scrapbook, undated newspaper clippings.
2. Petitions to President Roosevelt and Rep. Victor Metcalf in support of Harry N. Morse for U.S. Marshal, December 18, 1901–January 3, 1902, author's collection.
3. H. N. Morse to Joseph Miller, October 23, 1903, April 7 and 18, 1904, author's collection.
4. Marysville *Daily Appeal*, July 20, 21, 22, and 23, 1904; *San Francisco Chronicle*, July 20 and 21, 1904; Oakland *Herald*, July 20, 21, and 22, 1904.
5. Oakland *Enquirer*, July 21 and 22, 1904; *San Francisco Chronicle*, October 13, 14, 15, and 26, 1904.
6. H. N. Morse, *The Taxpayer's Appeal*, October 29, 1904; Morse, Scrapbook, various clippings regarding graft in Alameda County; Oakland *Times*, November 10, 1904; *San Francisco Chronicle*, November 9 and 10, 1904.
7. Huntington Library, Jules Callundan to Collis P. Huntington, January 9, 1897.
8. Norman E. Tutorow, *Leland Stanford: Man of Many Careers* (1971), 221ff.
9. Stanford University Archives, David Starr Jordan to Dr. Ray Lyman Wilbur, May 18, 1921.
10. *San Francisco Chronicle*, February 21, 1905.
11. San Francisco *Call*, February 21, 1905; *San Francisco Chronicle*, February 21, 1905.
12. The chemist's supplemental report is reproduced in the *San Francisco Call*, March 4, 1905.
13. Stanford University Library, *Coroner's Inquest In Re Jane L. Stanford*, testimony of Bertha Berner; see also Honolulu *Pacific Commercial Advertiser*, March 1, 1905.
14. *Coroner's Inquest In Re Jane L. Stanford*, testimony of Bertha Berner, May Hunt, and Dr. Francis H. Humphris; San Francisco *Call*, March 2, 1905; *Pacific Commercial Advertiser*, March 7, 1905.

15. *Coroner's Inquest In Re Jane L. Stanford,* verdict.

16. San Francisco *Call,* March 3, 1905.

17. Ibid., March 5, 1905.

18. Ibid., March 11, 1905.

19. Stanford University Library, statement of David Starr Jordan and Timothy Hopkins, postdated March 16, 1905; also published in San Francisco *Call,* March 15, 1905.

20. See, for example, San Francisco *Call,* March 16, 17, 18, 22, and 28, August 24, December 31, 1905.

21. Stanford University Library, Ernest C. Waterhouse to David Starr Jordan, March 14, 1905; *Pacific Commercial Advertiser,* March 7, 1905; Coroner's Inquest. The Cooper Medical College report has been long lost. Its summary is quoted in Bertha Berner, *Mrs. Leland Stanford: An Intimate Account* (1935), 209–10. Dr. Jordan briefly mentioned the contents of the report in an interview in the San Francisco *Call,* December 31, 1905.

22. David Starr Jordan to Mountford S. Wilson, March 22 and 23, 1905; David Starr Jordan to S. F. Leib, March 22, 1905; David Starr Jordan to Carl S. Smith, March 24, 1905. Stanford University Library.

23. For evidence that supports the poisoning theory, see *Coroner's Inquest* and Gary Ogle, "The Mysterious Death of Mrs. Leland Stanford," *Pacific Historian* 25, no. 1 (Spring 1981):1–7. On the natural causes theory, see "The Mystery of Jane Stanford's Death," *Stanford Observer* (June 1991): 24; and Gunther W. Nagel, *Jane Stanford: Her Life and Letters* (1975), 173–75.

24. Boyd G. Stephens to author, February 8 and 14, May 5, 1994; author's interview with Dr. Stephens, February 23, 1994.

25. San Francisco *Call,* March 3, 1905.

CHAPTER 21

1. Articles of Co-partnership between Morse and Callundan, April 19, 1906, in author's collection. The fire also destroyed Morse's voluminous scrapbooks, which he had painstakingly compiled since 1856 (and therefore made researching this book immeasurably more difficult). With donations from friends Morse put together a large scrapbook of newspaper clippings about his career, but it was a pale imitation of what he had lost.

2. Oakland *Herald,* May 24, 1907; Morse, Scrapbook, undated obituary notices; Morse, Journal of European trip (1907), author's collection.

3. H. N. Morse to George Pardee, April 13, 1905; this and Morse's

other letters to Pardee are in the Bancroft Library. On the San Francisco graft prosecutions, see Walton Bean, *Boss Ruef's San Francisco* (1972).

4. *San Francisco Call*, January 5 and 15, 1908; *Oakland Tribune*, August 27, December 25, 1908, March 29, 1909; *Sacramento Bee*, October 25, 1910; Morse, Scrapbook, undated clippings.

5. *San Francisco Chronicle*, March 17 and 20, 1911; Articles of Co-partnership between Harry M. Morse and Oda May Callundan, March 20, 1911, author's collection. The Morse Patrol and Detective Agency continued to do business in San Francisco until 1972 when it was bought out by a larger concern.

6. Emma de la Montanya, Scrapbook, undated clippings; *San Francisco Call*, January 12, 1912; *San Francisco Chronicle*, November 10, 1911, January 12, 1912; *Oakland Tribune*, January 14, 1912.

7. *Estate of Morse*, Last Will and Testament and Inventory and Appraisement, author's collection.

8. Charles G. Reed, "Resolutions of Respect to the Memory of Captain Henry N. Morse," author's collection.

Bibliography

THERE have been no previous books about Harry Morse, with the exception of Charles Howard Shinn's *Graphic Description of Pacific Coast Outlaws*, which was originally written as a feature story for the New York *Sun* in 1890. Nor has any historian previously done substantial research on his life. Thus this book was of necessity researched mostly from primary sources. Much important material came from systematic searching through the issues of the San Leandro, Oakland, and San Francisco newspapers. Morse's personal papers and records provided crucial source material. I was fortunate in acquiring many of Morse's surviving diaries, memoirs, records, and correspondence, which proved invaluable for the completion of this book. Of particular importance were Morse's memoirs, published in his own periodicals in the 1880s and 1890s: the *Pacific Monthly, California Police Record,* and *San Francisco Saturday Mercury.* The only known copies of these publications containing his recollections are in the author's collection. The principal sources are cited below.

BOOKS AND ARTICLES

Asbury, Herbert. *The Barbary Coast.* New York: Alfred A. Knopf, 1933.

Bancroft, Hubert Howe. *History of California.* 7 vols. San Francisco: History Company, 1888.

Bean, Walton. *Boss Ruef's San Francisco.* Berkeley: University of California Press, 1972.

Beers, George. *Vasquez; or, the Hunted Bandits of the San Joaquin.* New York: Robert M. DeWitt, 1875.

Bell, Horace. *Reminiscences of a Ranger.* Santa Barbara, Calif.: Wallace Hebberd, 1927.

Berg, Martin. "Snitch." *California Lawyer* (November 1991).

Berner, Bertha. *Mrs. Leland Stanford: An Intimate Account.* Stanford: Stanford University Press, 1935.

Bieber, Ralph P. *Southern Trails to California in 1849.* Glendale, Calif.: Arthur H. Clark, 1937.

Black, Esther Boulton. *Rancho Cucamonga and Dona Merced.* Redlands, Calif.: San Bernardino County Museum Association, 1975.

Boessenecker, John. *Badge and Buckshot: Lawlessness in Old California.* Norman: University of Oklahoma Press, 1988.

————. "George Hackett: Terror to Road Agents." *Old West* (Fall 1987).

————. "Pio Linares: Californio Bandido." *The Californians* (November–December 1987).

————. "Social Banditry's Righteous Rebels v. Common Criminals." *The Californians* (November–December 1987).

Boyer, Dick. "The Famous Selby Gold Robbery of 1901." *Crockett Signal* (January 1930).

Brown, Richard Maxwell. *No Duty to Retreat: Violence and Values in American History and Society.* New York: Oxford University Press, 1991.

Bullough, William A. *The Blind Boss and His City: Christopher Augustine Buckley and Nineteenth-Century San Francisco.* Berkeley: University of California Press, 1979.

Burnham, Alonzo M. [*sic*]. "I knew Vasquez." *Touring Topics* 22, no. 7 (July 1930).

Butler, Phyllis Filiberti. *The Valley of Santa Clara.* Novato, Calif.: Presidio Press, 1981.

Castillo, Pedro, and Albert Camarillo. *Furia y Muerte: Los Bandidos Chicanos.* Los Angeles: University of California, 1973.

Clough, Charles W., and William B. Secrest, Jr. *Fresno County: The Pioneer Years.* Fresno, Calif.: Panorama West Books, 1984.

Collins, William, and Bruce Levene. *Black Bart: The True Story of the West's Most Famous Stagecoach Robber.* Mendocino, Calif.: Pacific Transcriptions, 1992.

Davidson, Harold G. *Edward Borein, Cowboy Artist.* Garden City, N.Y.: Doubleday, 1974.

DeArment, Robert K. *Bat Masterson: The Man and the Legend.* Norman: University of Oklahoma Press, 1979.

DeMattos, Jack. *The Earp Decision.* College Station, Texas: Creative Publishing, 1989.

Dillon, Richard. *Wells Fargo Detective.* New York: Coward-McCann, 1969.

Dugan, Mark, and John Boessenecker. *The Grey Fox: The True Story of Bill Miner, Last of the Old-Time Bandits.* Norman: University of Oklahoma Press, 1992.

Duke, Thomas S. *Celebrated Criminal Cases of America*. San Francisco: James H. Barry, 1910.

Egan, Ferol. *Frémont: Explorer for a Restless Nation*. New York: Doubleday, 1977.

Ethington, Philip J. "Vigilantes and the Police: The Creation of a Professional Police Bureaucracy in San Francisco, 1847–1900." *Journal of Social History* 21 (Winter 1987).

Evans, W. McKee. *To Die Game: The Story of the Lowry Band, Indian Guerrillas of Reconstruction*. Baton Rouge: Louisiana State University Press, 1971.

Fanning, Pete. *Great Crimes of the West*. San Francisco: n.p., 1929.

Friedman, Lawrence M. *Crime and Punishment in American History*. New York: Basic Books, 1993.

Friedman, Lawrence M., and Robert V. Percival. *The Roots of Justice: Crime and Punishment in Alameda County, California, 1870–1910*. Chapel Hill: University of North Carolina Press, 1981.

Fritz, Christian G. *Federal Justice in California: The Court of Ogden Hoffman*. Lincoln: University of Nebraska Press, 1991.

Frusetta, Peter C. *Quicksilver Country: California's New Idria Mining District*. Published by author, 1990.

Glasscock, C. B. *Bandits and the Southern Pacific*. New York: Frederick A. Stokes, 1929.

Gorn, Elliott J. *The Manly Art: Bare-Knuckle Prize Fighting in America*. Ithaca: Cornell University Press, 1986.

Greenwood, Robert, ed. *The California Outlaw*. Los Gatos, Calif.: Talisman Press, 1960.

Guinn, J. M. *History of the State of California and Biographical Record of Oakland and Environs*. Los Angeles: Historic Record Co., 1907.

Halley, William. *Centennial Year Book of Alameda County*. Oakland, Calif.: William Halley, 1876.

Harlan, Jacob Wright. *California From '46 to '88*. San Francisco: Bancroft, 1888.

Heintz, William. *San Francisco's Mayors*. Woodside, Calif.: Richards Publications, 1975.

Hinkel, Edgar J., and William E. McCann, *Oakland 1852–1938*. Oakland, Calif.: Works Progress Administration, 1939.

A History of Tuolumne County. San Francisco. B. F. Alley, 1882.

History of Washington Township, 2d ed. Stanford: Stanford University Press, 1950.

Hoeper, George. *Black Bart, Boulevardier Bandit*. Fresno, Calif.: Word Dancer Press, 1995.

Horan, James D. *The Pinkertons: The Detective Dynasty that Made History.* New York: Crown, 1967.

Hoover, Mildred B., Hero G. Rensch, and Ethel Rensch. *Historic Spots in California,* 3d ed. Stanford: Stanford University Press, 1966.

Hume, James B., and John N. Thacker. *Robbers Record.* San Francisco: H. S. Crocker, 1885.

Issel, William, and Robert W. Cherny. *San Francisco, 1865–1932: Politics, Power, and Urban Development.* Berkeley: University of California Press, 1986.

Jackson, Joseph Henry. *Bad Company.* New York: Harcourt, Brace, 1949.

———. Ed. *San Francisco Murders.* New York: Duell, Sloan and Pearce, 1947.

Jackson, Joseph Henry, and Lenore Glen Offord. *The Girl in the Belfry.* Greenwich, Conn.: Fawcett, 1957.

Latta, Frank F. *Black Gold in the Joaquin.* Caldwell, Idaho: Caxton, 1949.

———. *Joaquin Murrieta and His Horse Gangs.* Santa Cruz, Calif.: Bear State Books, 1980.

Lees, I. W. *Full and Complete Statement of the Forgeries and Frauds of H. S. Tibbey.* San Francisco: Bunker & Hiester, 1879.

Lundberg, Ferdinand. *Imperial Hearst.* Westport, Conn.: Greenwood Press, 1939.

McKanna, Clare V. "Banditry in California, 1850–1880: Myth and Reality." San Diego Corral of the Westerners, *Brand Book Number Eight,* 1987.

———. "The Case of Bartolo Sepulveda: Mistaken Identity or Doctored Evidence?" *Pacific Historian* 27, no. 3 (Fall 1983).

———. "Crime and Punishment: The Hispanic Experience in San Quentin, 1851–1880." *Southern California Quarterly* 72, no. 1 (Spring 1990).

———. "Ethnics and San Quentin Prison Registers: A Comment on Methodology." *Journal of Social History, Carnegie-Mellon University* 18, no. 3 (1985).

———. "The Nameless Ones: The Ethnic Experience in San Quentin, 1851–1880." *Pacific Historian* 31, no. 1 (Spring 1987).

Messerve, Theodore. "The Log of a 49er." *Overland Monthly* (July–December 1914).

Monaghan, Jay. *The Great Rascal.* Boston: Little, Brown, 1951.

Moody, Ralph. *Stagecoach West.* New York: Thomas Y. Crowell, 1967.

Morn, Frank. *The Eye that Never Sleeps: A History of the Pinkerton National Detective Agency.* Bloomington: Indiana University Press, 1982.

Morrison, Annie L., and John H. Hayden. *History of San Luis Obispo County and Environs.* Los Angles: Historic Record Co., 1917.

Morse, Harry N. *Report of Harry N. Morse on Dupont Street Frauds.* n.p. 1879.

Mullen, Kevin J. "Founding the San Francisco Police Department." *Pacific Historian* 27, no. 3 (Fall 1983).

Munro-Fraser, J. P. *History of Alameda County, California.* Oakland, Calif.: M. W. Wood, 1883. Reprint, 1969.

Myers, John Myers. *San Francisco's Reign of Terror.* Garden City, N.Y.: Doubleday, 1966.

"The Mystery of Jane Stanford's Death." *Stanford Observer* (June 1991).

Nagel, Gunther W. *Jane Stanford: Her Life and Letters.* Stanford: Stanford Alumni Association, 1975.

Ogle, Gary. "The Mysterious Death of Mrs. Leland Stanford." *Pacific Historian* 25, no. 1 (Spring 1981).

Peixotto, Edgar. *Report of the Trial of William Henry Theodore Durrant.* Detroit: Collector Publishing, 1899.

Pitt, Leonard. *The Decline of the Californios.* Berkeley: University of California Press, 1966.

Powell, Janet, and Dan Powell. *La Puente Valley, Past and Present.* La Puente, Calif.: La Puente Junior Women's Club, 1937.

Prassel, Frank Richard. *The Western Peace Officer.* Norman: University of Oklahoma Press, 1972.

Record of the Families of California Pioneers. N.p.: Genealogical Records Committee, Daughters of the American Revolution, 1940.

Report of the Directors of the State Prison. Sacramento: James Allen, State Printer, 1856.

Reynolds, J. E., ed. *Graphic Description of Pacific Coast Outlaws.* Los Angeles: Westernlore Press, 1958.

Richardson, D. S. "Duels to the Death." *Overland Monthly* (August 1888).

Ross, Dudley. *Devil on Horseback.* Fresno, Calif.: Valley Publishers, 1975.

Sawyer, Eugene T. *Life and Career of Tiburcio Vasquez.* Reprint. Oakland, Calif.: Biobooks, 1944.

Shinn, Charles Howard. *Graphic Description of Pacific Coast Outlaws.* San Francisco: R. R. Patterson, ca. 1890.

———. *Mining Camps.* Reprint. New York: Alfred A. Knopf, 1948.

Secrest, William B. "The Beast in the Belfry." *True West* (November 1986).

———. *Dangerous Trails: Five Desperadoes of the Old West Coast.* Stillwater, Okla.: Barbed Wire Press, 1995.

———. "The Return of Chavez." *True West* (January–February 1978).

———. "Riders with Vasquez." *Real West* (October 1986).

———. "Who Died at Cantua Creek?" *Real West Special* (Spring 1985).

Smith, Wallace. *Prodigal Sons*. Boston: Christopher Publishing House, 1951.

Soulé, Frank, John H. Gihon, and James Nisbet. *The Annals of San Francisco*. New York: D. Appleton, 1855. Reprint, 1966.

Swanberg, W. A. *Citizen Hearst*. New York: Charles Scribner's Sons, 1961.

Thompson, Mark. "The Truth About the Lies." *California Lawyer* (February 1989).

Tutorow, Norman E. *Leland Stanford: Man of Many Careers*. Menlo Park, Calif.: Pacific Coast Publishers, 1971.

Vandor, Paul E. *History of Fresno County*. Los Angeles: Historic Record Co., 1919.

Walsh, James P., and Timothy J. O'Keefe. *Legacy of a Native Son*. Saratoga, Calif.: Forbes Mill Press, 1993.

COURT RECORDS

California State Archives. California Supreme Court Records. *Henry N. Morse v. Alameda County*.

———. *People v. Rodundo*.

———. *People v. Tibbey*.

California Supreme Court Reports. *Blythe v. Ayers* 96 Cal. 532 (1892).

———. *Estate of Blythe* 102 Cal. 254 (1893); 105 Cal. 357 (1894); 108 Cal. 124 (1895); 110 Cal. 226 (1895); 110 Cal. 229 (1895); 110 Cal. 231 (1895).

———. *Lent v. Tillson* 72 Cal. 404 (1887)

———. *People v. Durrant* 116 Cal. 179 (1897)

———. *People v. Irwin* 77 Cal. 494 (1888)

———. *People v. Ysidore Padillia* [sic] 43 Cal. 535 (1872).

———. *People v. Jonas Rodundo* [Tomás Redondo], 44 Cal. 538 (1872).

———. *People v Soto* 49 Cal. 467 (1874).

———. *People v Tibbey* 57 Cal. 153 (1880).

San Joaquin County Clerk, Stockton. *Inquest upon Frank Medina and Four Others*, December 10, 1869.

Santa Clara County Clerk. *People v. Pancho Galindo and Juan Soto*. County Court, case no. 1311.

———. *People v. Francisco Salazar, Jesus Sanchez and Juan Soto*. County Court, case no. 1081.

———. *People v. Juan Soto*. County Court, case no. 1304.

———. *People v. Juan Soto and Pancho Galindo*. County Court, case nos. 1311 1/2 and 1312.

Unpublished cases. *Morse v. Alameda County* (1979) 2 Cal. Legal Record 256.
U.S. Supreme Court Reports. *Lent v. Tillson* 11 S.Ct. 825, 140 U.S. 316 (1891).

UNPUBLISHED MATERIALS

Alameda County Sheriff's Department
    Daily Record of Current Events, 1870–1876.
Bancroft Library. University of California at Berkeley.
    Governor George Pardee papers.
    H. N. Morse. The Taxpayer's Appeal, October 29, 1904.
John Boessenecker collection.
    Edward Byram. San Francisco Police Journals, 1876–1908.
    Emma de la Montanya. Scrapbook.
    Harry N. Morse.
        "Aberisto Marquis." Handwritten manuscript.
        Diaries, 1864–78.
        Genealogical Records.
        Journal of European trip, 1907.
        Mining records.
        Miscellaneous correspondence.
        Miscellaneous Morse Detective Agency papers.
        Scrapbook.
        Sheriff's fee book, 1864–67.
        Will, probate, and estate documents.
    Charles G. Reed. "Resolutions of Respect to the Memory of Captain Henry N. Morse."
    Petitions in Support of Harry N. Morse for U.S. Marshal.
    Boyd G. Stephens, M.D., to author, February 8 and 14, May 5, 1994.
    Ben K. Thorn to Harry N. Morse, 1884.
California State Archives.
    Governor's Offers of Rewards.
    Governors Pardon Papers. Pardon Files of Bartolo Sepulveda and Ramon Romero.
    Muster Roll, Oakland Guard.
    San Quentin Prison Inmate Register.
    Tiburcio Vasquez reward file.

California State Library.
    Register of Deaths, 1936.
California State University Library, Hayward.
    Winfield Scott to Mrs. A. Py, November 5, 1930.
Census Population Schedules, 1860. Gilroy Township, Santa Clara County.
Philip Hudner collection.
    Statement of John Prewett, 1885.
Huntington Library, San Marino, California.
    Jules Callundan to Collis P. Huntington, January 9, 1897.
    Cave Coutts papers.
National Archives.
    Record Group 36. U.S. Customs Service. Special Agents Reports and
    Correspondence.
Stanford University Library.
    Coroner's Inquest In Re Jane L. Stanford.
    David Starr Jordan. Correspondence.
University of Santa Clara Archives.
    Baptismal records, Mission Santa Clara.
Wells Fargo Bank History Department, San Francisco.
    James B. Hume. Scrapbooks.

AUTHOR INTERVIEWS

John D. Gilchriese, February 20, 1993.
Bartolome Sepulveda, July 29, 1988.
Boyd G. Stephens, M.D., February 23, 1994.

NEWSPAPERS

Alameda County Gazette (San Leandro)
Alameda Democrat
Alta California (San Francisco)
California Police Gazette (San Francisco)
Contra Costa Gazette (Martinez)
Fresno *Republican*
Hayward *Weekly Journal*
Los Angeles *Star*
Marysville *Daily Appeal*

Monterey *Democrat*
Nevada City *Democrat*
New York *Sun*
Oakland *Daily News*
Oakland *Daily Transcript*
Oakland *Enquirer*
Oakland *Herald*
Oakland *Mirror*
Oakland *Times*
Oakland *Tribune*
Pacific Commercial Advertiser (Honolulu)
Sacramento *Bee*
San Diego *Union*
San Francisco *Alta California*
San Francisco *Bulletin*
San Francisco *Call*
San Francisco Chronicle
San Francisco Examiner
San Francisco *Post*
San Francisco *Real Estate Circular*
San Francisco *Weekly Chronicle*
San Jose *Daily Independent*
San Jose *Daily Patriot*
San José *Mercury*
San Jose *Semi-Weekly Tribune*
San Jose *Telegraph*
San Luis Obispo *Pioneer*
Santa Clara *Argus*
Stockton Daily Independent

Index